Library of
Davidson College

Applied Poverty Research

An interdisciplinary collection by sociologists, economists, and political scientists, this book takes an extensive look at the massive literature on poverty and poverty programs. The contributions show how poverty research is defined, organized, and utilized, and demonstrate to what extent and in what ways it benefits the nonpoor, the general public, the poverty program agency, and the researcher, as well as the poor themselves.

Applied Poverty Research

Edited by

RICHARD GOLDSTEIN
and
STEPHEN M. SACHS

ROWMAN & ALLANHELD
PUBLISHERS

ROWMAN & ALLANHELD

Published in the United States of America in 1984
by Rowman & Allanheld
(A division of Littlefield, Adams & Company)
81 Adams Drive, Totowa, New Jersey 07512

Copyright © 1983 by Policy Studies Organization

All rights reserved. No part of this publication may
be reproduced, stored in a retrieval system, or
transmitted in any form or by any means, electronic,
mechanical, photocopying, recording, or otherwise,
without the prior permission of the publisher.

Library of Congress Cataloging in Publication Data
Main entry under title:

Applied poverty research.

  Bibliography: p.
  1. Poverty−Research−United States−Addresses,
essays, lectures. I. Goldstein, Richard, 1964.-   .
II. Sachs, Stephen M., 1938.-   .
HC110.P6A73   1983   305.5′69′072073   83-16126
ISBN 0-86598-137-X

    84 85/10 9 8 7 6 5 4 3 2 1

Printed in the United States of America

TABLE OF CONTENTS

Acknowledgments ix

Part I. Defining the Problem 1
1. Introduction 3
   Richard Goldstein and Stephen M. Sachs
2. Toward A Political Economy of Poverty Research: A Critique from Right to Left 14
   Stephen M. Sachs
3. Who Really Benefits from Applied Poverty Research? Opening up a Question 29
   Richard Goldstein

Part II. Measuring Poverty 41
4. Introduction 43
   Richard Goldstein and Stephen M. Sachs
5. Limiting Poverty by Design: The Official Measure of Poverty 49
   Harrell R. Rodgers, Jr.
6. The Politics of Measuring Poverty Among the Elderly 64
   Lori B. Girshick and John B. Williamson
7. The Anti-Poverty Effect of In-Kind Transfers: A "Good Idea" Gone too Far? 77
   Timothy M. Smeeding
8. A Poverty of Government Services: Estimates 1962, 1972, 1977 102
   Thomas F. Stinson and Ronald B. Larson

Part III. Alternative Research Perspectives: Relating Needs to Solutions 115
9. Introduction 117
   Richard Goldstein and Stephen M. Sachs
10. Beyond the Quantitative Cul-de-Sac: A Qualitative Perspective on Youth Employment Programs 123
    Ray C. Rist
11. Welfare Terminations and Benefit Reductions: What Program Recipients can tell Policy Planners 138
    Arnold Vedlitz and Jon Alston
12. Explaining Away Black Poverty: The Structural Determinants of Black Employment 148
    Lou Ferleger
13. Uses of Microsimulation in Applied Poverty Research 175
    David Betson and David Greenberg
14. Evaluating Poverty Programs: The Usefulness of Dynamic Continuous Simulation Modelling 191
    John Dixon, Barry Nagorcka and James Cutt

Part IV.	**Alternative Policy Perspectives: The Subjects of Poverty Research**	209
15.	Introduction Richard Goldstein and Stephen M. Sachs	211
16.	Who Benefits from Knowledge About the Health of Undocumented Mexicans? Joseph Nalven	217
17.	Changing Public Attitudes about Public Welfare Clients and Services Through Research Leon H. Ginsberg	241
18.	Income Maintenance Experimentation: Cui Bono Kenneth J. Neubeck	253
19.	Employment Demonstrations: A Strategy for Policy Formulation Lee Bowes Fremont-Smith	260
20.	Social Welfare Programs: Lessons from Europe, the Need for Comparative Analysis Harrell R. Rodgers, Jr.	269
Part V.	**Conclusions**	285
21.	Politics, Ethics, and Poverty Research Stephen M. Sachs and Richard Goldstein	287
Index		295
Contributors		301

TABLES AND FIGURES

5.1	Poverty Standard: 1979	52
5.2	Poverty Schedule, Family of 4 (Non Farm): 1959-1979	53
5.3	Size of the Poor Population Under Current and Revised Poverty Cutoffs, 1974	57
5.4	Households Below the Poverty Level Under Alternative Income Definitions, Fiscal Year 1976	59
7.1	Income In-Kind "Major" Public In-Kind Transfer Programs vs. "Total" Private and Public Income In-Kind in 1980	80
7.2	Percentage of Persons with Income Below the Poverty Line: 1965-80	88
7.3	Characteristics of the Public Assistance System in the Poorest States	91
8.1	Progress Against Poverty of Government Services: 1962, 1972, 1977	106
11.1	Client Evaluations by Length of Time on Welfare Rolls	143
12.1	Industry of the Employed Population: 1962, 1970	152
12.2	Industry of the Employed Population: 1972, 1980	154
12.3	Median Usual Weekly Earnings of Full-Time Wage and Salary Workers, by Occupational Group and by Race, May 1978	156
12.4	Employed Blacks in Manufacturing by Occupational Group: 1972, 1980	158
12.5	Employed Blacks in Service Sector (including private household workers) by Occupational Group: 1972, 1980	159
12.6	Employed Blacks in Health Services (including Hospitals) by Occupational Group: 1972, 1980	160
12.7	Employed Blacks in Retail Trade by Occupational Group: 1972, 1980	162
12.8	Employed Blacks in Finance, Insurance and Real Estate by Occupational Group: 1972, 1980	163
14.1	A Set of Poverty Program Objectives and Related Performance Indicators	193
14.2	Feedback Loops	195
14.3	Causal Loop Diagram of the Whole Model	199
14.4	Income-Unit Sub-Model	201
14.5	The Structure of the Demand Sub-Model	203
14.6	The Structure of the Supply Sub-Model	204
17.1	School Clothing Allowances; Distribution Method Preferences	246
17.2	Public Employees Receiving Welfare Services by Agency	249

ACKNOWLEDGMENTS

This volume started as a special issue of Policy Studies Journal, though it has grown much larger. The special issue (Vol. 10, No. 3, March 1982) was made possible by funds provided by the Community Services Administration. Although CSA no longer exists we still want to thank them and particularly Robert Clark, Chief of the Evaluation Division at that time. We also thank the Indiana University President's Committee for financial assistance with the word processing, and the Policy Studies Organization and, in particular, Stuart Nagel, Secretary-Treasurer.

Several people provided help and encouragement for the project as a whole and with respect to the choice of articles. Richard Goldstein gives particular thanks to Lou Ferleger, Mike Martin, Bob McShea and Jennifer Wilton. Stephen M. Sachs gives his deepest thanks to Elizabeth Cohen for many ideas, thoughts and inspirations; to his colleagues at I.U.P.U.I.: Jim Simmons, Susan Sutton, Donna Kay Dial, Bob Kirk, Ain Haas, Lory Lampert, Ron Margolin, Ken Berger, Chuck Winslow, and Richard Freeland for numerous comments and suggestions; to Marsha Neawedde for outstanding secretarial support and assistance. Finally, we would like to thank the authors of the articles who put up with several delays and still provided invaluable help in finishing the book.

Richard Goldstein   Brighton, MA
Stephen M. Sachs   Indianapolis, IN

PART I

DEFINING THE PROBLEM

INTRODUCTION

Richard Goldstein
Stephen M. Sachs

The poor shall never cease out of the land.
Deuteronomy 15:11

For ye have the poor always with you.
Matthew 26:11

    The above does not affect the desire of some to abolish poverty and the desire of others to study either poverty or programs aimed at abolishing or alleviating poverty. Poverty has been studied (in the modern sense), in England and in the United States, at least since the latter part of the nineteenth century, but there has been an increase in the amount of this kind of study during the last fifteen years (the "War on Poverty"). One question rarely asked is, "what has been the value (if any) of these studies?"

    This volume is a first attempt at investigating this question. The authors of the papers included here have, in several ways, investigated the worth of previous poverty-related research. Sometimes this involves new research as a base for questioning previous research.

    Eventually, we want to answer the questions of (1) who has benefited from applied poverty research, and, (2) have the benefits to the poor outweighed the costs to the poor? No single volume can hope to answer these questions in their entirety. This volume does start to answer these questions, however, as well as opening up these questions and providing some ways of examining them, ways which will be pursued in future studies.

    It should be noted that the term "research" is, for the purposes of the analyses in this volume, broadly defined to include virtually all collecting, analyzing and communicating of information for the purposes of evaluating and/or making decisions concerning poverty programs. From this perspective, for example, gathering and analyzing data to determine who is poor or eligible for programs constitutes research.

    The articles in this volume are divided into sections based upon the type of attack that they provide to the issues. That is, there are a number of different ways that one could look at applied poverty research with the question of who benefits in mind, including:

- o What kinds of limits does the research place on itself (or have placed on it) with respect to the people to be studied and the data to be used?
- o What kinds of limits are placed on the research because of the methodological perspectives adhered to?
- o What kinds of limits are placed on the research because of the policy perspectives adhered to?
- o What kinds of limits are placed on the research because of the philosophical perspectives used or relied upon?
- o What has been the evolutionary history of forms of applied poverty research (or questions orienting or constraining applied poverty research), and how has this limited:
  (a) the forms and types of research attempted, and,
  (b) the types of research results that are possible?
- o What types of applied poverty research will be the next fad, and what does this say about previous research?
- o What is the quality of applied poverty research?

Not all of these questions, nor the others that one could ask, can be answered or even broached in one brief volume. The articles are placed into three sections, which deal, respectively, with:

(1) Measuring Poverty -- how do we determine who the poor are, and what problems, if any, are there with the methods used to make this determination?

(2) Alternative Research Perspectives -- Have there been methodological blinders that affected whole schools of applied poverty research?

(3) Alternative Policy Perspectives -- Policy perspectives here refers to both the policies that are studied and the policy perspective which is inherent in the method of study. This second part of the meaning is closely related to what is called Alternative Research Perspectives (above) in the sense that a research study that studies only individuals, say, is constrained in the types of policies that it can "see" as solutions to the problems studied.

In addition to these three sections, there is also an introductory section comprised of this essay and two others. The first, by Stephen Sachs, reviews various philosophical perspectives on poverty and how these perspectives influence poverty research. The second, by Richard Goldstein, lays out many of the issues that would be involved in a more complete examination of the question of who really benefits from poverty research. Finally, there is a brief concluding section in which we spell out some of the implications of the current situation both for society in general and for social researchers.

In the remainder of this essay, we provide a brief historical background and then spell out some of the overriding issues that are pointed up by this history and by the current situation.

AN HISTORICAL LOOK AT POVERTY RESEARCH

Although modern European poverty policy began in the fourteenth century with prohibitions of beggary, the study of poverty (at least in the West) did not begin until the late eighteenth century. Even these studies are generally not considered to be of acceptable quality today (Hobsbawm, 1968). The earliest attempts to conduct what we would now recognize as poverty studies, including the definition of a poverty line, took place in England during the second half of the nineteenth century. The most famous was conducted by Charles Booth and his colleagues. The first comparable study in the United States was published by Robert Hunter in 1904. (In addition to Hobsbawm, histories can be found in Cullen, 1975; Cole, 1972; Elesh, 1972; Lecuyer and Oberschall, 1978; and Rubinow, 1934.) At this time, there also appeared a number of books describing the conditions of the poor; the most famous are Jacob Riis' How the Other Half Lives, and Jack London's People of the Abyss.

From the turn of the century to today, a great volume of studies of the poor have been published. Virtually all, whatever their differences, have shared several themes, including: an emphasis on a distinction between the "deserving" and the "undeserving" poor (Gans, 1969; Patterson, 1981); an emphasis on the "culture" of the poor; and, an emphasis on the "prevention" of poverty (Patterson, 1981). In addition, at least with respect to poverty research in the United States, poverty was "re-discovered" many times (Patterson, 1981: 100, 201). The most recent re-discovery is usually denoted by the publication of Michael Harrington's book, The Other America, in 1962.

Whether Harrington's book helped to cause a re-discovery of poverty or just serves as a convenient marker, the period following publication of The Other America did see a rapid increase in poverty research. This increase was, at the least, spurred by funds from the War on Poverty. The increase in research was also spurred by the optimistic belief that success in applied physical science could somehow be transferred to such social problems as poverty. This optimism was signified by the widely asked question, "If they can put a man on the moon, why can't they do something about poverty?" Possibly the best answer, not only to this specific question but to the whole over-optimistic mood, was the (semi-) humorous "who needs poor people on the moon?"

On the question of how much of each re-discovery was really a repeat of the last generation's work and how much amounted to "standing on the shoulders of the last generation", it is instructive to read the article on Poverty in the 1934 Encyclopedia of the Social Sciences (Rubinow, 1934). This article compares very favorably with articles written in the 1960's and 1970's, including discussions of economic and non-economic senses of poverty (see the Introduction to the "Measuring Poverty" section, below), a discussion of the alleged causes of poverty, both individual and structural (see the Introduction to the "Alternative Research Perspectives" section, below), and a discussion of some policy implications of these views.

It is impossible here to over-emphasize the importance of some of the recurring trends in poverty research. The distinction between deserving and non-deserving poor makes virtually impossible the elimination of poverty, while the continuing emphasis on culture and on prevention feeds the fuel of programs aimed at changing the poor (as contrasted with programs aimed at ameliorating the situation of the poor). One of the material consequences of this is that we spend much more on poverty programs than would be necessary to eliminate the poverty gap (the gap between poor people's income and the poverty line).[1]

> Senator Abraham Ribicoff, the former Secretary of HEW, indicated in 1972 that there were some 170 anti-poverty programs sponsored by federal money at an annual cost of $35 billion. He noted that if one-third of the money was directed at the poor, there would no longer be any poverty in the nation (unless, of course, the poverty level was revised upward). Thirty five billion dollars is a lot of money, much more than most readers can conceive. Most of it never went to the poor, but to the people who ran the poverty programs. (Ornstein, 1974: 489-490; see also, Patterson, 1981: 113, 137; Plotnick, 1979: 282-3; Tuckman, 1973: 87-90; Tussing, 1975: 7; and Ulman, 1965: xv-xvi.)

Given this, social scientists (among others) must ask themselves what they mean by their desire to eliminate poverty. Some people might see this purported desire as irony. Instead of ending poverty do social scientists actually want to defuse objections to poverty? Before bellowing a "No" in answer to this question, we should at the very least be clear that this is not what we are doing.

That social scientists may be serving the needs of government (Helfgot, 1981:2) or of the wealthy is at least suggested by some German proverbs ("Poverty is the rich man's cow" and "Poverty is the hand and foot of wealth" (quoted in Hobsbawm, 1968:399)) and by Senator Long's comment (during the debate in Congress on President Nixon's Family Assistance Program) that he couldn't "get anybody to iron [his] shirts." (quoted in Patterson, 1981:194)

Further, Herbert Gans (1973: Chapter 4) has pointed out that poverty has many positive functions for the non-poor. Among these is that poverty

> makes possible the existence or expansion of "respectable" professions and occupations, for example, penology, criminology, social work, and public health. More recently, the poor have provided jobs for professional and paraprofessional "poverty warriors," as well as for journalists and social scientists, this author included, who have

Defining the Problem

> supplied the information demanded since public curiosity about the poor developed in the 1960s. (Gans, 1973:105)

Gans also points out how other non-poor groups are positively affected by other functions of poverty. (See also Danziger and Haveman, 1978: 12.) For example, it may be advantageous to employers for there to be a sizeable number of low-income people, many of whom are unemployed or under-employed, as a restraint upon worker demands for higher wages. (For a current example, see Williams, 1982.)

In come cases, it may be the existence of something called "research" which serves the needs of government, rather than the actual research. For example, in "What Will They Think of Next?" (1981: 3) it was reported that the state of Illinois is attempting to use the cover of "scientific inquiry" as a way to legitimate a new cost-cutting measure. This is apparently allowed under

> Sec. 1115 of the Social Security Act [which] permits the Secretary to suspend all sorts of beneficiary protections in the interests of scientific inquiry. It is a time-honored ploy of state governments seeking to cut back Medicaid programs to write up the whole idea as "an experiment" and apply for a waiver of the normal rules. Indeed one of the earliest attempts occurred in 1971 in California during the governorship of (you guessed it) R. Reagan.

All of this may point to the validity of characterizing the War on Poverty as a "war on the poor." (Graham, 1967: 224)

SOME QUESTIONS ABOUT POVERTY RESEARCH

If poverty can be ended at about one-third of what it costs to fund unsuccessful anti-poverty programs, why don't we just transfer the necessary funds? Why all of the emphasis on the distinction between the deserving and the undeserving poor? Why are structural causes of poverty ignored in our research and programs especially when our rhetoric recognizes the importance of structure? Why, if we think culture is a (or the) cause of poverty do we not test this supposition? This section briefly examines these four questions. We do not attempt to answer these questions here, but rather we attempt to justify them as legitimate queries and to sketch their implications.

First, what is meant by "structure"? Blau has recently argued that underneath all the different definitions is one common denominator:

> social structure refers to those properties of an aggregate that are emergent and that consequently do not characterize the separate elements composing the aggregate ... The

> sum of many trees is the same whether each stands in a different yard or they all are crowded together, but only in the latter case do they make a forest. (Blau, 1981: 9-10)

One of the important things to notice about structures is that there is interdependence between the elements that comprise the structure. This can lead to apparent paradoxes. One relevant to the discussion of poverty is

> a meritocracy where occupational chances largely depend on education. This makes every person interested in obtaining as much schooling as possible, raising educational levels, reducing educational inequality, and enhancing educational mobility. But . . . these changes will not appreciably improve chances of occupational mobility or diminish inequality in occupational status if the occupational distribution is exogenously determined by industrial conditions and economic demand. On the contrary, the result is that more education than before is required to achieve a given occupational status, contrary to the interests of job applicants, although it continues to be in the interest of every applicant to maximize his or her education, since doing so improves occupational opportunities, which repeats the process in the next generation by further raising the education needed to have the same occupational chances as one's parents. (Blau, 1981: 7; this example is taken by Blau from Boudon, 1981; see also Schelling, 1978.)

Many authors have recognized the potential importance of social structure in causing poverty (Hodge and Laslett, 1980; Korpi, 1980; Orcutt, et al., 1980; Pettigrew and Back, 1967; Rubinow, 1934). But few have actually studied the effect of structure, though (1) it is possible to do so, and (2) some authors have drawn conclusions to the effect that structure is important solely because they have failed to explain things on non-structural grounds (Abell and Lyon, 1979). However, it has been acceptable to study the effect of poverty programs on structure, particularly on economic growth, and usually to draw conservative conclusions about the alleged deleterious effects on the economy of coddling the poor. (For a less conservative example of this, see Gordon, 1963.) Examples of the few studies of structure include Davidson and Krackhardt (1977), Helfgot (1981), Tuckman (1973), and Wachtel (1971). Helfgot's study is particularly telling because he discusses a case where social scientists recognized the importance of structure in causing a certain problem, but then designed a non-structural "solution". (See especially page 54 in Helfgot, 1981; this example is discussed in detail in the Introduction to Part IV of this volume.)

The lack of sufficient or proper consideration of structural issues is raised by a number of the papers in this book. For example, Louis Ferleger examines the effect of structural factors in the labor market upon black employment and Harrell Rodgers presents a comparative analysis of European and U.S. poverty programs.

By contrast it may be argued that the lack of consideration of social and economic structural factors in much poverty research is justified because the primary causes of poverty are cultural (Lewis, 1966). If researchers really believe this, however, much of their research and policy-making efforts are misguided.

In Helfgot's example (above), and in most research on the "culture of poverty", a major problem appears to be the unwarranted assumption by social scientists that culture is an ever-present and unchanging feature of a locale or group of people. How else can one explain the failure (pointed out by Gans in 1971 and still true) to study changes in culture when the poor have attained higher incomes (indicated by Thackeray's Becky Sharp saying "I think that I could be a good woman if I had five thousand a year"), or the failure to study what happens to behavior when people escape from poverty?

Another possible reason for the relative lack of structural analysis in poverty studies may be the influence of politics upon researchers. First, it may be that those who fund and/or design studies of poverty and poverty programs do not believe that structural solutions are politically feasible. Dixon, Nagorcka and Cutt discuss some circumstances in which they believe that this might be the case in their examination of simulating the impacts of proposed income maintenance programs in Australia. Interestingly, Harrell Rodgers argues from the European experience that whether structural reforms are politically feasible depends at least in part upon the comprehensiveness of the programs (in his second article, "Social Welfare Programs").

Second, it may be that it is in the interests of many of those designing and/or funding poverty research projects to avoid structural considerations. This explanation is consistent with the discussions in the papers by Goldstein and by Neubeck in this volume. We need to consider what is the best explanation of:

- o our failures to perform these kinds of studies;
- o our insistence on distinguishing between deserving poor and undeserving poor;
- o our failure to consider structural explanations;
- o our insistence on poverty programs, rather than just income transfers.

Is it that we have been co-opted?

ETHICS

Two important ethical issues arise in applied poverty research: One, issues spawned by the fact of employment by a sponsor who is different from the subject of study. Two, "consideration of the consequences of [this] research, including the uses and misuses of scientific knowledge and the ethics of cross-disciplinary research." (Lamberth and Kimmel, 1981)

Too little thinking has gone into the ethical questions raised by allowing someone else, and especially someone who is not the subject of study, to set our research questions and hypotheses. It is not that no thinking has been done about these issues (see Angell, 1967; Glazer, 1972), but that much of our thinking on these issues has been nothing but a retreat behind the wall of "freedom of research." These issues are too large to deal with here, but we should at least realize that we have no right to impose our freedom of research on others' freedom not to be researched, especially since, "Too frequently, problem-oriented studies produce problems rather than alleviate them." (Kleymeyer and Bertrand, 1980; and the studies cited there.) Many of these issues are discussed in Boulay, et al. (1980) and Goldstein (1981), and in much of the debate surrounding the new regulations for the protection of human subjects (Department of Health and Human Services, 1981). One instance of ethical problems of research and their impact is discussed by Joseph Nalven in his article on problems of health involving undocumented Mexicans in the United States.

If our research is not generalizable, either across subjects or across time or across political boundaries (such as States), then it is unethical for us to try and make this kind of generalization. It is also unethical for us to implement the results of shoddy research. Much of our research is effectively worthless because it has never been replicated and it has not been suitably designed. (Datta, 1980; Levitan and Taggart, 1976; see Goldstein's article for more on this.)

CONCLUSION

At a time when social science funding is being cut, is it really appropriate to even investigate the question of who has benefited from poverty research? This question was asked of one of the editors of this volume (RG) by a potential contributor. This person seemed to feel that at a time when the government was making attacks on social science research and social science-associated programs, and being supported in public by social scientists (Mazur, 1981; Wyman, 1982), that what all good social scientists should do is fight back.

We believe, to the contrary, that what is needed is an examination of social science and its effects. If it has had deleterious consequences for people, or even if it has just been a waste of money, then it should not be supported, or at least it should not be supported in the traditional way. This is especially important if we want to fight against other administrative initiatives, initiatives that rather than fighting poverty directly seem actuated by the belief that:

> Unto every one that hath shall be given, and he shall have

abundance; but from him that hath not shall be taken away even that which he hath. (Matthew 25: 29)

NOTES

1. Strictly speaking, this may be an over-simplification due to inefficiencies and negative incentives. For example, if all families were guaranteed, say, $3,000 per year per adult and $2,000 per year per dependent child, would families earning less than this (or even slightly more than this) stop working? If so, this would raise the poverty gap. This question is very complex and very little relevant evidence exists. Fairly simplistic discussions of these issues can be found in Okun (1975: 108-109), and in Tussing (1975: 7, 140).

REFERENCES

Abell, Troy and Lyon, Larry (1979) "Do the Differences Make a Difference? An Empirical Evaluation of the Culture of Poverty in the United States." American Ethnologist 6:602-621.
Angell, Robert C. (1967) "The Ethical Problems of Applied Sociology." In The Uses of Sociology, edited by Paul F. Lazarsfeld, William H. Sewell and Harold L. Wilensky. New York: Basic Books, Inc.
Blau, Peter M. (1981) "Introduction: Diverse Views of Social Structure and Their Common Denominator." In Continuities in Structural Inquiry, edited by Peter M. Blau and Robert K. Merton. Beverly Hills: Sage Publications.
Boudon, Raymond (1981) "Undesired Consequences and Types of Structures of Systems of Interdependence." In Continuities in Structural Inquiry, edited by Peter M. Blau and Robert K. Merton. Beverly Hills: Sage Publications.
Boulay, Harvey, Goldstein, Richard, and Zisk, Betty (1980) "Protecting Human Subjects of Research: Proposed Amendments to HEW Policy: Comments on Pool's Analysis." PS 13:202-203.
Cole, Stephen (1972) "Continuity and Institutionalization in Science: A Case Study of Failure." In The Establishment of Empirical Sociology, edited by Anthony Oberschall. New York: Harper & Row, Publishers.
Cullen, Michael J. (1975) The Statistical Movement in Early Victorian Britain: The Foundations of Empirical Social Research. New York: Barnes & Noble Books.
Danziger, Sheldon and Haveman, Robert (1978) "An Economic Concept of Solidarity: Its Application to Poverty and Income Distribution Policy in the United States." Research Series No. 37. Geneva: International Institute of Labour Studies.
Datta, Lois-ellin (1980) "Interpreting Results: Values and the Case of Reports on Federal Programs Supporting Educational Change."

In *Problems in American Social Policy Research*, edited by Clark C. Abt. Cambridge: Abt Books.

Davidson, Leonard and David Krackhardt (1977) "Structural Change and the Disadvantaged: An Empirical Test of Culture of Poverty/Situational Theories of Hard-Core Work Behavior." *Human Organization* 36:304-309.

Department of Health and Human Services (1981) "Final Regulations Amending Basic HHS Policy for the Protection of Human Research Subjects." 46 Federal Register 8390.

Elesh, David (1972) "The Manchester Statistical Society: A Case Study of Discontinuity in the History of Empirical Social Research." In *The Establishment of Empirical Sociology*, edited by Anthony Oberschall. New York: Barnes & Noble Books.

Gans, Herbert J. (1969) "Culture and Class in the Study of Poverty: An Approach to Anti-Poverty Research." In *On Understanding Poverty*, edited by Daniel P. Moynihan. New York: Basic Books, Inc.

Gans, Herbert J. (1971) "Social Science for Social Policy." In *The Use and Abuse of Social Science*, edited by Irving Louis Horowitz. New Brunswick: Transaction Books.

Gans, Herbert J. (1973) *More Equality*. New York: Pantheon Books.

Glazer, Myron (1972) *The Research Adventure*. New York: Random House.

Goldstein, Richard (1981) "On Deceptive Rejoinders About Deceptive Research: A Reply to Baron." *IRB: A Review of Human Subjects Research* 3:5-6.

Gordon, Margaret S. (1963) *The Economics of Welfare Policies*. New York: Columbia University Press.

Graham, Elinor (1967) "The Politics of Poverty." In *The Great Society Reader*, edited by Marvin E. Gettleman and David Mermelstein. New York: Random House.

Helfgot, Joseph H. (1981) *Professional Reforming*. Lexington: Lexington Books.

Hobsbawm, E.J. (1968) "Poverty." In *International Encyclopedia of the Social Sciences*, edited by David L. Sills. New York: Crowell Collier and Macmillan, Inc.

Hodge, Robert W. and Laslett, Barbara (1980) "Poverty and Status Attainment." In *Poverty and Public Policy: An Evaluation of Social Science Research*, edited by Vincent T. Covello. Cambridge: Schenkman Publishing Co.

Kleymeyer, Charles D. and Bertrand, William E. (1980) "Towards More Ethical and Effective Carrying Out of Applied Research Across Cultural or Class Lines." *Ethics in Science & Medicine* 7:11-25.

Korpi, Walter (1980) "Approaches to the Study of Poverty in the United States: Critical Notes from a European Perspective." In *Poverty and Public Policy: An Evaluation of Social Science Research*, edited by Vincent T. Covello. Cambridge: Schenkman Publishing Co.

Lamberth, John and Kimmel, Allan J. (1981) "Ethical Issues and Responsibilities in Applying Scientific Behavioral Knowledge."

New Directions for Methodology of Social and Behavioral Science 10:69-79.
Lecuyer, Bernard and Oberschall, Anthony R. (1978) "Social Research, The Early History Of." In International Encyclopedia of Statistics, edited by William H. Kruskal and Judith M. Tanur. New York: The Free Press.
Lewis, Oscar (1966) "The Culture of Poverty." In Anthropological Essays, by Oscar Lewis (1970). New York: Random House.
Levitan, Sar A. and Taggart, Robert (1976) The Promise of Greatness. Cambridge: Harvard University Press.
Mazur, Allan (1981) "Evaluating the Social Sciences." Science 212:875.
Okun, Arthur M. (1975) Equality and Efficiency: The Big Tradeoff. Washington: The Brookings Institution.
Orcutt, Guy, et al. (1980) "Poverty Research on Family Determination of Labor Income." In Poverty and Public Policy: An Evaluation of Social Science Research, edited by Vincent T. Covello. Cambridge: Schenkman Publishing Co.
Ornstein, Allan C. (1974) "The Cost of Federal Funding: Who Benefits?" Education and Urban Society 6:469-496.
Patterson, James T. (1981) America's Struggle Against Poverty 1900-1980. Cambridge: Harvard University Press.
Pettigrew, Thomas F. and Back, Kurt W. (1967) "Sociology in the Desegregation Process: Its Use and Disuse." In The Uses of Sociology, edited by Paul F. Lazarsfeld, William H. Sewell and Harold L. Wilensky. New York: Basic Books, Inc.
Plotnick, Robert D. (1979) "Social Welfare Expenditures: How Much Help for the Poor?" Policy Analysis 5:271-289.
Rubinow, I.M. (1934) "Poverty". In Encyclopedia of the Social Sciences, edited by Edwin R.A. Seligman. New York: The Macmillan Company.
Schelling, Thomas C. (1978) Micromotives and Macrobehavior. New York: W.W. Norton & Company.
Tuckman, Howard P. (1973) The Economics of the Rich. New York: Random House.
Tussing, A. Dale (1975) Poverty in a Dual Economy. New York: St. Martin's Press.
Ulman, Lloyd (1965) "Foreword." In Poverty in America, edited by Margaret S. Gordon. San Francisco: Chandler Publishing Company.
Wachtel, Howard M. (1971) "Looking at Poverty from a Radical Perspective." Review of Radical Political Economics 3:1-19.
"What Will They Think of Next?" (December 1981) Health Advocate: Newsletter of the National Health Law Program 127:3.
Williams, Daniel (14 February 1982) "The strike a city took to its heart." Boston Sunday Globe: All, A20.
Wyman, Anne C. (1982) "The Study of Human Society, its Promise and its Limits." The Boston Globe (January 4):2.

TOWARD A POLITICAL ECONOMY OF POVERTY RESEARCH: A CRITIQUE FROM RIGHT TO LEFT

Stephen M. Sachs

The way in which one looks at research on poverty is directly related to one's political and economic philosophy which in turn is usually connected to how one perceives his/her own interest. Therefore, in embarking upon an evaluation of poverty reseach, it is useful to survey the philosophical spectrum to consider how poverty research is seen from each major political-economic viewpoint.

Beginning on the contemporary "right,"[1] with capitalist libertarians[2] and extreme "clasical liberals" like Friedrich Hayek (Hayek, 1944 and 1960),[3] we find those who believe in minimal government with the state acting merely as umpire to see that private interests compete fairly. In this view the state should not intervene in the economy through either an administrative process of regulation or the provision of public goods and services. In the extreme example of this range of positions even the operation of fire departments and schools and the building and maintenance of streets and highways should be left to private initiative (Machan, 1972; Hospers, 1974). Hence poverty policy should be a private, largely charitable, concern in which government has no legitimate role. In the minimalist state a limited amount of privately supported poverty research would be useful to assist private charitable organizations. Privately sponsored research relating to the poor would also be legitimate as part of general economic research to provide information to businesses, consumers, and workers so that they could make more informed decisions. For example, research into where there are large numbers of unemployed people might be useful to business to find locations in which to find low cost labor, while research into what fields offer numerous job openings in specific localities would aid workers in obtaining employment. Such research might properly be funded through sale of publications or subscription to services summarizing its results. Thus the free market would determine the nature and direction of poverty research as well as directing the production and consumption of all other commodities (Von Mises, 1962).

In the current U.S. context, in which the minimalist sees public poverty programs as constituting illegitimate welfare statism, research concerning poverty, and other fields in which government is improperly involved, is appropriate to the extent that it shows the flaws in public programs and can support the argument that such programs do not work and should be abandoned. Aubry Robinson "Government and Public Health," and Lynn Kinsky "The FDA and Drug Research" (both in Machan, 1975) are illustrative of this kind of research.

Free market proponents such as Ronald Reagan (Reagan, 1981, and Gilder, 1981, Ch. 11) and Jack Kemp (Kemp, 1979, Ch. 5) lean toward minimal goverment, but believe that some public intervention in the economy is necessary, including a "safety net" of welfare and social security services. They, along with more moderate conservatives such as Richard Nixon (Nixon, 1970) see a legitimate, but limited, role for government social programs, although the private sector would continue to have primary duty for combatting poverty through efficient business practices and personal initiatives (Gilder, 1981, Chs. 2, 3 and 6). In this view the state has a supporting responsibility to provide minimum support for the few deserving poor (Gans, 1969; Patterson, 1981) whose financial difficulties cannot be adequately assisted by private means and for those who have earned the few legitimate public benefits (e.g., social security) (Reagan, 1981, pp. 40-41). From this perspective poverty research is appropriate that helps make programs more efficient, eliminating disincentives to work in on-going programs,[4] and removes ineligible recipients from the roles of those receiving public benefits. Since many conservatives of these types (and many minimalists as well) believe that a person's economic success is largely a function of his/her character development (and ability) in which education plays a part, research into the psychology and culture of poverty would be encouraged. Such research is seen both as an aid to moral education and support for the argument that, except for the few deserving poor, the solution to poverty lies in the poor themselves and not in government giveaways.

Many neoconservatives, such as Daniel Patrick Moynihan in the early and mid-seventies (Steinfels, 1979, Ch. 6; Coser and Howe, 1977, pp. 29-63 and 181-192; Moynihan, 1966; Kristol, 1978, Chs. 14, 25, 27, 28 and 29; Bell, 1976; Rainwater and Yancey, 1967; Glazer, 1966) and Platonist conservatives like Leo Strauss (who generally share the neoconservative view of social programs)[5] have taken a similar position on research concerning the culture of poverty, and have to a lesser extent supported investigation which might lead to reforms limiting the scope of anti-poverty measures. However, where those to their right approve, at most, a small government intervention into the economy to deal with poverty, neoconservative concerns about expanding social welfare services are often largely tactical. Many neoconservatives like Moynihan, Irving Kristol and Daniel Bell in the 1970's developed political positions in reaction to what they feared were the excesses of the Great Society in the 1960s. They believed that Johnson's extensive War on Poverty raised the expectations of the lower classes far beyond the ability of government to deliver, thereby threatening the legitimacy of the entire socio-economic-political system. Their main concern was stability (Steinfels, 1979, Chs. 2 and 3). Yet they agreed with the analysis of many liberals and some socialists (Steinfels, 1979, Chs. 2, 4-7; Moynihan, 1968) that the contemporary private economy could not meet the needs of society without considerable intervention from the state (Steinfels, 1979, Chs. 3, 5, 6, 7 and 9). Where libertarians and classical liberals generally represent a small business perspective, neoconservatives have usually represented large corporate interests (Steinfels, 1979, pp. 7-15). Reminiscent of the conservative Bismarck's initiation of the world's first social security program in Germany in the 19th century (Palmer and Colton, 1960, pp. 585-588), many neoconservatives perceive that the United States is burdened with a large underclass which must be provided with welfare programs if its support for the system is to be maintained (Steinfels, 1979, Chs. 3, 5, 6, 7 and 9). Hence neoconservatives often support research concerning the causes of poverty and other issues which might lead to new or expanded programs. But they have preferred that such research be undertaken quietly and technically by a few trusted researchers in order that it not be used to attack existing programs or raise destabilizing public demands for new measures (Steinfels, 1979, Chs. 6 and 10).

Toward the ideological center there are the moderate liberals, including those of the New Deal persuasion such as Hubert Humphrey (Humphrey, 1964), who have faith in the free enterprise system but believe that the current economy of giant scale business requires considerable government intervention to keep it in balance and to redress its shortcomings (Clark, 1939). Engaging much support from organized labor, big business, and the professions, liberals of this type believe extensive social welfare measures are necessary to keep post-industrial capitalism humane and viable. This approach requires research into the causes of poverty and into better ways of overcoming those causes, from technical adjustments of program administration to innovative policy. The debate over how to measure poverty discussed in Section II of this volume contains numerous examples of research suggesting technical improvements in existing programs. Stinson and Larson, for instance, argue that benefits provided to low income people would be more adequate and a larger number of those in need of benefits would be eligible if the quantity and quality of government services in a community were included in eligibility measurements since public services tend to be less available and of lower quality in low income areas.[6] Much of the experimentation with income maintenance programs discussed critically by Kenneth Neubeck in Part IV exemplifies innovative liberal research.[7] The largest number of studies from the liberal perspective are of the poor themselves. Usually these have been undertaken to increase understanding of why they as individuals are impoverished. (For example see Sheppard, 1970, Section II; Will and Vatter, 1970, Sections I, III, IV and V; and Morrill and Wohlenberg, 1971).

Consistent with a general outlook of evolutionary progress through rational analysis and discussion, liberals usually view the development of programs, and hence of research, as a slow progressive process with only rare major departures from previous programs and concerns. From this perspective research continually should lead the way to reform in an orderly manner (e.g., Kershaw, 1970). While a very small portion of research should explore the wide spectrum of alternative possibilities, so that there may be some preliminary information available in case these might eventually become relevant, the great bulk of exploration ought to be into those questions that have arisen from recent program experience (Lindblom, 1959, and Etzioni, 1967 and 1968, Ch. 11 and 12). This is the view of most of the mainstream foundations which fund research as well as of the majority of established academics who receive the overwhelming majority of major research grants. Hence the bulk of policy related poverty research has been concerned with narrow evaluations of ongoing programs and limited reforms suggested by essentially friendly program review (Lipsky, 1980).

Most of the top professional administrators in federal, state and local agencies generally agree with this moderate liberal view. However, they and their supporters among their clientele have vested interests, primarily in maintaining, and secondly, in enlarging, the work of their agencies, that is likely to influence their research perspectives. Research that will lead to program improvement is desirable, and studies showing a need to expand agency operations are welcome, but information seriously challenging the work of an agency is to be feared. Hence there is a self-interest in narrow, technically defined, non-repeatable research.

Many liberals will agree that there is potential for self interest in research, but counter that measures such as requiring program evaluation by reviewers outside of the agency, the development of legislative staffs and staff agencies such as G.A.O., together with the wide spectrum of active interest groups including public interest research organizations, plus a competitive, free press representing a broad range of views, is sufficient to provide for adequate, if imperfect, pluralism and checks and balances in research. A number of instances of such checks and balances are set forth in Leon Ginsberg's article in Section IV. These liberals would agree that if research too often is overly narrow, excessive and parochial, it is because agencies and those most concerned about their work have a tendency to lose perspective in the course of dealing with individual, day-to-day issues, and that a lack of resources, notably time and money, inhibits their ability to see clearly beyond the expedient to re-examine basic premises (Lindblom, 1959). These liberals would assert their hope that in time reforms resulting from the operation of checks and balances in this essentially open system would bring improvement through reform.

Left liberals, socialists and collective anarchists[8] (as well as many capitalist libertarians and classical liberals) would respond that while there is some truth in the moderate liberal apology, the fundamental problem is that the system is not truly open; that despite a few Ralph Naders and Common Causes, configurations of interest and gross inequalities in power keep most research, particularly the bulk of research which most directly influences government decision-making, in the interest of establishment groups and not of society as a whole.[9] Poverty research is in the interests of the rich at the expense of the poor (Katznelson and Kesselman, 1975, Chs. 1-5, 11-14; Cloward and Piven, 1971, 1979, 1982; Piven, 1974; Roby, 1974; and Dreitzel, 1974).

From a left radical perspective the primary causes of poverty in the United States are fundamental problems in the existing capitalist economy (Rodgers, 1979, Chs. 2, 3, 8 and 9; Rose, 1972). (Some capitalist libertarian and classical liberals would agree, but unlike left critics, see the cause of this difficulty in government intervention in the economy with the solution a return to a free market (Machan, 1975).) Left political economists believe that the difficulties with the existing capitalist system are so severe that mere reform through regulation and a supporting welfare system is inadequate to address its basic defects including the pervasiveness of poverty. They hold that programs that really would solve the problems of poverty if undertaken under the existing system would be so costly that they would undermine the current economic structure, while effective less costly solutions would involve direct transformation of the economy. Therefore, the dominant institutions cannot permit a truly effective poverty policy (Katznelson and Kesselman, 1975; Lerner, 1973, Ch. 1). At best, they may allow enough regulation and welfare to temporarily keep the existing system from breaking down into open interclass warfare. Liberal anti-poverty programs temporarily maintain the liberal state by alleviating the worst excesses of post-industrial capitalism while creating the illusion that those who wish to do so can escape poverty (Katznelson and Kesselman, 1975, Chs. 12, 13 and 14).

Left critics argue that one of the ways in which the established interests protect themselves is by controlling poverty research in fact while claiming an open system of research and discussion with academic freedom and freedom of the press (Katznelson and Kesselman, 1975, Ch. 11 and Piven, 1974). Although left thinkers disagree about to what extent this control is exerted consciously (Mills, 1956), and to what degree it is the result of unconscious inculturation following the forces of self interest (Lerner, 1973: 27-29), left critics agree that through possession of position and resources the dominant institutions actually direct the course of the great bulk of research in all its phases: the collection, dissemination, interpretation, and utilization of information. It is the wealthy interests who finance the major foundations that support research, donate most to political campaigns, lobby most effectively with all branches of government, own the preponderance of newspapers, magazines, radio and television stations to whom they provide the bulk of income through advertising. This combination of influences has the effect of directing the preponderance of public discussion and professional research along a limited set of lines generally favorable to establishment interests (Lerner, 1973, Ch. 1; Katznelson and Kesselman, 1975,, Chs. 2, 5, 8, 9, 11-14; Sweezy, 1942, Ch. XIII; Wolfe, 1976). Those on the boards of foundations and in key decision-making positions in government usually come either from large corporations or are established academics. One usually becomes established as an academic by receiving research grants and by publishing in prestigious professional journals. The choice of what articles to publish in prestigious professional journals is made by established academics. Thus, it is argued, the process involves a vicious circle in which the interest of the dominant institutions pervades. Most often this control is exerted subtly, only occasionally is it exercised directly; but the result is that the mainstream of research supports the needs of the established few with only enough dissent to make established claims of openness appear legitimate. It is for this reason that so much investigation is technical and narrow with little examination of significant alternatives. This in turn helps keep the discussion of public policy in the press, by the general public, and in government, focused within a narrow perspective (Piven, 1974; Katznelson and Kesselman, 1975, Chs. 2-4, 11-13).

In general, those on the left contend that the proper role of poverty research is to provide a critical analysis of poverty policy, showing its shortcomings and linkage to an inadequate and unjust economic system.[10] Left liberals, socialists and collective anarchists also emphasize exposing and re-examining unstated assumptions in established research[11] and comparative analysis of alternative research modes and policies.[12]

Numerous Marxists and some others on the left argue that further study of the poor should be abandoned, except to the extent that information showing the extent of the problems of poverty is important for public education concerning the inadequacies of the present economic system, including the failure of ongoing poverty policies.[13] They argue that even as anthropology arose as a discipline in the 19th century in imperialist western countries as a conduit of information for enhancing colonial control of third world possessions (Asad, 1973) so a great deal of social reseach of low income people assists the dominant elite in an internal colonization while resulting in little more than token benefits to the subjects of the studies (Katznelson and Kesselman, 1975, Ch. 12). According to this point of view, expressed in this volume by Kenneth Neubeck, poverty related research should focus instead on elite analysis[14] of the poverty policy process exposing the harsh realities of its decision-making and operation to the public.[15]

When society begins to change fundamentally to a more legitimate form the role of poverty research is also transformed. So long as research is undertaken primarily for the benefit of the few at the expense of the many, it is to be opposed. But when it becomes an instrument for the benefit of all, when it is undertaken in the general rather than the particular interest (as Rousseau would state it (Rousseau, 1965)), poverty research is to be supported. Followers of all public philosophies that assert the primacy of a general interest will agree with this general proposition.[16] For those on the contemporary left that means moving away from a society divided by class toward one in which differences of interest remain, but all are essentially on an equal footing. Various left liberals, socialists, anarchists and other progressive radicals each have their own vision of what constitutes the legitimate society and what the appropriate transition to it is in given conditions.[17] But once the transition is clearly in motion (to the orthodox Marxist this would mean once the capitalist system has been left behind and at least the first stages of socialism have begun (Lenin, 1963)), then proper poverty research, and indeed all policy and social research, shifts from opposition to support of the process of transformation. At that point the question whether or not to pursue culture of poverty research or any other line of questioning loses some of its political character and questions of psychology, metaphysics, and epistemology come to the fore in making research choices. But, even in the best regime following the most enlightened policy, a large degree of politics remains in research decisions and critical research remains a necessity (Kettler, 1974). This is true not only for Marxists,[18] or adherents of left philosophies, but in general; for change the definitions of legitimate and enlightened to fit the particular perspective and it becomes clear that there are analogues to this problem for all political positions that accept the existence of the public good. In every situation there are people who will benefit and/or suffer loss as a result of social research. The researcher, relevant agencies and their clientele, the subjects of the research, the general public -- everyone concerned -- has an interest in whether, and in what way, the inquiry will be undertaken, how the information gained will be processed, distributed, and ultimately utilized, or disregarded, in making public and private decisions. Evaluation of poverty and other social research, then, cannot be responsibly made solely on the basis of abstract questions of methodology and epistemology -- as important as those concerns are. We have a responsibility to look further to estimate the impact of inquisitorial acts.[19] In the context of this volume we must begin to ask, "Who benefits from poverty research?"

NOTES

1. The author recognizes that labeling terms like right, left, liberal, conservative, Marxist, while often helpful, are clearly oversimplifications. Each such category includes a wide number of issues and questions. Lack of space prevents our delving into many of the important questions and distinctions within, and exceptions from, each of the general positions

2. discussed here. I hope, however, that if my categorization is taken with a great deal of salt, it will be more helpful than confusing.
2. A good anthology of relevant libertarian writings is Tibor Machan, editor, The Libertarian Alternative, 1975. See Jerome Tucelle, 1972, It Usually Begins With Ayn Rand for a good survey of libertarian thought.
3. Other examples of classical liberals are Barry Goldwater (1960, pp. 68-75), Milton Friedman (1968, 1970 and 1972), James Buchanan (1967 and 1970), and Henry Simons (1948). Many "New Right" thinkers and politicians take a similar, non-interventionalist approach to government regulation of the economy and provision of social welfare services. For example, see Helms, 1976.
4. For a recent example, see Greene, 1981.
5. Strauss may never have done this directly, but it is consistent with his position which is essentially the same in practice as that of many neoconservatives. Some of Strauss' leading associates like Martin Diamond (Steinfels, 1979, p. 5) are often labeled neoconservatives and a number of those associated with Strauss have taken this kind of position on the advancement of the poor (e.g., Herbert Storing, whose work on Black Americans including, What Country Have I, 1970, was intended to encourage blacks to win equality through developing and asserting their own virtue). Strauss' conservative philosophy can be gleaned in part in his volumes, What is Political Philosophy, 1959 and Natural Right and History, 1953.
6. The debate over how to measure poverty also includes research from a wide variety of non-liberal positions. Timothy Smeeding's piece in Section II discusses, and opposes, the arguments of conservative researchers who argue that benefits provided to low income people should be reduced by including in-kind benefits received in calculating a person's income; while Harrell Rodgers' critique, "Limiting Poverty by Design: . . . " is an example of a socialist approach to this issue.
7. It is important to note that not only liberals supported income maintenance experiments. Some conservatives like Nixon (Moynihan, 1973) and Milton Friedman favored the idea of direct payments to the poor as a way to reduce the poverty bureaucracy while numerous socialists backed the idea as a progressive development in establishing a right to a minimum income.
8. The range of positions and groups squeezed into the label, "the left" for the limited purposes of this essay is extremely broad. It includes what we here term left liberals, who usually join with social democrats calling for a mixed economy of private and publicly owned businesses with private enterprise controlled, rather than merely regulated, by government (Carnoy and Shearer, 1980, Parts II and III), and the full

spectrum of socialists, collective anarchists (or libertarian socialists), syndicalists, etc. Clearly, within this extensive collection of positions there are tremendous differences in program strategy and the details of critiquing current U.S. society. In very broad terms, however, their critiques of the United States socio-political-economic system are generally similar in that they all complain of the unjust dominance of the system by a small set of interests because of an inequity of power. Moreover, all of these groups include some kind of class analysis in their critique, though the view of what constitutes class, or its equivalent, is quite varied and not necessarily limited to economic class in the sense that Lenin used the term (e.g., some radical feminists substitute sex for economic class as the core characteristic around which to build their analysis, while a number of "unorthodox Marxists" consider economics, kinship, authority and community relations as independent core characteristics in analysis (Albert and Hahnel, 1978, ch. 3)). There are sufficient analogues in their positions to consider these groups together in this brief discussion of poverty research if we bear in mind the differences underlying their apparent unity suggested by the high level of abstraction of this discussion. Extreme anarchists, who believe in no government whatsoever, with society organized entirely on the basis of volunteer cooperation (Dolgoff, 1974; Krimerman and Perry, 1966; Apter and Joll, 1972) (collective anarchists believe in a very decentralized and participatory socialism) also tend to agree with much of the left critique of the existing political-economic-social system, but like capitalist libertarians see the solution of the problems of poverty through a cessation of government action, through voluntary collectivism rather than in a competitive free market.

9. The dominance of capitalist society by a wealthy ruling class is central to the Marxist perspective (for a good survey of Marxist classics see Tucker, 1972; Mendel, 1963). Good U.S. studies supporting this position are Mills, 1956; Domhoff, 1967, 1971, 1979 and 1980; Kolko, 1976. A good left liberal discussion along these lines is Newfield and Greenfield, 1972. Rodgers, 1979 is an example of a political economic analysis specifically of the relationship between capitalism and the continuation of extensive poverty in the United States. Other works of this type include James, 1972, Bachrach and Baratz, 1970, Rose, 1972, Tussing, 1975, Roby, 1974 and Cloward and Piven, 1971, 1979 and 1982. Katznelson and Kesselman, 1975 discuss the built-in limitations on poverty policy and of the questions that can receive serious public consideration concerning such policy in the course of a political-economic analysis. A good general left critique of the politicization of social research is Dreitzel, 1974.

10. Examples of this kind of research are Roby 1974, Kotz, 1971, Rose, 1972, Bachrach and Baratz, 1970, Cloward and Piven, 1971, 1979 and 1982, Edwards, 1978 and Pious, 1974.
11. For an example of this kind of critique see Ryan, 1971, pp. 3-22.
12. For examples of this kind of research see Harrell Rodgers' article on alternative approaches in this volume and Carnoy and Shearer, 1980.
13. Deutsch and Howard, 1970 contains a number of critiques of this character.
14. Domhoff, 1967 and Mills, 1956 are classic examples of this kind of research.
15. Roby, 1974, Rose, 1972, and Dreitzel, 1974 are examples of this kind of critique.
16. Only if one takes a position like that of Thrasymachus in Book II of Plato's Republic, in which Thrasymachus argues that justice is the will of the stronger, would one oppose this proposition (and even then one might support it when he/she, or his/her party, were in power).
17. Newfield and Greenfield, 1972, Raskin, 1974, Carnoy and Shearer, 1980, Harrington, 1973, Lerner, 1973, Katznelson and Kesselman, 1975, Ch. 14, Lynd and Alperovitz, 1973, and Albert and Hahnel, 1978 give some idea of the range of views on these questions.
18. This raises the question of praxis, the progressive dialectic between theory and practice in which research plays an important role. For an interesting, innovative view of Praxis see Albert and Hahnel, 1978, Ch. 3 and 4.
19. Some of the issues involved here are discussed in the introduction and conclusion of this volume as well as in Nalven's article, "Who Benefits from Knowledge about the Health of Undocumented Aliens." See also Helfgot, 1981; Gans, 1973; Williams, 1982; Lamberth and Kimmel, 1981; Angell, 1967; Glazer, 1972; Boulay, et al, 1980; Goldstein, 1981 and Rule, 1978.

REFERENCES

Albert, Michael and Hahnel, Robin (1978). Unorthodox Marxism: An Essay on Capitalism, Socialism and Revolution. (Boston: South End Press).

Angell, Robert C. (1967). "The Ethical Problems of Applied Sociology," in Lazersfeld, Paul E., William M. Sewell and Harold L. Wilensky, The Uses of Sociology. (New York: Basic Books).

Apter, David E. and James Joll (eds.) (1972). Anarchism Today. (Garden City: Anchor Books).

Asad, T. (ed.) (1973). Anthropology and Colonial Encounters. (London: Ithica Press).

Bachrach, Peter and Baratz, Morton (1970). Power and Poverty: Theory and Practice. (New York: Oxford University Press)

Bell, Daniel (1976). *The Cultural Contradictions of Capitalism*. (New York: Basic Books).

Boulay, Harvey, Richard Goldstein and Betty Zisk (1980). "Protecting Human Subjects: Proposed Amendments to H.E.W. Policy: Comments on Pool's Analysis," in *PS*, Vol. 13, pp. 202-203.

Buchanan, James (1967). *Public Debt in a Democracy*. (Washington, D.C.: American Enterprise Institute).

——— (1970). *The Public Finance; An Introductory Textbook*. (Homewood, Illinois: R.D. Irwin).

Carnoy, Martin and Shearer, Derek (1980). *Economic Democracy*. (Armonk, N.Y.: M.E. Sharpe, Inc.).

Clark, John M. (1939). *Social Control of Business*. (New York: McGraw-Hill Book Co.).

Cloward, Richard and Piven, Frances Fox (1971). *Regulating the Poor*. (New York: Pantheon Books).

——— (1979). *Poor People's Movements*. (New York: Random House, Inc.).

——— (1982). *The New Class War: Reagan's Attack on the Welfare State and Its Consequences*. (New York: Pantheon Books).

Coser, Lewis and Howe, Irving (1977). *The New Conservatives: A Critique from the Left*. (New York: Meridian Books).

Deutsch, Steven and Howard, John, eds. (1970). *Where It's At: Radical Perspectives in Sociology*. (New York: Harper and Row Publishers).

Dolgoff, Sam (1974). *The Anarchist Collectives: Workers' Self-Management in the Spanish Revolution 1936-1939*. (Brooklyn, New York: Free Life Editions).

Domhoff, G. William (1967). *Who Rules America?* (Englewood Cliffs, N.J.: Prentice Hall, Inc.).

Domhoff, G. William (1971). *The Higher Circles: The Governing Class in America*. (New York: Vintage Books).

Domhoff, G. William (1979). *The Powers That Be: Process of Ruling Class Domination in America*. (New York: Vintage Books).

Domhoff, G. William (1980). *Power Structure Research*. (Beverly Hills, CA: Sage Publications).

Dreitzel, Peter (1974). "Social Science and the Problem of Rationality," in Katznelson, Ira, Adams, Gordon, Brennen, Philip and Wolfe, Alan, *The Politics and Society Reader*. (New York: David McKay Co.).

Edwards, Richard A. (1978). "Who Fares Well in the Welfare State," in Edwards, Richard C., Reich, Michael and Weisskopf, Thomas, *The Capitalist System*. (Englewood Cliffs, New Jersey).

Etzioni, Amitai (1967). "Mixed Scanning: A 'Third' Approach to Decisionmaking," *Public Administration Review*, vol. 27, pp. 385-392.

——— (1968). *The Active Society: A Theory of Societal and Political Processes*. (Glencoe: The Free Press).

Friedman, Milton (1968). Dollars and Deficits: Living with America's Economic Problems. (Englewood Cliffs, New Jersey: Prentice Hall, Inc.).

———— (1970). The Counter Revolution in Monetary Theory. (London: Institute of Economic Affairs).

———— (1972). An Economist's Protest: Columns in Political Economy. (Glen Ridge, N.J.: T. Horton).

Gans, Herbert J. (1969). "Culture and Class in the Study of Poverty: An Approach to Anti-Poverty Research," in Moynihan, Daniel, On Understanding Poverty. (New York: Basic Books).

———— (1973). More Equality. (New York: Pantheon Books).

Gilder, George (1981). Wealth and Poverty. (New York: Basic Books, Inc.).

Glazer, Myron (1972). The Research Adventure. (New York: Random House).

Glazer, Nathan (1966). "The Grand Design of the Poverty Program," New York Times Magazine, February 27.

Goldstein, Richard (1981). "On Deceptive Rejoinders About Deceptive Research: A Reply to Barron," IRB: A Review of Human Subjects Research, vol. 3, pp. 5-6.

Goldwater, Barry (1960). The Conscience of a Conservative. (Sheperdsville, KY: Viltor Publishing Co., Inc.).

Greene, Leonard (1981). Free Enterprise Without Poverty. (New York: W.W. Norton and Co.).

Harrington, Michael (1973). Socialism. (New York: Bantam Books).

Hayek, Friedrich (1944). The Road to Serfdom. (Chicago: University of Chicago Press).

———— (1960). The Constitution of Liberty. (Chicago: University of Chicago Press)

Helfgot, Joseph H. (1981). Professional Reforming. (Lexington, MA: Lexington Books).

Helms, Jesse (1976). When Free Men Shall Stand. (Zonderzan Publishing House).

Hospers, John (1974). "What Libertarianism Is," in Machan, Tibor (ed.), The Libertarian Alternative. (Chicago: Nelson Hall Publishers).

Humphrey, Hubert (1964). The Cause is Mankind: A Liberal Program for Modern America. (New York: Praeger).

James, Dorothy (1972). Poverty, Politics and Change. (Englewood Cliffs, N.J.: Prentice Hall, Inc.).

Katznelson, Ira and Kesselman, Mark (1975). The Politics of Power: A Critical Introduction to American Government. (New York: Harcourt, Brace, Jovonovich, Inc.).

Kemp, Jack (1979). An American Renaissance: A Strategy for the 1980s. (New York: Berkeley Books).

Kershaw, Joseph, assisted by Paul J. Courant (1970). Government Against Poverty. (Chicago: Markham Publishing Co.).

Kettler, David (1974). "The Vocation of Radical Intellectuals," in Katznelson, Ira, Adams, Godron, Brenner, Philip, and Wolfe,

Alan, <u>The Politics and Society Reader</u>. (New York: David McKay Co.).
Kolko, Gabriel (1976). "The Man of Power," in Etzkowitz, Henry and Schwab, Peter, <u>Is America Necessary?</u> (St. Paul: West Publishing Co.).
Kotz, Nick (1971). <u>Let Them Eat Promises: The Politics of Hunger in America</u>. (Garden City, N.Y.: Anchor Books).
Krimerman, Leonard and Lewis Perry (eds.) (1966). <u>Patterns of Anarchy: A Collection of Writings on the Anarchist Tradition</u>. (Garden City, New York: Anchor Books).
Kristol, Irving (1978). <u>Two Cheers for Capitalism</u>. (New York: Mentor Books).
Lamberth, John and Allan J. Kimmel (1981). "Ethical Issues and Responsibilities in Applying Scientific Behavioral Knowledge," in <u>New Directions for Methodology of Social and Behavioral Science</u>, vol. 10, pp. 69-79.
Lenin, Vladimir (1963). <u>The State and Revolution</u>. reprinted in Mendel, Arthur P. (ed.), <u>Essential Works of Marxism</u>. (New York: Bantam Books).
Lerner, Michael (1973). <u>The New Socialist Revolution</u>. (New York: Dell Publishing Co.).
Lindblom, Charles E. (1959). "The Science of Muddling Through," <u>Public Administration Review</u>, vol. 19, no. 1, pp. 79-88.
Lipsky, Michael (1980). "Poverty and Administration: Perspectives on Research" in Vincent T. Covello, <u>Poverty and Public Policy: An Evaluation of Social Science Research</u>. (Cambridge: Schenkman Publishing Co.).
Lynd, Staughton and Alperowitz, Gar (1973). <u>Strategy and Program: Two Essays Toward a New American Socialism</u>. (Boston: Beacon Press).
Machan, Tibor (ed.) (1975). <u>The Libertarian Alternative</u>. (Chicago: Nelson Hall Publishers).
_____ (1972). "Freedom Through Capitalism," in James, Dorothy, <u>Outside Looking In</u>. (New York: Harper and Row).
Mendel, Arthur (1963). <u>Essential Works of Marxism</u>. (New York: Bantam Books, Inc.).
Mills, C. Wright (1956). <u>The Power Elite</u>. (New York: Oxford University Press).
Morrill, Richard and Ernest M. Wohlenberg (1971). <u>The Geography of Poverty in the United States</u>. (New York: McGraw-Hill Book Co.).
Moynihan, Daniel Patrick (1966). "The Case for a Family Policy," <u>America</u>, September 18.
_____ 1968. "The Democrats, Kennedy, and the Murder of Dr. King," <u>Commentary</u>, May.
_____ 1973. <u>Politics of a Guaranteed Income: The Nixon Administration and the Family Assistance Plan</u>. (New York: Random House).

Newfield, Jack and Greenfield, Jeff (1972). The Populist Manifesto: The Making of a New Majority. (New York: Warner Paperback Library).

Nixon, Richard M. (1970). "Welfare Alternatives," excerpts from August 8, 1969 Address to the Nation on Welfare Reform, in Will, Robert and Vatter, Harold Poverty in Affluence. (New York: Harcourt, Brace & Word, Inc.).

Palmer, R.R. and Colton, Joel (1960). A History of the Modern World. (New York: Alfred A. Knopf, Inc.).

Pious, Richard (1974). "Policy and Public Administration: The Legal Services Program in the War on Poverty," in Katznelson, Ira, Adams, Gordon, Brenner, Philip, and Wolfe, Alan, The Politics and Society Reader. (New York: David McKay Co.).

Piven, Frances Fox (1974). "Social Science and Social Policy," in Roby, Pamela, The Poverty Establishment. (Englewood Cliffs, N.J.: Prentice-Hall, Inc.).

Rainwater, Lee and Yancey, William (1967). The Moynihan Report and the Politics of Controversy. (Cambridge, MA: M.I.T. Press).

Raskin, Marcus (1974). Notes on the Old System. (New York: David McKay, Inc.).

Reagan, Ronald (1981). Rendezvous With Destiny. (Salt Lake City, Utah: Osmund Publishing Co.).

Roby, Pamela (ed.) (1974). The Poverty Establishment. (Englewood Cliffs, N.J.: Prentice Hall).

Rodgers, Harrell (1979). Poverty Amid Plenty: A Political and Economic Analysis. (Reading, MA: Addison-Wesley Publishing Co.).

Rose, Stephen M. (1972). The Betrayal of the Poor: the Transformation of Community Action. (Cambridge: Schenkman Publishing Company).

Rousseau, Jean Jacques (1965). The Social Contract. (New York: Harper Publishing Co.).

Rule, James B. (1978). Insight and Social Betterment: A Preface to Applied Social Science. (New York: Oxford University Press).

Ryan, William (1971). Blaming the Victim. (New York: Pantheon Books).

Sheppard, Harold L. (ed.) (1970). Poverty and Wealth in America. (Chicago: Quadrangle Books).

Simons, Henry (1948). Economic Policy for a Free Society. (Chicago: University of Chicago Press).

Steinfels, Peter (1979). The Neoconservatives: The Men Who Are Changing Americas Politics. (New York: Touchstone Books).

Storing, Herbert (ed.) (1970). What Country Have I: Political Writings by Black Americans. (New York: St. Martin's Press).

Strauss, Leo (1953). Natural Right and History. (Chicago: University of Chicago Press).

_____ (1959). What is Political Philosophy and Other Studies? (Glencoe, Illinois: The Free Press).

Sweezy, Paul (1942). *The Theory of Capitalist Development*. (New York: Monthly Review Press).

Tucelle, Jerome (1972). *It Usually Begins with Ayn Rand: A Libertarian Odyssey*. (Briarcliff Manor, N.Y.: Stein and Day).

Tucker, Robert (ed.) (1972). *The Marx-Engels Reader*. (New York: W.W. Norton).

Tussing, Dale (1975). *Poverty in a Dual Economy*. (New York: St. Martin's Press).

Von Mises, Ludwig (1962). *The Free and Prosperous Commonwealth: An Exposition of the Ideas of Classical Liberalism*. (Princeton, N.J.: D. Van Nostrand).

Will, Robert E. and Vatter, Harold G. (1970). *Poverty in Affluence: The Social Political, and Economic Dimensions of Poverty in the United States*. (New York: Harcourt, Brace & World, Inc.).

Williams, Daniel (1982). "The Strike a City Took to Its Heart," *Boston Sunday Globe*, February 14, pp. A 11 and A 20.

Wolfe, Alan (1976). "The Professional Mystique," in Etzkowitz, Henry and Schwab, Peter, *Is America Necessary?* (St. Paul: West Publishing Co.).

WHO REALLY BENEFITS FROM APPLIED POVERTY RESEARCH?: OPENING UP A QUESTION*

Richard Goldstein

INTRODUCTION

> "Another study! Hell, they just don't want to do anything."
> "Another study! Why don't they give the money to us so we can do something with it, rather than wasting it on more research?"
> "They study us again and again, but they never tell us what they have learned."

These complaints about research on poverty have been heard again and again, from both poor people and their representatives (see, for example, Farmer, 1967). Usually, bureaucrats and researchers just brush the complaints aside as meaningless. Yet, the frequency with which these complaints have been heard keeps alive the idea that they are not meaningless, as does the continuing existence of widespread poverty.

The idea that poverty research does not benefit the poor is not limited to the poor or their representatives. Judge David Bazelon made the following statement in a 1972 address to correctional psychologists:

> You must ask yourselves whether your help is really needed, or whether you are merely engaged as magicians to perform an intriguing side show so that spectators will not notice the crisis in the center ring. In considering our motives in offering you a role, I think you would do well to consider how much less expensive it is to hire a thousand psychologists than to make even a miniscule change in the social and economic structure. (Quoted in Caplan and Nelson, 1974: 104.)

---

* I would like to thank Louis Ferleger, Stephen Sachs and Jennifer Wilton for their comments on earlier drafts.

This does not imply that the establishment is the only or even the prime beneficiary of this research. As several authors have pointed out, social scientists have also benefited, at least in the sense of increased money and jobs (Guttentag, 1970; Helfgot, 1981; and Ridgeway, 1967), and in the sense of an expansion of the number of and types of legitimate research questions (Gramlich, 1980). Further, there may be costs to these or to other actors that outweigh the benefits. Of course, that social scientists benefit does not imply anything about the extent to which the poor and society at large also benefit from this research.

Notice also, that the question of who benefits, if anybody does, is not coincident with the question of whether the research is used. Regardless of whether the research of the psychologists referred to by Bazelon is used, his statement stands. Specifically, individualistic research, and the programs based on this research, are much less expensive than structural changes to society.

In this article we open up the question of who really benefits from poverty research, illuminating some of the issues involved in this question. The articles which follow delve more deeply into specific aspects of the broader problem, providing partial answers to portions of this question while suggesting lines of inquiry that we hope will be pursued in future studies.

BACKGROUND

Many believe that the correct answer to our question "Who Really Benefits?" is one of the following two questions:

"Hasn't this already been investigated?"
"Isn't it obvious that poor people will benefit in the long-run, and probably already have benefited?"

Our answers are that this question has barely been asked in the past and has certainly not been answered, and that, no, it is not obvious that poor people have generally benefited or will generally benefit from research on poverty. It is, after all, possible that no one will benefit from this research, or even that only the bureaucracy, or politicians, or social scientists, or wealthy interests, will benefit.

Although many researchers have investigated the distribution of the benefits of poverty programs, very few have asked the same questions about their own work. Nathan Caplan and Stephen Nelson are among the exceptions. They asked whether blacks were likely to benefit from being studied. To answer this, they investigated the work listed in Psychological Abstracts for the first six months of 1970. They found that 82% of the relevant studies were person-oriented and only 16% were situation oriented (while the remainder were mixed). The person-oriented studies could only help those in power control those out of power -- they could not help the blacks.

This was of course a limited investigation and it used a possibly biased sample, but it is suggestive.

Possibly more informative is an anecdote told about a situation that Caplan actually found himself in at one time. Caplan was studying a job development program and found that punctuality was a problem. He could obtain funding to study the "deficient time perspectives" of the subjects, but could not obtain money to purchase alarm clocks for these same people, even after discovering that less than one-fourth of them had access to clocks. No one was interested in discovering whether this simple situational fact had any bearing on the punctuality problem, but there was plenty of interest in discovering possible psychological causes. (Caplan and Nelson, 1974: 101-102)

There has also been some investigation of the positive results of social science research both for the poor and in general. In its recent report on poverty research, the National Academy of Sciences spent some time discussing the actual past substantive uses of research on poverty in policy-making. These uses included: the creation of a few important general data sources which have influenced policy debate; a shift from human capital programs to income maintenance measures; changes in program administration, including for example, relevant definitions (such as that of the household); the raising of new questions (such as the target efficiency of programs). (Committee on Evaluation of Poverty Research, 1979: 24-28) Unfortunately, regarding none of these did the Committee inquire into its effect on poor people. Though the positive effects of some of these may seem obvious, there have occurred enough perverse experiences in the history of anti-poverty programs to warn us that even such a change as getting people to look at the target efficiency of a program may have negative effects for the poor. (See Galliher and McCartney, 1973; Gramlich, 1980; and Moore, 1973.)

A similar caveat may be in order regarding Adam Yarmolinsky's (1976:272) example of social science producing new, useful information: The President's Crime Commission found that there was a probability of .5 of any male in the U.S. being arrested for a non-traffic offense some time during his life. This led to, among other things, the removal of questions about arrests from the standard Civil Service Employment forms. For this information and result to have been helpful to poor people means that those doing the hiring using these forms were prejudiced against those who had been arrested (or possibly they were prejudiced against those who had been arrested and whose forms contained certain other information, for example, information showing them to be poor and "thus" not "worthy" of further consideration), and that the lack of this information meant that either these people were now operating in a non-prejudicial manner or that different prejudices, less harmful to poor people, were now operating. Yarmolinsky presents no information relevant to these assumptions, and I know of none. It is even possible that the above change hurt poor people because those doing the hiring previously helped those poor who had never been arrested, and thus were "worthy", and now no aid is provided to any poor applicants since the "worthy" cannot be distinguished from the "not worthy".

In fact, what Yarmolinsky thinks is undeniably a benefit may be a cost. This is in general true concerning the effects of social science on policy. Some critics of this relationship have levied strong charges against social scientists in the policy arena. For example, Caplan and Nelson (1974:100) charge that, "Repeatedly reform-minded social scientists have unwittingly compounded the problems they set out to solve." Moore (1973), in an article reviewing research on minorities in the U.S., found several deleterious consequences for minorities, including:

- exclusion from participation in programs;
- mis-design of programs;
- the sustenance and even the generation of stereotypes.

Another deleterious effect has been that "On balance, the scholarly community made the public discourse not less but more venomous." (Frankel, 1976:14) To the extent that Frankel is correct, the reason may be the failure of social scientists to see that social problems represent situations of conflict of interests, rather than just a "technocratic" problem. (Rule, 1978)

Part of the evidence presented in support of the above quotes are arguments concerning the way in which research is organized and arguments about the perspective(s) of researchers. These arguments are clearly relevant to the question of who benefits from this type of research. They include:

- Social scientists follow the lead of non-scientists (politicians and bureaucrats); that is, social scientists let the basic questions to be researched be formulated by non-scientists (this applies to "basic" research as well as to applied research). (See Aaron, 1978; Denzin, 1970; Helfgot, 1981; Partridge, 1978; Sanger, 1979; and Williams, 1971.)
- Social scientists study only those who are too weak to protect themselves (at least regarding the non-public parts of people's lives.) (Jones, 1980).
- Social scientists are ambitious, attempting to get ahead by doing what those in power want done.

Popular culture has even noticed some of these issues as evidenced by the comic strip "Motley's Crew", in which one character says:

> The government's got an unbeatable system! First, they screw things up so bad that a bunch of blue-collar workers get laid off. That lets 'em hire a bunch of white-collar people to help those blue-collar workers find a job. Then

the government turns around and brags that white-collar unemployment is going down!!!

Thus, we see that the issue of utilization of poverty research is not the same as the issue of who benefits from, and who pays the costs of, poverty research -- there are many intervening steps. These steps can mean, for example, that a piece of research can have more benefit (less cost) for poor people if it is never used than it would if used. This may be especially true of research that is person-oriented. Structural research or theorizing would at least tell one that in a competitive system there must be some losers. This knowledge should help prevent researchers from blaming losers for their condition, since changing their condition can only mean, at best, that one is changing who the losers are. (For more on this, see the Introduction.)

Also relevant are more broadly-based studies of who benefits. For example, Clark Abt has presented a number of papers on questions relating to the benefits of applied social research, and how these benefits could be increased. In one paper, Abt (1976a) concludes that the benefits of applied social research and development and of social programs exceed their costs. Unfortunately, in addition to the general problems of cost-benefit analysis (deciding what is a cost and what is a benefit; "monetizing" non-monetary events and happenings so that incomparables can be compared), Abt's work has some other problems. The most important for us is that he ignores the costs to the program recipients of the programs and of the research and development efforts. Abt also ignores some other potential costs, including one of the points that we started with, that of using program money for research rather than for the program or other form of aid.

In another paper, Abt (1976b:1) presents a model which illustrates the bias of his approach:

> A simple model of the productivity of social policy-relevant evaluation research, and indeed most government applied social research, includes variables of <u>issue prioritization</u>, <u>research question selection</u>, <u>research design validity</u>, <u>research execution competence</u>, <u>findings communication effectiveness</u>, and <u>policy application</u> effectiveness, all divided by the costs of doing the research. (Emphasis in original.)

For Abt, the costs of doing the research are <u>solely</u> the monies spent annnually by the federal government. Yet, clearly there are other costs involved (including the opportunity costs of the money spent on the research).

One of these other costs is clearly pointed to by Abt in the same paper. There, he reports on a conversation he had with a Cabinet Officer. Abt asked what the result would be if an evaluation researcher openly published the results of a study inimical to the policy aims of the agency and without the permission of the agency. The response was that all subsequent contract and grant awards to the <u>offender</u> would be reviewed at the highest level of the agency with the intent of finding some good reason for not making the award. The Cabinet Officer did not have any memory of this actually happening, but that may well be because this is exactly what researchers would expect to occur and therefore they would not publish that kind of information (Abt, 1976b:7-8; see also Brickell, 1978). It may also never have occurred because of the propensity that many researchers appear to have of finding what the agency wants them to find. Clearly Abt's work is important as far as it goes. But, it does not go far enough.

Finally, investigations made by Representative Green's staff and by the General Accounting Office (Green, 1972a; 1972b; see also Ornstein, 1974)

> found educational organizations taking money for work not done, for studies not performed, for analyses not prepared, for results not produced. Over and over again, we have found educators using public funds for research projects that have turned out to be esoteric, irrelevant, and often not even research. (Green, 1972a:13)

Certainly, research funds for which the sponsor receives no return cannot generate benefits to the poor. But, research that is so esoteric that its results cannot be generalized or implemented also generates no benefits for program recipients.

OTHER RELEVANT WORK

There are two other areas from which work relevant to the question of "Who really benefits?" comes. One, studies of physical science research, and, two, studies of the rate of decay of either knowledge or of the benefits derived from knowledge that is generated by research.

With respect to studies of physical science research and development, the results do not bode well for our concerns:

> Are the advisory efforts of scientists effective in informing the democratic decision-making process? The answer... is a resounding No!... problems stem to a large extent from institutional arrangements and are not peculiar to individuals. (Primack and Von Hippel, 1974:4)

That is, the fact that advice and information is only available to part of the government and is not available to all to the public makes it easy for bureaucrats and politicians to ignore and/or distort the advice given by the scientists. What makes this institutional is that laws and regulations decree that much of this information not be made public and not be available even to other branches of government.

Regarding the second issue, there are as yet no studies concerning the knowledge gained from applied poverty research. There are, however, extensive studies into the rate of decay (or conservation) of traditional capital. Rate of decay here refers to the rate at which, for example, benefits accrue from research over time. Normally one would expect the rate of return to decline over time both because conditions change and because invalidity of the original research impedes over-time generalizations. Investigations into the rate of decay of revenues due to new knowledge, especially knowledge that is useful in business, such as product or process innovation, are starting to appear. These latter studies might be useful to our concerns. These studies basically conclude that new-knowledge-related revenues decay faster than does the knowledge that the revenues are based on, for two reasons. One, it is difficult to maintain the ability to appropriate the benefits from the knowledge. Two, new innovations are developed which partly or entirely displace the original innovation (Pakes and Schankerman, 1978).

These points can be translated into our area of concern as follows: One, that it is difficult to maintain the ability to appropriate benefits means, among other things, that research can be used by both friends and foes of the poor because knowledge can be used by persons other than those who generated the knowledge. Knowledge alone does not generate benefits, only the appropriate use of knowledge generates benefits. Two, that new innovations are developed means, among other things, that what was true yesterday may not be true tomorrow. For example, more education may lead to a higher paying job now, but when everyone has more education, not everyone will obtain a higher-paying job. This may mean that any benefits that do accrue to the poor from research on poverty will be very short-lived, while the costs may not be short-lived.

ARE THERE INHERENT METHODOLOGICAL PROBLEMS?

Lee Cronbach (1976:147) has said that,

> The social scientist is trained to think that he does not know all the answers. The social scientist is not trained to realize that he does not know all the questions. And that is why his social influence is not unfailingly constructive.

An example of this inability occurs in the recent National Academy of Sciences' evaluation of federal support for poverty research. In their conclusion, the Committee on Evaluation of Poverty Research (1979:70) says that,

> Our committee has accepted the institute's [The Institute for Research on Poverty at the University of Wisconsin] view of itself strictly as a research vehicle. Acting as such it serves essential interests of all parties to the arrangement: the university, the researchers, and the government.

And where are the poor? They are to be the subjects and objects of research but are not to be party to an arrangement that provides core funds to a research institute specializing in poverty research. Nor does anyone appear concerned about whether the poor will receive any benefits from this arrangement. (Also, see Guttentag, 1970.) Furthermore, where is the general public? Is this research, or at least this arrangement, really in the public interest?

Datta (1980) argues that the problems are not inherent but arise because we have not used well-known remedies for the biases in our research. The two remedies that she is referring to are (1) replication, and (2) strong inference; that is, the design of studies that will critically and systematically test all plausible alternative hypotheses. As Datta points out, these two remedies are both widely used in the physical and life sciences and could be used in the social sciences. But they are not used.

At another level, some have argued that it is not our research but our inferences from the research which is at fault. Levitan and Taggart (1976:6), for example, say

> In the late 1960s, the reservations were reread with more care, revealing that most findings were neither rigorous nor clearcut. Ironically, the discovery that the emperor was naked did not damage the reputation of social scientists and their techniques as much as it did the subjects of their evaluation: if evaluations could not conclusively prove the value of governmental programs, then the programs must not have been worthwhile.

Many others have noted that both evaluative and non-evaluative research tend to have a conservative and/or negative bias (Becker and Horowitz, 1972; Berk and Rossi, 1977; Carter, 1971.) Whether this bias is inherent is, however, still an open question. Horowitz (1971:2) appears to believe it is not inherent but that all parties must have access to all stages of the study, and then have use of the study in the formulation of policy. Similarly, Williams (1971:58) argues that the problem is an emphasis on macronegative results, that is, results that indicate how certain groups are disadvantaged as to jobs, income, education, etc., but do not indicate how to overcome these problems.

On the other hand, possibly the strongest indication that this type of research is biased inherently is the absence of unbiased studies.

CONCLUSION

Clearly we are not yet ready to answer the questions of who really benefits from applied poverty research. Yet, the evidence presented above, and in other articles in this volume, is enough to make if doubtful that poor people and the general public benefit very much. If virtually all poverty research follows the lead of non-scientists, then what can poverty research add, especially if it is biased? It appears that the most that poverty research can add is hints for individuals with respect to how they can improve their situation. Poverty research has also been used to suggest new programs or revisions in programs before the existing programs have even had a chance to work. The Special Impact Program (Title VII of the Economic Opportunity Act) is an example of this. ("The Abt Evaluation: What Happened", 1977; see also (for other examples) Becker and Horowitz, 1972; Berk and Rossi, 1977; Moore, 1973.) Used in this way, poverty research, or any form of evaluation, is aptly described by Voltaire: "The best is the enemy of the good."

REFERENCES

Aaron, Henry J. (1978) Politics and the Professors. Washington: The Brookings Institution.

Abt, Clark C. (1976a) "Toward the Benefit/Cost Evaluation of U.S. Government Applied Social Research and Social Programs, and the Marginal Productivity of Their Components, 1965-1975." Presented to the International Economic Association Conference on "Econometric Contributions to Public Policy", Urbino. Mimeo.

Abt, Clark C. (1976b) "Notes for a Strategy for Big and Small Social Research." mimeo.

Becker, Howard S. and Horowitz, Irving Louis (1972) "Radical Politics and Sociological Research: Observations on Methodology and Ideology." American Journal of Sociology 78:48-66.

Berk, Richard A. and Rossi, Peter H. (1977) "Doing Good or Worse: Evaluation Research Politically Reexamined." In Evaluation Studies Review Annual, Volume 2. Edited by Marcia Guttentag with Shalom Saar. Beverly Hills: Sage.

Brickell, Henry M. (1978) "The Influence of External Political Factors on the Role and Methodology of Evaluation." In Evaluation Studies Review Annual, Volume 3. Beverly Hills: Sage.

Caplan, Nathan and Nelson, Stephen D. (1974) "Who's to Blame?" Psychology Today 99-104.

Carter, Reginald K. (1971) "Clients' Resistance to Negative Findings and the Latent Conservative Function of Evaluation Studies." The American Sociologist 6:118-124.

Committee on Evaluation of Poverty Research (1979) Evaluating Federal Support for Poverty Research. Washington: National Academy of Sciences.

Cronbach, Lee J. (1976) "Five Decades of Public Controversy Over Mental Testing." In Controversies and Decisions: The Social Sciences and Public Policy. Edited by Charles Frankel. New York: Russell Sage Foundation.

Datta, Lois-ellin (1980) "Interpreting Results: Values and the Case of Reports on Federal Programs Supporting Educational Change." In Problems in American Social Policy Research. Edited by Clark C. Abt. Cambridge: Abt Books.

Denzin, Norman K. (1970) "Who Leads: Sociology or Society?" The American Sociologist 5:125-127.

Farmer, James (1967) "The Controversial Moynihan Report." In The Moynihan Report and the Politics of Controversy. Edited by Lee Rainwater and William L. Yancey. Cambridge: The M.I.T. Press.

Frankel, Charles (1976) "The Autonomy of the Social Sciences." In Controversies and Decisions: The Social Sciences and Public Policy. Edited by Charles Frankel. New York: Russell Sage Foundation.

Galliher, John F. and McCartney, James L. "The Influence of Funding Agencies on Juvenile Delinquency Research." Social Problems 21:77-90.

Gramlich, Edward M. (1980) "Future Research on Poverty and Income Maintenance." In Poverty and Public Policy: An Evaluation of Social Science Research. Edited by Vincent T. Covello. Cambridge: Schenkman Publishing Co.

Green, Edith (1972a) "The Educational Entrepreneur -- A Portrait." The Public Interest 28:12-25.

Green, Edith (1972b) "Education's Federal Grab Bag." Phi Delta Kappan 54:83-86.

Guttentag, Marcia (1970) "Introduction." Journal of Social Issues 26:1-13.

Helfgot, Joseph H. (1981) Professional Reforming. Lexington: Lexington Books.

Horowitz, Irving Louis (1971) "Introduction." In The Use and Abuse of Social Science. Edited by Irving Louis Horowitz. New Brunswick: Transaction Books.

Jones, Delmos (1980) "Accountability and the Politics of Urban Research." Human Organization 39:99-104.

Levitan, Sar A. and Taggart, Robert (1976) The Promise of Greatness. Cambridge: Harvard University Press.

Moore, Joan W. (1973) "Social Constraints on Sociological Knowledge: Academics and Research Concerning Minorities." Social Problems 21:65-77.

Ornstein, Allan C. (1974) "The Cost of Federal Funding: Who Benefits?" Education and Urban Society 6:469-496.

Pakes, Ariel and Schankerman, Mark (1978) "The Rate of Obsolescence of Knowledge, Research Gestation Lags, and the Private Rate of Return to Research Resources." Harvard Institute of Economic Research, Discussion Paper Number 659.

Partridge, William L. (1978) "Uses and Nonuses of Anthropological Data on Drug Abuse." In Applied Anthropology in America. Edited by Elizabeth M. Eddy and William L. Partridge. New York: Columbia University Press.

Primack, Joel and Von Hippel, Frank (1974) Advice and Dissent: Scientists in the Political Arena. New York: Basic Books, Inc.

Ridgeway, James (1967) "Simulating Poverty: Input and Output." In The Use of Social Research in Federal Domestic Programs, Part II. A Staff Study for the Research and Technical Programs Subcommittee of the Committee on Government Operations. Washington: U.S. Government Printing Office.

Rule, James B. (1978) Insight & Social Betterment: A Preface to Applied Social Science. New York: Oxford University Press.

Ryan, William (1971) Blaming the Victim. New York: Vintage Books.

Sanger, Mary Bryna (1979) Welfare of the Poor. New York: Academic Press.

"The Abt Evaluation: What Happened" (1977) In A Review of the Abt Associates, Inc., Evaluation of the Special Impact Program. Cambridge: Center for Community Economic Development.

Williams, Walter (1971) Social Policy Research and Analysis: The Experience in the Federal Social Agencies. New York: American Elsevier Publishing Company, Inc.

Yarmolinsky, Adam (1976) "How Good Was the Answer? How Good Was the Question?" In Controversies and Decisions: The Social Sciences and Public Policy. Edited by Charles Frankel. New York: Russell Sage Foundation.

PART II

MEASURING POVERTY

INTRODUCTION

Richard Goldstein
Stephen M. Sachs

Annual income twenty pounds, annual expenditure nineteen nineteen six, result happiness. Annual income twenty pounds, annual expenditure twenty pounds ought and six, result misery.

<u>Dickens</u>

One important element in any poverty research strategy, or in any strategy for alleviating or eliminating poverty, is knowledge either of who is poor or of a criterion for determining who is poor. The U.S. currently has an "official" poverty line (actually a set of lines, called a matrix), called the Orshansky index (matrix) after its originator, Mollie Orshansky of the Social Security Administration. This measure was devised in the early 1960's, is updated every year (since 1969 the update has been via the Consumer Price Index), and has been determined back to 1959. During the first 15 years of this definition's life, challenges to it appeared intermittently. In the last few years, challenges have appeared more often, on broader grounds, and from widely divergent sources. The articles in this section criticize the Orshansky matrix primarily from the perspective of "The index should be changed (or supplemented) in the following ways if the index is to be more consistent with the stated objectives." Because of the complexity of, and the number of, issues, we present a brief organizing scheme. Our organizational scheme uses the six traditional questions of the journalist (Who, What, When, Why, Where, and How), and some possible answers to these questions.

<u>Who</u> must be counted to obtain a measure of the extent of poverty? There are two classes of answers: the type of person to be counted, and the groupings of that type of person. The official measure counts only poor people (that is people whose incomes are below a certain level), and counts these people in their families, or, if they do not live in a family, counts them as unrelated individuals.

Regarding the first class, other possible answers include: everybody, the non-poor, and various special groups, such as the elderly. By choosing just to count the poor, the government can only obtain a measure of the extent of poverty by using an "absolute" (or quasi-absolute) criterion that can independently be applied to people.

(Absolute vs. relative measures are discussed in several of the papers in this section, especially the paper by Harrell Rodgers.) It is of course possible to devise such a criterion and the official measure uses the criterion of money income. However, if one thinks either that poverty should be measured relatively, or that a single monetary criterion is not satisfactory, then one would want to measure something about everybody in the country. The paper by Timothy Smeeding, which deals with in-kind benefits, is relevant to the decision about measuring only the poor or measuring everybody. Lori Girshick and John Williamson, in their paper, discuss some of the same issues with respect to one particular group, the elderly.

The second class of answers deals with the grouping of people. One could group people with their resident families as the government does now, or one could group people by households (that is, by the people that they live with regardless of relationship), or one could group people by the spending unit that they belong to (that is, we could stop assuming both that family members do spend their money together, and that unrelated individuals living together do not spend their money together), or people could be grouped by the community in which they live, or, we could even decline to group people. Each of these procedures would provide different answers to the question of who is poor. The spending unit grouping and the non-grouped individual answers have rarely if ever been investigated because of the large amounts of new data that would be required.

Grouping by household has been investigated. Changing to a household definition would affect the demographic profile of those classified as poor and, at least in 1974, would also have decreased the number of people counted as poor (McNeil, et al., 1976; Department of Health, Education and Welfare, 1976: 101). However, it is also possible that changing to a household definition would change the behavior of some people, thus reducing the credibility of the estimates cited above. Lerman and Townsend (1974: 206) suggest that this kind of change "could discourage economies achieved when households are shared. A low-income family could lose its benefits if it moved in with a moderate-income family." Since living together does not necessarily mean the sharing of either resources or expenditures, this new definition could result in inequities.

Stinson and Larson discuss and exemplify the possibility of grouping by community. Many authors have discussed the narrowness of looking only at goods and services at the individual level. Global services which affect the quality of life, such as education and street cleaning, can also differ in their quality and even in adequacy. Stinson and Larson provide one way in which this difference can be measured and in which decisions about the "poverty" of these services can be determined. This paper is important because many poor people live in communities that include mostly poor people and it is essential to determine whether in addition to individual problems and disadvantages these poor people also suffer from collective disadvantages, such as a poor educational system. A poverty of collective services would appear to make it much harder for poor people to escape from poverty. (For a review, from an analytic perspective, of litigation on the issue of school finance, see Sherman, 1981).

<u>What</u> does one count or measure to determine the extent of poverty? While the official measure is a straight-forward money line, there have been numerous suggested changes or additions, including:

- o The poverty gap: the total amount of money by which poor people are below the poverty line.
- o The (monetary) extent to which various percentages of the poor are below the appropriate poverty line.
- o Non-monetary differences between the situation of the poor and of the non-poor, for example:
  - access to services;
  - quality of life issues;
  - quality of those services that are accessible;
  - the "ease" with which people at various income levels can increase their incomes, including the "permeability" of the poverty line.
- o The effect of in-kind benefits which is discussed in some detail, at least with respect to benefits received by the poor, in Timothy Smeeding's paper; one criticism of calling the cost of in-kind benefits "income" to the poor recipients is that

  > not all in-kind benefits are improvements in one's standard of living. Medical care, for example, is available only when someone . . . is ill. It is a bit strained to argue that a family's life style has improved if it collects $2,000 in medical benefits because someone needed an operation. ("Are There Any Poor People? Do They Have A Pretty Good Life?", 1981: 11).

- o The costs of goods and services often differ for people who live in areas where most residents are poor as compared to the cost for people in other areas. This is often discussed as strictly a geographic issue: are some parts of the country more expensive than other parts, and if so, should the poverty line be affected by this? But, the issue is broader: are some parts of a city, for example, more expensive than other parts? There is evidence that some parts of certain cities are more expensive than other parts of those same cities (Caplovitz, 1967). There is even stronger evidence that the Consumer Price Index rises at different rates for various groups of the population. For evidence that the CPI for various groups of the poor rises faster than does the overall CPI, and that the CPI for the wealthy rises slower, see Department of Health, Education and Welfare (1976: 93) and, National Social Science and Law Project (1980).
- o Program eligibility levels, which often differ from the poverty line. As Girshick and Williamson show with respect

to programs for the elderly, program lines are lower than the poverty line.

Third, are we concerned to measure the extent of poverty at any particular point in time and make our decisions based on this cross-sectional measure, or are we concerned with multi-year, even life-time, measures? As Lerman and Townsend (1974: 208) say,

> Short accounting periods allow government payments to be most sensitive to current needs at the cost of reduced equity over the long run and reduced savings incentives. Again, at the root of the conflict is the extent to which a family has control over its consumption flow.

There have been attempts to solve these problems through measures that abstract from income fluctuations. For example, Garfinkel and Haveman (1974: 196) suggest a measure of what they call "earnings capacity" which is based on "a family's ability to generate income when it uses its human and physical capital at capacity." The problem with this measure as with all long-term measures is that we have no way of telling if people are going to be able to use their capacities to the fullest since this is not in the control of individuals or families.

<u>Why</u> do we want to measure poverty? The answer undoubtedly differs for different people, but we can classify the different types of answers that one might come across as follows:

- o Politics, for example to convince people that poverty is not really a very serious problem, or, to argue that it is an extensive problem requiring considerable governmental intervention (Goodman, 1982).
- o Programs, for example to set up eligibility or assessment lines (but see the paper by Girshick and Williamson).
- o Academic or intellectual, for example because we want to know the answer to the question of how many poor people there are, or what income distributions or life style variations exist.
- o History, that is to make historical comparisons. To do this we either need to keep the same definitions, or we need to ensure that data exists at each point in time so that several definitions could be used. (Recall that the Orshansky index is only useful back to 1959.) We know that studies of how many people are poor have gone on since at least the end of the nineteenth century. We also know that over time the poverty line definition has changed to provide for increased living levels (Appelbaum, 1977; Patterson, 1981: 12, 19, 45, 161), but, the "status of these families relative to the rest of society has remained static. In this, the poverty line reflects not what the poor need, but what those who determine such things believe they should have." (Appelbaum, 1977: 514)

Measuring Poverty

<u>Where</u> are the poor? This question can refer to either geographical differences (widely discussed; see Department of Health, Education and Welfare, 1976) or to different living arrangements. Girshick and Williamson provide an excellent discussion of some of the implications for poor elderly people who live in institutions and the effect of this on programs for the elderly and on basic counts of poverty among the elderly.

Finally, our sixth question is "<u>How</u> is poverty measured, or, how are the poor counted?" The official poverty lines are based on a number of assumptions which greatly ease the determination of the lines. Thus, poverty is basically equal to three times the cost of food under the Department of Agriculture's Thrifty Food Plan. This line is compared to the estimates of income based on the March supplement to the Current Population Survey. There are a number of methodological and technical problems with this survey, not the least of which is that measuring poverty is not its purpose (its purpose is to provide labor force information quickly). As Fendler and Orshansky (1979: 640) say, "The speed with which the data must be collected, as well as the limited space on the survey questionnaire, make the CPS undesirable as the vehicle for the collection of extensive new data on noncash income." Further, other possible sources of this information are felt by many to be of even lower quality. For example, in its discussion the Department of Health, Education and Welfare claims that estimates of income from the decennial Census, which are "apparently" inconsistent with CPS estimates are of lower quality than are the CPS estimates. (Only a cynic would feel that HEW says this because the Census estimates show more poverty than do the CPS estimates. See Department of Health, Education and Welfare, 1976: 13-14.)

As the above makes clear, there are many potential revisions that one could make. Some of these are discussed in the articles included in this section:

- o The use of a relative measure (Rodgers);
- o The use of measures of in-kind benefits (Smeeding);
- o The use of non-monetary incomes or assets (Girshick and Williamson);
- o The use of measures of the availability and adequacy of government-supplied collective services (Stinson and Larson).

In discussing possible revisions, all the authors make clear the political purposes served by the current definition. This is also recognized by the author of the official index who has said,

> Realistically, the acceptability of a "new" or "revised" index of poverty will stem as much from the number and characteristics of those it classifies as poor as from the inherent logic of the measure itself. (Fendler and Orshansky, 1979: 643).

REFERENCES

Appelbaum, Diana Karter (1977) "The Level of the Poverty Line: A Historical Survey". Social Service Review 51:514-523.
"Are There Any Poor People? Do They Have A Pretty Good Life?" (1981) Jobs Watch 1:11.
Caplovitz, David (1967) The Poor Pay More. New York: The Free Press.
Department of Health, Education and Welfare (1976) The Measure of Poverty. Washington: U.S. Government Printing Office.
Fendler, Carol and Orshansky, Mollie (1979) "Improving the Poverty Definition." American Statistical Association Proceedings of the Social Statistics Section.
Garfinkel, Irwin and Haveman, Robert (1974) "Earnings Capacity and the Target Efficiency of Alternative Transfer Programs." American Economic Review 64:196-204.
Goodman, Ellen (4 February 1982) "Rif' em--that's how the White House handles bearers of bad news." Boston Globe: 13.
Lerman, Robert I. and Townsend, Alair A. (1974) "Conflicting Objectives in Income Maintenance Programs." American Economic Review. 64:205-211.
McNeil, John M., Sater, Douglas K., and Winard, Arno I. (1976) "Effect of Using a Poverty Definition Based on Household Income." American Statistical Association Proceedings of the Social Statistics Section.
National Social Science and Law Project (1980) "Recent Proposed Changes to the Official Definition of Poverty." Clearinghouse Review 14:736-738.
Patterson, James T. (1981) America's Struggle Against Poverty, 1900-1980. Cambridge: Harvard University Press.
Sherman, Joel D. (1981) "Equity Measurement and School Finance Litigation." Law & Policy Quarterly 3:442-463.

LIMITING POVERTY BY DESIGN:
THE OFFICIAL MEASURE OF POVERTY

Harrell R. Rodgers, Jr.

Nations measure poverty in a variety of ways. The choice of measure has numerous implications. Some measures greatly reduce official estimates of poverty, providing a justification for a less vigorous anti-poverty policy, and less generous welfare programs. Some measures increase the official estimate of poverty, putting pressure on public officials. The cost of estimating poverty also varies with the sophistication of the measures. An attempt to be precise is much more expensive than estimates based only on reported incomes. The Smeeding and the Girshick and Williamson papers presented here certainly indicate how complex poverty measurement can be. Some measures also provide insight into more than just the poverty rate. For example, a measure might yield insights into the distribution of income or wealth in a society.

ABSOLUTE MEASURES

Measures of poverty can be divided into two broad categories -- absolute and relative. An absolute standard attempts to identify the basic, even subsistence, resources required to live above the poverty level. A relative standard defines poverty in relationship to the median living standards of the society. A relative standard shows not only how many people live below the average standard in a society, it also provides insights into the distribution of income and wealth among the population. In 1969 the President's Commission on Income Maintenance in the United States (p. 8) concluded that:

> The community's decision as to what is "essential" is dictated in general by its social conscience. If society believes that people should not be permitted to die of starvation or exposure then it will define poverty as the lack of minimum food and shelter necessary to maintain life.... As society becomes more affluent it defines poverty as not only the lack of the components of a subsistence level of living, but also the lack of opportunity for persons with limited resources to achieve

the quality of life enjoyed by persons with an average amount of resources. The definition of poverty progresses from one based on absolute standards to one based on relative standards.

The irony of the Commission's reasoning is that while America is certainly an affluent nation, it still defines poverty in absolute, subsistence terms.

There was no official measure of American poverty until the mid-1960's. In 1964 the Council of Economic Advisors (CEA) formulated a crude measure of poverty. The CEA standard relied on a Social Security Administration (SSA) study of the income needs of four-person, nonfarm families. The SSA study first used as its base a "low-cost" food budget prepared by the Department of Agriculture. The low-cost food budget was designed to provide a poor family with the minimum diet required to avoid basic nutritional deficiencies. The budget allowed twenty-eight cents per person per meal, or $3.36 per family per day. Since a 1955 Department of Agriculture study had shown that poor families spend about one-third of their budget on food, the food budget was multiplied by three to determine the poverty standard. This calculation produced a poverty threshold of $3,995.

Since $3,995 was considerably higher than welfare expenditures for poor families, CEA decided to formulate a lower poverty standard. The new standard was based on an "economy" budget, which equalled about 80 percent of the low-cost diet. The new budget allowed expenditure of twenty-three cents per person per meal, or $2.76 per family per day. When the new budget was multiplied by three, the poverty threshold was $3,022. Relying on this less expensive budget, CEA set the poverty standard for families at $3,000, and decided that half this amount would serve as the poverty line for a single individual (Orshansky, 1963). Using this rough guide, the CEA reported that 35 million people (about 20 percent of the total population) were poor in 1962 (Wilcox, 1969:27).

In 1965, the Social Security Administration attempted to improve upon the CEA standard, but decided to continue to base the standard on the estimated cost of an "adequate" diet for families of various sizes. Using an Economy-Food budget formulated by the National Research Council, a poverty standard was computed for various family sizes, with an adjustment for urban or rural residence. It was assumed that food costs represented 33 percent of the total income needs of families of three or more, and 27 percent of the total income required by two-person households. This standard, known as the Orshansky index after its author, was quickly adopted as the federal government's official measure of poverty.

Table 5.1 shows the 1979 SSA poverty standard for various family sizes. Note that the standard varies by family size, the sex of the family head, and the family's place of residence. Farm families are presumed to need only 85 percent of the cash income required by nonfarm families (until 1969 they were presumed to need only 70% as much). The rate for single persons is adjusted up to compensate for

Limiting Poverty by Design   51

the higher cost of living alone (the food budget is multiplied by 5.92 rather than by 3.0). The food budget for couples is multiplied by 3.88 to compensate for their higher costs. Female-headed families receive slightly less and two-person elderly families are presumed to need 8 percent less than nonelderly two-person families.

Table 5.2 shows the SSA poverty threshold for a nonfarm family of four backdated to 1959, and the number of persons counted as poor by year using the standard. Until 1969, the yearly changes in the poverty standard reflect changes in the cost of the Economy-Food budget. Since 1969 the standard has been adjusted yearly according to changes in the Consumer Price Index. Taken at face value, the SSA standard suggests that substantial progress was made toward reducing poverty in the 1960s with some reversals occurring in the 1970s. In 1959 there were almost 40 million American poor, but the count dropped to 25.4 million by 1963. The count remained basically steady until 1973 and 1974 (revised figures) when poverty declined to about 23 million. However, in 1975 poverty increased by 2.5 million persons and actually exceeded poverty for every year back to 1967. Between 1976 and 1979 the count stabilized at about 25 million poor. In 1980 and 1981 the poverty count rose dramatically.

An analysis of the actual computation of the official poverty standard for one family size is illustrative. In 1979 the poverty threshold for a nonfarm family of four was $7,412. This standard allowed $1,853.00 per person per year, or $5.08 per day, one third being the allocation for food ($1.69). The family could spend a total of $2.25 per meal for all four persons, or $47.32 per week on food. A budget for a four-person family would look like this:

<u>$2,470.66 for food:</u> $1.69 a day (56¢ per meal) per
                                  person; $11.83 per week per person.

<u>$2,470.66 for shelter:</u> $205.89 a month for rent or
                                  mortgage for four persons.

<u>$2,470.66 for necessities:</u> $51.47 a month per person for
                                  clothing, furniture, transportation,
                                  health care, utilities, taxes, enter-
                                  tainment, etc.

The first thing one notices about the standard is that the estimates are extremely low. It is highly doubtful that anyone could prepare a nutritious meal for four persons for $2.25, or that a family of four could be adequately fed on $47.32 a week. The allowances for rent or mortgage and other necessities are also extremely low. The same is true, of course, for other family sizes. Notice on Table 5.1 that an elderly urban resident is allowed only $3,479. Clearly one intention of the SSA is to define poverty in a manner that keeps the

Table 5.1 Poverty Standard: 1979

Size of Family Unit	Non Farm			Farm		
	Total	Male Head	Female Head	Total	Male Head	Female Head
1 person (unrelated individual)	$3,683	$3,689	$4,855	$3,556	$3,138	$3,236	$3,001
15 to 64	3,773	3,778	3,912	3,619	3,254	3,324	3,076
65 yrs. & over	3,472	3,479	3,515	3,468	2,963	3,988	2,948
2 persons	4,702	4,725	4,737	4,669	3,981	3,991	3,917
Head 15 to 64 yrs.	4,858	4,878	4,905	4,762	4,156	4,163	4,027
Head 65 yrs. & over	4,364	4,390	4,394	4,362	3,730	3,732	3,686
3 persons	5,763	5,784	5,820	5,624	4,917	4,928	4,680
4 persons	7,386	7,412	7,416	7,381	6,329	6,332	6,261
5 persons	8,736	8,775	8,785	8,690	7,492	7,492	7,509
6 persons	9,849	9,914	9,922	9,843	8,424	8,428	8,309
7 persons and more	12,212	12,280	12,322	12,037	10,533	10,547	10,178

Source: U.S. Bureau of the Census, "Money Income and Poverty Status of Families and Persons in United States: 1979 (Advance Report)," Current Population Reports, Series P-60, No. 125, 1980; p. 28.

Table 5.2
Poverty Schedule
Family of 4 (Non Farm): 1959-1979

	Standard	Millions of Poor	Percent of Total Population	Median Family Income	Standard as a % of Median Family Income
1959	$2,973	39.5	22 %	$5,417	54.8
1960	3,022	39.9	22	5,620	53.7
1961	3,054	39.9	22		
1962	3,089	38.6	21		
1963	3,128	36.4	19		
1964	3,169	36.1	19		
1965	3,223	33.2	17		
1966	3,317	30.4	16		
1966*	3,317	28.5	15		
1967	3,410	27.8	14		
1968	3,553	25.4	13		
1969	3,743	24.1	12		
1970	3,968	25.4	13	9,867	38.0
1971	4,137	25.6	12.5	10,285	40.2
1972	4,275	24.5	12	11,116	38.4
1973	4,540	23.0	11	12,051	37.6
1974	5,038	24.3	12	12,836	34.2
1975*	5,038	24.3	11.5	12,902	39.0
1975	5,500	25.9	12	13,719	40.0
1976	5,815	25.0	12	14,958	30.8
1977	6,200	24.7	12	16,009	38.7
1978	6,662	24.7	11.4	17,640	37.7
1979	7,412	25.2	11.6	19,680	37.6
1980	8,414	29.3	13	21,020	40.0
1981	9,287	31.8	14	22,388	41.5

Source: Derived from Bureau of Census, "Characteristics of the Low-Income Population," Current Population Reports, Series P-60, Various Years.

poverty count as low as possible. Notice on Table 5.2 that the poverty standard has not increased at anything like the rate of growth in personal income. In 1959 the standard was 53 percent of median family income. By the 1970s it averaged only about 39 percent of the family income, and had dropped to 37.6 percent by 1979. Much of the decline in the poverty count between 1959 and 1968 may be the result of the failure of the standard to keep pace with the growth of personal income, rather than from families actually escaping poverty. As the authors of a recent Organization for Economic Co-operation and Development (OECD) (1976: 63) study note:

> It is not surprising . . . that the percentage of the United States population that falls below the official poverty line has declined considerably over the last decade or more (from 22.4 percent of total population in 1959 to 11.9 percent in 1973). For, as long as poverty is defined in absolute terms, economic growth is likely to be enough to eliminate much of it without any special income maintenance programs . . . .

The unrealistic nature of the SSA standard is suggested by the research of another government agency. The Bureau of Labor Statistics (BLS) annually estimates the income families need to live at a "lower-level" standard of living, a "middle-level" standard, and a "higher-level" (Monthly Labor Review, 1980). The BLS estimated that in 1978 an urban family of four would have had to gross $18,622 to live at a "middle-level" or moderate standard. A "lower-level" standard of living, the BLS said, would have required $11,546 -- almost $5,000 more than the poverty standard. The BLS concluded that a lower-level standard in 1978 would have required $3,574 for food, $2,233 for housing, and $5,739 for such items as transportation ($856), clothing ($847), personal care ($301), medical care ($1,065), Social Security ($719), and taxes ($935). For the same size and type of family, the SSA poverty standard for 1978 allowed only $2,221 for food, or $1.52 per person per day. The BLS standard allowed $2.44 a day for each person's food needs; a higher but hardly extravagant sum. As the above figures show, the BLS allowance for necessities other than food and shelter were modest, but they total more than twice the SSA's allowance for necessities. In fact, the assumptions of the BLS standard for "lower-level" families are quite spartan. For example, the BLS assumes that families at the "lower-level" live in rental housing without air conditioning, relies heavily on public transportation where it is available and owns an eight year-old car where it is not, performs most services for itself, and utilizes free recreational facilities (Monthly Labor Review, 1969).

Thus, by the BLS estimates the poverty standard is clearly a bare subsistence level, one that leaves the poor far below the living standards of even lower-income families, and far from a moderate standard of living. This would be true even if the poor had as much money as the poverty standard allows. However, the income figures collected yearly by the Census Bureau reveal that most poor families have incomes that fall considerably below the poverty level. For example, in 1979 the average poor family fell $2,185 below the poverty threshold. For white families the median deficit was $2,008, for black families it rose to $2,458 (Current Population Reports, 1979: 37).

Critics have raised a large number of additional criticisms about the SSA standard. The major ones are these:

Regional Variations: There are no adjustments in the index to compensate for the rather substantial variations in cost-of-living across the nation.

Rural vs. Urban: The 15 percent reduction for farm families is not supported by empirical evidence. While some persons in rural areas may be able to grow some of their own food and may incur lower housing costs, many necessities in rural areas are more expensive.

The Food Budget: Since the food plan is the base of the poverty standard, its calculation is critical. Quite clearly, SSA did not decide to use the Economy budget as a base because it was deemed adequate for poor people's needs. Wilcox (1969: 27) reports that SSA originally designed the Economy budget for temporary or emergency use only, but decided to use it permanently because more adequate budgets showed too much poverty. In July, 1975 the SSA substituted a Thrifty-Food budget for the Economy budget. The new budget reflects changes in RDA food standards, in public purchasing habits, and food manufacturing (Peterkin, 1976). The new budget, however, will mean little as far as the poverty standard is concerned.

The Multiplication Rate: The assumption that food expenditures acount for one-third of poor people's budgets is based on a 1955 study. More recent studies (Miller, 1971) indicate that poor people spend about 28 percent of their income on food. Thus, critics argue, the food budget should at least be multiplied by a factor closer to 3.4 than to 3 (See Girshick and Williamson). This would increase the poverty standard and count substantially.

Table 5.3 provides some examples based on a 1976 study by the Department of Health, Education, and Welfare (since renamed the Department of Health and Human Services). The figures show that the poverty standard would be substantially affected by changing the food budget ratio, and/or by substituting a more generous food budget. All the figures in Table 5.3 are based on a multiplier of 3.4 rather than 3. Notice that with this multiplier and the Thrifty-Food budget, 39.9 million persons would have been counted among the poor in 1974 (the threshold for an urban family of four would have been $6,360). If the food budget was based on only about 80 percent of the more generous Low-Cost Food Plan, and a multiplier of 3.4 used, the poverty count would have been 41.4 million (the threshold would have been $6,494 for an urban family of four). If the Low-Cost budget had been completely substituted for the Thrifty-Food Plan and 3.4 multiplier used, the poverty threshold for an urban family of four would have been raised to $8,118 and would have yielded a staggering poverty count of 55.4 million. Notice on Table 5.3 that only changing the multiplication factor increases the number of poor by 15.6 million persons. Changing both the budget and the multiplication factor increases the number of poor by 31.1 million persons.

These figures are particularly telling because the Low-Cost Food Plan represents an adequate, but very frugal diet for average families. It is the most economical of three plans developed by the USDA for nonpoor families. Compared to the more expensive Moderate and Liberal plans, the Low-Cost Plan calls for smaller amounts of most foods (especially meats, milk, and vegetables), and larger amounts of cereal, flour, and bread. It also calls for cheaper cuts of meat and prudent choices from all food groups (Peterkin, 1976:8-9). Thus, the Low-Cost Plan is a very modest diet, but if it was substituted for the Thrifty-Flood Plan the poverty count would increase very substantially.

Pretax Income: The poverty standard reflects gross not net income. An urban family of four with an income of $7,412 in 1979 would not have been considered poor by the SSA standard, but their net pay would have been considerably less than the poverty standard after deductions for taxes, social security, retirement and insurance.

In-kind Benefits and Assets: While cash-income-security payments (e.g., Social Security and Unemployment compensation) and cash assistance benefits (e.g., AFDC, SSI and general assistance) are included in SSA's measure of income, neither assets or in-kind benefits such as food stamps and Medicaid are included. Since it is conceivable that some families may have low incomes but assets they can draw on, the failure to include assets may distort poverty calculations to some extent (Weisbrod and Hansen, 1968).

The failure to include in-kind benefits is the most severe problem. In-kind benefits such as food stamps are quite expensive, go to a large number of people, and definitely improve the life of recipients. A recent study by Smeeding concluded that if the poverty figures were adjusted for underreporting of income by the poor, taxes paid, the receipt of in-kind benefits, the number of persons below the poverty line would have been 8.7 percent of all persons in 1968 (rather than 13%), 8.0 percent in 1970 (rather than 13%), and 5.4 percent in 1972 (rather than 12%). This would have dropped the poverty count to around 17 million in 1968 and 1970, and some 11 million in 1972 (Smeeding, 1975). Smeeding's estimates are updated in his essay in this volume.

A study by the Congressional Budget Office reached similar conclusions for fiscal year 1976 (See Table 5.4). Before any transfer income, 20.2 million households (25.5% of all households) were below the poverty threshold. Social insurance (Social Security) reduced the number of poor households to 11.2 million. Adding cash assistance reduced the poor households to 9.1 million. In-kind aid reduced the

Table 5.3

Size of the Poor Population Under Current and Revised Poverty Cutoffs, 1974
(in millions)*

	U.S. Population	Using Official Poverty Cutoffs	Using Revised Poverty Cutoffs			
			80% of Low-Cost Plan Condensed Family Size	Thrifty Plan	80% of Low-Cost Plan	Low-Cost Plan
Persons	209.3	24.3	39.2	39.9	41.4	55.4
Families	55.7	5.1	8.8	8.7	9.0	12.8
Unrelated Individuals	18.9	4.8	8.4	8.2	8.4	9.2
Children Ages 5-17	49.8	7.5	10.4	11.1	11.6	15.4

* Source: U.S. Department of Health, Education and Welfare, The Measure of Poverty (Washington, D.C.: Government Printing Office, 1976, p. 77.

** The poverty level for a nonfarm family of four would be $6,494 under the 80% condensed family budget; $6,366 under the Thrifty budget; $6,494 under the 80% of the low-cost budget; $8,118 under the low-cost budget.

number to 5.3 million, and adjustments for taxes paid raised the number slightly to 5.4 million households. This would leave 6.9 percent of all households, or about 14.2 million persons, in poverty in 1976. Of course, both the CBO and Smeeding's analysis are based on the assumption that the poverty threshold has been reasonably measured.

Those critics of SSA's standard who believe that the government overestimates poverty base their argument on the failure of SSA to count in-kind benefits (Browning, 1976). While the figures above clearly indicate that the failure to include in-kind benefits does distort the calculations, those who believe SSA's standards underestimate poverty make two points. First, that while in-kind benefits, or some proportion of their value, should be included in the calculations, the poverty threshold should also be adjusted upwards substantially. These scholars argue that the unrealistic poverty threshold underestimates poverty much more severely than the failure to consider in-kind benefits increases the count.

This seems to be a valid point. As noted above, when adjustments for in-kind benefits, unreported income, and taxes paid are made, the number of poor is reduced by about 10 to 15 million. Adjustments in food budgets and the multiplication factor, however, show that the poverty standard underestimated the poor by anywhere from 15 to 31 million. Since most in-kind benefits go to persons in the lowest income quintile, those persons not counted in the poverty estimates because of the low thresholds are unlikely to be receiving in-kind aid. Thus, many scholars (Harrington, 1977; Rodgers, 1978) argue, a much improved measure that considered in-kind benefits, taxes paid, underreporting of income and raised the food budget and multiplication factor would probably show anywhere from 5 to 20 million additional poor.

A second point often raised is that the value of the in-kind service or aid to the recipient may not be equal to the government's cost. Medicaid services are a good example. Medicaid services, which are often dispensed by Medicaid mills, may be expensive yet worthless or even harmful to recipients. Additionally, a dying person who receives expensive Medicaid services would be pushed over the poverty threshold, perhaps even into some upper-income group. But, of course, the person could hardly be said to have escaped poverty because of an expensive, lingering illness or death. Smeeding's article in this volume discusses many of the other problems encountered in attempting to quantify the value of in-kind benefits.

ALTERNATIVE APPROACHES TO THE MEASUREMENT OF POVERTY: RELATIVE MEASURES

In most industrialized nations, poverty is defined in a relative, rather than an absolute manner. A relative standard defines poverty not in terms of the basic resources required for subsistence but in

Table 5.4

Households Below the Poverty Level Under
Alternative Income Definitions
Fiscal Year 1976

Households In Poverty	Pre-Tax/ Pre-Transfer Income	Pre-Tax/ Post-Social Insurance Income	Pre-Tax Post-Money Transfer Income	Pre-Tax Post-In-Kind Transfer Income		Post-Tax/ Post Total Transfer Income
				I[a]	II	
Number in Thousands	20,237	11,179	9,073	7,406	5,336	5,446
Percent of All Families	25.5	14.1	11.4	9.3	6.7	6.9

Source: Congressional Budget Office, Poverty Status of Families Under Alternative Definitions of Income (Washington, D.C.: Government Printing Office, 1977), p. XV.

[a] Excludes Medicare and Medicaid Payments.

relationship to the modal standards of living in a society. Townsend (1974: 15) describes the spirit of a relative standard:

> Individuals, families and groups in the population can be said to be in poverty when they lack the resources to obtain the type of diets, participate in activities and have the living conditions and amenities which are customary, or are at least widely encouraged or approved in the societies to which they belong.

The most usual manner of formulating a relative definition is by pegging it to median income (OECD, 1976: 64-67). The poor are defined as those who earn less than some percentage of the median income for their family size. The percentage is generally in the 50 to 66 percent range. If this approach was adopted in America, it would substantially raise the poverty standard and the poverty count. For example, in 1979 the official poverty threshold for an urban family of four was $7,412. The median income for four-person families was $22,617. If half the median income was used as the poverty standard, the relative standard would have been $11,308 -- an increase in the poverty standard for four-person families of more than 50 percent. Roughly estimated, a relative standard of this type for all family sizes would yield a poverty count of 50 to 60 million American poor. The great increases in the poverty count perhaps explains in part why the American government has resisted the adoption of such a standard.

A relative standard might also prove embarassing because it would more clearly delineate the overall distribution of wealth in America. A recent study by the Department of Health, Education and Welfare (Peterkin, 1976: xxiv) revealed that if the poverty line was based on 50 percent of median family income, it would show that about 19 percent of all families were poor during every year back to 1959. This indicates little change in the distribution of income, although in-kind benefits are not taken into consideration. A relative standard also draws attention to the fact that millions of Americans live just above the poverty line for their family size. In 1979, for example, 35.4 million Americans lived below 125 percent of the poverty level for their family size (Current Population Reports, 1980: 32).

A recent OECD (1976: 67) study formulated a much more modest, and basically very crude, relative standard, and compared it to private and public measures of poverty in ten industrialized nations. Regardless of the measure used, the data revealed a significant amount of poverty in all but three nations (West Germany (3%), Denmark (5%) and Sweden (3.5%)). The standardized data for eight of the nations shows the highest rates of poverty in Canada (11%), the United States (13%) and France (16%).

By far the most sophisticated attempt to measure poverty is Townsend's (1979) recent study of British poverty. Townsend altered the traditional measures in two important ways. First, he developed a measure of resources in place of cash income. Townsend's measure of resources consisted of five components: cash income, imputed as well as actual income from the ownership of wealth, and three types of in-kind assistance: employer welfare benefits, public social services, and private income. Townsend also measured style of living (rather than simple consumption) to determine the levels at which resources were so low as to constitute deprivation. Townsend's measure showed a great deal more poverty than official government statistics. The official British government measure of poverty (based on supplemental benefit levels) has in recent years shown that about 7 percent of all households live in poverty. Townsend's deprivation standard showed that about 25 percent of all British households are poor (1979: 272).

Girshick and Williamson's article in this volume discusses many of the other variables that could be studied to define poverty. Obviously the options are numerous, and sophisticated efforts quickly become very complicated. Their analysis, for example, reveals that a sophisticated measure would have to consider the special needs of each of the major groups within the poverty population. Clearly there would be a point at which the cost-benefits of a sophisticated measure of poverty would be negative. It would, in other words, cost more to be really accurate than the information would be worth. This is especially true since the measurement of poverty is clearly so political. Any measure that showed more poverty would certainly meet resistance from an administration determined to reduce welfare costs. As Girshick and Williamson note, the official poverty standard is not even used to determine eligibility for welfare programs. While the standard varies by program, generally a lower standard is used to reduce the number of recipients and hold program costs down.

CONCLUSIONS

The measurement of poverty is highly political. Most industrialized nations have not given the matter much consideration, and some that have manifest a clear bias toward measuring poverty in a manner that underestimates deprivation. Townsend's research has set the standard for quality measurement of poverty, but his efforts are unlikely to be emulated by governments that would find serious studies of poverty embarassing.

No nation is more guilty of purposefully underestimating poverty than the United States. There is considerable evidence that serious studies of American poverty would reveal that the problem is considerably more extensive then official figures indicate. By underestimating poverty, public officials diminish the seriousness of the problem. The less serious a social problem can be made to seem, the less pressure officials feel to resolve or at least substantially alleviate it. Given the very considerable costs of current welfare programs (about $60 billion a year) and the failure of these efforts to reduce poverty below the 25 million level in recent years, research showing that poverty is actually as extensive as it officially was in 1959 would be politically unsettling. Of course, a relative measure of poverty would also prove embarassing because it would greatly increase the poverty count, it would emphasize the maldistribution of wealth and income in America, and the failure of social policies and tax laws to significantly alter this distribution.

To justify the government's currently flawed and basically futile approach to poverty alleviation SSA and CBO officials have for years discussed including in-kind benefits in income calculations for the poor, without alterations in the food budget or multiplication ratio. This would produce an appearance of poverty reduction, and lessen the official significance of poverty as a social problem. But the poor in all their terrible numbers would still be with us.

REFERENCES

Browning, E.K. (1976). "How Much More Equality Can We Afford?" The Public Interest. July, 1976: 90-103.

Current Population Reports (1979). "Money Income and Poverty Status of Families and Persons in the United States: 1978 (Advance Report)." Series P-60, No. 120.

Current Population Reports (1980). "Money Income and Poverty Status of Families and Persons in the United States: 1979 (Advance Report)." Series P-60, No. 125.

Harrington, M. (1977). "Hiding the Other America." The New Republic. February, 1977: 15-17.

Harrington, M. (1962). The Other America. Penguin Books, New York.

Miller, H. P. (1971). Rich Man, Poor Man. Thomas Y. Crowell, New York City, New York, p. 120.

Monthly Labor Review (1969). "New BLS budgets provide yardsticks for measuring family living costs." 92: April, 3-16.

Monthly Labor Review (1980), 103, January, 1980: 44-47.

The Organization for Economic Co-operation and Development (OECD) (1976). Public Expenditure on Income Maintenance Programmes. OECD, Paris, France.

Orshansky, M. (1965). "Counting the Poor: Another Look at the Poverty Profile." Social Security Bulletin. 27: 3-39.

Orshansky, M. (1963). "Children of the Poor." Social Security Bulletin. 25: 2-21.

Peterkin, B. (1976). The Measure of Poverty. HEW, Washington, D.C., pp. 33-61.

The President's Commission on Income Maintenance Programs (1969). Poverty Amidst Plenty. Government Printing Office, Washington, D.C., p. 8.

Rodgers, H. R. (1979). *Poverty Amid Plenty: A Political and Economic Analysis*. Addison-Wesley Publishing Co., Reading, Mass.

Rodgers, H. R. (1978). "Hiding Versus Ending Poverty." *Politics and Society*. 8: 253-266.

Smeeding, T. M. (1975). "Measuring the Economc Welfare of Low Income Households and the Anti-Poverty Effectiveness of Cash and Non-Cash Transfer Programs." Unpublished Ph. D. Dissertation, University of Wisconsin, Madison, Wisconsin.

Townsend, P. (1979). *Poverty in the United Kingdom: A Survey of Household Resources and Standards of Living*. University of California Press, Berkeley, California.

Townsend, P. (1974). "Poverty as Relative Deprivation: Resources and Style of Living." In *Poverty, Inequality and Class Structure*, D. Wedderburn (Ed.) Cambridge University Press, London.

Weisbrod, B. and Hansen, W. L. (1968). "An Income-Net Worth Approach to Measuring Economic Welfare." *American Economic Review*. 58: 1315-1329.

Wilcox, C. (1969). *Toward Social Welfare*. Irvin-Dorsey, Homewood, Illinois.

THE POLITICS OF MEASURING POVERTY AMONG THE ELDERLY

Lori B. Girshick
John B. Williamson

The choice of procedures for measuring poverty often reflects political compromises and unstated political agendas. If a group of experts using what they consider objective scientific procedures comes up with a poverty line that is "too high," government policymakers who have commissioned the research are likely to find an excuse for revising the line downward to make it more "acceptable" politically. Those who support efforts to redistribute income will tend to favor poverty lines based on "relative" incomes and those who do not support redistributive efforts are more likely to favor measures based on some "absolute" standard that does not take into account overall increases in living standards. The method of measurement depends upon who is doing the counting and for what purpose. Theoretically, policymakers could set levels low enough to "eliminate" poverty altogether (Huber, 1974; U.S. House, 1978).

Our focus in the present analysis is on special problems associated wtih efforts to measure the extent of poverty among the elderly. This effort can be viewed as a contribution to the new extensive literature on problems of measuring poverty more generally. For reviews of this literature see the Smeeding and Rodgers articles in this volume, Osmond and Durkin (1979), U.S. Department of Health, Education and Welfare (1976), Williamson and Hyer (1975), and Watts (1969).

There are many ways to count the elderly poor. However, it is becoming increasingly evident that more than income statistics are needed. For this reason some measures take into consideration a variety of non-income sources of economic well-being. Adjustments to income measures are called for because different groups in the population have their own particular needs and resources. Unfortunately, as we shall see, these efforts at adjustment often introduce new sources of error.

Of particular interest in the present analysis is the practice of basing eligibility for various government social programs on income criteria other than the official government poverty line. We will argue that this practice of using different and sometimes lower poverty lines for program eligibility can be interpreted as constituting an alternative set of implicit or operational poverty lines.

We begin our analysis with a brief evaluation of "official" government measures of poverty. We then consider the implications of the most commonly used measure for efforts to count the elderly poor and assess trends in poverty rates.

OFFICIAL GOVERNMENT MEASURES OF POVERTY

The most widely used measures of poverty among the elderly are the Social Security Administration's (SSA) poverty lines and the Bureau of Labor Statistics' (BLS) Budgets for Retired Couples. The poverty lines constructed by Orshansky (1965) for the SSA were based on a "scientific" study of the income needed to meet specified nutritional standards associated with the Department of Agriculture's "Economy Food Plan." The amount of money a family would need for that food plus other necessities was estimated based on the determination that one-third of family income was spent on food. However, this determination is no longer valid. The Bureau of Labor Statistics, for example, estimates that a multiplier of four rather than three would be more accurate today (Schulz, 1980). In 1979 the poverty threshold for an elderly couple was $4,390, for an elderly individual, $3,479 (U.S. Bureau of the Census, 1980). However, as Rodgers (this volume) points out, the SSA purposefully defined poverty in a way that would keep the number of poor low. The SSA poverty measure was actually adopted because it was low enough to be politically acceptable, not because it assured an adequate diet.[1]

Mollie Orshansky herself claims that today more should be allowed for nonfood items (U.S. House, 1978; Fendler and Orshansky, 1979). She and Fendler argue that the income thresholds for the elderly should be 40 percent higher than they are, to reflect the "Thrifty Food Plan." This plan replaced the "Economy Food Plan" in 1975, but the food cost to total living cost ratio was not adjusted. In 1977, their "adjusted" poverty line[2] for an elderly couple was $5,080, and for a single aged individual it was $4,064. This contrasts with the 1977 official aged poverty cutoffs set at $3,666 for couples and $2,906 for single persons (Fendler and Orshansky, 1979).

An additional problem with the SSA poverty rates is that they are based on samples from the Current Population Survey, which excludes persons who are institutionalized. Since 5 percent of the elderly are in institutions and 70 percent of such persons have incomes below the poverty line (U.S. House, 1978), a case can be made that if these institutionalized elderly were counted the poverty rate for the elderly would be greater than estimates based on Current Population Survey data suggest.[3]

The Retired Couples' Budget developed by the BLS represents an average urban elderly family living at a modest level. This family is assumed to have the average clothing, furnishings, and other major items of families. Three budget levels, a lower, an intermediate, and a higher, were developed in 1971, replacing the original one budget level first set in 1946-47. Annual updates reflect not only CPI changes, but also adjustments for changes in living standards. Budget levels are based on spending patterns (as measured by consumer spending surveys) which reveal a change from buying "more" to buying "better" (Schulz, 1980). The Retired Couples' budgets for an urban elderly couple in autumn of 1978 were set at $5,514 (Lower), $7,846 (Intermediate), and $11,596 (Higher) (Bureau of the Census, 1980). There is no inherent logic in choosing the BLS lower budget over the intermediate budget as a poverty line; thus, political considerations can easily influence the actual choice made.

While the BLS lower budget is sometimes used as a poverty line, by far the most common measure is the SSA poverty line. In the next section we consider some of the implications of using this measure to count the elderly poor and trace trends in elderly poverty rates.

A PROFILE OF THE ELDERLY POOR

In 1979 some 15 percent of the elderly were poor compared with 12 percent of the total population (U.S. Bureau of the Census, 1980). Based on the same SSA thresholds 35 percent of the elderly were poor in 1959, 25 percent were poor in 1969, and 15 percent were poor in 1979. During the twenty year period between 1959 and 1979 there was a sharp decline in the proportion of elderly poor, but between 1978 and 1979 the percent of the elderly who were poor did increase from 14 to 15 percent (U.S. Bureau of the Census, 1980).

While the absolute economic status of the elderly has improved during the past twenty years as reflected in the preceding poverty rate statistics, there has not been a long-term improvement in the relative economic status of the elderly (Williamson, 1979). During the past thirty years there has been no significant long-term increase in the median income of the elderly relative to other age groups (Johnson and Williamson, 1980). The United States is somewhat unique among advanced industrial nations in its emphasis on absolute as opposed to relative measures of poverty. Most other advanced nations emphasize relative measures of income inequality. If an absolute measure is used, the evidence suggests that the problem will eventually be eliminated through long-term economic growth (and with it an increase in the standard of living); but if a relative measure is used, such as one-half of the median income, the evidence suggests that the condition can only be eliminated through income redistribution. The political implications of these alternatives are profound.

To say that 15 percent of the elderly are poor does not accurately capture the marked variations in risk of poverty among various subgroups of the elderly. In 1979, 36 percent of elderly blacks as opposed to 13 percent of elderly whites were poor. Some 11 percent of elderly males were poor compared with 18 percent of elderly females, and 27 percent of elderly black males were poor compared with 10 percent of elderly white males. Some 42 percent of elderly black females were poor compared with 16 percent of elderly white females. The sharpest contrast is between elderly black females, with 42 percent poor, and elderly white males, with 10 percent in poverty (U.S. Bureau of the Census, 1979, 1980).

In 1981 over 90 percent of the elderly (22.5 million people) were receiving Social Security benefits (U.S. Department of Health and Human Services, 1981). Since 1975, benefit levels have been automatically adjusted according to changes in the CPI. The CPI attempts to reflect major price changes pertaining to all segments of the population living in different parts of the country. However, the elderly have different spending patterns than the non-elderly. Not only is there a change in income amount and source due to retirement, but less money is spent on transportation, recreation, housing, and education, while more money is spent on medical expenses, food, and household needs (Borzilleri, 1978).[4] In view of this it is relevant to ask how the average prices for the elderly rise in comparison to the price rate increases measured by the CPI. Other studies of the CPI have also found that prices rose faster for the elderly and the poor than was reflected in the CPI (Hollister and Palmer, 1969; Lamale, 1963; Mirer, 1975). The implications of these studies is that different indices should be designed for different target groups.[5]

Cash transfers are the most important source of economic well-being for the elderly. While the majority of the elderly rely on one or more government programs as their primary source of income, many remain poor even after these benefits are taken into consideration. Of those whose only source of income was Social Security, 34 percent of elderly families and 62 percent of aged individuals remained below the poverty level. Some 80 percent of aged individuals who received only SSI remained below the poverty line. Even when Social Security and SSI were combined, almost 47 percent of aged families and 56 percent of unrelated individuals still remained below the poverty level if these were the only sources of income (U.S. Bureau of the Census, 1980).

The impact of income and non-income benefits on poverty status is illustrated by a Congressional Budget Office (1977) study. In 1976, before taking into consideration Social Security, government pensions, unemployment, AFDC, and SSI, 58 percent of aged families would have been classified as poor. But after taking these benefits into account only 19 percent were considered poor. This figure can be further reduced to 4 percent after transfers and in-kind benefits, such as food stamps, Medicare, and housing assistance are added in.

If we add in the medical care, food stamps, housing subsidies and other in-kind benefits that the aged poor receive, it might seem that very few of the aged really are poor. A major flaw in this line of reasoning is that it fails to take into consideration the various non-income benefits for the non-poor. The middle class receives health insurance, vacations, educational tuition, and, most important of all, income tax benefits, to name a few. Indeed, non-income transfers go mainly to the non-poor (Orshansky, 1969). So, rather than the adjustments for non-income resources resulting in a decrease in estimates of the number of elderly poor, a more appropriate response would be to establish a higher poverty line to reflect the relative resources of all age and income groups.

ADJUSTING FOR NON-INCOME SOURCES OF ECONOMIC WELL-BEING

To more adequately measure the economic well-being of the elderly, non-income variables need to be considered in addition to income variables. Researchers at the University of Wisconsin's Institute for Research on Poverty argue that economic well-being should not measure actual levels of consumption or actual levels of income, but the attainable consumption of the family (Moon and Smolensky, 1977b). While Moon (1976) states that the ideal measure of economic welfare is the level of satisfaction families achieve by their control over buying goods and services they want to buy, the attempt to rank "satisfaction" encounters problems of arbitrariness similar to trying to establish minimum standards of living. In this sense, then, economic well-being cannot be measured objectively. However, by assessing the level of consumption a family could hope to maintain over its lifetime rather than over one particular year, the resource position of the aged can be more accurately portrayed.

Both net worth (assets minus liabilities) and income are important influences on economic well-being. Converting net worth into an annuity value and adding it to current income is advocated by some as an improvement to current income measures alone. Since annuity value is a function of the amount of net worth, the life expectancy of the person involved, and the rate of inflation, the distribution of well-being by age will change if a combined income-net worth measure is used. Since older people have higher ratios of net worth to current money income and shorter life expectancies, their economic position will "appear" most improved (Weisbrod and Hansen, 1968).

The life-cycle hypothesis of consumption holds that you save money when you are young and spend money when your are old (also known as dissaving). Adding annuitized net worth to income to measure well-being is consistent with dissaving. However, if used alone the measure is of limited applicability because so few elderly have significant assets other than their homes.[6] Fluctuating inflation rates, the arbitrary nature of choosing an annuity rate, and the argument that no one particular income net worth measure is clearly preferable to several plausible alternatives weakens the utility of this approach for adjusting poverty measures (Projector and Weiss, 1969).

Incorporating human capital (or future earnings potential) into the measurement of economic well-being results in a "lowering" of well-being for the aged. Work disincentives inherent in Social Security and SSI policies affect the earnings potential of the elderly. Social Security allows an individual to keep $5000 in earnings before being taxed at a rate of 50 percent on the remainder (until the pension benefit is reduced to zero), and SSI also has a high tax on all sources of income. In addition, ill health, transportation problems, and decreased flexibility regarding work schedules contribute to a lower human capital rate for the elderly (Moon and Smolensky, 1977a).

Accurate measurement of in-kind transfers, which include Medicare, Medicaid, public housing, and Food Stamps, is difficult. To add the dollar value of these benefits to income measures they can be valued either at the cost to the government or at the amount the recipient would spend to fulfill the need. (For a third approach and more elaboration on the preceeding two, see Moon and Smeeding, 1981.) Which measure is used to set a value on these transfers depends upon the political priorities of policymakers. For example, government cost may lead to an "overstatement" of the welfare gain since the recipient may place a lower value to the commodity being measured. The recipient may wish to spend more on food and less on health care, but in-kind transfer benefits do not allow such choices.

Intrafamily cash transfers are included in current income measures, but most certainly are underreported. The lack of recordkeeping, the absence of dollar amounts for certain shared family resources, and the desire not to jeopardize program eligibility may influence the accuracy of answers to survey questionnaires and program applications.

While net worth, human capital, in-kind and intrafamily transfers all ideally aid in capturing well-being, and thus in theory can be used to improve upon our measures of poverty, in practice such efforts typically involve the introduction of new sources of error. For example, in the determination of program eligibility and poverty status for the elderly it would seem reasonable to take into consideration intrafamily in-kind transfers. But potential recipients are going to be aware of the implications of reporting such transfers and understate them. It is possible that the resulting poverty measure would in practice be less accurate than one which did not attempt to take into consideration this source of well-being.

SOCIAL PROGRAM ELIGIBILITY CRITERIA

A great deal of effort goes into the determination of the official federal government poverty level, but federal and state governments often choose not to use this measure in connection with social program eligibility. When alternative income criteria are substituted, they have the effect of redefining poverty often at a lower level. These income criteria become the operational measures of poverty used by federal and state governments, based on pragmatic, political considerations as opposed to "objective" need. Some programs have high income lines (or no income criteria), but their resources are generally quite limited. Such programs may seem generous until we take into consideration how few of the potentially eligible are actually able to obtain program benefits. Two quite different approaches have been found for keeping down spending on welfare state programs for the aged. One is to impose stringent income and assets criteria as in the case of SSI. The other is to limit the supply of the benefit being provided as in the case of subsidized housing.

The different eligibility criteria create a variety of problems for the elderly poor who are dependent on government-funded social programs. These problems stem from (1) lack of coordination between programs which can result in an increase in benefits from one program source triggering automatic reductions in benefits from others; (2) penalties for applicants who have limited resources; (3) programs with eligibility levels set below the poverty line so that access to benefits is limited; and (4) differing eligibility requirements between states creating great inequities in benefits provisions. To illustrate these points we will briefly consider the Supplemental Security Income (SSI), Medicaid, Food Stamps, and subsidized housing programs.

To be eligible for SSI benefits, a person must be either 65 or older, blind, or disabled, and have limited resources and limited income. The asset limit has been set since 1974 at $1500 for an individual and $2250 for a couple. The income limit as of 1981 was $3176 per year for an individual and $4764 for a couple.[7] The 1981 income limit of $3176 is below the 1979 poverty line of $3479 and it would be even further below were we to take into consideration the 1980 and 1981 CPI poverty line adjustments.

SSI eligible persons are penalized in several ways. When living with relatives a flat one-third reduction from calculated benefits is automatic if both food and shelter are provided. If relatives from the household earn income, the benefit payment is further reduced, the amount varying by household composition and source of income. Both of these reductions occur independent of how much the recipient actually is sharing in these resources (U.S. Department of HEW, 1978). These standards function to keep SSI recipients permanently in poverty. Automatic reductions and the low maximum levels provide serious disincentives for maintaining family networks and promote institutionalization for those who cannot afford to live independently on these benefit levels. If Medicaid pays more than 50 percent of the cost of institutionalization, the SSI benefit drops to $25 under the assumption that basic needs are being met and SSI funds aren't necessary.

The elderly pay more for health care than any other age group, spending about three times the amount per person that is paid out by non-aged adults. While Medicare is believed by some to be a comprehensive health plan, it pays less than 40 percent of the elderly's health care bill. This is not adequate considering that health costs more than tripled between 1966 and 1977. Expenses not covered by Medicare include: prescription drugs, eyeglasses, hearing aids, dentures, custodial care, and preventive care (Davis and Schoen, 1978; U.S. House, 1978). Medicaid, therefore, is the major source of health care coverage for the aged poor.

Eligibility for Medicaid is automatic for SSI recipients in all but 15 states. So here again the implicit poverty line is well below the official poverty line. While the Federal government sets minimum guidelines for state Medicaid programs, which include, for example, inpatient hospital services, lab and x-ray services, skilled nursing facility services, and home health care services, state variations in

The Politics of Measuring Poverty Among the Elderly 71

eligibility requirements and the actual services they provide create great inequity in the coverage.

The rate of functional disability for the elderly is 15 times greater than for the non-elderly. From the standpoint of the elderly, the lack of long-term care in both health and social services is the weakest point in the health care system. Nonavailability of services, lack of qualified personnel, and financial barriers restrict access to adequate care. Medicaid's institutional bias in the provision of long-term care is revealed in the statistic that 73 percent of Medicaid expenditures for the elderly are received by skilled nursing or intermediate care facilities. Home health care, on the other hand, received less than two percent of Medicaid's long-term care coverage. Of the elderly who need long-term care, 83 percent could be cared for under a home health program, but Medicaid regulations to qualify for that coverage are strict, and even then it is too limited to be effective. Almost 70 percent of all nursing home residents are below the poverty level. Of these, 48 percent were not initially poor, but were forced to "spend down;" that is, they had to spend their income and assets down to the SSI (poverty) level in order to qualify for Medicaid (U.S. House, 1978; Lowy, 1980).

In 1979, of the five percent of all elderly households in public or subsidized housing, 70 percent were above the poverty line. The Section 202 housing program[8] provides 40-year Federal loans to non-profit borrower corporations who represent the elderly or handicapped. The housing is primarily for low income persons who may also qualify for Section 8 (or other) housing assistance, which stipulates that no more than 25 percent of income can go towards rent. Section 8 is aimed at "lower-income" families with adjusted family incomes which do not exceed 80 percent of the median income of the area, and at "very low-income" families with adjusted income not exceeding 50 percent of the median. Adjustments are made to account for family size and unusual medical expenses. The maximum income limit to qualify for Section 8 assistance, which varies by local housing authority, can be quite high. For example, the income limit for an elderly couple in Boston in 1980 was $8700. While the implicit poverty line for subsidized housing tends to be high, many of the elderly spend years on waiting lists without ever being assigned an apartment. This restriction of the supply of subsidized housing can be just as effective as stringent income criteria in limiting the cost of the program. For example, the Boston Housing Authority estimates that the 2,000 elderly on their waiting lists underestimates the number who would sign up if more housing were available by some 3,000 to 4,000 people. A similar situation exists for most large cities around the country.

Testimony heard by the U.S. Senate (1979) has emphasized the relevance of housing policy to programs designed to help the elderly live independently and avoid or at least delay institutionalization. The lack of subsidized housing is one factor tending to increase rates of institutionalization.

The elderly historically have had a low level of participation in the Food Stamp program. This is true even though these stamps can be used for food in stores, to pay for home delivered meals, and for hot meals at an Elderly Nutrition Program meal site. Only 17 percent of Food Stamp households were 65 or older in March of 1980 (U.S. Bureau of the Census, 1981). Eligibility is based on household resources and current monthly income.[9] Households receiving public assistance are automatically eligible. SSI recipients are similarly eligible for Food Stamps in most states. But less than one-third of the eligible elderly participate in the program. Reasons for non-participation include the stigma of welfare, misinformation about eligibility, and lack of information on how they can use their Food Stamps.

Recent legislation has been very generous to the elderly and the disabled. The 1979 Food Stamp Act amendments allow the elderly to deduct medical expenses over $35 which are not covered by Medicare or insurance and "excess shelter" costs which are housing, fuel, and utilities expenses over 50 percent of income after all other deductions up to $115. Present law sets income limits using _net_ income at 100 percent of the poverty line. Proposed law, which has passed the Senate and is expected to pass the House, uses _gross_ income at 130 percent of the poverty line as the new limit. Recently the Senate voted to exempt the elderly and disabled from the new gross income limit, which is to their advantage since it hits one and two person households harder than does the present net income limit.

While Congress has already voted to cut the Food Stamp program by $1.5 billion in 1982, it seems reluctant to cut benefits for elderly (and disabled) recipients. One reason is that the elderly, the disabled, and their advocates constitute a stronger lobby than do Food Stamp recipients more generally. In addition policymakers can provide concessions to the elderly cheaply; for example, exemption of the elderly from the proposed gross income limit would cost only $35 million because the elderly constitute such a small proportion of program recipients.

CONCLUSION

We have argued that the official government poverty lines are based as much on political criteria as on "objective" and "scientific" criteria. This is reflected in the procedure used to construct the original SSA poverty lines. While it is clear that income alone is not an adequate measure of economic well-being, it is also evident that the various modifications of income measures have their own sources of error. Some measures of well-being tend to create the perception that the elderly are better off than is actually the case (e.g., net worth measures) and others the perception that they are worse off (e.g., human capital measures). Intrafamily and in-kind transfers need to be taken into consideration, but such efforts risk substantial error.

We have described the political nature of the eligibility criteria associated with various social programs. In measuring the poverty among the elderly, the real (or operational) poverty line is found by looking at the income eligibility criteria associated with various social programs. We have seen that SSI eligibility levels are used for most Food Stamps and Medicaid programs. We suggest that SSI levels can be considered an implicit poverty line, used for counting the number deemed sufficiently poor to justify state assistance.

Eligibility standards reflect what the State is willing to pay. While the system has cost-effectiveness as a goal, exclusion criteria often push the elderly into dependence rather than towards independence. "Independence" for the elderly is often synonymous with not being institutionalized. Yet, eligibility criteria which result in a need to spend down to reach low levels of eligibility contribute to the weakening of family ties and an increase in the risk of institutionalization. The problem of social isolation which such policies contribute to can be even more oppressive than that of dependency itself.

The government funds spent do not help the elderly poor to improve their economic well-being to the extent one might hope. In today's political environment it is not possible to meet all the legitimate needs of the elderly poor, but even at present levels of expenditure it should be possible for a greater proportion to achieve lives of independence and dignity. However, in their effort to hold costs down, balance the increasing demands on government by the different constituent groups, and still try to appear responsive to the public, policymakers trap many of the elderly in a cycle of poverty, thus increasing dependence on the State.

NOTES

1. The original poverty threshold derived strictly on the basis of a "scientific" assessment of nutritional needs was deemed too high to be politically acceptable to government policymakers. The Council of Economic Advisors decided, therefore, to devise a lower poverty standard, set at 80 percent of the "low-cost food budget" developed by the Department of Agriculture (Orshansky, 1963).
2. Orshansky's adjustments are based on the following changes: changed nutrient allowances; an increase in the ratio of nonfood consumption to food consumption to reflect current consumption patterns; cost increases associated with the new Thrifty Food Plan; use of actual age-sex composition of family members rather than simulations; and the elimination of differential estimation within families for farm-nonfarm residence, sex of head, and number of children. The new ratios become 1 to 3.4 (instead of 1 to 3) for families of 3 or more, and 1 to 4.3 (instead of 1 to 3.7) for 2 person families (Fendler and Orshansky, 1979).
3. An official poverty line has not actually been established for the institutionalized elderly. For this group there are special considerations to take into account such as setting dollar amounts on the value of Medicare and Medicaid transfer payments.

4. Borzilleri's study (1978) of consumer prices increases from January 1970 to March 1977 showed that on the average, prices for the elderly rose about 4 percent faster than for the population in general. Comparing the first three automatic adjustment periods (1975, 1976, 1977) for Social Security benefits as indicated by the CPI with the Older Person's Index (OPI) constructed by Borzilleri, the CPI showed increases of 8.0%, 6.4%, and 5.9%, while the OPI indicated higher increases of 8.2%, 6.8%, and 6.3%.
5. For an opposite view, see Michael (1979).
6. Approximately 70 percent of the elderly do own their own homes, but these homes are more likely to be deteriorating or substandard than is the case for other age groups (Harris, 1978).
7. The actual determination of income limits is more complex than these figures suggest due to some twenty-one possible exclusions. Most of the elderly do not have earned income, but for those who do the SSI benefit is not reduced to zero until earned income reaches $7373 per year. More common are those with only unearned income for whom the SSI benefit reduces to zero at $3416 per year when certain of the exclusions are taken into consideration.
8. Section 202 was first introduced as part of the Housing Act of 1959 to provide direct Federal long-term loans for the construction of housing for the elderly and the handicapped. It was originally aimed at the elderly whose incomes were above public housing budgets, but low enough to be inadequate for housing in the private market. In 1974 it was amended by the Housing and Community Development Act, which changed the method of determining the interest rate, and provided Section 8 housing assistance payments for these projects.
9. The resource limit for most households is $1500; if one person is over 60 in a 2-person or more household, the limit is $3000. Maximum monthly net income for an individual is $316.

REFERENCES

Borzilleri, Thomas C. (1978) "The Need for a Separate Consumer Price Index for Older Persons: a Review and New Evidence." Gerontologist 18 (3): 230-36.

Congressional Budget Office (1977) "Poverty Status of Families Under Alternative Definitions of Income." Background Paper No. 17 (Revised). Washington, D.C.: U.S. Government Printing Office.

Davis, Karen, and Cathy Schoen (1978) Health and the War on Poverty. Washington, D.C.: The Brookings Institution.

Fendler, Carol, and Mollie Orshansky (1979) "Improving the Poverty Definition." Proceedings of the Social Statistics Section, Washington, D.C. American Statistical Association.

Harris, Charles S. (1978) Fact Book on Aging: A Profile of America's Older Population. Washington, D.C.: National Council on the Aging.

Hollister, R.G., and John L. Palmer (1969) The Impact of Inflation on the Poor. Madison, Wisconsin: University of Wisconsin Institute of Research on Poverty.

Huber, Joan (1974) "Political Implications of Poverty Definitions." Pp. 71-80 in J. Huber and P. Chalfant (eds.). The Sociology of American Poverty. Cambridge, Massachusetts: Schenkman Publishing Company.

Johnson, Elizabeth S., and John B. Williamson (1980) Growing Old. New York: Holt, Rinehart and Winston.

Lamale, Helen H. (1963) "The Impact of Rising Prices on Younger and Older Consumers." Bureau of Labor Statistics, Report No. 238-2. Washington, D.C.: U.S. Government Printing Office.

Lowy, Louis (1980) Social Policies and Programs on Aging. Lexington, Massachusetts: Lexington Books.

Michael, Robert T. (1979) "Variations Across Households in the Rate of Inflation." Journal of Money, Credit, and Banking 2 (February): 32-46.

Mirer, Thad W. (1975) "The Distributive Impact on Purchasing Power of Inflation During Price Controls." Quarterly Review of Economics and Business 15(2): 93-96.

Moon, Marilyn (1976) "The Economic Welfare of the Aged and Income Security Programs." Review of Income and Wealth 22 (September): 253-69.

Moon, Marilyn and Timothy Smeeding (1981) "Medical Care Transfers, Poverty and the Aged." Journal of Health Politics, Policy and Law 6(1): 29-39.

Moon, Marilyn and Eugene Smolensky (1977a) "Income, Economic Status, and Policy Toward the Aged." Discussion Paper No. 350-76. Madison, Wisconsin: Institute for Research on Poverty.

_____ (1977b) (eds.) Improving Measures of Economic Well-Being. New York: Academic Press.

Orshansky, Mollie (1963) "Children of the Poor." Social Security Bulletin 25: 2-21.

_____ (1965) "Counting the Poor: Another Look at the Poverty Profile." Social Security Bulletin 28(1): 3-29.

_____ (1969) "How Poverty is Measured." Monthly Labor Review 92 (February): 37-41.

Osmond, Marie, and Mary Durkin (1979) "Measuring Family Poverty." Social Science Quarterly 6(1): 87-95.

Projector, Dorothy, and G. Weiss (1969) "Income-Net Worth Measures of Economic Welfare." Social Security Bulletin 32 (November): 14-17.

Schulz, James H. (1980) The Economics of Aging. Second edition. Belmont, California: Wadsworth.

U.S. Bureau of the Census (1979) "Social and Economic Characteristics of Older Population: 1978 (Special Studies)." Current Population Reports, Series P-23, No. 85. Washington, D.C.: U.S. Government Printing Office.

_____ (1980) "Money Income and Poverty Status of Families and Persons in the United States: 1979." Current Population Reports, Series P-60, No. 125. Washington, D.C.: U.S. Government Printing Office.

_____ (1981) "Characteristics of Households and Persons Receiving Noncash Benefits: 1979 (Special Studies)." Current Population Reports, Series P-23, No. 110. Washington, D.C.: U.S. Government Printing Office.

U.S. Department of Health, Education and Welfare (1976) The Measure of Poverty: A Report to Congress as Mandated by the Education Amendments of 1974. Washington, D.C.: U.S. Government Printing Office.

_____ (1978) Social Security Handbook. Sixth edition, Washington, D.C.: U.S. Government Printing Office.

U.S. Department of Health and Human Services (1981) Social Security Bulletin 44(5). Washington, D.C.: U.S. Government Printing Office.

U.S. House of Representatives Select Committee on Aging (1978) Poverty Among America's Aged. Washington, D.C.: U.S. Government Printing Office.

U.S. Senate Subcommittee on Housing and Urban Affairs (1979) The Elderly in Housing. Washington, D.C.: U.S. Government Printing Office.

Watts, Harold W. (1969) "An Economic Definition of Poverty." Pp. 316-29 in D. Moynihan (ed.), On Understanding Poverty. New York: Basic Books, Inc.

Weisbrod, Burton A. and W. Lee Hansen (1968) "An Income-Net Worth Approach to Measuring Economic Welfare." American Economic Review 8 (December): 1315-29.

Williamson, John B. (1979) "The Economic Status of the Elderly: Is the Problem Low Income?" The Journal of Sociology and Social Welfare 6 (September): 673-700.

Williamson, John B., and Kathryn M. Hyer (1975) "The Measurement and Meaning of Poverty." Social Problems 22(5): 652-63.

THE ANTI-POVERTY EFFECT OF IN-KIND TRANSFERS:
A "GOOD IDEA" GONE TOO FAR?*

Timothy M. Smeeding

> The 'war on poverty' that began in 1964 has been won. The growth of jobs and income in the private economy, combined with an explosive increase in government spending for welfare and income transfer programs, has virtually eliminated poverty in the United States. Any Americans who truly cannot care for themselves are now eligible for generous government aid in the form of cash, medical benefits, food stamps, housing, and other services.
>
> Martin Anderson
> Welfare (p. 15)

Is poverty really dead? Have we won the war on poverty with in-kind transfers as Martin Anderson (1978) and others[1] suggest? And if so, can we feel assured that President Reagan's proposed budget reductions will not hurt the "truly needy" -- whoever they are?[2] Based on applied poverty research of the 1970s it is tempting to answer all of these questions in the affirmative. But this paper will show that to do so is to jump to an unwarranted conclusion, one based on questionable studies of the extent of income poverty which have apparently been more or less accepted by many policymakers and journalists with little or no critical review. To be sure, these studies have played a major role in recent policy debates. For example, Martin Anderson's 1978 book, Welfare, from which the opening quote

---

* This paper was supported by the American Statistical Association (ASA) through funds granted them by the National Science Foundation and was written while I was an ASA Research Fellow. I would like to thank Sheldon Danziger, Richard Goldstein, Roger Herriot, and Robert Plotnick for their comments and suggestions, and G. William Hoagland for making available unpublished data. I claim credit for all errors, omissions, and transgressions.

was taken, played a role in scuttling the Carter Administration's welfare reform package: The Program for Better Jobs and Income (PBJI).[3] Even more recently, the belief that we have licked poverty has led the Reagan Administration to conclude that "welfare" spending can be reduced wtih little or no effect on poor families. However, we will show that even if one accepts the notion that poverty has been eliminated (or at least satisfactorily reduced to statistical insignificance) by cash and in-kind transfers, the facts of the matter lead to the conclusion that if these transfers have reduced poverty then reducing these transfers will in turn increase poverty. For the affected family, increased earned income is theoretically an alternative to reduced transfers. However, most of the poor are aged, disabled, or single parent families with young children, who cannot be expected to "earn their way out of poverty" in a short time, if at all.

The purposes of this paper are: to review the arguments of those who feel that poverty is a statistical artifact and the grounds on which their arguments are based; to try and identify the progress against poverty which has been made so far and its implications for policy; and finally to indicate the way in which current and future applied poverty research might accurately reflect this progress such that future pro-poverty (i.e., poverty creation) and anti-poverty (poverty reduction) policies can be accurately evaluated in terms of their impact on low income families.

Before we begin this exercise, two matters which are not directly dealt with in the remainder of the paper need to be addressed. These issues are: 1) the significant differences and biases created when analyzing all types of income in-kind as compared to only the "major" in-kind transfers which we deal with below; and 2) the issue of whether or not the official poverty line used in this study need be changed to account for the nonmoney income received by the nonpoor. In the first column of Table 7.1, "major" in-kind transfer benefits in the form of food (Food Stamps, School Lunch), housing (public and subsidized housing), and medical care (Medicaid and Medicare) are shown.

The next two columns include aggregate estimates of "other" unaccounted for in-kind benefits. They may take the form of public or private sector, free or below-market price subsidization of each type of good (including income tax subsidization[4]) or they may be the more traditional type of income in-kind, food received as pay, for instance. No account is taken of private interfamily transfers in-kind (e.g., housing and food provided to an elderly parent who lives with their children). The sources of all estimates and the items included are shown at the bottom of the table. While these are hardly precise or complete estimates -- indeed, if precise estimates of their market value were available we might also be able to impute their value to individuals -- they are close enough to provide the reader with an appreciation of the implicit "selectivity bias" associated with counting only a limited set of in-kind transfer benefits in income. In total, the market value of in-kind transfer benefits counted in this exercise (and in similar previous exercises), is only a little more than one-third of those in-kind benefits which theoretically should be included if we want to estimate the total effect of these types of benefits on the income size distribution. In each case the value of public and private food, housing, and medical benefits not counted exceeds the value of in-kind benefits which are counted.

The fifth and sixth rows in Table 7.1 differentiate between means-tested and nonmeans-tested benefits. "Major" in-kind transfers include 87.0 percent of all means-tested benefits as compared to 20.7 percent of nonmeans-tested transfers. Thus the items which we are including bias measures of income distribution in the sense that they are primarily directed toward low income persons. The table suggests that the simulation models which are described below have so far only literally scratched the surface in terms of developing a more comprehensive estimate of the income size distribution.

The second, and related issue, deals with the question of whether or not the current official poverty line need be adjusted to account for the "other" sources of income in-kind which are shown in Table 7.1. Several individuals, including Mollie Orshansky herself, argue that the current poverty standard is based on a cash or money income concept, and a change in the income definition to include in-kind benefits necessitates a change in the poverty standard definition as well. While a good case can be made for such a change (see Rodgers, this volume; 1978; Harrington, 1977) policymakers are not yet ready to consider this matter. In fact, a recent Senate Budget directive (U.S. Senate, 1980:33-34) instructs the Census Bureau to publish a series of reports which assess the impact of the "major" types of in-kind transfers in Table 7.1 on the official measure of poverty, beginning no later than October 1, 1981. Several authors (including Girshick and Williamson, and Rodgers, both this volume) find other major difficulties with the current poverty line measure. A major problem centers around the fact that the current poverty line has been adjusted only for increases in the Consumer Price Index since 1963. From an intertemporal perspective, it is indeed an "absolute" poverty line, one which does not reflect the fact that since its inception it has not risen with the incomes of the rest of the population. For instance, in 1963 the poverty line for a four person family was 44 percent of the median family income of this same size family, but by 1979 it had fallen to 33 percent. Thus, if the income distribution maintains its relative shape, and if real incomes rise (as they have since 1963), poverty will be reduced just by the fact that the "absolute" poverty line does not change with real income. A relative poverty line, e.g., one that remained at 44 percent of median family income, would show a larger number of poor persons.[5] There are, of course, several other reasons why one might want to change the current official poverty measure[6] which will not be reiterated here.

TABLE 7.1

Income In-Kind "Major" Public In-Kind Transfer Programs
VS "Total" Private and Public Income In-Kind in 1980[1]

Row	Type of Benefit	"Major" In-Kind Transfer Benefits[2]	"Other" In-Kind Income Public	"Other" In-Kind Income Private[3]	"Total" Value of Benefits	"Major" as a Percent of "Total"
1.	Food	$12.1 [4]	$ 1.2 [5]	$16.6 [6]	$ 29.9	40.4%
2.	Housing	5.4 [7]	35.7 [8]	13.4 [9]	54.9	9.9
3.	Medical Care	58.6 [10]	25.9 [11]	50.7 [12]	135.2	43.3
4.	TOTAL	$76.1	$62.8	$80.7	$219.6	34.7%
5.	TOTAL MEANS TESTED BENEFITS	$40.3 [13]	$ 3.6 [14]	$ 2.4 [15]	$ 46.3	87.0%
6.	TOTAL NON-MEANS TESTED BENEFITS	$35.8	59.2	78.3	173.3	20.7

Sources: Social Security Bulletin (1981), U.S. Budget, FY 1982 (1981); Survey of Current Business (1979); U.S. Chamber of Commerce (1981)

Notes:
1. 1980 estimates unless otherwise noted.
2. Includes public in-kind transfer benefits from the program mentioned in notes 4, 7, and 10 below. This is also the set of in-kind transfer benefits whose effect on poverty is analyzed in the remainder of this paper.
3. Includes some employer provided benefits, philanthopic transfers, and some sources of nonmarket income in-kind, but excludes private interfamily in-kind transfers, e.g., the medical bills of the elderly which are paid by their children or the free housing and food provided for an elderly parent who lives with their children. In 1979 these benefits totalled roughly $20.0 billion (Lampman and Smeeding, 1981), but we are not able to separate food from housing benefits.
4. Includes $9.1 billion in Food Stamps and $3.0 billion in School Lunch benefits.
5. Includes several U.S. Department of Agriculture programs (e.g., Women's Infant's and Children's Special Food Program (WIC), School Milk, etc.) for 1980.

6. Includes $6.6 billion in food produced and consumed on farms and food received as pay in 1978, plus $10.0 billion in employer provided "business lunches".
7. Includes $5.4 billion in public and subsidized housing for low income families under various public programs including: Low Rent Public Housing and Sections 8, 235, 236, 101 and 202b of the 1937 Housing Act.
8. Includes $28.8 billion in tax expenditures for mortgage interest, property tax deductibility and tax exempt bonds to finance mortgages; $3.9 billion in FHA, VA, FHMA mortgage subsidies for 1980 only (i.e., no account taken of prior years subsidies which are still in effect); and $3.0 billion in rent control subsidies.
9. Includes $13.4 billion in net imputed rental income for owner occupied residences in 1978. This estimate is gross rental value minus property taxes, depreciation, and other maintenance costs.
10. Includes $23.6 billion in Medicaid and $35.0 billion in Medicare vendor payments.
11. These include $22.7 billion vendor payments for medical services under several public programs, including CHAMPUS, Veteran's Health Care, Worker's Compensation, Maternal and Child Health Care, Public Health Services, etc. in 1979. Also included are $3.2 billion in tax expenditures for tax deductible health and medical expenses. Estimates do not include medical research or construction expenditures.
12. Includes $50.7 billion in employer provided group health insurance contributions for private sector and government employees in 1979.
13. Excludes "paid" School Lunch benefits and Medicare. Virtually all children who eat hot school lunches receive a basic subsidy under this program, even if they pay "full" established price. This subsidy accounts for about 25 percent of total School Lunch benefits. Another 75 percent of benefits go to those who either receive the lunch for free or pay a reduced price of 10-20 cents per meal. Medicare covers all elderly Social Security beneficiaries and a large group of the nonaged disabled, primarily those receiving Social Security benefits. About 15 percent of Medicare benefits accrue to poor elderly persons, but Medicare is not a means-tested transfer program.
14. Includes expenditures for USDA income tested programs such as WIC; expenditures for Maternal and Child Health Care; and one-half of mortgage interest guarantees (which because they accrue to households with incomes above the median, are "income-tested" only in the broadest sense).
15. Includes health care vendor payments made by charitable organizations ($2.0 billion) and charitable food and housing expenditures ($0.4 billion). Because these payments are generally for the benefit of the indigent, they were included under means-tested benefits.

To conclude, there is reason to be concerned about both omitted types of income in-kind and the validity of the poverty line once one introduces nonmoney income. At the present time it is not possible to accurately distribute the nonmoney income of the nonpoor -- the other income in-kind in Table 7.1 -- among the recipient population. In addition, experimenting with different poverty measures clearly lies beyond the scope of this paper. But the arguments which are made below would also apply to a "new" poverty line which was based on the total value of nonmoney income.[7]

POVERTY IS DEAD: THE BASIS OF THE ARGUMENT

The inadequacies of the U.S. Census Bureau's poverty statistics are by now widely known. In particular, the omission of in-kind transfers limits their usefulness and reliability.[8] Martin Anderson (1978:19) has gone so far as to label this omission a "deliberate 'cover-up' of the true extent of poverty in the U.S."

Edgar Browning (1975:29-30) was among the first to claim that "because the Census Bureau's statistics on income distribution and official poverty counts ignore in-kind transfers (e.g., Food Stamps, Medicaid), they are largely useless as a basis for rational analysis of questions concerning income distribution..." He argues further that: "the total value of resources consumed by the poor in 1973 was enough to raise every officially poor family 30 percent above its poverty line." On average, then, we spend more than enough to eradicate poverty altogether. However, there are two basic problems with this estimate. The first problem is that few in-kind transfer beneficiaries are average. Not every poor person benefits from all of these transferred resources -- some benefit a lot, others not at all. Recent data for 1979 (U.S. Census, 1981:20) indicates that 28 percent of the official poor did not benefit from any public in-kind transfers, while 22 percent benefited from at least three programs. When benefit nonrecipiency and benefit variance is taken into account, many remain poor. The second problem with Browning's estimate is that he divided total means-tested cash and in-kind transfers by the official or "after cash transfer" poor. He should have both subtracted benefits that did not go to the poor from the numerator and divided by the pre-transfer poor in the denominator. Thus he spread too many transfers over a group of poor who had already been reduced by these same benefits! However, Browning's paper did serve to identify and highlight the potential impact of in-kind transfers on poverty.

In 1977, the Congressional Budget Office (CBO) indicated that the poverty rate had fallen to 8.2 percent of the population (compared to the Census Bureau estimate of 11.7 percent), once one had added the market value of Food Stamps, School Lunch, and several public housing programs to cash income; and further to 5.9 percent once medical transfer benefits (Medicare and Medicaid) had been distributed among recipients.[9] In an almost identical later study, G. William Hoagland (1980) predicted that the poverty rate would fall to 4.1 percent in fiscal year 1980 once all of these benefits were taken into account. Both the original CBO study and the later Hoagland paper were based on sophisticated microsimulation models for in-kind transfers which were coupled with modified versions of the Census' March CPS to impute in-kind benefits to eligible individuals for each of the forementioned programs. Because, for budgetary purposes, Congress always needs to know what will happen to expenditures on a given program next year, rather than what actually did happen last year, both of these studies are based on earlier years' March CPS which were "aged" forward (i.e., projected) to reflect household structure and macroeconomic conditions in the year in question.[10] While reliance on microdata provides the capability to accurately simulate the structure of benefits for each program type, the CBO and Hoagland studies contain at least three shortcomings, any one of which could seriously bias their results.

First, the data "aging" process is subject to two types of error. For one, the accuracy of the general methodology itself has never, to my knowledge, been substantiated by going back to reexamine the aged data vis-a-vis the actual year's data which it forecast. For instance, one could compare actual 1976 income as reported in the March CPS 1977 with the "aged" data for 1976 which was constructed from an earlier year's data set. The second type of error with data aging processes is the necessity of relying on macroeconomic forecasts of unemployment, national income, and inflation to adjust factor market income (earnings, interest, etc.) to reflect forecast market conditions. In recent years, predictions based on macroeconomic forecasting models have differed substantially from actual occurrences. Thus even if the aging process were technically perfect, plugging in the wrong economic assumptions produces the wrong answers. While data aging may be necessary for estimating the future budgetary impact of a given change in a program, these data are not well suited for estimating the extent of poverty.

The second shortcoming is the lack of data on patterns of multiple recipiency for cash and in-kind transfer benefits. Sometimes multiple benefit status determination is straightforward, i.e., the fact that virtually all AFDC recipients and most SSI recipients[11] are covered by Medicaid. However, there is little or no administrative data which reflects patterns of multiple in-kind benefit recipiency. Only very recently have surveys provided such information on a nationwide basis.[12] Thus <u>all</u> current studies of poverty and in-kind transfers are flawed by this shortcoming, including Smeeding (1975) and Plotnick and Smeeding (1979), which are mentioned below, as well as the CBO and Hoagland papers. Without multiple beneficiary data, the researcher can only simulate program eligibility and benefit recipiency for each particular in-kind benefit program in isolation from other programs. Thus in studies like these the value of Medicaid, Food Stamps, Medicare, Public Housing, etc., are each individually imputed to the basic CPS money income data for each separate program. Patterns of multiple recipiency simply "fall out" of such simulations, i.e. they are created as a statistical byproduct. However, because multiple benefit recipiency can be crucial in assessing who is poor (not poor) after receipt of such benefits, one cannot at all be sure of the accuracy of the results of such efforts.[13]

The final, and probably most crucial flaw in the CBO and Hoagland studies is their reliance on valuing in-kind benefits at their market value. That is, they measure control over resources via dollar cost of benefits provided and not the value which recipients place on those resources. In assessing the budgetary impact of proposed program changes, it makes sense to utilize market value as a measure of benefits, simply because the aggregate market value of benefits (plus administrative overhead) is conceptually synonymous with program appropriations. However when assessing the effect of a program on individual households' economic well-being and their poverty status, the recipient value is the appropriate construct for measuring the impact of the program in question. In some cases, e.g., for Food Stamps, the recipient value of the in-kind transfer is very close to the market value. However, recipient valuation is particularly crucial in the case of medical transfer benefits, i.e., Medicaid and Medicare. In 1979 the price which the government would need to charge a person covered by such plans to just break even was about $1,000 per coveree for each program.[14] If the government group rated such insurance policies it would need to charge more to elderly and disabled Medicare recipients and less to children and non-disabled younger adults. But this does not mean that such beneficiaries value these benefits at this amount.

For instance, an elderly individual covered by both Medicare and Medicaid insurance plans had "command over medical resources" of $2,981 during 1979. That is, they held a Medicare insurance policy which cost $1,011[15] and a Medicaid policy which cost $1,970 (roughly three-quarters of which, or $1,550, covers them against the need for institutionalization in a nursing home or in an intermediate care facility). Both the earlier CBO study and the Hoagland paper treat this $2,981 just as if it were more flexible cash income, adding it to the money incomes of eligible individuals. If the recipient individual would not put such a high value on this policy, it would be worth considerably less to them. The problem is, of course, the determination of how much less. The essence of the problem is not a lack of alternatives. In fact, there are several ways to solve this problem (Smeeding and Moon, 1980). The theoretically preferred method is to determine how much a recipient would be willing to pay for such a policy by considering out of pocket medical insurance and medical care expenditure by similar families who do not benefit from such policies. However, virtually all elderly persons benefit from Medicare, hence the "similar families" do not exist in this case. Moreover, willingness to pay for insurance against institutionalization is largely unmeasured altogether. That is, there is little evidence dealing with actual expenditures for such insurance.[16] In short, while it is safe to assume that recipients value medical transfers at less than cost, determining the precise amount of cash income for which the recipient would trade their medical benefits is a difficult task.

A somewhat easier but more limited method is to restrict the value of medical transfers to no more than the amount which is "allowed for" in the poverty income budget. That is, of the $3,410 (4360) which separated poor elderly individuals (couples) from nonpoor individuals in 1979, I estimate that about $380 (497) is budgeted for medical care.[17] If we limit the value of medical care to no more than this amount, the results will be quite different than if we added the entire $2,981 ($5,962!) to the cash incomes of elderly individuals (couples). Poverty status determination is quite sensitive to this issue. For instance, in a recent study (Smeeding and Moon: 1980) only 1.5 million elderly persons were poor in 1974 once medical benefits were counted at market value, while 2.5 million of the elderly were poor if the value of medical benefits was limited to the poverty line budgeted amount. Neither the CBO nor Hoagland consider these alternatives. As an alternative, they have published estimates of the poor both with and without medical care transfers counted in income, not recommending either measure as being preferred over the other.

The importance of this point cannot be overestimated. More than two-thirds of the total market value of in-kind transfers counted in the 1977 CBO study were medical transfers. Our largest means tested income transfer program, Medicaid, accounts for almost a third of <u>all</u> means tested transfer benefits (including cash welfare) all by itself. Counted at their market value in 1979, $2,981 worth of medical benefits would almost make a single elderly person unpoor all by themselves, even if this person had little other income to fulfill more basic needs. Thus, unless one accepts the fact that the poor can count on eating wheelchairs and burning crutches for heat, the valuation of medical benefits is a crucial element in measuring the antipoverty effects of benefits in-kind. In the CBO study, 13.5 (16.7) percent of all (elderly) families[18] were poor before counting benefits in-kind. After counting these benefits the poverty rate dropped to 8.1 (6.1) percent in 1976. Fully 3.2 (8.0) percentage points of this total 5.4 (10.6) percentage point decrease in poverty, of 59 (75) percent of the impact of in-kind transfers, can be attributed to medical transfers alone.

In sum, because of these three flaws, the CBO and Hoagland estimates need be treated with some caution. In my own research (Smeeding 1975; Plotnick and Smeeding, 1979), like the CBO, I also used microsimulation techniques to allocate in-kind transfer benefits to individual families using CPS data for 1968, 1970, 1972, and 1974. While I did not use "aged" data, and while my estimates did adjust for recipient willingness to pay for medical benefits and other in-kind transfers (Food Stamps and Public Housing), they omitted School Lunch benefits and Public Housing benefits (except for 1972), and lacked outside information on patterns of multiple in-kind benefits recipiency. The most recent of these estimates, for 1974, indicates that benefits from Food Stamps, Medicaid and Medicare were large enough to reduce the poverty rate from 11.2 percent (the Census figure) to 7.8 percent. In 1972, the corresponding rates were 11.9 and 6.2 percent (including the effects of Public housing in 1972).

The most widely cited set of estimates of poverty rates after receipt of in-kind benefits are those of Morton Paglin (1979a, 1979b), possibly because Paglin presents a set of estimates which run all the way from 1959 to 1975 in one piece of research. Unfortunately his estimates are also the most questionable. The major technical flaw in Paglin's work is its reliance on published money income distribution figures. While such a restriction was necessary to compile the time series of estimates which he presents, working with published data presents several seemingly insurmountable problems. It is impossible to determine which persons benefited how much and from what programs with any acceptable degree of accuracy. Interestingly, while it is hard to imagine how Paglin can be at all sure of the benefit distribution for any one in-kind program (or its effect on poverty) he argues (Paglin 1979b:45) that he has accounted for patterns of multiple benefit recipiency.[19] Finally, because he cannot simulate individual eligibility for benefits, Paglin is forced to use inferior estimates of the number of recipients of any program who are poor.[20] Like the CBO, he relies only on market value as a measure of the value of benefits to recipients. After adjusting for taxes, underreporting and income sharing by unrelated persons living together as well as adjusting for in-kind transfers, Paglin's final estimates for 1975 indicates that only 3.6 percent of the population was poor.

ANOTHER LOOK AT THE NUMBERS

As mentioned above, there are several shortcomings in virtually all current studies of poverty and transfers in-kind. However, because not all existing studies have the same shortcomings, they can be adjusted to a roughly comparable basis. In Table 7.2, I have made such adjustments. In-kind benefits for food (Food Stamps, School Lunch), housing (several public housing programs), and medical care (Medicare and Medicaid) are included, and counted at their recipient, i.e., their "cash equivalent" value.[21] Adjustments for cash income underreporting and federal income and payroll tax liability were also made. The new Census data on multiple benefit recipiency has not been used to adjust these figures. Estimates are presented for all in-kind transfers, and then for all such transfers excluding medical care transfers.[22] The results of Paglin's research (for 1965-1974); the CBO study (for 1976); and the Hoagland study (for 1980) are also presented for comparison. Further comparisons can be made to the official Census Bureau estimates of poverty and to estimates based on pre-(cash and in-kind) transfer factor market income.

The conclusions to be drawn from this table are straightforward. If it were not for the rapid growth of government cash and in-kind transfers, poverty would not have changed much, if at all, since the war on poverty began in 1965.[23] Thus all of the net[24] progress against poverty which was made during the 1965-1980 period can be attributed to transfer payments. The Census income figures indicate that poverty has declined by roughly 25 percent over this period with most, if not all, of this progress occurring between 1965 and 1972. Since then, little if any progress has been made. The adjusted income data indicate that by 1980 poverty rates were roughly 45 percent below Census estimates if one includes medical benefits, and about 30 percent lower based on food and housing transfers. In-kind benefits have indeed reduced poverty below official estimates. However, the downward trend in adjusted poverty rates has, in a fashion quite similar to the Census figures, made little progress since 1972. While income transfers have grown tremendously over this period, the economy has deteriorated and increasing numbers of low income elderly, disabled, and female headed families have emerged to offset this growth. Based on the 1979-80 figures (and on a 1980 population estimate of roughly 225 million persons), America still has a significant poverty problem. Between 13.7 and 18.0 million people remain in poverty, depending on whether medical care benefits are included or excluded from the incomes of the poor. The much quoted Paglin-CBO-Hoagland figures indicate a much lower level of poverty, with a slight jump where, for 1976 and 1979-80, Table 7.2 substitutes the CBO and Hoagland estimates, respectively, for Paglin's estimates. Using Paglin's techniques for years beyond the final year of his study (1975) would result in a poverty rate of no more than 3 percent and a poverty count of 6.7 million persons this year.

Based on the Hoagland results for 1980 and on my own research, the remaining poor live largely in the South (roughly half), many in rural areas and are largely made up of female headed families with young children and the families of disabled adults. Many of the so-called "working poor" (mainly in the rural South) are also very close to the poverty line economic margin. However, the demographic make-up of the Southern poor is fast becoming similar to that of the poor in other regions: mainly single parent families and families with disabled adults. The income transfer system has succeeded in raising the incomes of most elderly units above the official poverty line, but not by a great deal. Elderly Southern non-white single individuals remain the exception to this general rule.

POLICY IMPLICATIONS

The Reagan Administration has suggested that they will be able to reduce income transfer payments for 1982 by $18.4 billion and not hurt the "truly needy". Of these cuts, at least $7.0 billion are

TABLE 7.2

Percentage of Persons with Income
Below the Poverty Line: 1965-80

Year	Factor[1] Market Income	Census Income[2] (Official Measure)	Adjusted Income[3] Including Medical Transfers	Adjusted Income[3] Excluding Medical Transfers	Paglin/ CBO[4] Adj. Income Estimates
1965	21.3	15.6	12.1	12.1	13.3
1968	18.2	12.8	9.9	10.9	7.3
1970	18.8	12.6	9.3	10.7	6.4
1972	19.2	11.9	6.2	8.3	4.7
1974	20.3	11.6	7.2	9.0	3.8
1976	21.0	11.8	6.7	8.3	5.9
1979-80	20.0	11.6	6.1	8.0	4.1
Percentage changes					
1965-1979-80	-6.1	-25.6	-49.6	-34.4	-69.1
1965-72	-9.9	-23.7	-48.8	-32.0	-64.6
1972-1979-80	4.1	-2.5	-1.6	-3.6	-15.9

Sources: Unless otherwise noted, the data were tabulated from the Survey of Economic Opportunity (for 1965), various March Current Population Survey Data Tapes, and from tabulations provided by William Hoagland.

1. Factor Market Income is defined as Census income less all government cash transfers. The data for 1965-1976 are taken from S. Danziger and R. Haveman (1981). The 1979-80 estimate is for 1979 and was compiled by the author using the March 1980 CPS.

2. Census figures are taken from various issues of the Current Population Reports P-60 series. The 1979-80 estimate is for 1979.

3. Adjusted income adjusts Census money income for under-reporting, adds in-kind public transfers at their cash equivalent value, and subtracts federal payroll and income taxes. The data for 1956-1974 are as in Plotnick and Smeeding (1979), adjusted to include public housing and School Lunch benefits. The 1976 and 1979-80

estimates are based on data provided by William Hoagland and Hoagland (1980) adjusted for the overly optimistic macroeconomic assumptions used in the income aging process, and for the cash equivalent value of in-kind transfer benefits. The column excluding medical transfers is exactly equal to the column including medical transfers, except for the fact that the impact of the cash equivalent of Medicare and Medicaid has been excluded.

4. The final column is taken from Paglin (1976b) for 1965-1974, and Hoagland (1980) for 1976 and 1979-80. It should be noted that the 1976 estimate is for fiscal year 1976 and not calendar year 1976. Similarly, the 1979-80 estimate is for fiscal year 1980.

planned for means-tested in-kind food, housing, and medical transfers; the rest coming from cash transfer programs such as AFDC and Social Security. The presumption is that "welfare cheats, chiselers and rip-off artists" will be eliminated from the rolls of the poor and forced to go to work to support themselves.[25] A three year cut in the Federal personal income tax is planned. The majority of the benefits would go to high income families. The non-working poor are usually not liable for personal income or payroll taxes, and for the working near-poor, increases in Social Security taxes and inflation would wipe out any income tax savings which they would realize.

In the future, the Reagan administration plans to return welfare to the state level by means of a system of block grants. While the details of such a proposal are yet to be worked out, the clear intent of the program is to allow states to set their own benefits standards for AFDC and related programs, and to rely more heavily on state and local revenue sources to finance future increases in such expenditures. Such a philosophy is diametrically opposed to the idea of a nationwide minimum income guarantee such as that proposed in President Cater's <u>Social Welfare Reform Amendments</u> (SWRA) of 1979 or in President Nixon's 1969 <u>Family Assistance Plan</u>.

While it is difficult to determine the specific effects of the Reagan budget reduction unless and until they are implemented, a few general predictions can be made from the data presented above. First, because it has been income transfers that have reduced poverty over the last 15 years, reductions in income transfers will increase poverty levels. Most poor people are dependent on the welfare system, and because they are elderly, disabled, or have home responsibilities for preschool children, poverty today is highest in those states which provide the fewest income transfers for the poor. Table 7.3 documents this fact. As officially measured, the 13 states with the highest poverty rates contain nearly 40 percent of all poor. All but one are Southern States, most with large concentrations of rural poor. The characteristics of their welfare systems and its "nonbeneficence" are clear from the table. In <u>every</u> state, AFDC maximum payments are far below the national average; none of these states supplement federal SSI payments; only two have AFDC-UP programs. Food Stamp participation rates are below the national average,[26] as is percent of state budget spent for public welfare. Medicaid participation and benefits are generally below national averages, etc. . . . From this table it is clear that the reason there is so much poverty in the South is because the Southern states do not choose to spend to aid those with lowest incomes. <u>Each</u> of these thirteen states would have been required to increase welfare benefits above present levels had the Carter SWRA plan with its combined cash and Food Stamp minimum benefit of 65 percent of the poverty line passed. Only one other state (Arizona) would have had to raise their current benefits. Returning welfare to these states in a block

Characteristics of the Public Assistance System in the Poorest States

	Poverty in 1975		Cash Public Assistance				Medicaid				Food Stamps	Welfare Effort
State	Persons (Millions) Who Are Poor (1)	Percent of Persons Who Are Poor (Rank) (2)	Maximum AFDC Benefits (1975) (3)	AFDC-UP Program? (1978) (4)	SSI Supplements? (1978) (5)	Recipients as % of State Poor (1978) (6)	Average Payments Per Beneficiary (1976) (7)	Recipients as % of Poverty Population (1972) (8)	State Medically Needy Option? (1978) (9)		Participation Rates (1978) (10)	Percent of State Budget Spent for Public Welfare (1979) (11)
TX	1.870	15.2 (10)	$ 140	No	No	34.4%	$632	18%	No		29.4%	15.5%
GA	.883	18.0 (5)	153	No	No	56.7	497	35	No		35.7	16.8
NC	.788	14.7 (12)	200	No	No	43.4	496		Yes		37.8	10.5
MS	.607	26.4 (1)	60	No	No	50.5	326	16	No		44.5	12.4
KY	.596	17.7 (6)	235	Yes	No	47.5	281	43	No		51.4	17.2
FL	1.227	14.4 (13)	170	No	No	33.1	448	27	Yes		48.8	9.7
LA	.720	19.3 (3)	158	No	No	53.0	361	23	No		46.1	13.1
TN	.660	15.3 (9)	132	No	No	52.2	384	19	Yes		49.5	15.0
SC	.478	17.2 (7)	117	No	No	46.2	284	16	No		40.2	9.9
AL	.587	16.4 (8)	135	No	No	53.3	406	17	No		40.2	13.3
AR	.392	18.5 (4)	140	No	No	49.7	505	10	Yes		37.4	16.2
WV	.270	15.1 (11)	249	Yes	No	43.0	231	35	Yes		55.2	11.8
NM	.223	19.3 (2)	206	No	No	39.0	381	28	No		39.9	9.5
National Total/ Averages	23.991	11.4%	$278	Yes-26 States	Yes-26 States	59.2%	$549	59%	Yes-30 States		46.9%	19.3%

Sources (by column number)

1,2. U.S. Bureau of the Census, Survey of Income and Education, special tabluation (latest year with state specific estimates).
3. U.S. Department of Health, Education and Welfare, 1969:9.
4. National Rural Center, 1978:94.
5. National Rural Center, 1978:101 (states which supplement payments to the aged maintaining their own residences).
6. National Rural Center, 1978:124-125 (includes AFDC, AFDC-UP, or SSI recipients as Public Assistance recipients).
7. U.S. Department of Health, Education and Welfare, 1978:79.
8. Davis and Schoen, 1978:68.
9. Davidson, 1979:60, Table 3.
10. U.S. Department of Agriculture, 1979:36 (percentage of all eligible households which receive stamps).
11. National Rural Center, 1978:70.

grant form would not only increase poverty, but also increase the interregional poverty rate differential as well.

A key element of recent welfare reform proposals, beginning with President Carter's PBJI, is the importance of "workfare" as an alternative to welfare. That is, low income able-bodied two-parent families, single individuals, and low income single parent families without preschool children should be expected to rely mainly on earnings as a source of income, and not on welfare benefits alone. The Carter PBJI plan would have provided such families with minimum wage PSE jobs supplanted with welfare grants, had they not found private sector employment within a given period. After <u>PBJI</u> was defeated, as an accompaniment to the 1979 <u>SWRA</u> plan, the Carter Administration proposed the <u>Work and Training Opportunities Act</u> (WTOA) of 1979 which would have also provided job assistance and training to these same groups, though on a smaller scale than PBJI. The Reagan Administration would go further. They plan to force[27] AFDC recipients without preschool children, and possibly also qualifying Food Stamp recipients, to work just to maintain their benefits and not for any additional pay. Clearly, for low income families such as these, the majority of whom are either poor or barely over their poverty lines, the long term solution to poverty is stable employment and earnings, not welfare. Thus employment assistance is clearly a necessary part of any comprehensive welfare reform proposal. Shrinking job opportunities for low skill workers manifest themselves in high youth and minority unemployement rates. Without adequate training and placement assistance it is difficult for the 30 percent of the poor who <u>are</u> largely able bodied adults (or teenage children in those families) to obtain adequate permanent employment. Job training, job placement, and employer subsidies to hire these workers are sorely needed if they are to succeed in the labor market of the 1980s.

It is more important to recognize that in most cases, at least for a temporary period of two to five years, the large majority of the poor cannot be counted on to work their way out of poverty! The major reason why they cannot do so is quite clear once one looks at the composition of the poor. A full 70 percent of the official poor (and a similar fraction of the adjusted income poor) are in families headed by a single female parent with at least one preschool child, an aged person, or a disabled adult (Schiller, 1981). These cannot, at least in their current circumstance, be expected to support themselves wholly with earnings, and clearly the vast majority are not cheats, chiselers or rip-off artists. They need the help of the welfare system; for many of them income transfers are not only a temporary means of avoiding poverty but also a long term solution to their poverty problem.[28] For any given female headed family with very young children, income transfers are clearly a temporary end; when the children are of school age the mother should, with employment and childcare assistance, become more reliant on earnings. But, if present trends continue, another female headed family with preschool children will be there to take her place. The low income aged and permanently disabled cannot be required to rely on earnings alone; for them a sufficient income support system is necessary to combat poverty. Even minimal welfare reform/workfare proposals like <u>SWRA</u> would have helped both of these groups in general, and Southern and rural poor in particular (Chernik and Holmer, 1979) had they passed.

WHERE DO WE GO FROM HERE

The level and trend of poverty in America should be one of our most important social indicators. However in recent years official Census Bureau poverty estimates have not been very useful. Primarily because they do not record the impact of in-kind transfers these figures overestimate the level of poverty. But recent efforts to "adjust" for this omission have exaggerated the amount by which in-kind transfers have reduced poverty, leading many to falsely assume that we no longer have a poverty problem. The solution is to make legislators aware of the true nature and extent of poverty, and the way to do so is to create an official government measure of poverty which does take account of in-kind transfers, in an equitable fashion, and which is annually tabulated and updated. Applied poverty research has laid the groundwork for such a measure. Now the government must put aside its inertia and use this research product to create the necessary indicators for assessing both our progress toward eliminating income poverty, and for designing strategies to address the problems which still remain. For instance, the poverty estimates shown above indicate that even a limited welfare reform/workfare program such as that proposed by the Carter Administration would have been extremely beneficial to those who remain in poverty, had it been passed. Perhaps an even more important need for an accurate and timely poverty estimate lies before us. If President Reagan is successful in his efforts to emaciate the current welfare system, as seems highly likely at this point, policymakers need to be informed of the <u>increasing</u> number of poor in the 1980s which, I believe, these policies will foster.

NOTES

1. See also Morton Paglin (1979a, 1979b); Michael Boskin (1981); Edgar Browning (1975); and the <u>Wall Street Journal</u> (1981).
2. The Reagan Administration has never bothered to define truly needy. Under questioning, Karna Small (1981), Deputy White House Press Secretary, ventured that it was even possible that a family with income beneath the official poverty line might not be "truly needy", thus implying that need and poverty status are not necessarily synonymous.

3. Copies of Anderson's book were distributed to Congressmen by those critical of the Carter program while it was still under consideration. While various people have offered differing explanations of why PBJI was defeated (e.g., Califano, 1981), many attribute at least some credit to the Anderson book.
4. Indeed indirect income tax subsidization of a particular type of expenditure whether by exclusion from tax, by deduction from the tax base, or by tax credit, is generally no different than a direct subsidy of the same amount for the same expenditure. In fact, a truly thorough analysis of government subsidization would include such items as "energy" tax credits and deduction for state and local sales tax which are in-kind transfers (i.e., indirect consumption subsidies) for which there is no direct subsidy equivalent. That is, if there were a program which provided the poor with an identification card to exempt them from state sales taxation, a direct subsidy equivalent to the indirect income tax subsidy for retail sales taxes would exist.
5. In a recent paper Fendler and Orshansky (1979) update the official poverty line using the same methodology on which it was originally based, but later years data. That is, they take the U.S. Department of Agriculture (USDA) Thrifty Food Budget (instead of the Economy Food Plan on which poverty is currently based) and divide it by the reciprocal of the food expenditure to after-tax money income ratio from the 1965 USDA Household Survey (which was .29 as compared to the 1955 ratio of .33). On this updated basis, the number of persons in poverty increased by 50 percent (as compared to the official poverty count). Interestingly the new updated poverty line for a four person family was 44 percent of the median family income for the same size family which, as noted above, is exactly the same fraction of the median income for a four person family as was the current poverty line in 1963. Unfortunately this updated poverty line has not to my knowledge even been discussed, (much less adopted) by policymakers.
6. For instance, anyone who advocates such a change might want or need to reconsider: that the poverty line multiplier is based on after-tax income; that it is a consumption needs standard and maybe consumption (not money income) is the correct comparable measure of well-being; that one can ignore wealth; that the income sharing unit is properly defined; that we should rely on a food based poverty line; etc.
7. The reader might also recognize that rough estimates of the size distribution of "other" nonmoney income items for 1972 (Smeeding, 1979) indicate that if we were to include all forms of nonmoney income in our estimates, the income share of the poor would still increase relative to that of the rich.
8. Besides failure to account for in-kind income, other difficulties with Census income and poverty data include: 1) failure to

adjust Current Population (CPS) income for underreporting; 2) failure to subtract payment of income and payroll taxes; 3) failure to account for income sharing among unrelated persons who are living together; 4) the fact that the Census data on which poverty is based undercounts blacks, Hispanics and other low income persons; 5) that they count among the poor a substantial number of illegal aliens who are ineligible for most types of government transfers and who, some feel, should not be included among the poor; and 6) that about six percent of the poor report at least one type of negative income which usually indicates substantial positive net worth. The extent of the effect of these last three problems on the Census poverty count is not yet well documented. The net effects of the first three: income underreporting, taxes, and income sharing would, on net, reduce the poverty count 15 to 25 percent. Because these issues are of secondary importance to the main aim of this paper, they are not discussed below. However, the data in Table 7.2, as with almost all of the studies reviewed below, do adjust for these three factors. A prolonged discussion of these and other related issues (e.g., the effect of the underground economy on poverty) is not properly within the scope of this paper and is not so important or controversial as in-kind transfers.

9. The original CBO study (1977) presented family poverty data. But Hoagland (1980) later recomputed this same data base to estimate the extent of poverty on a persons basis.

10. For instance the 1977 CBO study reports fiscal year 1976 income, but is based on the March 1975 CPS which contains income data for calendar year 1974. Similarly, the Hoagland (1980) study reports fiscal year 1980 results based on calendar year 1977 income from the March 1978 CPS.

11. In sixteen states receipt of SSI does not automatically confer eligibility for Medicaid.

12. The March 1980 <u>Current Population Survey</u> (U.S. Bureau of the Census, 1981) and the Income Survey Development Panel (MacDonald, 1981) both provide this capability for the 1979 income year. While there are few multiple benefits studies in earlier years to begin with, e.g., U.S. Joint Economic Committee (1973), National Urban League (1980), and Lyon, et al. (1976), none of these covered the entire U.S. population. The Joint Economic Committee study covered only six "low income areas" in 1971, while the Urban League study covered only blacks in 1978, and the Lyon et al. study covered only New York City.

13. Sensitivity tests could be designed to assess how different patterns of multiple recipiency affect chosen measures (e.g., the poverty rate or the poverty gap), but I am not aware of any such efforts. Smeeding (1981) suggests several causes of bias which may produce large differences between macrosimulation

models for in-kind benefit recipiency and the CPS recipiency data for 1979.

14. It might be mentioned that the 1977 CBO study allocated medical care transfer benefits according to amount of medical service consumed. Such a benefit allocation implies that the sicker you are the better off you are due to additional medical benefits paid for by these programs. In the absence of data on health status which might provide a means by which one could measure the value of medical services consumed, a more legitimate methodology would treat these programs as insurance policies provided to cover families regardless of their actual usage of medical care services; the benefit concept used in Hoagland (1980) and Smeeding (1975). However because of lack of data on actual usage of medical care services used by recipients, the CBO simulation gave each type of recipient: aged, blind or disabled, adults, and children the average expenditure per recipient in their state. Because the insurance value is equal to average expenditures (plus overhead) per coveree for each type of beneficiary in each state, the actual measure of benefits used in the CBO study is much less damaging than its methodological basis might indicate.

15. The $1,011 is gross of the $101.40 premium which the elderly pay for Medicare Part B Supplemental Medical Insurance.

16. In fact, because one must be nearly totally without income or financial resources (savings) before Medicaid pays for nursing home services, and because other income transfers are automatically reduced to nursing home residents (e.g., SSI benefits drop from between $275 and $500 per month to $25 per month), the policies may be worth little to such individuals.

17. These figures are derived from the 1960-61 U.S. Bureau of Labor Statistics, Consumers Expenditure Survey by considering the budget share spent on medical care and medical insurance by elderly families with incomes equal to the poverty line income for this type of family in 1960-61. These budget shares for medical care: 11.0 percent for single elderly and 11.4 percent for elderly couples, were then used to determine the amount which is budgeted for medical care. We chose 1960-61 instead of a similar 1972-73 data, because it was the closest data of its type to 1963 -- the year for which the poverty line was constructed, and because neither Medicare nor Medicaid were in existence in 1960-61. Thus the program whose benefits we seek to evaluate have not already biased the data which is being used to evaluate them.

18. Unrelated individuals are counted as single person families.

19. Paglin's multiple benefit recipiency allocation formulae are based on the 1973 U.S. Joint Economic Committee study of benefits in six low income areas. This study warned that "this paper is based on low income areas only ... Thus the sample proportions receiving public welfare benefits exceed the

comparable national figures." (p. 2) The study (p. 29) reveals that anywhere from 33 to 71 percent of sample households received any benefit at any sample site. Altogether of the 2,100 low income area households surveyed, only 1,006 or 47.9 percent received at least one in-kind benefit in 1971. One of these study conclusions bears repeating here (p. 3): "Nonetheless all of these benfits have not eliminated poverty, for even among the households receiving five or more benefits, there were those at every site with total incomes (including in-kind benefits at market value) below the poverty standard."

20. For instance, Paglin uses a 1973 Council of Economic Advisor's (Economic Report of the President, 1974:176) estimate that 70 percent of Medicaid recipients were poor. On this basis Paglin allocates 70 percent of all Medicaid benefits to the poor. Using Paglin's own definition of pretransfer poor, my 1974 estimates find that 52 percent of Medicaid recipients were poor and that they received 47 percent of all Medicaid benefits.

21. The "cash equivalent" value is the amount of cash income which would make an in-kind transfer beneficiary just as well off as the in-kind benefit which they actually receive. In other words, it measures the amount of money income for which a family would trade their in-kind benefits. See Smeeding and Moon (1980) for a more complete treatment of this concept.

22. These adjustments were made using computer tabulations of the distributions of various types of income in-kind by recipient type and income level. The CBO and Hoagland (1980) data was provided by G. William Hoagland. Ratios of cash equivalent value to recipient value for these same programs and recipients at various income levels from my own data for 1968-1974 were also used. The aging bias in the CBO and Hoagland data was adjusted for by increasing their pre-transfer poverty rates by 1.0 percent to make them consistent with other estimates of pretransfer poverty based on unaged data.

23. While factor market income might have changed somewhat if there were no government transfers, it would not have changed nearly enough to offset the flat roughly 20 percent figure in this table. For more on this topic, see Danziger, Haveman, and Plotnick (1981), and Lampman and Smeeding (1981).

24. Several complicated demographic and social trends underly this net figure. No doubt the increase in aged and single parent families over this period would have increased market income based poverty if they alone had occurred. On the other hand, increased earnings for black male headed families and low income Southern families, if taken alone, would have reduced this rate below 20 percent. However, these two opposing forces have roughly netted out. See Danziger and Plotnick (1977) for more on demographic change and poverty.

25. At the same time that these chiselers are supposed to return to work Reagan plans to phase out most public service

employment (PSE) slots and much of the CETA program along with it.

26. The latest year for which Food Stamp participation rates are available is 1978. However, there is some evidence that since the Food Stamp purchase requirement was removed on January 1, 1979, the <u>number</u> of participants in the South and in rural areas has increased dramatically. If the participation <u>rates</u> have increased as well, as seems likely, the Food Stamps participation rates in Table 7.3 may now be close to the national average. If so, the point of the effectiveness of national vs state controlled income support systems would be even more forcefully made.

27. At this writing Congress had modified the Reagan proposal to give states the option of enforcing this provision.

28. One additional factor may affect the work behavior of the poor. Many of the aged, disabled, and single parent poor participate in two or more in-kind transfer programs. In 1979, 45 percent of all poor households received at least two of the major types of in-kind transfer benefits mentioned above; 22 percent benefited from three or more such programs. Moreover, nearly 80 percent of the poor households who received cash public assistance also received two or more types of in-kind benefits (U.S. Bureau of Census, 1981: 21). Regardless of the jobs skills or job opportunities of these beneficiaries, multiple cash and/or in-kind transfer receipt may create severe work disincentives because of the cumulative "tax rate" problem which they present. That is, for all of these in-kind programs except for Medicare, and for all types of cash public assistance (e.g., AFDC and SSI), benefits fall or eligibility may be threatened altogether (e.g., Medicaid) as earnings increase. An additional dollar earned may produce a total 40-70 cent reduction in benefits once all programs have adjusted their benefits to account for this earnings increase. In general, the greater the number of programs that one participates in, the less the net income gain from increased work effort. Thus the transfer system itself discourages work effort. However, the extent to which these programs discourage work effort -- particularly among the aged, disabled, and single parent households is not known at this time (Danziger, Haveman, Plotnick, 1981).

REFERENCES

Anderson, M. (1978) <u>Welfare</u>. (Palo Alto: Hoover Institution Press).

Boskin, M. (1981) "Prisoners of Bad Statistics" <u>Newsweek</u>. January 26:15.

Browning, E. (1975) <u>Resdistribution and the Welfare State</u>. Washington, D.C.: American Enterprise Institute.

Califano, J. (1981) <u>Governing America</u>. (New York: Simon and Schuster).

Chernick, H. and M. Holmer (1979) "The Urban and Regional Impacts of the Carter Administration's 1979 Welfare Reform Proposal". Mimeo. June.

Congressional Budget Office (1977) <u>Poverty Status of Families Under Alternative Definitions of Income</u>. Background paper #17 (Revised). Washington: U.S. Government Printing Office.

Danziger, S. and R. Plotnick (1977) "Demographic Change, Government Transfers, and Income Distribution", <u>Monthly Labor Review</u>. April.

Danziger, S. and R. Haveman (1981) "The Reagan Budget Cuts: Implications and Alternatives", <u>Challenge</u>. May/June.

Danziger, S., R. Haveman and R. Plotnick (1981) "How Income Transfer Programs Affect Work, Savings, and the Income Distribution: A Critical Review," <u>Journal of Economic Literature</u>, September.

Davidson, S. (1979) "The Status of Aid to the Medically Needy", <u>Social Service Review</u>, March.

Davis, K. and Schoen, C. (1978) <u>Health Care and the War on Poverty</u>. Washington: Brookings Institution.

<u>Economic Report of the President</u> (1974) Washington, D.C.: U.S. Government Printing Office.

<u>Employee Benefits: 1979</u> (1981) Washington: U.S. Chamber of Commerce.

Fendler, C. and M. Orshansky (1979) "Improving the Poverty Definition". Proceedings of the American Statistical Association. December.

Girshick, L. and J. Williamson (1983) "The Measurement of Poverty: The Case of the Elderly" (this volume).

Harrington, M. (1977) "Hiding the Other America", <u>New Republic</u>. February.

Hoagland, G.W. (1980) "The Effectiveness of Current Transfer Programs in Reducing Poverty", presented at Middleburg College Conference on Economic Issues.

Lampman, R. and T. Smeeding (1981) "Interfamily Transfers as an Alternative to Government Transfers to Persons". April. Mimeo.

Lyon, D.W. et al. (1976) <u>Multiple Welfare Benefits in New York City</u>. Rand Corporation Study #R-2002, August.

MacDonald, M. (1981) "Multiple Benefits of Food Stamp Participants and Nonparticipants: Recipiency Patterns, Income Adequacy, and Work Disincentives". University of Wisconsin. May. Mimeo.

National Rural Center (1978) <u>The Rural Stake in Public Assistance</u>, Vol. 10. Washington, D.C. National Rural Center.

National Urban League (1980) <u>The Myth of Income Cushions for Blacks</u>. Washington, D.C.: National Urban League.

Paglin, M. (1979a) "Poverty in the United States: A Reevaluation", Policy Review. Spring.
Paglin, M. (1979b) Poverty and Transfers In-Kind. Palo Alto: Hoover Institute Press.
Rodgers, H. (1978) "Hiding vs Ending Poverty", Politics and Society. Vol. 8.
_____. (1983) "Limiting Poverty by Design: The Official Measure of Poverty" (this volume).
Plotnick, R. and T. Smeeding (1979) "Poverty and Income Transfers: Past Trends and Future Prospects", Public Policy. Vol. 27, No. 3. Summer.
Schiller, B. (1981) "Welfare: Reforming Our Expectations", Public Interest. Winter.
Small, K. (1981) Washington Post. March 9.
Smeeding, T.M. (1975) "Measuring the Economic Welfare of Low Income Households and the Anti Poverty Effectiveness of Cash and Noncash Transfer Programs". Ph.D. dissertation. University of Wisconsin-Madison, August.
Smeeding, T.M. (1977) "The Antipoverty Effect of In-Kind Transfers", Journal of Human Resources. Summer.
_____. (1979) "On the Distribution of Net Income", Southern Economic Journal. January.
_____. (1981) "Estimating In-Kind Income Using the CPS: Survey vs Pure Microsimulation Approaches". Mimeo. June.
_____ and Moon (1980) "Valuing Government Expenditures: The Case of Medical Care Transfers and Poverty", Review of Income and Wealth, September.
Social Security Bulletin (January, 1981).
Survey of Current Business (June, 1979).
U.S. Budget FY 1982 (1981) Washington: U.S. Government Printing Office.
U.S. Bureau of the Census (1981) Characteristics of Households and Persons Receiving Noncash Benefits. Current Population Reports, Series P-32, No. 110, March.
U.S. Department of Agriculture (1979) Annual Food Stamp Program Evaluation, Fiscal Year 1978, prepared for U.S. House of Representatives Committee on Agriculture, Nutrition, and Forestry, September.
U.S. Department of Health, Education, and Welfare (1979) The Measure of Poverty. Washington: U.S. Government Printing Office.
Aid to Families With Dependent Children Statement for Basic Needs, July 1975 (1976) Social and Rehabilitation Service. NCSS Report D-2. Washington: U.S. Government Printing Office.
U.S. Department of Health, Education, and Welfare (1978) Medicaid Statistics FY 1976. Health Care Financing Administration. Washington: U.S. Government Printing Office.
U.S. Joint Economic Committee (1973) "How Public Welfare Benefits are Distributed in Low Income Areas". Studies in Public

Welfare, Paper #6. Washington: U.S. Government Printing Office. March 26.

U.S. Senate (1980) "Departments of State, Justice, and Commerce, The Judiciary, and Related Agencies Appropriation Bill, 1981", No. 96-949. 96th Congress, 2nd session. September 16: 33-34.

Wall Street Journal (1981) "Budget Flinch?" February, 13.

A POVERTY OF GOVERNMENT SERVICES: ESTIMATES 1962, 1972, 1977

Thomas F. Stinson*
Ronald B. Larson

In 1964 the United States formally declared war on poverty. A national consensus emerged which held that individuals lacking access to a minimum set of goods and services were disadvantaged, and that it was appropriate for federal, state, and local governments to pursue programs designed to increase opportunity for the disadvantaged. Translating that general objective into effective public policy, however, has not been easy.

One stumbling block to effective anti-poverty policy has been the way poverty has been defined. The current income measure used has focused attention on a narrow definition of poverty. Other elements which may be equally important in improving economic opportunity for the disadvantaged are ignored.

One neglected dimension of the poverty problem is examined in this paper.[1] Specifically, our concern is that a definition of poverty based solely on the income needed to purchase a minimum market basket of privately produced goods and services implicitly assumes that there is no need to insure access to minimal levels of the goods and services -- such as education -- produced by local government. Since providing access to an adequate level of public goods may be an effective and cost-efficient way of achieving long-run reductions in the poverty population, omitting public goods from consideration may limit the success of anti-poverty programs.

Communities with large percentages of their population below the income poverty line might be expected to be those offering low levels of government services, but such need not be the case. State and federal aids to localities are a significant portion of local government revenues. Those aids may be distributed to insure that all local governments offer services at a minimum adequate level. Estimates of the extent of government services poverty then can

---

* Views expressed are those of the authors and not necessarily those of the U.S. Department of Agriculture.

provide a crude measure of the success of compensatory aid programs of state and federal governments in redirecting revenues to local governments in low-income communities.

This issue has a special relevance at present. If access to a minimum adequate level of local government goods and services is considered to be part of a minimum endowment guaranteed all citizens, proposed reductions in federal aid to State and local government may substantially weaken the safety net under the most vulnerable in society. Consolidating programs which funnel resources to those local governments serving a high percentage of low income residents into a limited number of block grants may have similar effects. The long-term impact of a period of inadequate funding for schools and other public services -- of increasing the number who do not have access to adequate levels of government services -- may well be an increase in the number of poor.

This paper traces the nation's progress against government services poverty. Per capita local government expenditures in county areas are used in the comparisons. Changes in access to minimal levels of local government services are noted by comparing the number of counties and the population below a local government services poverty line in 1972 and 1977, with those below in 1962. One set of rather surprising results emerge. Under one definition, local government services poverty is found to be virtually eliminated by 1977. The paper concludes with a discussion of the forces which may have produced the changes, and of the likely effects of federal budget cutbacks.

DRAWING A POVERTY LINE FOR LOCAL GOVERNMENT SERVICES[2]

Several methods exist for calculating a poverty line for government services. One could, for example, specify in physical terms the inputs needed to produce a minimally adequate level of services, then cost each out at market prices in the years desired for comparison. A major problem with this approach, illustrated by the continuing debate over what constitutes quality education, is that experts often disagree over what constitutes an adequate service level. Further, the cost and content of such a package will vary across the nation, making national comparisons difficult. Consequently, this method -- similar in approach to the way the income poverty line was developed -- was rejected.

A second approach, more closely related to the relative poverty lines described in Rodgers' and Smeedings' essays in this volume, is also possible. Government services in a locality might be defined to be inadequate when per capita expenditures are in the lowest quartile or decile of expenditures nationally. Here though, no progress is possible -- the lowest decile will always contain 10 percent of the counties. An alternative is to select an arbitrary percentage below the mean level of expenditure. With this approach progress is possible, although the researcher's initial assumptions about the approximate size of the population below the standard can influence the level chosen as a poverty line.

This paper uses a third method based on the revealed preference approach to explaining consumer behavior.[3] It depends on the assumption that consumers can assess the adequacy of the local government services they receive, given their budget constraints, and that through the political process the level of services available can be controlled. Under these assumptions local governments will provide services at the level desired by their residents and the preferences of the community for public services can be assumed to be revealed by the amount spent by the locality. In effect, it is assumed that, in the absence of reasons to suspect otherwise, public sector spending in a community is an accurate reflection of the demand for public services by that community's residents.

With this framework, a minimum adequate standard for local government services can easily be identified. All that is required is the selection of a set of localities where no apparent barriers -- such as rapid population growth -- prevent the effective realization of citizen preferences for government services, and where there are no reasons -- such as size economies -- to expect expenditures to be unusually high or low. The range of expenditures which remains reflects a distribution of adequate levels of local government services. A minimum standard can then be set by identifying a lower bound for that expenditure distribution.

To improve the interstate comparability of the data only the sum of expenditures by all types of local governments within a county area was considered. Separate estimates for cities, counties, and school districts were not attempted, although a separate standard for education expenditure was computed. Expenditures where state and private sector responsibilities differ greatly -- welfare, highways, and health and hospitals -- were excluded as were all capital expenditures. A lower bound of the mean expenditure less one standard deviation was chosen as an estimate of the poverty line.

Alternative poverty lines for local government services were calculated using eight samples of counties, each chosen so that there would be no reason to suspect that local public service levels would be below a minimum adequate level. Although a case could be made for choosing the results from any one of the samples as the poverty line, the lowest was chosen as the measure to be used in this study. Such a choice, it was felt, would be less susceptible to the charge of overstating the percentage of the population living in counties where local government spending is inadequate. Estimates of the poverty line were not greatly different, however. Six of the eight local expenditure lines were within a range of $8, and six of the eight education expenditure lines were within $10.

Results: 1962

Estimates of the extent of government services poverty in 1962 were produced by comparing actual per capita local expenditures with the poverty line described above. Data on current local government expenditures (less those on welfare, highways, and health and hospitals but including education), and on current local education expenditures by county area, taken from the 1962 Census of Governments were used.

Slightly more than ten percent of the nation's counties -- 334 counties in 16 states -- were below the poverty line for local government expenditures. Two hundred counties in 19 states were below the education expenditure standard. Counties with expenditures below the local government services poverty line had 1960 populations totaling 7.7 million; those below the education line, 7.0 million. One hundred sixty-four counties with populations of 4.4 million were below both standards. Approximately four percent of the nation's population in 1962 lived in counties where spending for either local government services or public education appeared inadequate. More than two percent lived in counties where spending for both education and all local services were below the standards.

Local government expenditures in 1962 were below the poverty line in 30 percent or more of the counties in Alabama, Arkansas, Kentucky, Mississippi, South Carolina, Tennessee and Virginia. But, only three states -- Arkansas, Mississippi and Tennessee -- had 30 percent or more of their counties below the education expenditure line. Counties falling below either poverty line were concentrated almost entirely in the South.

Counties below the government services poverty line were, as might be expected, those with relatively low incomes. Nearly 60 percent were in the bottom two deciles (the poorest 20 percent) when counties were ranked on the percent of families with incomes less then $3000 in 1960. More than 75 percent were in the bottom three deciles. Nearly 70 percent of the counties below the education line were in the bottom three deciles.

Counties below the government services poverty lines also had a larger than average percentage of nonwhite residents. More than 50 percent of the counties below the local government standard were in the first three deciles in 1970 percent nonwhite, and more than 55 percent of those below the education line were in those same three deciles. More than 78 percent of the counties falling below the local government standard and 67 percent of those below the education spending line were in the lowest three deciles when counties were ranked on the basis of the percent of the 1970 population, age 25 or greater, who were high school graduates.

Other demographic characteristics seemed to have little effect. Rankings on the basis of population, population density, and percent urban failed to identify particular sets of counties where there was a higher than average likelihood of low spending for local services or

Table 8.1. Progress Against Poverty of Government Services: 1962, 1972, 1977

	Persons Below	Counties Below	States with at least one County Below
Absolute Standard			
Current local government expenditure			
1962	7,657,828	334	16
1972	397,855	24	9
1977	212,995	10	7
Current educational expenditure			
1962	6,999,705	200	19
1972	203,804	16	11
1977	249,390	14	11
Both local government and educational expenditure			
1962	4,433,622	164	14
1972	200,273	14	9
1977	212,995	10	7
Dynamic Standard			
Current local government expenditure			
1962	7,657,828	334	16
1972	5,793,502	288	21
1977	3,186,329	184	20
Current educational expenditure			
1962	6,999,705	200	20
1972	10,290,618	373	29
1977	13,112,904	396	28
Both local government and educational expenditure			
1962	4,433,622	164	14
1972	4,956,106	239	20
1977	2,847,104	161	20

education. However, noticeably fewer counties in the first and tenth deciles on each of these three measures were below the government services poverty line.

The use of average per capita expenditure by county area as a measure of local government service adequacy is not fully satisfactory. Problems with using any expenditure measure as a proxy for quality of services are well-known and will not be dealt with here (Stinson, 1981). For our purposes a more distressing problem is that significant intra-county differentials in service levels are hidden. Counties falling below a government services poverty line may have localities in which services are more than adequate, while counties above that line may have areas where services are substandard.

These problems with determining the number of people receiving less than a minimum adequate level of government services leave one hesitant to emphasize the absolute size of estimates of that population. But, such estimates, with all their problems, are useful standards for measuring the nation's progress in improving the level of local government services available. The next two sections discuss changes in that population between 1962 and 1977 under two alternative sets of assumptions.

Progress to 1972 and 1977: Absolute Standard

One way the 1962 government services poverty lines could be updated is to adjust only for price increases. This assumes that the minimum service level set in 1962 remained relevant through 1977. An absolute standard, it allows for no changes in tastes over time nor for the possibility of technological change allowing the accomplishment of the same tasks at lower cost. It simply measures the cost of producing the same market basket of public goods and services using the same sets of inputs and technology. To create new absolute standards, the 1962 poverty lines were inflated to reflect 1972 and 1977 price levels using appropriate implicit GNP deflators for state and local governments from the Survey of Current Business.

When the absolute standards were applied to 1972 and 1977 Census of Government reports of expenditures by county area, the changes were dramatic. Only 24 counties (398,000 people) were below the local government poverty line in 1972, and 10 counties (213,000 people) below in 1977 (Table 8.1). For education the results were similar -- 16 counties (204,000 people) below in 1972 and 11 counties (249,000 people) in 1977.

Closer examination of the 10 counties below one or both of the poverty lines for government services in 1977 revealed that in almost every instance the low per capita expenditures reported by Census could be attributed to either unusual institutional circumstances -- such as Indian reservations or military bases -- or problems of allocating local government expenditures for cities and school districts which cross county lines. If one accepts the absolute standard based on the 1962 data, it appears that by 1977 virtually everyone in the United States lived in a county where expenditures exceeded the level thought minimally adequate in 1962, adjusted for inflation. Either consciously (through increased federal and state aid to local government) or accidentally, access to a minimum level of public services has been improved dramatically.

Results 1972 and 1977: Dynamic Standard

Those critical of the use of an absolute poverty line argue that a fixed standard produces misleading and meaningless comparisons when used over a long period of time. While such a measure identifies the extent to which access to a particular set of goods and services had changed, it says nothing about whether that market basket of goods and services is still the appropriate one to consider.

Changes in technology, tastes, and real income are all important reasons why an absolute measure adjusted for price changes may not produce an accurate estimate of changes in public services poverty. One way to create a dynamic measure which continually adjusts for current tastes, technology, income and prices is to re-estimate the poverty lines for government services using the same technique as in 1962, but using 1972 and 1977 data.

Re-estimation appears particularly important since major changes have occurred in all of the elements which might affect perceptions of a minimum adequate level of government services. Improvements in technology, particularly in the data processing, electronics, and communications areas, are probably most noticeable to the casual observer of local government. These changes, however, have probably had only a modest effect on perceptions of a minimum adequate level of local government services. Changes in tastes and increased real incomes were likely to have had more significant impacts.

The period 1962-1977 spans the initiation of the Great Society programs with their increased emphasis on government's responsibility to solve the nation's social ills. The environmental movement with its emphasis on protecting the local environment, and the consumer movement where all levels of government were urged to take a more active role in protecting consumers also emerged during that period. All these activities reflected a popular demand for government to assume a more active role than it had in the past. Given the expanded role expected of government, the level of services thought adequate in 1962 was not likely to be considered sufficient in 1977. While the assumption of constant tastes and preferences is common in economic models, it appears inappropriate here.

Increased real incomes also contribute to a changing perception of the minimum adequate service level. As incomes increase consumers demand more of all goods, including publicly provided

A Poverty of Government Services

goods. While there is only limited information about how much desired consumption of local government services increases given additional income, all studies indicate that amounts consumed increase. For an absolute standard to be correct, other things equal, increases in income must have no effect on the public's perception of a minimum adequate standard of local government services.

Results obtained using a dynamic measure were quite different from those obtained using the absolute standard (see Table 8.1). There was still a sizeable reduction in the number of counties below the poverty line for local government services, however. The number of counties below that line dropped from 334 in 1962 to 288 in 1972 and 184 in 1977, a decrease of 45 percent. The number of people living in counties where spending was low decreased by nearly 60 percent, from 7.7 million in 1962 to 3.2 million in 1977.

Local government expenditures were below the poverty line in 30 percent or more of the counties in only two states in 1977 -- Arkansas and Kentucky. Three other states had between 10 and 20 percent of their counties below that line. Compared to 1962, when seven states had more than 30 percent of their counties below the line, this shows considerable progress. Success under this measure does not, however, approach that shown under the absolute standard discussed earlier.

Results for local education expenditures are much less encouraging. The number of counties below that poverty line increased from 200 in 1962 to 373 in 1972 and 396 in 1977. Populations in those counties went from 7.0 million in 1962 to 10.3 million in 1972 and 13.1 million in 1977. Between 1962 and 1977 the number of counties spending less than the poverty level increased by nearly 90 percent, the number of people living in those counties by 85 percent.

Six states had more than 30 percent of their counties below the education poverty line in 1977 -- Alabama, Arkansas, Kentucky, Mississippi, South Carolina and Tennessee. Two of those states -- Alabama and Tennessee -- had more than 60 percent of their counties below the line. In 1962 only three states had 30 percent of their counties below the line and none had 60 percent or more. Although the counties below the poverty lines for local government services were still heavily concentrated in the South, nearly ten percent of those below the education standard came from midwestern and western states.

Mitigating circumstances may exist in some counties. Increased use of private schools and radical shifts in the ratio of school age children to the total population could produce an artificially low level of per capita spending which does not accurately reflect the true quality of the local schools. However, there appears to be little doubt that access to a minimally adequate public elementary and secondary education system has not improved, and has probably worsened.[4]

Counties below the 1977 poverty line for local government services continued to be low income counties, although not quite in the same proportion as in 1962. Only 45 percent of those below the line for all services were in the top two deciles of counties in percent of families below the 1969 poverty line. More than 60 percent of the 1962 counties below had been in the top two deciles of counties in percent of families below the 1960 poverty line. Another major change was in the proportion of counties with large percentages of nonwhite residents below the line. In 1962 more than 50 percent of those below the government services line were in the first three deciles in 1970 percent nonwhite. In 1977 those same deciles contained only 37 percent of the counties below the line.

The characteristics of counties below the education line also changed. Here, however, the change was due to the counties entering the group rather than those escaping. The percent in the top three deciles when counties were ranked by percent of families below the income poverty line declined from nearly 70 percent in 1962 to 54 percent in 1977. Similarly the percent of counties below the education line and in the top three deciles in percent nonwhite decreased from 55 percent to 47 percent.

SOURCES OF CHANGE -- IMPLICATIONS FOR THE FUTURE

Perceptions of the nation's progress toward insuring everyone access to a minimum adequate market basket of publicly provided goods and services depends on which measures of local service adequacy are chosen. But, whether the absolute or the dynamic standard is accepted, the number of counties in which local government expenditures were substandard dropped significantly between 1962 and 1977.

The results are less clear when spending for public elementary and secondary education is considered. If an absolute standard is used virtually all counties in the U.S. are above the poverty line, while if a dynamic standard is used the number below nearly doubles from 1962 to 1977. This wide divergence may accurately reflect the effect of changing tastes and incomes in the demand for public education, and the difficulty that less prosperous counties have in keeping up with the new standard. Or, this change may be largely artificial, caused by measurement problems associated with the increased use of private schools in some counties. Any final judgement on progress in this area will require careful examination of the characteristics of those counties below the line.

Similar studies of counties moving from below to above either standard will be required to identify the reasons for the improvements which occurred. In general, those counties which moved from one side of the line to the other appear to be a rich data set for testing some hypotheses about local fiscal behavior. Studies relating changes in local government expenditures to the whole range of socio-economic characteristics contained in social accounting frameworks would also appear to be of considerable interest.

Preliminary examination of these counties has led to some initial hypotheses. The most important is the strong presumption that increased federal and state aids made a major contribution toward reducing the number of counties below the local government expenditure standard, and that these aids may have kept the number below the education standard from becoming even greater. Between 1962 and 1977 intergovernmental aid rose from 30 percent to 48 percent of local government revenue. This increase was due primarily to an expansion of a wide array of federal and state programs providing aid to local governments, not to federal revenue sharing which accounted for less than two percent of local revenues in 1977.

Programs targeting funds directly to localities with a large concentration of the poor may have been particularly important in reducing the incidence of government services poverty. Two pieces of evidence lend support to that position. First, when counties are ranked on the percentage of families with incomes below the poverty line, the number in the tenth decile (the poorest ten percent) who were also below the minimum standard for all local government services shrunk from 124 to 42, a decrease of 66 percent. For education alone, the decrease was from 69 to 51, or 26 percent. Using an alternative definition of low income counties -- the U.S. Department of Agriculture's list of Persistent Low Income (PLI) counties (Davis, 1979) -- 104 of the 225 PLI counties were found to be below the 1962 local government standard, but only 61 in 1977. The number of PLI counties below the education line increased by 45 percent during that same period, however. For all counties (not just those with large concentrations of the poor) there was a 45 percent decrease in the number below the local expenditure standard and a 98 percent increase in those below the education poverty line.

Another finding of some interest is that the number of counties below the government services poverty lines which are in the first decile of counties in 1970 percent nonwhite dropped dramatically between 1962 and 1977. The number below the local government standard fell from 65 to 13, those below the education standard, from 81 to 54. These results may provide an indication of the impact of some of the 1960's civil rights activity, including that dealing with voting rights, on access to local government services.

The apparent ties between increases in federal aid and reductions in the extent of poverty of government services raises important questions about the impact of current proposals to restrict future federal spending. If compensatory programs -- such as the Elementary and Secondary Education Act (ESEA) -- have been successful in increasing expenditures in low income areas, cuts in these programs probably will plunge more counties below the poverty line, and further limit access to public services in those counties already below. The result will be a widening of the gap between the poor and the rest of the nation in access to public services.[5]

A Poverty of Government Services

Econometric studies have attempted to identify the effect of increased federal and state aids on local government spending (Inman, 1979, Gramlich, 1969). They indicate that local government expenditures typically do not increase by the full amount of aid received. Instead, a portion of the aid substitutes for local taxes. Feldstein (1977) found that funds distributed under Title I of ESEA increased local expenditures by as much as 72 cents for each dollar of aid distributed. The same study estimated that unrestricted and unmatched state foundation aid for education added only about 13 cents to spending for each dollar of aid. These findings suggest that local expenditures will not decrease dollar for dollar with cuts in federal aid, since local governments are likely to increase property taxes, where constitutionally possible.

But, proposed cuts in federal aid still will almost certainly increase the number of counties below a government services poverty line. Counties where service levels are currently only slightly above the minimum adequate standard may fall below even if local taxes are increased to replace 80 or 90 percent of lost federal aids. Other communities receiving significant amounts of compensatory aid will simply lack the financial resources necessary to replace those aids. Suggested elimination of targeting provisions and the consolidation of aid programs into a small number of block grants could further worsen the outlook for those living in less prosperous counties by placing poorer counties at a disadvantage compared to counties with more political clout.

A rough indication of the sensitivity of estimates of the extent of government services poverty to changes in local government revenues can be obtained by moving the poverty line higher and comparing the number under the new line with those under the old. An increase in the 1977 local government services line of $50 per capita (slightly less than 20 percent) increases the number of counties below from 184 to 616, and the number of people from 3.2 to 12.8 million. The results for education seem even more sensitive. There an increase of $3 per capita (less than two percent) brought an additional 56 counties with 2.7 million residents under, increases of 15 and 20 percent respectively.

These results offer reason for concern that across the board cuts in federal aid programs may substantially increase the number of counties where less than a minimally adequate level of public sevices is available. Such aid cutbacks may produce further barriers to the disadvantaged as they try to enter the mainstream of society. At the least, reducing access to such publicly provided goods and services as education seriously weakens the social safety net under the most vulnerable in society.

NOTES

1. Others have noted problems with the narrow definition of poverty and attempted to specify a multi-dimensional definition of poverty in some detail. See for example "Social Goals and Indicators for American Society," 1967, especially S.M. Miller et. al, "Poverty, Inequality, and Conflict."
2. This section is a shortened version of Stinson (1968).
3. In simplified form the revealed preference approach argues that when rational consumers choose a particular set of goods, that particular mix is revealed to be preferred by those consumers to all other combinations of those same goods which could be purchased for the same amount or less. That this result holds can be seen by noting that at the time of purchase all other combinations of the goods in question which cost the same total amount could have been chosen, but were not. For a summary of revealed preferences and the theory of demand see any graduate economic textbook such as Baumol (1965) or Henderson and Quandt (1971). More detail may be found in Samuelson (1948).
4. Changes in the distribution of expenditures in the group used to define the poverty line could artificially inflate estimates of the number of counties below a government services poverty line (Andrea Lubov, personal communication). This does not appear to have happened in this instance, however, since the percentage increase in the number of counties in the reference groups which were below the line was substantially less than the percentage increase in those below for counties outside the reference group.
5. There are, however, those who argue that federal aid to education has not allowed school districts with a large proportion of the poor to increase their spending relative to wealthier districts. Some even argue that federal aid may have decreased equality. If this is true higher federal aid payments may have helped cause the growth in the number of counties below an education expenditures poverty line. This would suggest that cuts in aid, although reducing education expenditure in all counties, might increase equality. See Berke, 1972, and Carroll, 1979.

REFERENCES

Baumol, W.J. (1965) <u>Economic Theory and Operations Analysis.</u> Prentice Hall, Inc.: Englewood Cliffs, NJ.

Berke, J.S. (1972) <u>Federal Aid to Public Education: Who Benefits.</u> Lexington Books: Lexington, MA.

Carroll, S.J. (1979) <u>The Search for Equity in School Finance: Summary and Conclusions.</u> Rand Corp.: Santa Monica, CA.

Davis, T.F. (1979) Persistent Low Income Counties in Rural America. Rural Development Research Report No. 12, U.S. Department of Agriculture: Washington, D.C.

Feldstein, M.S. (1977) The Effect of a Differential Add-on Grant: Title I and Local Educational Spending, National Institute for Education, Department of Health, Education, and Welfare, ED 157-174.

Gramlich, E.M. (1969) "The Effects of Federal Grants on State-Local Expenditures: A Review of the Econometric Literature," Proceedings National Tax Assoc., pp. 569-593.

Henderson, J.A. and Quandt, R.E. (1971) Miocroeconomic Theory A Mathematical Approach. McGraw Hill: New York, NY.

Inman, R.P. (1979) "The Fiscal Performance of Local Governments: An Interpretative Review" in P.B. Mieskowski and M.L. Strazheim eds., Current Issues in Urban Economics, Johns Hopkins University Press: Baltimore, MD, pp. 270-321.

Samuelson, P.A. (1948) "Consumption Theory in Terms of Revealed Preference" Economica Vol. 15, pp. 243-253.

"Social Goals and Indicators for American Society" (1967) Annals of the American Academy of Political and Social Sciences, Vols. 371 and 373, May, Sept.

Stinson, T.F. (1968) "Drawing a Poverty Line for Government Services: An Initial Attempt." American Journal of Agricultural Economics, Vol. 50, No. 5, December, pp. 1416-1420.

_____ (1981) "The Fiscal Status of Local Governments" in A.T. Hawley and S.M. Maize, eds., Non-Metropolitan America in Transition, University of North Carolina Press: Chapel Hill, pp. 734-781.

U.S. Department of Commerce, Bureau of the Census (1962, 1972, 1977) Census of Governments.

PART III

ALTERNATIVE RESEARCH PERSPECTIVES: RELATING NEEDS TO SOLUTIONS

INTRODUCTION

Richard Goldstein
Stephen M. Sachs

The thirteenth stroke of a clock is not only false of itself, but casts grave doubts on the credibility of the preceding twelve.
Mark Twain

Improvement that you have to take a statistical microscope to discover does not amount to anything.
Henry George

Reviews of poverty research consistently provide results similar to Mark Twain's clock. However, with research, a new result does not automatically mean that one should distrust the earlier results; rather, the situation might have changed so much that the results should change. In fact, if the quality of our research were consistently high, new results could fit with old results to provide us with powerful grounds for powerful theories, telling us what are the important causal conditions. Unfortunately, poverty research is not generally of that high a quality, and therefore, a new and different result means new questions and doubts about both past and current results.

In this section we present articles that question, on varying grounds, the value of previous research results. To provide a context for these articles we briefly present one type of organizing framework for "alternative research perspectives." This framework is composed of eight questions and the different types of answers that can be given to each of these questions.

One, what is it that we want to make conclusions about? For the purpose of examining alternative research perspectives, there are two sub-questions that need to be asked:

a) Does one want a yes/no answer or a broader and deeper answer with respect to the relationship being investigated? That is, is one only interested in whether a relationship exists in a certain form, or is one interested in whether there is any relationship, and if so what the nature and quality of the relationship is? For example, Michael Lipsky (1980:183) says, "research on poverty and administration usually does not take as problematic the effect of administration on the poor, but instead often assumes that the government objective is to ameliorate poverty," and therefore this research often focuses on "the extent to which the objectives of the program are achieved." If the actual, though never made public, objective is to control the poor or to sidetrack either lay or professional criticism of the government, then the researcher who limits the question to this type of a yes/no question may actually be serving the interests of government and opposing the interests of the poor. This view is consistent with the analysis in Kenneth Neubeck's paper in this section. (See also the Introduction to this volume (Part I), and Michelson, 1973:94.) Sometimes a yes/no question is appropriate, but often, especially in a situation of much ignorance, it is not.

b) Is the research designed to (1) identify the problem, (2) propose a solution, or, (3) test possible implementations of a solution? (See Szanton, 1981:72.) These are very different and the techniques used to answer them are also very different. Further, it is not the case that identifying a problem will automatically and uniquely point the way to the solution; the causes of a problem do not have to be integrally related to the solution. Similarly, a solution does not entail any particular implementation of that solution. The vast majority of poverty studies have been part of the "identification of the problem" class. It is very doubtful that most of this has been either necessary or desirable. According to Harold Watts,

> One category of research which might... be dispensed with is any further simple cataloging... of facts about the poor. It is hard to imagine what can be gained from a more minute documentation of the unsatisfactory consequences of trying to meet the needs of four persons with less than $60 a week. (Watts, 1967:267; $60 in 1967 would be about in $163 in 1981 when one adjusts for inflation using the Consumer Price Index.)

Two, what types of data do we need, behavioral, attitudinal, physiological, or relational (among the many possibilities)? Poverty research has tended to place great emphasis on attitudinal data even when another data type was more appropriate. This has especially been the case when behavioral or relational data was necessary to answer the question being asked. (For examples, see Goldstein, 1977.)

Three, concerning what types or levels of units do we need this information? Poverty research has emphasized information about individuals, though some work has been done with naturally appearing groups such as school classes. Little or no work has been concerned with institutions and their effect, even though this effect can dominate individual effects.

Louis Ferleger's article in this section argues that studies of employment, underemployment and unemployment that do not take certain structural factors into account cannot (except accidentally) lead to programs that will help. That is, research that is based on just information about those who have employment problems cannot lead to solutions because there are structural elements to these problems and these structural elements cannot be discovered except through studies of labor market structure. Ferleger deals with the structure of black employment to exemplify his argument. (The Introduction to Part I presents more material on the need for structural analyses in poverty research.)

Four, what type of time factor (cross-sectional or longitudinal) do we require information about? A longitudinal data base can cover anything from a few years to decades or even centuries. Among other assertions, the lack of any long-term longitudinal data makes the assessment of the argument that the poverty of the 1960's and 1970's is "new" very difficult to evaluate, although there is some evidence that this argument is wrong (Patterson, 1981:12-13). On another level of concern, cross-sectional studies contain the (usually implicit) assumption that the current situation is in equilibirum (if this assumption were denied, then the statistical analyses usually used would be faulty). This assumption is rarely if ever true, which may go a long way to explaining why many of our best efforts to explain and to eradicate poverty have failed abysmally.

Five, what forms of data collection are appropriate for the types of data needed? This question in large part refers to the old question of "qualitative" vs. "quantitative". That is, are we sure that we know the domain within which the answers to our research questions exist? If we are sure, then quantitative (or "closed") forms of data collection are appropriate. If we are not sure, then qualitative (or "open") forms of data collection are not only appropriate, they are necessary. In his paper, Ray Rist argues that the lack of qualitatively gathered data has resulted in an inability to learn from either previous research or from previous programs. He provides an example based on his study of a youth employment program that could not be adequately studied through non-qualitative means, and argues that this form of research is necessary if we are to discover *why* programs do or do not work, and if we are to base future programs on actual knowledge rather than on guesses. (Also, see Lee Fremont-Smith's paper in Part IV.) Arnold Vedlitz and Jon Alston develop further the issue of how to pursue qualitative analysis in their paper, "Welfare Terminations and Benefit Reductions: What Program Recipients Can Tell Policy Planners." They argue that a program's target population is an invaluable but often untapped source of information for evaluations.

Six, what kinds of alternative hypotheses are plausible, and how are they being eliminated or guarded against? It is unfortunate but true that most poverty research seems to be completely unaware of this problem. It is as though we believe that we have very strong theories and these theories are definitely correct, and therefore, we only want to measure the parameters to better specify the theory. However, we don't even know if behavior is a consequence of poverty or a cause of poverty, or if it can possibly be either depending on the situation. To solve problems such as this, we have to add several types of guards (or controls) to our research, including:

- control groups or control situations;
- subject, researcher, and situational variability;
- strong statistical controls;
- studies of process (including comparisons of the expected or postulated process and the actual process; see Goldstein, 1980).

One consequence of not using these forms of control is that there are few if any generalizable conclusions that we can safely draw from our research.

Seven, what forms of data analysis are appropriate for the types of data collected and in the form in which they were collected? Rather than delving into issues of choice of statistical technique, we limit ourselves here to two small but very important points related to strategies of statistical testing:

a) It has long been recognized that there is a logical asymmetry in statistical testing due to the non-equivalence of the power of a test (the probability of correctly rejecting the null hypothesis) and the level of significance used (where level of significance refers to the probability of incorrectly rejecting the null hypothesis). In practical terms this often amounts to a bias in favor of the null hypothesis. This causes problems given our propensity to choose a null hypothesis of "no difference" or of "no effect". Given the importance of many of these issues, it might be much more desirable to choose a null hypothesis that postulates a difference or an effect. This would amount to changing our research assumption from, "the program is worthless unless proven otherwise" to one of, "efforts meeting recognized and critical needs are worthwhile unless proven otherwise." (Levitan and Taggart, 1977:283; also 275-6.) One could view this as a choice similar to the one made in our criminal justice system that people are innocent until proven guilty. The question is, where is the burden of proof to be placed?

b) There is also a logical problem in many of our statistical tests. If our hypothesis is, "If A then B" (If people behave in a certain way then they are poor in an economic sense, for example), and we find that B is true, this does not tell us that A is true (there could be another cause of B). Even more, were we to look at persons for whom B is true and find that for these people A is also true, the results would not tell us that the relationship hypothesized is true. Making this kind of a jump is a logical fallacy. To test the hypothesis, one would want to look at people who are A and see if all of them are also B, and then try to eliminate other (non-A) causes of B. Testing the conclusion (B) does not test the hypothesis. Thus, for example, the Culture of Poverty literature, which looks only at poor people, cannot be an adequate test of its own hypothesis. (This argument, though with different examples, is presented in Mahoney, 1976:137-140, 147.)

Eight, what guards or awareness of possible statistical problems, such as low power (little ability to reject the null hypothesis when it is false), or multiplicity (an increased chance of false rejection of the null hypothesis due to the large number of statistical tests) is shown? Here again, it is unfortunately true that poverty researchers have shown little awareness of these possible problems. For example, many studies perform many, many statistical tests, virtually guaranteeing that some will be falsely significant (have Type 1 error).

Lack of awareness of the issues opened above leaves a great deal of room for alternative research perspectives. Sometimes, as with the articles by Ferleger and Rist, these alternatives take the form of different choices within the research design (answers to the eight questions discussed above effectively spells out a research design), which means the research will have different results or at least different explanations for the results. In other cases, the alternative perspective takes the form of disagreeing with a conclusion, and re-interpreting the results of the study, something that is possible because the holes in the study design leave room for new interpretations. As pointed out by Aaron (1978:79), this is exemplified by the first Coleman report. (See also the articles in Mosteller and Moynihan, 1972.)

However, another type of alternative research perspective is to build on what is already available. One way in which this can be done is via computer simulation. Two articles in this section present arguments in favor of computer simulations of very different types.

David Betson and David Greenberg discuss microsimulation. This is the simulation of what individuals and families (households) will do in response to changing circumstances, including changing government policies.

John Dixon, Barry Nagorcka and James Cutt discuss macrosimulation. This is the simulation of the macroeconomic consequences of a program. These consequences include changes in employment levels, tax receipts, and GNP.

These two techniques require very different levels of data, but otherwise they are similar in some important ways: they implement certain assumptions about what people will do in response to certain conditions. To the extent that these assumptions are "correct" (or at least lead to the same results as would the correct assumptions), we learn about the likely consequences of certain actions. That is, we learn this *if* an additional assumption is made. This additional assumption *is* that the changes in the conditions will not themselves lead to new forms of response. (See Betson and Greenberg.) To some extent the robustness of the simulation results can be measured by sensitivity analyses. However, the question will always remain of "How can we learn when our assumptions (theories) about people's responses are no longer valid?" This is a problem that continually needs to be re-assessed. Computer simulations have a tremendous power to produce results that are convincing regardless of their validity. Amid the mass of data and the myriad of results, mistakes, including mistaken assumptions, are often difficult to detect. But when the assumptions are appropriate and the data correct, simulations have great power to "test" conjecture.

REFERENCES

Aaron, Henry J. (1978) *Politics and the Professors.* Washington: The Brookings Institution.

Goldstein, Richard (1977) "A General Framework for Data-Gathering." In *A Review of the Abt Associates, Inc., Evaluation of the Special Impact Program.* Cambridge: Center for Community Economic Development.

Goldstein, Richard (1980) "P.S.R.O., Quality of Care, and Research." *Evaluation & The Health Professions* 3:461-472.

Levitan, Sar A. and Taggart, Robert (1976) *The Promise of Greatness.* Cambridge: Harvard University Press.

Lipsky, Michael (1980) "Poverty and Administration: Perspectives on Research." In *Poverty and Public Policy: An Evaluation of Social Science Research,* edited by Vincent T. Covello. Cambridge: Schenkman Publishing Co.

Mahoney, Michael J. (1976) *Scientist as Subject: The Psychological Imperative.* Cambridge: Ballinger Publishing Co.

Michelson, Stephan (1973) "The Further Responsibility of Intellectuals." *Harvard Educational Review* 43:92-105.

Mosteller, Frederick and Moynihan, Daniel P. (eds.) (1972) *On Equality of Educational Opportunity.* New York: Vintage Books.

Patterson, James T. (1981) *America's Struggle Against Poverty 1900-1980.* Cambridge: Harvard University Press.

Szanton, Peter (1981) *Not Well Advised.* New York: Russell Sage Foundation and The Ford Foundation.

Watts, Harold W. (1967) "Response." In *The Use of Social Research in Federal Domestic Programs, Part II -- The Adequacy and Usefulness of Federally Financed Research on Major National Social Programs,* A Staff Study for the Research and Technical Programs Subcommittee of the Committee on Government Operations. Washington: U.S. Government Printing Office.

BEYOND THE QUANTITATIVE CUL-DE-SAC: A QUALITATIVE PERSPECTIVE ON YOUTH EMPLOYMENT PROGRAMS

Ray C. Rist*

INTRODUCTION

The youth employment situation in the United States is a matter of the utmost national concern. With unemployment rates for all youth approximately 20 percent and those of minority youth nearly double that figure, the country is in the midst of seeing literally hundreds of thousands of young people pass into adulthood without ever having been employed. The implications of this schism between the young and the world of work are not encouraging. As has been documented in a growing number of studies, the relation between long-term unemployment and the work experiences of persons while young is clear: Those who are marginal to or completely outside the labor force while they are young tend to be in the same predicament when they are adults (cf. Adams and Mangum, 1978). The process appears to be a cumulative one, and the cycle of unemployment persists.

It should also be stressed that the size of this population is not insignificant. During 1977, for example, 1.6 million young people between the ages of 16 and 19 were unable to find jobs, and their unemployment rate was almost three times that for persons 20 years and older. Stated differently, youth account for approximately one-tenth of the labor force, but almost one-quarter of all unemployed. In his address of January 10, 1980, announcing new initiatives in the area of youth unemployment, former President Carter stated that there were:

> 2 million high school students in lower income school districts alone who are at least two years behind in their basic skills that are taken for granted in today's job market, and I need not tell you that the 2-year measurement is much better than many of these young peoples'

---

* The views expressed here are solely those of the author and no support or endorsement by the U.S. General Accounting Office or the United States Congress is intended or should be inferred.

educational level demonstrated. A large number of high school graduates in the United States of America are still functionally illiterate. They cannot read or write. They cannot add or subtract well enough to hold a simple job.

There is a second large group of disadvantaged young people also, coincidentally, about two million, who are already out of school but having severe problems getting a job, and if they ever get a job, on holding a job.

In sum, there is an "at risk" population in these two categories alone of nearly 4 million youth who are likely candidates for the unemployment rolls.

The response to this situation by the federal government has been through the initiatives contained in the Youth Employment and Demonstration Projects Act (YEDPA) of 1977. Created with a specific focus on the needs of youth, the effort was to signal a quantum leap in the support of youth employment and training projects. The Act has been funded at nearly one billion dollars per year. Indeed, in its first two years (1977-1979) YEDPA programs accounted for one-fourth of the measured employment growth for all teenagers and approximately three-fourths of all employment growth for black teenagers.

The Act was particularly concerned with overcoming the barriers between school and work by more closely linking education, employment, and training institutions. It has sought to forge new relationships (Taggart and Ganzglass, 1980). One of the four programs authorized by YEDPA was the Youth Employment and Training Program (YETP). This was the largest of the four programs in terms of budget support -- a full 500 million dollars per year. This program was designed to provide a range of work experiences and skills necesary for future employment, especially for those low-income youth, 16 to 21 years of age, who are in school or out of school and unemployed or underemployed. Certain YETP provisions have also allowed designated forms of participation by youth 14 and 15 years old, as well as by youth who are not economically disadvantaged. Approximately 150,000 youth have participated each year in various YETP funded programs.

What provides a sense of urgency to this effort is that there is a desperate need both to improve the education of low-income minority youth and to find the means by which to create more employment for them (Ginzberg, 1979). The evidence on this point is both conclusive and sobering: The situation for poor minority youth, as compared with white middle-class youth, has steadily deteriorated over the past 15 years. Whether one measures employment rates or labor force participation rates, the disparities have grown and continue to do so. This is in spite of all the education, employment, and training programs initiated since the mid-1960's and carried on to the present (cf. Adams and Mangum, 1978:19-34).

YEDPA was to be more than simply ameliorative -- desperately as such ameliorative efforts were needed. There had to be a coherent intellectual framework for assessing the persistence of

Beyond the Quantitative Cul-De-Sac   125

youth unemployment, the reason being, as Mangum and Walsh (1978) have cogently stated, that little or no systematic effort has been made over the past years to learn from previous efforts, either positive or negative. The information on which to base decisions on what programs to instigate, what policies to pursue, and what objectives to seek have heretofore not been made available. Their rather somber assessment includes much of what they understand to be in the YEDPA initiatives as well. They note:

> It is ironic that after 17 years of experimentation with employment and training programs for youth, Congress found it necessary to legislate activities and programs aimed at discovering the causes of youth unemployment and its potential solutions. It seems fair to ask whether the assumptions upon which past youth programs were based were faulty, or whether the programs themselves were poorly designed or mismanaged. Yet, aside from the research provisions of the Youth Employment and Demonstration Projects Act (YEDPA), the programs authorized by the Act are the same as those which have been implemented over the past 17 years -- work experience on community improvement and conservation projects, institutional and on-the-job training, counseling, placement and other kinds of supportive services ... Congress undoubtedly hoped that programs initiated under YEDPA would be innovative and would unearth heretofore untried techniques, but one of the criticisms of past programs has been that they have been almost exclusively experimental. Experiment has been piled upon experiment, but a concerted, overall policy for treating youth unemployment and transitional problems has never emerged. (p. 11)

If Mangum and Walsh are correct in their assessment that, "aside from the research provisions", few new or innovative program efforts could be anticipated from the YEDPA effort, then, of necessity, attention should focus on what the research sponsored by YEDPA might yield both in the way of new theoretical insights and programmatic initiatives.

THE "EXEMPLARY IN-SCHOOL DEMONSTRATION PROJECTS"

In recognition that present approaches to reduce youth unemployment are imperfect, both in design and implementation, the Secretary of Labor was authorized through YEDPA to allocate up to one-fifth of YEDPA funds on demonstration projects to support knowledge development. The mandate from the Congress in the YEDPA legislation was clear:

> Sec. 321. It is the purpose of this part to establish a variety of employment, training, and demonstration programs to explore methods of dealing with the structural unemployment programs of the nation's youth. The basic purpose of the demonstration programs shall be to test the relative efficacy of the different ways of dealing with these problems in different local contexts.
> Sec. 348. ... to carry out innovative and experimental programs, to test new approaches for dealing with the unemployment problems of youth, and to enable eligible participants to prepare for, enhance their prospects for, or secure employment in occupations through which they may reasonably be expected to advance to productive working lives. Such programs shall include, where appropriate, cooperative arrangements with educational agencies to provide special programs and services. . .

The remaining 80 percent formula monies were to be distributed among the local sponsors of programs for youth to alleviate some unemployment and "buy time". Yet there was little confidence that, in the end, these projects would either address the long-term needs of the youth or provide new insights into how programs might be more effectively organized and implemented so as to have a greater impact. New ideas, new approaches, and new actors would have to be on the scene if innovative and pathbreaking approaches were to be found.[1] And while it was not explicit in the legislation, it can be surmised that if successful projects could be located where jobs were created and the youth were prepared to assume them, then perhaps cities and states would be encouraged to redirect portions of the 80 percent formula funds towards projects of this kind. Thus, the discretionary projects could achieve a ripple effect throughout the infrastructure of youth employment and training programs.

To learn more about one aspect of the complex set of relations between education and present/future employment opportuniites, the Department of Labor set aside in Fiscal Year (FY) 1979 and again in FY 1980 from the discretionary funds within YETP approximately $15 million for "Exemplary In-School Demonstration Projects". These grants were to explore the dynamics of in-school projects and their effectiveness. They also would be awarded to promote cooperation between the education and the employment and training systems.

As a result of a five-tier evaluation process designed to select from among the more than 520 submitted proposals, forty-eight projects were chosen. The first contracts were signed and projects began operation in September 1978. Forty-seven of the projects did become operational. Programs were funded in one of four substantive areas: Academic Credit for Work Experience, Expanded Private Sector Involvement, Career Awareness, and Job Creation Through Youth-Operated Projects (cf. Rist, et al., 1980a).

The individual local programs selected for this demonstration project were slated to operate from between nine and eighteen months, specifically, between September 1978 and March 1980.

Programs could include summer activities in 1979 if those activities were shown to be a logical extension of the school year program. The projected size of the youth populations to be served in the programs varied from a low of 35 to a high of 10,000. Sites were located across the nation in 31 states and in locations that ranged from rural to metropolitan areas. Individual grant awards were approximately $175,000 to $400,000 with the average being near $300,000. Additional funding during FY 80 from the DOL enabled twenty-five of the sites to continue beyond their original termination dates.

THE YOUTHWORK NATIONAL POLICY STUDY

In September 1978, a group of researchers at Cornell University was requested to undertake a longitudinal qualitative research study of the entire cohort of funded projects. The Youthwork National Policy Study (YNPS) was conceptualized as a continuing series of intensive qualitative research evaluations of key policy questions. These questions were to be mutually agreed upon by Youthwork, Inc. (a non-profit intermediary providing assistance to the projects), the appropriate legislative committees in the Congress, staff on the Domestic Council at the White House, and staff at the U.S. Department of Labor. The approach was one of building upon the longitudinal perspective, but asking time-bounded and policy-relevant questions that could best be answered through continuous interaction with the sites.

A significant departure from traditional qualitative research was instigated with this study. Rather than send the observers into the field and wait for the "emergent issues" to become apparent, time constraints as well as specific policy questions necessitated the pre-definition of the areas of investigation. Six "analysis packets" were written, each of which focused on a particular area of study. The six included: Program Implementation, CETA-School Collaboration, The Views of Youth, Private Sector Involvement, Interinstitutional Linkages, and Employment Training Alternatives. The analysis packets did not specify _how_ the data relevant to the various policy issues should be collected, only _what_ were the areas of concern. As such, each packet provided the conceptual frameworks within which data were gathered. Throughout the study, observers remained responsible for determining, in the context of the packets, the important events and activities at their respective project sites and for insuring that these events were faithfully reported in their field notes.

Perhaps more important to stress than the changes made within the methodology was the fact that qualitative research was used at all. The application of this method to the study of the Exemplary In-School Projects represented a profound break from traditional approaches to the study of youth education and employment training. Rather than rely on the models of "input-output" evaluations, or those which stress summative approaches, the analyses were based on the study of social processes and day-to-day realities not amenable to quantification. <u>Key aspects of these projects could not be evaluated through mathematical formulas or standardized testing.</u> An in-depth <u>familiarity, a closeness to the staff and students, a longitudinal perspective that permitted the observer to study changes over time were all strengths derived from a qualitative research approach.</u>

The Youthwork National Policy Study chose the qualitative research approach because of its flexibility in design and execution and, most important, because qualitative data are most useful in capturing the processes and on-going problems and successes of program development and implementation, areas around which the key policy questions revolved. In addition, these types of data easily lend themselves to a formative feedback design essential to the improvement of employment and educational programs for low-income in-school youth. The field work drew heavily from the methodologies traditionally associated with anthropology, sociology and social psychology (Rist, 1980).

THE POTENTIAL OF QUALITATIVE RESEARCH

There is a growing consensus among those involved in large-scale policy evaluations that there is an important, indeed critical, role to be played by qualitative research. Too often in the past, the assumption has been made that statistical realities coincide with cultural realities. That this is not so has been the Achilles heel of many efforts at evaluating employment and training programs. As Weiss had already noted in 1970:

> One hopeful direction is to place less stress on evaluation of over-all impact, studies that come out with all-or-nothing, go/no-go conclusions. More resources should be allocated to evaluations that compare the effectiveness of variant conditions within programs (different emphases and components of programs, attributes of sponsoring agency structure and operation, characteristics of participants) and begin to explain which elements and sub-elements are associated with more or less success. Such an approach produces data of interest across a wide range of programs and has high utility in pointing direction for further program development.

In reviewing a large number of studies of the utilization (or lack thereof) of program evaluations, Alkin and Daillak (1979) concluded that the utilization of process evaluations is hindered by the attempt to translate complex and multi-dimensional variables into linear and discrete variables. Program persons themselves know this can fundamentally distort any analysis of the impact of their program. Thus they increasingly tend not to place much reliance on such data. In the end, it is of little benefit to program operators and policy makers to have to rely on artificially created "clean" data in a complex and messy world. Alkin and Daillak also conclude:

> In a very real sense, there is another major finding of the study: an enhanced conviction on our part that naturalistic methods are the most powerful and appropriate methodology for the study of utilization (p. 49).

I would concur and suggest that there are yet additional contributions to be made by qualitative research to the study of education and youth unemployment. The remaining pages of this paper will elaborate upon them.

A Respect for Complexity

It is a truism in social science research that the perceptions, values and attitudes one holds about various issues are highly influenced by one's location in the social structure. Stated differently, not everyone holds the same definitions of reality. While this may at first glance appear somewhat facile, the multiplicity of ways in which the world might be viewed has not influenced the efforts of many researchers. They assume that to "know" is to look through a window rather than a prism. Data collection that is predicated upon believing everyone shares a common set of assumptions, that everyone "knows" X is always X and never Y is a strategy that often misses more than it illuminates.

Critical to these missed opportunities to explore the diversity and complexity of the social world are the <u>a priori</u> assumptions of those in research who work from an experimental (or quasi-experimental) model. Outcomes are anticipated and "good research" is then a rigorous measure of whether, in fact, they appear. Indeed, this is the underlying epistemology of the classic pre-test, post-test methodology. Given the post-test is but a repetition (after treatment) of the pre-test, the research must of necessity anticipate what outcomes are likely from the intervention. Yet what has rendered nigh unto useless so much of this research is that the respondents interpret and respond to the interventions in ways differently than those anticipated by the researchers. The outcome, then, of measured effects on the post-test is the ubiquitous finding of "no effect." But as our own observations of youth employment programs made clear, there were countless effects that were not those expected by program researchers or operators (Rist, et al., 1980b).

Qualitative research is particularly appropriate to the articulation of the multiple ways in which people understand their world and react to it. First, qualitative research is longitudinal. It necessitates spending time, considerable amounts of time, with the various actors. As Erving Goffman has so forcefully demonstrated, what occurs "front stage" may have little or no connection to what is happening "back stage." Qualitative rersearch is predicated upon the long-term building of trust and familiarity that then allows the researcher to go backstage and participate in events, discussions, and interactions that never meet the public eye.

A longitudinal perspective also allows the researcher to observe events as they unfold over time. This vantage point, in contrast to the cross sectional approach of most survey and attitudinal research, respects the fact that the values, beliefs, and behaviors of individuals can and do change. What quantitative research treats as static is, in fact, fluid and constantly evolving.

A second aspect of qualitative research that contributes to this more complex (but more accurate) mosaic of reality is that neither behaviors nor beliefs are examined other than <u>in context</u>. What young people say and what they do are both influenced by and impinge upon the social setting in which they live. Not to examine the diversity and variation in the ways that the young come into adulthood is to presume to "hold constant" the environment. While a great deal of employment research is predicated upon precisely this assumption -- that critical differences will emerge if enough demographic and ecological variables are held constant -- the approach is a limited one. Youth and the context in which they mature is constantly changing. It is critical, therefore, to observe, document, and respect this change if the cross-pressures and currents on young people are to be understood. That so little of this has happened speaks to why we continue to rediscover the wheel when we create education and employment training programs (Berg, 1971).

A third important contribution of committing one's research to a longitudinal perspective is, and this is especially true of studying programs funded on "soft" monies, that staff turnover is so great as to frequently allow the researcher to become the program historian. At several of the Exemplary In-School sites, the observer remained while three generations of senior staff came and went. To have this perspective allowed the researchers to observe countless starts and stops of initiatives, of the manner in which program objectives were constantly muted and transformed with each new set of actors. Further, it became apparent that this constant "musical chairs" among staff rendered absolutely useless research predicated upon an assumed set of clear program goals and procedures. Indeed, instances were documented where the second and third sets of senior staff had not even read the original funded proposal. To have observed program implementation as a constant set of improvisations was to observe actors in search of a script.

<u>A Check on Statistical Portrayals</u>

Qualitative research can tell us the status of the emperor's clothes in a way that any number of surveys of persons with downcast eyes along the parade route never could. To ask young people what they think of the society, of their place in it, and what opportunities it might hold provides one form of data. It is quite another to observe them, to participate with them in school, on the streets and, for those who are fortunate, at the work place. For the young, as for the rest of us, the schism between words and deeds is often very great. As noted earlier, statistical realities do not necessarily coincide with cultural realities. Thus to rely on statistical definitions of situations, to assume that the intricate cultural systems of the young can be accurately captured with linear processes of quantification, and that quantified "facts" represent shared meanings is to make a leap of faith.[2]

Beyond the matter of whether, in quantitative research, there is shared understanding of the concepts and measures, there is the concern with interpretation. Statistical data can often lead to mathematically correct but socially disputed conclusions (Sieber, 1973). As but a brief example, consider the study of the black family undertaken by Daniel Moynihan. That the Department of Labor statistics suggested there were few black men in parenting roles in the black community need not have been taken at face value, had the qualitative literature on the black community been consulted. Statistical portrayals of this "problem" were at odds with qualitative reports of the manner in which members of the black community saw themselves and the manner in which they "knew" that males were participating in parenting activities. "Facts" only become "facts" in a social context, and variations in context can thus result in quite different beliefs about what is true or correct.

As but another example of the role qualitative research can play to clarify and interpret quantitative data, observers at the Exemplary In-School projects found the Management Information System (MIS) data being sent to the Department of Labor (DOL) often varied considerably from the actual levels of student involvement in the programs. Indeed, this worked both ways, i.e., to cover failure and to obscure success. On the one hand, students were frequently counted as participants when they were not. This was done to ensure levels of participation acceptable to the DOL. On the other hand, low levels of student program completion were reported honestly at one site and DOL reacted quite negatively, believing the program to have been ineffective. But qualitative date indicated that the reason for this low level of course completion was not program failure, but that the students were being hired away before the program ended as they were in such demand. In either set of circumstances, statistical data provided an inaccurate understanding of the programs and their impact on young people.

Commenting on a recent publication detailing the findings of the New Jersey Income Maintenance Experiments, Irwin Deutscher has written (1979:238):

> As for the policy persuasiveness of such data (econometric models), I submit that many legislators and policy-makers are more likely to be persuaded by the touching anecdote than by the test of significance. For that, I am grateful.

In contrast to statistical portrayals, qualitative research is in a distinctive position from which to capitalize on the "human dimension" that pervades the political milieu of the policy-making process. In the complex and politically charged world of policy-making, the fixation on charts, graphs, and tables is simply not sufficient to be persuasive. They may be informative, but they are not always so and are seldom likely to mobilize action.

The contrast to data which qualitative research can supply is striking. To systematically study programs, the lives of participants, the evolving changes in neighborhoods, schools and families, and to portray these data so that the policy-maker has a "feel" for the issue can be persuasive in a way that reams of statistical printouts can never match. Time and again during our conversations with federal policy-makers, we were asked, "What is really going on out there?" These individuals have a sense that the conventional data coming back to them lacks authenticity and congruity to the way in which programs are actually being conducted and the impacts evident in the lives of the young. The constant litany of "no effect" rings false to their own instincts. The political arena in which policy is formulated is one where the key actors are not researchers. They are politicians or generalists, individuals who, of necessity, must "stay in touch," "cover their bases," "stay close to the folks back home" and any number of other such stock phrases. The point being that, as a group, politicians function as arbitrators, mediators, reconcilers, and referees over the allocation of our collective resources. Qualitative research can speak to them with an authenticity, with a sense of "how things really are" that can allow them to utilize information relevant to their policy-making roles.

Examining the Unanticipated

The earlier discussion on respecting the complexity of the social world challenged the view that social scientists can hold the world still long enough to maintain their experimental controls. The fact that such rigor is ever elusive allows for events, situations, and outcomes not under "control" to emerge. In short, there are opportunities for unanticipated consequences. Program managers know that confronting the unanticipated is an incessant part of their daily effort. Putting out "brush fires" is but another way of acknowledging that events, persons, and situations have a tendency to go their own way, not to act as predicted, and not according to the original script.

Research strategies not sufficiently flexible and open-ended to accommodate this ever-present serendipitous aspect of human behavior are doomed to reflect only that which stood still long enough to be measured in conventional ways. The irony of this is that these static aspects of the environment are often the least interesting, the least critical, and the least amenable to change (Bronfenbrenner, 1979). A research strategy that can only capture the stationary because of the epistemological assumptions upon which it is built is a strategy in an intellectual cul-de-sac.

Qualitative research puts no such constraints upon itself. The observation and study of behavior in natural settings emphasizes non-intervention, a willingness to use the natural setting as a research site, and a willingness to allow events to go as they will (Rist, 1977, 1979). It is in this way that non-contrived aspects of situations can be studied. Unanticipated events occur. Some are episodic and marginal. Others take on a central and profound importance in the social setting. A close-in and longitudinal familiarity with the setting can not only document that such unanticipated consequences and events do indeed occur, but can also determine the relative importance of these events upon the long-term adaptation and response of persons and organizations.

THE MATTER OF IMPLEMENTATION

In their 1978 assessment of the YEDPA legislation, Mangum and Walsh posed the following question:

> It seems fair to ask whether the assumptions upon which past youth programs were based were faulty, or whether the programs themselves were poorly designed or mismanaged (p. 11).

The answer, they later suggested, is unknown. In large part this is because research has never been conducted to answer a simple question: What youth programs were actually implemented? The process of moving from establishing goals to achieving them through program implementation is a process of which those involved in youth employment efforts are woefully uninformed. It is in this area, as many others, that little attention has been paid to the process of implementation (Hargrove, 1975). Indeed, Hargrove sees it as the "missing link" between policy formation and program operation.

We have, in a sense, completed the circle when we focus upon the implementation process. As the recent (and massive) Rand Corporation study of federal program implementation made clear, programs are seldom implemented as they were designed (Berman and McLaughlin, 1978). The clean and crisp organization charts developed by new programs start to disintegrate often before the ink is dry. Any number of unanticipated events, circumstances, and interactions tend to deflect the program off in other directions. The complexities of program administration seldom conform to the Weberian models of 19th Century Prussia.

Data from the Exemplary In-School Projects suggest that program managers knew very little about the processes of implementation and strategies most appropriate to achieve successful program operation. They sought to enhance the delivery of services to youth, but the rationale and methodology were not clear. As Pressman and Wildavsky have stated in this regard (1979:xxi):

> Policies imply theories. Whether stated explicitly or not, policies point to a chain of causation between initial conditions and future consequences. If X, then Y. Policies become programs when, by authoritative action,

the initial conditions are created. X now exists. Programs make the theories operational by forging the first link in the causal chain connecting actions to objectives. Given X, we act to obtain Y. Implementation, then, is the ability to forge subsequent links in the causal chain so as to obtain the desired results.

Given that the projects were to be "demonstration projects," i.e., trying new and different ways of addressing the needs of high risk youth, it is perhaps not surprising that prior to the beginning of the programs, there was little sense of how to "forge subsequent links in the causal chain so as to obtain the desired results." The consequence was an ongoing set of improvisations -- some of which were successful and more of which simply perpetuated the problems first generated by the lack of a coherent methodology.

Qualitative research is well suited to the study of the implementation process. The three rationales noted earlier for employing qualitative research -- respecting the complexity of the social system, providing a check on statistical interpretations, and studying the unanticipated consequences of social change -- all are appropriate in the analysis of implementation. They become key components of research that addresses itself to how results, desired or otherwise, are obtained. The more the recognition that the implementation process has to be treated as an independent variable in any program assessment, the more imperative a qualitative perspective. That we know so little about viable youth employment programs after having tried so long suggests something of the tragic loss we have garnered as a result of our misplaced emphasis upon quantitative research (Rist, 1980). It simply is an inappropriate research strategy for the critical questions that continue to demand answers.

POSTSCRIPT

We are into a period where the politics of scarcity prevail. Human service programs will be scrutinized more closely and with less presumption of effectiveness than in any recent administration. How to implement programs well, to "obtain the desired results" mentioned by Pressman and Wildavsky, will be of paramount concern. The shotgun approach of throwing programs at problems is past. The new agenda is fewer programs with fewer resources. Thus what remains must be used with the greatest care and with the greatest assurances of being the most appropriate allocation of effort.

The credibility of researchers to be heard in this area will rest upon their willingness to address the difficult issues of program implementation and evaluation. The applied research agenda for the 1980's ought to be one that seeks both to systematically explore the "black box" of program implementation and design appropriate measures of program effectiveness. These twin concerns -- efficiency and effectiveness -- are the bottom line for those policymakers who would seek input from the research community. Research that would be applicable should be cognizant of such concerns.

But having said this, it should be immediately noted that policymakers and researchers alike are in something of a quandary with youth employment programs. On the one hand, though there have been multiple efforts to address the very real situation of youth unemployment, very little is known from them as they have not been systematically evaluated or documented. That task now must be undertaken, post hoc as it is. On the other hand, it can be concluded that the persistence of youth unemployment demonstrates the ineffectiveness of current approaches. The alternative is to begin with new actors, new institutional arrangements, and new definitions of the problem.

The reality is that we know so little from previous efforts that we have no systematic idea of what worked when or why. Indeed, we are not even certain of what the efforts consisted. Consequently, there is no firm basis from which to make the policy decision on the continuation or eliminiation of previous efforts -- a classic instance of the "baby and bath water" analogy.

The de facto decision made by the Department of Labor was to opt for the instigation of new programs predicated upon new institutional arrangements. (That this is the same department that administered the previous efforts as well is an irony not to be lost.) The presumption has been made that previous DOL efforts were not successful -- whatever those efforts might have been. New DOL efforts with new evaluative strategies has become the order of the day.

What remains to be seen is whether the presence of a large body of newly generated research findings will have any influence upon the policy process. There simply has not been sufficient passage of time to allow us to ascertain if the absence of knowledge in the past -- and its presence now and in the near future -- will make any difference in either the implementation of youth programs or, more importantly, the continuing crisis of youth unemployment.

NOTES

1. As but one indication of the disenchantment with current approaches, witness the efforts of the Carter Administration to cut by almost $200 million the funding during FY 1979-1980 for vocational educational programs. Then-Secretary Califano called vocational education one of HEW's "least effective" programs (Carnegie Council on Policy Studies, 1979:146).
2. A lack of sensitivity to the variations in the life experiences and perceptions of young people pervades much of the research on youth employment. Consider the highly influential report of the President's Science Advisory Committee, Youth: Transition into Adulthood (1973). In this report, no special attention was given to those youth who were Black, Hispanic, or were female.

Rather, the authors rather blithely indicated that their analysis and findings were applicable to "youth" in the aggregate. The myopic nature of such a view is self evident.

REFERENCES

Adams, A. and G.L. Mangum (1978) <u>The Lingering Crisis of Youth Unemployment</u>. Kalamazoo, MI: W.E. Upjohn Institute.

Alkin, M.C. and R.H. Daillak (1979) "A Study of Evaluation Utilization," <u>Education Evaluation and Policy Analysis</u>. Vol. 1, No. 4, July-August, 41-50.

Berg, I. (1971) <u>Education and Jobs: The Great Training Robbery</u>. Boston: Beacon Press.

Berman, P. and M.W. McLaughlin (1978) <u>Federal Programs Supporting Educational Change, Vol. VIII</u>. Santa Monica, CA: The Rand Corporation.

Bronfenbrenner, U. (1979) <u>The Ecology of Human Development</u>. Cambridge, MA: Harvard University Press.

Carnegie Council on Policy Studies in Higher Education (1979) <u>Giving Youth a Better Chance</u>. San Francisco, CA: Jossey-Bass.

Deutscher, Irwin (1979) "The Great Experiment," <u>Contemporary Sociology</u>. Vol. 8, No. 3, March, 237-239.

Ginzberg, E. (1979) <u>Good Jobs, Bad Jobs, No Jobs</u>. Cambridge, MA: Harvard University Press.

Hargrove, E. (1975) <u>The Missing Link: The Study of the Implementation of Social Policy</u>. Washington, D.C.: The Urban Institute.

Mangum, G. and J. Walsh (1978) <u>Employment and Training Programs for Youth: What Works Best for Whom?</u> Employment and Training Administration, Office of Youth Programs, Washington, D.C.

President's Science Advisory Committee (1973) <u>Youth: Transition to Adulthood</u>. Washington, D.C.: U.S. Government Printing Office.

Pressman, J.L. and A. Wildavsky (1979) <u>Implementation</u>. (Second Edition). Berkeley: University of California Press.

Rist, R.C. (1977) "On the Relations Among Educational Research Paradigms: From Disdain to Detente," <u>Anthropology and Education Quarterly</u>. Vol. 8, No. 2, May, pp. 42-50.

Rist, R.C. (1979) "On the Means of Knowing: Qualitative Research in Education," <u>New York University Education Quarterly</u>. Vol. 10, No. 4, pp. 17-21.

Rist, R.C. (1980) "Confronting Youth Unemployment in the 1980s: Sorting Out the Issues and Trends" in R. Rist, ed., <u>Confronting Youth Unemployment in the 1980s</u>. Elmsford, NY: Pergamon Press.

Rist, R. et al. (1980a) <u>Targeting on In-School Youth</u>. Cornell University, Ithaca, NY: Youthwork National Policy Study.

Rist, R. et al. (1980b) <u>Patterns of Collaboration: The CETA-School Linkage</u>. Cornell University, Ithaca, NY: Youthwork National Policy Study.

Sieber, S. (1973) "The Integration of Fieldwork and Survey Methods," American Journal of Sociology. Vol. 78, No. 6, pp. 1335-1359.

Taggart, R. and E. Ganzglass (1980) "Youth Employment: A Challenge for the 1980s" in R. Rist, ed., Confronting Youth Unemployment in the 1980s. Elmsford, NY: Pergamon Press.

Weiss, C.H. (1970) "The Politicization of Evaluation Research," Journal of Social Issues. Vol. 26, No. 4, pp. 57-68.

WELFARE TERMINATIONS AND BENEFIT REDUCTIONS: WHAT PROGRAM RECIPIENTS CAN TELL POLICY PLANNERS

Arnold Vedlitz
Jon Alston

There are a large number of factors to be considered when evaluating the merits of any public program. Some of the more notable of these include product costs, observable benefits (social and political), management efficiency, program range and depth, expenditure levels, resource competition, implementation concerns, and waste estimates. However, all of the above tend to be technical, cost-benefit oriented analyses largely devoid of concerns about the relationship between policy and client. That is, the human element affected most by programs has generally been overlooked in such program evaluations. To use Max Weber's phrase, bureaucratic programs tend to be "iron cages" which make the individual secondary in relation to technical interests. In response to this individual-mechanistic dichotomy, we focus here on an analysis of the consequences of AFDC client terminations and reductions from the point of view of the clients themselves, and on how their experiences and evaluations might provide useful information to welfare policy planners.

Few public policy areas have a greater direct impact upon their consumers than does welfare. The marginality of welfare consumers and the importance of various welfare programs to their every day existence make welfare clients continually vulnerable to and concerned about programmatic and policy changes. Welfare reform in the United States is as old as welfare itself. However, given today's political and economic realities, modifications in the welfare system will to a large degree probably consist of decreasing benefits and a stiffening of eligibility requirements. We expect many future "welfare reforms" to consist of attempts to reduce the number of welfare recipients. Also, welfare policy planning will probably increasingly involve the assumption that decreased levels of services will be necessary as welfare budgets are held constant or even decreased (Garfinkel, 1979:87). Such contraction of services will most likely be targeted among those potential and actual welfare recipients who are currently marginally eligible. In addition to general service contractions, it is likely that stricter rules (role of stepfathers; work requirements; allowable income levels; etc.) will be utilized to decrease welfare participation among the marginally poor.

Given the likelihood of reduced welfare funding levels, it would seem that information obtained from affected program recipients could be very important to policy makers as they attempt to target scarce program resources.

The purpose of this study is to examine participants in one such welfare area -- Aid to Families with Dependent Children. Specifically, we will look at those AFDC recipients who have been terminated or had their benefits reduced. We will examine the reasons for such reductions, the respondents' attitudes toward and evaluations of the AFDC program, their degree of understanding of the AFDC administrative process, their functional responses to the loss or reduction of assistance, and what their behaviors, experiences, and opinions can tell policy planners about future welfare reduction strategies.

The current study is based on a national stratified quota sample of 339 female AFDC recipients who, in 1978, had their benefits reduced or terminated. Approximately 35 such respondents were interviewed in each of nine states throughout the nation.[1] Two-thirds of the respondents were interviewed in person, either at home or in the welfare office and the remainder were interviewed by telephone. The sample of respondents included 49% white, 38% black, and 10% Hispanic. Basically equal proportions of the respondents were married, divorced, separated, or never married. While the sample is well distributed across population categories found within the AFDC program, the reader should use caution in generalizing to such populations. However, we feel that the sample mix is broad and can provide a valid picture of program enrollees who have been reduced or terminated. It will also be very useful in making between group comparisons of relevant AFDC attitudes and behaviors, for such terminated and reduced clients.

We first look at our respondents' feelings toward the AFDC program. Previous research has indicated that welfare recipients are generally supportive of the programs in which they are enrolled. For example, Handler and Hollingsworth (1969) found that Wisconsin AFDC recipients were not negatively oriented toward the program's eligibility requirements. In her analysis of the welfare literature, Macaulay (1977) reports that "... the negative character of the [welfare] system is experienced by a minority and not by the majority [of the welfare beneficiaries]." In a broader context, Katz and associates report generally positive evaluations by participants in most government service programs (Katz, et al., 1975).

However, recipient evaluations of welfare programs are usually obtained in studies which base their findings on samples of clients enrolled in ongoing or current programs. Also, these studies have tended to focus on narrow program elements and on groups of respondents from only one or two counties. The current study broadens the knowledge base of welfare recipient attitudes toward welfare programs by focusing on terminated beneficiaries, by evaluating a broader array of program components, and by utilizing a sample base more nationwide in scope.

What about our respondents, then? How did they feel they were treated generally? What do they feel were the strengths and weaknesses of the program and its employees? Do they understand the system and the reasons for their benefit reductions? As Handler and Hollingsworth (1969) suggest, we might expect that our terminated and reduced AFDC recipients would be bitter toward the program. After all, such individuals who have had their benefits reduced or stopped would naturally be upset by this and such feelings might be generalized to negative assessments of the program staff and program operations.

While this assumption may seem reasonable, it is somewhat superficial. It suggests that all recipients of welfare expect to get benefits indefinitely and that continuous, long-term beneficiaries are the rule rather than the exception. It also assumes that the termination decision is the only one which consumers are likely to consider in evaluating the AFDC staff and operations. These are largely unwarranted assumptions. Membership on welfare rolls, such as AFDC, is often transitory, as is poverty status itself (Levitan, Rein, and Marwick, 1972:50). Former HEW Secretary Joseph A. Califano has reported that during 1967-1972, some 21 percent of Americans were poor during at least one of these years; by contrast, only three percent were poor during all six years (Weil, 1978:29). Levitan, et al. (1972:40-50) have reported that there is great dynamism in the AFDC caseload:

> During 1970 some 750,000 cases were closed -- including nearly 40% of the 1.9 million AFDC households on the rolls at the beginning of the year. Thus, the 1.3 million families who received AFDC payments during all of 1970 accounted for less than one-half of the caseload at the beginning of 1971. Most families join and leave the AFDC rolls quickly. In recent years approximately one-quarter of the cases left within six months; 30 percent left within a year; half closed within two years; and three-fifths closed within three years.

In addition to this high client turnover, termination or reduction does not necessarily mean that a particular recipient will never again be eligible for AFDC benefits. There is a high proportion of current AFDC recipients who have received benefits at some earlier time that were not continuous with their current program status. Levitan, et al. (1972:50) report that

> In both 1961 and 1971 one AFDC family in three had previously received assistance. Of those in 1967 who had previously received aid, two-thirds had been on the rolls only once before and one-third had been on at least twice.

Moreover, one-fifth had been denied assistance at some (earlier) time.

Our own data support this trend. Nearly two-thirds of our respondents reported that they had previously received AFDC benefits. Also, of the respondents who actually had their benefits denied, over 50 percent said they plan on reapplying.

With this more complete perspective of AFDC recipient mobility in mind, we look at the attitudes of terminated and reduced program participants. We examine a number of client attitudes which provide a direct evaluation of AFDC program performance and implementation processes. First, how do these respondents feel, generally, about the AFDC program and staff? In spite of the fact that their benefits have been reduced or terminated, most were positively oriented toward the program. The AFDC on-line employees seemed to be viewed quite favorably. A significant majority of these AFDC clients felt that the agency workers were polite and helpful and that the workers did not attempt to discourage them. For most respondents, the client/worker relationship was not seen as an antagonistic one. There was, however, some doubt expressed by many clients about how fairly the agency treated all clients. A substantial minority of respondents felt the workers treated people differentially. Twenty-five percent said they felt the worker would bend the rules to help clients they liked while 36 percent believed the workers would make it harder on clients they disliked. Overall, however, 65 percent of the respondents were generally satisfied with the services they received from the agency and nearly 83 percent said they would refer someone else to AFDC for assistance.

Looking at how well these respondents understand the program and its requirements, we saw no evidence which would indicate that these clients were uncomprehending of the specific AFDC bureaucratic environment. Eighty-two percent said the agency's letter explaining their benefit reduction or denial was clear and for the 209 respondents for whom independent accuracy checks were possible, 91 percent had correctly identified the reason for their particular aid reduction. Of the various reasons given for benefit reductions, the two most commonly cited by respondents were too much income (46%) and non-completion of verification forms and processes (18%). In addition, most of these clients knew the system well enough to take advantage of the internal agency appeals process. Most knew of their appeal rights and the majority of those who chose not to exercise these appeal rights did so because they felt sure they were no longer eligible for benefits under the program. It seems that the AFDC bureaucratic workers and process are not seen by the majority of respondents as unfeeling or unnecessarily complex.

In spite of these relatively positive findings, however, many of the clients did identify problems with the system and with the AFDC workers. Some had problems obtaining all the documentation necessary to properly process a claim and many others felt the case workers were hard to contact. When asked what they would change in AFDC, over 20 percent of those responding said worker-related style or worker fairness.

While there were no significant racial or marital status differences among the respondents in their evaluations of the AFDC program, interesting variations did emerge between long- and short-term beneficiaries, a finding found by others (see Macaulay, 1977). The long-term recipients are generally felt to be more pathologically poor and dependent. Whether they got this way because of welfare or whether they stay on welfare longer because they are already this way is still an open question, and one beyond the scope of our analysis. What we can add to this general discussion, however, is that our longer-term enrollees also tend to be more cynical about and more negative towards the AFDC program. Table 11.1 arrays key client responses toward the program by the recipients' number of years on welfare.[2] While all of these responses do not show a perfectly monotonic relationship, it is clear that longer beneficiaries are generally more negative. There are several reasons why this may be the case. It is possible that long-term dependency, with its accompanying feelings of helplessness, might breed resentment among long-term AFDC beneficiaries. Researchers, however, have found little evidence to support this assertion (Macaulay, 1977). A more plausible explanation for such negative feelings among longer program enrollees may simply be that having had longer contact wtih the program and its employees they 1) have run into more bureaucratic snafus and rule problems and 2) have been interacting with the staff for so long that the staff views them in a more routinized, casual, less concerned manner.

Whatever the stimulus for such negativism, however, longer term respondents were more likely, in their interviews, to volunteer such statements as the following:

> "They strip you of every ounce of pride by the time you're through here."

> "They don't seem to care for a person's problems."

> "There's too much detail on the forms. Too many questions that don't have anything to do with your current problems."

Although there were many such comments, we wish to reiterate that most of the clients, even most longer term ones, were relatively positively oriented towards the case worker and were generally satisfied with the quality of services they did receive.

However, foremost among the problems clients did identify was the fact that the AFDC agencies seemed to provide little direct guidance to the client after termination or reduction in benefits.

Table 11.1. Client Evaluations by Length of Time on Welfare Rolls

Percentage Answering That:[1]	Years on Welfare[2]		
	Less than 1	1 to 3	More than 3
Workers polite or very polite	91.0	77.3	39.5
Workers helpful or very helpful	84.2	76.8	79.5
Workers treat all fairly	49.1	28.2	38.9
Workers bend rules for some	19.0	36.6	36.0
Workers make it hard for those they dislike	17.2	45.1	52.2
They (the respondents) are satisfied or very satisfied	75.4	69.5	62.9

[1] Each variable entry selects from one response pole of a contingency table with bi-polar options. Cell entries, therefore, should interpreted in the following way (looking at the first cell entry): Of those on welfare less than one year, 91% said workers were polite or very polite -- by inference, the table shows that 9% of those on welfare less than one year felt workers were rude or very rude. Each entry, then sums with its implied opposite pole to equal 100% and can, therefore, be compared to the responses given on that variable by the other categories of welfare recipients.

[2] Information on previous years on welfare was available for 219 of the 339 respondents. Fifty-eight (26.5%) were on less than one year, 71 (32.4%) were on one to three years, and 90 (41.1%) had been on the roles more than three years. With allowances for missing data on individual questions, these were the pools from which Table 11.1's cell entrees are drawn.

While the agency was quite likely to apprise reduced or terminated clients of their appeal rights, the agencies did not seem to provide much help to clients in locating other sources of support or in generally adjusting to the loss of AFDC benefits. Seventy-five percent of the clients said they received no advice from AFDC on other possible sources of aid.

The AFDC program, as it is currently administered, seems to be limited in its view of discontinued clients. When labeled as no longer eligible, it seems as though AFDC assumes the former client is now self-supporting. Hence, little follow-up or alternative aid has been offered. Whether AFDC personnel actions really grow out of such beliefs about the clients is immaterial. Regardless of its justification, such a posture can be especially harmful to those clients whose non-eligibility falls only slightly below agency criteria. In many such cases, marginal status beneficiaries may actually be substantially worse off after termination.

The client data suggest that more thought be given to those who have recently become ineligible for AFDC support. Such continuation of concern for former clients, in the form of self-help instruction, family guidance, or public and private aid referrals might reduce the cycles of on-again/off-again welfare status that seem to be occurring. Our data clearly indicate that reduced and terminated AFDC beneficiaries perceive a need for a more extended time perspective on the part of the AFDC agencies. One solution would be a greater effort by AFDC agencies to positively equip reduced beneficiaries for the problems they are likely to encounter and the possible assistance available to them. This effort is particularly significant since most recipients experience a cycle of alternating states of need and non-need with the differences in well-being between those eligible and those who are not sometimes being quite small. One may no longer be eligible for welfare assistance and yet be very close to meeting welfare criteria. The difference may be more of an administrative determination than a question of actual economic security.

We next sought to examine the adaptive responses of our reduced and terminated welfare recipients. The public's stereotype of welfare recipients is that people are on welfare because something is wrong with them -- that they are lazy, dependent, and non-individualistic. This is certainly the current myth and one we see repeated over and over again in public opinion polls (see Feagin, 1975:91-130). The public would likely expect, then, that reduced and terminated AFDC recipients would really have no successful adaptation to the loss of public aid.

The fact is, of course, that this is not an accurate description of welfare mothers. While many do not or can not work, in 1971, 28 percent of all AFDC mothers were either in the labor force or training, and for some states, like Florida, the figure was over 40 percent (Levitan, et al., 1972:54). In our own sample, over 25 percent of the welfare mothers reported they had a job at the time of their benefit reduction. Another 14.5 percent found a job after denial and over 20 percent reported they were looking for employment.

Whites were more likely to have a job than blacks (45% to 30%) but blacks were more likely to be seeking employment (45% to 36%). Divorced and separated respondents were much more likely to have a job and to be seeking a job than were married recipients (50% to 24%; and 44% to 26%, respectively).

Thus, we emerge with an image of reduced and terminated AFDC recipients which pictures them as less passive and "idle" than is commonly assumed. Again, these figures suggest that welfare programs should be increasingly concerned with preparing the welfare recipient for her post-welfare period.

It is clear, though, that employment per se is not enough to provide self-sufficiency even for those AFDC recipients working full time. There are many working poor who work full time and yet remain below or near the poverty level. While we don't have the figures for our sample, previous researchers argue persuasively that welfare mothers are usually only able to find marginal employment. Levitan, et al. (1972:54) believe that "An examination of the characteristics of (welfare) recipients suggests that for many on relief, achieving full economic independence is an unrealistic goal."

What other sources of help were available to, and taken advantage of, by these recipients? These respondents did not get much help from formal federal, state, local, or even private welfare agencies, with less than 15 percent reporting such aid. Surprisingly though, and on the positive side, over 20 percent of these respondents received help from their immediate family, extended family, or friends. Most previous studies, especially those focusing on the black family, lead us to believe that because of family disorganization and disintegration, welfare mothers could not expect much help from familial sources.[3] However, Heiss (1975:23-24), in his study of the black family, argues that controlling for the availability of kin able to help, blacks and white report about equal numbers who got start-up aid from some relative (although the figures did not seem to be larger than 25% for either group).

As we stated earlier, we found a substantial amount of help coming from familial sources. In comparing family help patterns across racial groups in our sample, we found that blacks and whites were about equally likely to receive help from immediate family members, but whites were almost three times more likely to receive help from their extended family.

CONCLUSIONS

In our study of reduced and terminated AFDC recipients, we found several patterns which should be of interest to policy planners. First, most AFDC recipients are relatively satisfied with AFDC employees and procedures, although some questions regarding fairness and equity were mentioned. This high level of support was forthcoming even from a sample of respondents who might, on some accounts, be expected to be more negative. However, there was an awareness by these respondents that the reduction or termination of aid was a relatively abrupt break. That is, the agency did not concern itself with preparing or helping individuals to adjust to the state of reduced or lost benefits. Perhaps more awareness of the need to better cushion and prepare terminated or reduced recipients could be considered. Given the repetitive on-again/off-again welfare status we referred to earlier, such agency preparation might enable more of those entering the off cycle to not have to return to the active welfare roles.

We also learned that these recipients were involved in seeking or were already holding jobs. More research and attention is needed on the welfare-job transition process and on ways to facilitate this movement to self-sufficiency.

We saw a relatively high level of familial assistance for these reduced and terminated AFDC beneficiaries. It seems clear that reduced welfare support affects an extended familial network involving many more persons than just the recipient and her children. To help, other family members are making adjustments -- financial and otherwise -- when welfare support ends or declines. We see that welfare termination or reduction has repercussions beyond the immediate recipient and a greater awareness of this fact can hopefully result in a more equitable and more effective welfare program.

And finally, we hope this effort has demonstrated that information obtained from program beneficiaries, like these AFDC mothers, can be quite useful to policy planners and decision-makers as they attempt to gather all the relevant information needed to properly evaluate the tough social welfare policy choices which lie ahead.

NOTES

1. The states surveyed include: Texas, New York, Pennsylvania, Maryland, Minnesota, Michigan, California, Louisiana, and Nevada. Prospective respondents were identified from welfare records in three local welfare sites in each of the nine states and sample respondents were selected in order to obtain a balanced cross-section of program recipients. The data were provided by the U.S. Department of Health, Education, and Welfare, Region VI.

2. One hundred twenty of the 339 respondents failed to say how long they had been on the AFDC roles, so while their responses are included in the overall question breakdowns, they do not appear in the bivariate presentation in Table 11.1. Therefore, some response breakdown levels in Table 11.1 may not jibe perfectly with known, whole sample parameters.

3. For an elaboration of the position arguing family disintegration among the poor, especially black, families, see Moynihan, et al., 1965.

REFERENCES

Feagin, Joe R. (1975) Subordinating the Poor: Welfare and American Beliefs. Englewood Cliffs: Prentice-Hall, Inc.

Garfinkel, Irwin (1979) "Welfare Reform." In The Social Welfare Forum, 1978. National Conference on Social Welfare. New York: Columbia University Press, pp. 80-95.

Handler, Joel F. and Ellen J. Hollingsworth (1969) "How Obnoxious is the 'Obnoxious Means Test'? The Views of AFDC Recipients." Madison: Institute for Research on Poverty, University of Wisconsin.

Heiss, Jerold (1975) The Case of the Black Family: A Sociological Inquiry. New York: Columbia University Press.

Katz, Daniel, Barbara A. Butek, Robert L. Kahn, and Eugenia Barton (1975) Bureaucratic Encounters: A Pilot Study in the Evaluation of Government Services. Ann Arbor: Survey Research Center, University of Michigan.

Levitan, Sar R., Martin Rein, and David Marwick (1972) Work and Welfare Go Together. Baltimore: Johns Hopkins University Press.

Macaulay, Jacqueline (1977) "Stereotyping Child Welfare." Society, Vol. 14, 2 (Jan./Feb.), pp. 47-51.

Moynihan, Daniel P., Paul Barton, and Ellen Broderick (1965) The Negro Family: The Case for National Action. Washington, D.C.: Office of Policy Planning and Research, U.S. Department of Labor.

Weil, Gordon L. (1978) The Welfare Debate of 1978. White Plains, NY: The Institute for Socioeconomic Studies.

EXPLAINING AWAY BLACK POVERTY: THE STRUCTURAL DETERMINANTS OF BLACK EMPLOYMENT*

Lou Ferleger

INTRODUCTION

Over the last twenty years the structure of the U.S. labor force has changed considerably. One of the most important changes is in the pattern of black employment. While some blacks have moved into middle-income occupations in the last two decades, a large and growing portion of the employed labor force has found themselves in poorly paid jobs. These jobs have been characterized not only by low pay but also by limited prospects for promotion and advancement. This paper analyzes the pattern of black employment since 1960 and examines the dominant theories offered to explain the persistence of black poverty. In addition we present an alternative model for understanding why employed blacks continue to be located in poorly paid jobs.

Studies of why some blacks receive low incomes and have a different pattern of occupational mobility than other groups of workers have grown in recent years. The bulk of this research centers on human capital-oriented explanations. While this model is appropriate under certain circumstances, these explanations tend to obscure more than they explain. Specifically they tend to overlook the changing nature of the U.S. economy. One key factor overlooked

---

* This study was assisted by a grant from the University of Massachusetts. I owe a debt of appreciation to the Office of Employment Analysis, Department of Labor, for providing unpublished data from the Current Population Survey. I am very grateful to Carol Kearns for encouraging me to seriously reconsider dominant theories of black poverty. Carol Ivan deserves special attention for helping me clarify my views. The same is true for Richard Goldstein. I would also like to thank William Lazonick, Esther Kingston-Mann, Jay Mandle, Steve Sachs and Mary Stevenson for their constructive comments and criticisms which improved the arguments in this paper.

has been the structural change that the economy has undergone from being manufacturing-based to being service-oriented. As a result, there has been a dramatic change in the structure of employment. While many commentators on the economic status of blacks have spent their time arguing over theoretical and empirical differences in their human-capital models, they have missed the significant change in the work patterns of employed blacks. As we demonstrate, this has led to an overemphasis on changes within particular labor markets with overall labor market trends being downplayed or neglected.

THEORETICAL FRAMEWORK

The growth of the service sector has significantly influenced the labor markets in which blacks find themselves. In the last twenty years black workers were increasingly located in particular service industries (as clerical or service workers) which have been characterized by low pay and limited opportunities to gain skills. At the same time the economy has undergone a major transformation that has dramatically increased the number of service-oriented jobs available to potential workers. Other sectors of the economy have not grown nearly as fast nor employed as many black workers. Despite governmental programs which have increased the number of blacks employed by local, state and federal governments and the emergence of private and public sector jobs for the black middle class, the black population continues to find employment limited in high-paying industries and occupations and, consequently, must seek employment in the low-paying industries and service-oriented occupations.

Since World War II, black labor has increasingly been concentrated in the service sector of the economy for several reasons. Blacks, who could no longer seek employment in the blackbelt of the South after cotton production was mechanized, migrated in large numbers to the North and Midwest. This provided some blacks with greater economic opportunities for securing higher-paying jobs than agricultural related activity had yielded. Yet the bulk of the black labor force found few high-paying jobs because, as Mandle has hypothesized, they were late arrivals in the competition for well-paid work, in addition to suffering from discriminatory practices (Mandle, 1978: 99). Another important factor was the failure of the manufacturing sector to provide more jobs for black workers prior to 1960. Thus, blacks moved primarily from agricultural work to service-oriented occupations, both of which were characterized by low pay and low levels of productivity. This latter factor is characteristic of large segments of the service sector and tends to make it more difficult for blacks to ascend to higher-paying occupations. The low level of advances in labor productivity characteristic of the service sector tends to make the economy increasingly prone to inflation (a topic not discussed here) and makes it less likely that blacks can escape service-oriented employment.

Two aspects of the performance of the American economy during this period contributed to the growth of black employment. First is the long period of prosperity experienced because of the stimulative fiscal and monetary policies consistently adopted by the government. Given the institutional structure of American capitalism, mobility is only possible if the economy experiences long-term growth. Economic growth has been a characteristic feature of the American economy since World War II, but especially so during the 1960s and the early 1970s. The resulting increase in employment in the economy at large was particularly important for blacks who found employment possibilities expanding in the manufacturing, government, and service sectors. For some blacks this meant a lessening of the rigidity of the job structure system and a changing structure of job possibilities. This point is documented below in Table 12.1.

Second, in the 1970s, the principal growth area in employment was in services: three industries -- eating and drinking places, health services, including private hospitals, and business and repair services -- accounted for 40 percent of the jobs created from 1973 to 1980 (Rothschild, 1981: 12).

This shift into service employment has been documented by others (O'Connor, 1973; Castels, 1980). But human capital-oriented theorists have consistently under-valued the importance of these changes. It is important to note here that shifts in the industrial structure of the labor force occur because of one or both of two reasons. On the one hand, labor shifts into those sectors of the economy which are experiencing the most rapid rates of expansion. On the other hand, labor tends to move out of those parts of the economy experiencing the most rapid rates of productivity advance. (This assumes that these industries are not rapidly expanding industries because if they are, then employment growth and productivity advance could occur simultaneously. However, rapid rates of increase in both productivity and employment are the atypical case.) Thus a sector such as services characterized at once by a relative increase in overall production, but a relatively slow rate of increase in output per hour worked, would tend to see a greater than proportionate growth in its labor force. Just such a trend is evident from the American experience.

Today more than three out of every five workers are in the service sector (an increase from about two in five, recorded in 1956). In addition, labor productivity in services is considerably below overall labor productivity trends in other industrial sectors (Rothschild, 1981: 14). The direction of change in the economy towards services and away from manufacturing tends to heighten the extent to which certain segments of the labor force are located in this sector. This is particularly true of the black labor force.

DATA

One problem with many studies in this area is that they do not take into account what is happening concurrently in both industrial and occupational categories.[1] Poverty research in this area relies heavily upon elaborate econometric tests to ascertain whether economic success has been achieved by blacks (Oaxaca, 1977). In this regard, econometric tests can be useful in specifying the particular earnings/occupational structure of the employed black population. Yet this research tends to overlook the aggregate problem of analyzing what is happening to the whole employed black labor force simultaneously.

By analyzing industrial categories, it is possible to locate where blacks and whites are employed by industrial designations: agriculture, manufacturing and construction, services, etc. For the 1972-80 period, it is also possible to break down each category into occupational headings (white collar, blue collar, service workers) and then determine which group of industries and which occupations within industries have been characterized by lower or higher earnings (on the average). Additionally, it is possible to identify those sectors that are characterized by relatively high productivity growth and low productivity advances. Theoretically, high productivity jobs are rewarded by high wages and vice versa. In the case where more workers are in industries characterized by low levels of productivity advance and these industries experience rapid growth, it is less likely that these workers will be able to find employment elsewhere.

Prior to 1960 the salient characteristic of black employment was that blacks were employed in low-wage occupations and industries (Mandle, 1978: 102). However, the 1960s witnessed a dramatic change in the industries in which blacks were employed (excluding self-employed). This trend is clearly evident in Table 12.1. In 1962 the majority of non-white workers were employed in three sectors: 48 percent in service industries (including retail trade), 18 percent in manufacturing and 12 percent in agriculture. (Blacks account for 89 percent of the non-white labor force.)[2] These industries employed 78 percent of the non-white labor force. The figures on whites in Table 12.1 reveal a somewhat different trend. In 1962, 38 percent of the employed labor force was in services (including retail trade), 27 percent in manufacturing, and 7 percent in agriculture. For whites, 72 percent of the employed population worked in these industries.

By 1970 a significant change had occurred for non-white workers in manufacturing. Now 25 percent of the employed non-whites worked in manufacturing jobs. For whites, no such shift occurs. The change in the manufacturing sector, both in the aggregate and within the categories, is slight for white workers.

In service industries, however, there is less of a change for non-white workers. Industries specializing in services still account for 35 percent of the employed work force (46 percent including retail trade). Yet there were some important changes that did occur within

Table 12.1

Industry of the Employed Population: 1962, 1970
(percent)

		1962*		1970	
		Nonwhite**	White	Nonwhite	White
(1)	Agriculture, forestry & fisheries	12	7	5	5
(2)	Mining	-	1	-	1
(3)	Construction	6	6	5	6
(4)	Manufacturing	18	27	25	27
	(5) Durable goods	10	15	14	16
	(6) Motor vehicles & equipment	1	1	2	1
	(6a) Other	9	14	12	15
	(7) Non-durable goods	8	12	11	11
	(8) Food & kindred products	3	3	3	2
	(8a) Other	5	9	8	9
(9)	Transportation, communication and other public utilities	5	7	6	7
	(10) Transportation	4	4	4	4
	(10a) Other	1	3	2	3
(11)	Wholesale trade	3	4	2	4
(12)	Retail trade	11	16	11	16
	(13) Eating and drinking places	4	3	3	3
	(13a) Other	7	13	8	13
(14)	Finance, insurance and real estate	2	5	3	5
(15)	Service industries	37	22	35	25
	(16) Personal services, including private households	22	6	13	4
	(17) Business services	1	1	2	2
	(18) Repair services	2	1	1	1
	(19) Entertainment and recreation	1	1	1	2
	(20) Professional and related services	12	12	19	16
	(21) Health services, including hospitals	6	4	8	5
	(22) Education	4	6	8	8
	(23) Other professional services	2	3	2	3
(24)	Public administration	5	5	7	6

Source: Current Population Survey, U.S. Department of Labor, unpublished data.

* Before 1967 the labor force includes Blacks 14 years and over. Later years refer to 16 and over.

** Approximately 89% of the Nonwhite population is black.

particular industries. In one of the lowest-paying industries (personal services, including households) there was a significant drop in overall employment, from 22 percent to 13 percent. Correspondingly, there was a sharp rise in the professional and related services subgroup. Twelve percent of all employed non-whites worked in these industries in 1972; by 1970, the figure was 19 percent. The two areas of employment growth within this subgroup were education and health services (including hospitals).[3] Other industries within this category remain virtually unchanged.

Finally, non-white employment declined significantly in agriculture. The trend that was evident in the 1950s continued throughout the 1960s and as a result fewer workers were located in the agricultural sector. This was true for both non-white and white workers.

These figures indicate that some blacks moved into labor markets that were characterized by higher paying jobs even though a substantial fraction of the work force was still primarily employed in service industries. Yet these trends did not necessarily occur only because of affirmative action programs or because of a lessening of individual or institutional racial discrimination. One important contributing factor was that the 1960s was a period of prosperity and rapid expansion of the employed labor force for both black and white workers.

The shift in the structure of black employment led to more blacks being employed in the manufacturing sector than prior to 1962. This shift did not get incorporated into many studies that were commissioned to examine the labor market status of blacks.[4] The failure to acknowledge this structural change means that research has been carried out that does not focus on the changing labor force patterns in manufacturing (while service employment remained relatively stable).

The pattern of employment that prevailed in the 1960s did not continue into the 1970s. During the 1960s one major area of employment growth for blacks was the manufacturing sector. However, manufacturing employment for blacks did not grow during the 1970s. Blacks employed in manufacturing accounted for 24 percent in 1972 and dropped slightly to 23 percent in 1980 (Table 12.2). Within the manufacturing sector, the decline occurred in motor vehicles and equipment. This is significant because this industry is characterized by higher wage levels than other industries. (The raw data indicates an absolute as well as a relative decline in employment between 1972 and 1980.)

The service sector continues in the 1970s to be the principal sector of employment for working blacks.[5] But some important changes occurred within this sector over the years. One, there has been a steady increase in employment in health services, including hospitals. This trend was also present during the 1960s and continues to be characteristic of black employment in the 1970s. In addition, three other industries employed more blacks in the 1970s: business

Table 12.2

Industry of the Employed Population: 1972, 1980
(percent)

			1972		1980	
			Black	White	Black	White
(1)	Agriculture, forestry & fisheries		4	4	2	4
(2)	Mining		-	1	-	1
(3)	Construction		6	7	5	7
(4)	Manufacturing		24	24	23	22
	(5)	Durable goods	14	14	13	14
		(6) Motor vehicles & equipment	2	1	1	1
		(6a) Other	12	13	12	13
	(7)	Non-durable goods	10	10	10	9
		(8) Food and kindred products	2	2	2	2
		(8a) Other	8	8	8	7
(9)	Transportation, communication and other public utilities		7	7	8	7
	(10)	Transportation	4	4	4	4
	(10a) Other		3	3	4	3
(11)	Wholesale trade		2	4	3	4
(12)	Retail trade		11	17	11	17
	(13)	Eating & drinking places	3	4	4	4
	(13a) Other		8	13	7	13
(14)	Finance, insurance and real estate		3	6	5	6
(15)	Service industries		36	26	36	28
	(16)	Personal services including private households	12	4	7	3
	(17)	Business services	2	2	3	2
	(18)	Repair services	1	1	1	2
	(19)	Entertainment and recreation	1	1	1	2
	(20)	Professional & related services	21	17	24	20
		(21) Health services, including hospitals	9	6	11	7
		(22) Education	9	8	10	8
		(23) Other professional services	3	4	4	4
(24)	Public administration		7	5	7	5

Source: Current Population Survey, U.S. Department of Labor, unpublished data.

Explaining Away Black Poverty

services, repair services and eating and drinking places. Together, these four industries accounted for 15 percent of black employment in 1972 and grew to 19 percent by 1980. The industry which experienced a sharp decline was personal services, including private households. Education also rose between 1972 and 1980 as did other professional services.[6]

This shift in these three sectors could be conceived of as positive if these jobs were characterized by high wages, better working conditions, or occupational advancement. But as Rothschild and others point out, these jobs tend to be precisely those that offer limited or nonexistent opportunities for advancement, low pay, and unstable employment. Furthermore, blacks moved from an occupation characterized by low wages (personal services) to other occupations (clerical and service workers) characterized by equally poor wages (Hedges and Mellor, 1979: 36).

One industry experiencing a relatively large increase in black employment in the 1970s was finance, insurance and real estate. While particular occupations within this industry are characterized by higher wages, the bulk of the black labor force was not employed in these particular occupations. Rather, blacks were employed as service workers and within the white collar groupings as clerical workers. Finally, it is important to recognize that a large share of the employed black clerical workforce is composed of black women rather than black men.

Employed whites also experienced a similar transformation in job prospects. White employment in the manufacturing sector had steadily declined from 27 percent in 1970 to 22 percent in 1980. Furthermore, the only growth area for any new labor entrants appears to be in the service sector.[7] Service employment has grown since 1970 and now accounts for 28 percent of the employed white labor force. Thus the service sector was the major area of growth for white workers in the 1970s, and its impact influenced employment trends for whites as well as blacks (Rothschild, 1981: 13).

For the 1972-80 period, it is possible to break down some of the data in Table 12.2 by occupational groupings: white-collar, blue-collar, and service occupations and sub-categories. In addition data is presented that shows the median usual weekly earnings of full-time wage and salary workers by occupational group. These figures are presented in Tables 12.3 - 12.8. Detailed breakdowns are given for the manufacturing sector, service sector (including private households), health services (including hospitals), retail trade, and finance, real estate and insurance.

Before we look at the occupational groupings of these industries, we can list those occupations that on the average can be characterized as having high (low) wages. Four occupational groupings are associated with high wages: professional and technical workers, managers and administrators, craft and kindred workers, and transport operatives. Low wages are associated with the following occupations: clerical, sales, factory operatives, nonfarm laborers,

Table 12.3

Median Usual Weekly Earnings of Full-Time Wage and Salary Workers, by Occupational Group and by Race, May 1978

Occupational Group	White	Black	Earnings of Blacks as a Percent of White
Managers and administrators (except farm)	$325	$281	86
Professional and technical workers	296	251	85
Craftworkers	283	237	84
Transport equipment operatives	260	200	77
Salesworkers	234	168	72
Nonfarm laborers	198	172	87
Operatives (except transport)	197	168	85
Clerical workers	174	182	105
Other service workers	155	141	91
Farmworkers	144	110	76
Private household workers	54	*	
TOTAL	$232	$181	78

Source: Hedges and Mellor, 1979, Table 3, p. 36.

Note: Hedges and Mellor also calculated median hourly earnings and stated that "Black men had median hourly earnings at least 95 percent those of white men in four of the six major occupational groups for which meaningful comparisons could be made: clerical workers, service workers, factory operatives and nonfarm laborers." The same was true for black women (excluding factory operatives), except that in some instances they earn more than white women (Hedges and Mellor, 1979, 38).

* Median not available.

and service workers. The difference in earnings is presented in Table 12.3. The data indicates that black workers consistently receive lower median earnings than whites in the same occupational group. The only two occupations (clerical and other service workers) where blacks receive comparable weekly earnings (especially when comparing blacks with white women, rather than comparing them with white men) are very low-paying occupations.

In the manufacturing industry the percentage of blacks employed as professional and technical workers rose over the years, as did the percentage for craft and kindred workers (Table 12.4). This trend indicates that even though employment slowed in manufacturing over the seventies (relative to other industries) blacks were able to make some in-roads into higher-paying occupations. At the same time there was a slight increase in managers and administrators and a slight decline in transport workers. Together, these four high wage groupings accounted for 22.3 percent of the employed labor force in 1972 and this rose to 26.5 percent in 1980. However, the majority of the workers within this industry remained located in the factory operative category which experienced a moderate decline over the years, but still accounted for slightly more than 50 percent of all workers in 1980. Finally, clerical workers grew between 1972 and 1980 while nonfarm labor declined.

The next industry examined is the service sector (Table 12.5). In general there have been important developments within this sector. The data indicates that there has been substantial growth in professional and technical workers, as well as a slight rise in the share of employed blacks who were classifed as managers and administrators. As will be shown shortly, this does not imply that more blacks are necessarily employed in higher-paying occupations. Other occupations that significantly changed within these groupings were clerical workers (increasing) and service workers (decreasing).[8] The former occupation is a major growth area for blacks across industries. Together, service and clerical workers account for close to 65 percent of all workers in this sector.

Table 12.6 presents data on health services (including hospitals). Earlier we stated that the health service sector was a major source of employment growth during the 1970s. Thus, this industry can be considered an important one in gauging the progress that blacks made in penetrating higher-paying occupations. From the figures, it appears that professional and technical workers experienced the largest growth over the years. In Table 12.5 this was represented as a substantial rise in professional and technical workers within the service sector in general. However, these numbers are somewhat misleading. In this occupational group (within this industry), there are several occupations where the differential in pay is quite drastic. This occupational group includes physicians, dentists, nurses, dieticians and therapists. While it is not possible to break down the data by particular occupation, nurses, dieticians and therapists are likely to comprise a majority of the workers in this industry rather

Table 12.4

Employed Blacks in Manufacturing by Occupational Group: 1972, 1980
(percent)

Total Employed = 100		1972	1980
(1)	White Collar	11.0	15.8
(2)	Professional and technical	2.6	4.3
(3)	Managers and administrators	0.9	1.6
(4)	Sales workers	0.4	0.6
(5)	Clerical	7.1	9.3
(6)	Blue Collar	84.0	80.1
(7)	Craft and kindred	12.6	15.6
(8)	Factory operative	53.8	51.3
(9)	Transport operative	6.2	5.0
(10)	Nonfarm labor	11.4	8.2
(11)	Service Workers	5.0	4.1

Source: Tables 12.4-12.8, see Table 12.1.

Table 12.5

Employed Blacks in Service Sector (including private household workers) by Occupational Group: 1972, 1980
(percent)

Total Employed = 100		1972	1980
(1)	White Collar	31.2	40.6
(2)	Professional and technical	17.6	22.0
(3)	Managers and administrators	2.6	3.6
(4)	Sales workers	-	-
(5)	Clerical	10.8	14.8
(6)	Blue Collar	11.4	11.0
(7)	Craft and kindred	2.7	3.4
(8)	Factory operative	4.4	3.8
(9)	Transport operative	1.1	1.1
(10)	Nonfarm labor	3.2	2.6
(11)	Service Workers	57.3	48.4

Table 12.6

Employed Blacks in Health Services (including Hospitals)
by Occupational Group: 1972, 1980
(percent)

Total Employed = 100		1972	1980
(1)	White Collar	25.0	34.6
(2)	Professional and technical	13.7	20.3
(3)	Managers and administrators	0.5	1.7
(4)	Sales workers	-	-
(5)	Clerical	9.9	12.4
(6)	Blue Collar	5.6	5.8
(7)	Craft and kindred	1.1	2.0
(8)	Factory operative	2.9	2.1
(9)	Transport operative	0.5	0.4
(10)	Nonfarm labor	1.1	1.2
(11)	Service Workers	69.4	59.7

than doctors and dentists. As Hedges and Mellor (1979: 35) point out, nursing is one of the lowest-paying occupations. The fact that nurses and dieticians account for a large share of the rise in professional and technical workers mitigates the impact this change in occupational groupings could have had on earnings. At the same time the percent of service workers significantly declined while the percent of clerical workers grew and all other categories remained about the same. Again, while service workers and clerical workers accounted for over 80 percent of the jobs of employed blacks in health services in 1972 and dropped to 70 percent in 1980, these occupational groupings still accounted for a substantial share of the employed work force.[9]

The occupational groupings of employed blacks in retail trade industries is reported in Table 12.7. In retail trade blacks did not do as well as in manufacturing in the seventies. There was virtually no change in professional and technical workers and only a slight increase in managers and administrators. The percentage of blacks who were classified as transport operatives and craft and kindred workers also declined slightly between 1972 and 1980. In addition, factory operatives decreased somewhat and sales workers increased slightly. However, the most important occupational grouping in this industry was clerical workers. Between 1972 and 1980 there was a sharp increase in the percent of blacks employed as clerical workers. Finally, even though there was a slight drop in the percent of blacks employed as service workers, this category still accounted for almost 30 percent of all workers within this industry in 1980. The data in Table 12.7 indicates that there have been no major inroads into high-paying occupations for blacks between 1972 and 1980 in this industry. The majority of workers are still employed in service-related occupations. Clerical employment was the only subgroup to increase over the years.

Another industry where black employment grew in this period was finance, insurance, and real estate (from three percent to five percent). However, employment growth within this industry did not lead to significant changes in occupational groupings (Table 12.8). While professional and technical workers and managers and administrators both experienced employment growth, the largest absolute increases occurred in the clerical category. This increase in clerical workers almost completely offset the equally sharp drop in service workers. In this group of industries some blacks were able to penetrate higher-paying occupations; however, most new workers in this industry could not, so that by 1980 over 70 percent of the workforce was still employed in service-oriented jobs. This is important because it implies that even though black employment grew sharply in this industry, the majority of blacks were unable to improve their income position by moving into higher-paying occupations.[10]

Table 12.7

Employed Blacks in Retail Trade by Occupational Group: 1972, 1980
(percent)

Total Employed = 100		1972	1980
(1)	White Collar	40.0	45.9
(2)	Professional and technical	0.7	0.9
(3)	Managers and administrators	9.8	10.7
(4)	Sales workers	14.4	15.4
(5)	Clerical	15.3	19.0
(6)	Blue Collar	29.0	24.5
(7)	Craft and kindred	6.2	5.9
(8)	Factory operative	7.5	5.4
(9)	Transport operative	5.6	4.4
(10)	Nonfarm labor	9.7	8.7
(11)	Service Workers	31.0	29.6

Table 12.8

Employed Blacks in Finance, Insurance and Real Estate
by Occupational Group: 1972, 1980
(percent)

Total Employed = 100		1972	1980
(1)	White Collar	67.2	80.0
(2)	Professional and technical	3.0	5.7
(3)	Managers and administrators	6.4	8.4
(4)	Sales workers	7.9	7.9
(5)	Clerical	49.8	57.7
(6)	Blue Collar	9.4	6.6
(7)	Craft and kindred	3.8	3.2
(8)	Factory operative	0.4	0.9
(9)	Transport operative	0.8	0.5
(10)	Nonfarm labor	4.5	2.0
(11)	Service Workers	23.3	13.8

CRITIQUE OF ALTERNATIVE MODELS

Historically analysts of black labor markets have approached the problems besetting blacks from different theoretical frameworks. Two dominant schools of thought have emerged -- human capital-oriented studies and the dual or segmented labor market approach. The bulk of the research carried out, however, tends to focus on neoclassical considerations such as the lessening of labor market discrimination and the degree of success associated with affirmative-action and government sponsored programs.[11]

It was not surprising, then, that in the 1960s many policy makers believed that blacks could only achieve economic gains (with respect to earnings and occupational advancement) if the government intervened legislatively. The intent of this legislation was to introduce a set of programs with rigid requirements (that lessen the likelihood of non-compliance) to reduce the gap between white and black earnings and occupational status. Almost all of the proponents of these programs believed that the labor market problems faced by black Americans could be accounted for by the effects of labor market discrimination and insufficient investments in human capital. Thus, one of the thrusts of the Great Society programs and the Civil Rights Act was to provide more training programs, more funds for educational programs to upgrade marketable skills and the promulgation of affirmative action programs in industry and government.

These programs generally centered on changing either the worker, or the job environment. One of the first programs used for these purposes was the Manpower Development and Training Act (MDTA). This set of programs was initially intended for retraining workers who had experienced job displacement because of automation. Some analysts argue that there was a considerable difference in the intent and functioning of these programs over time. The major difference was in the types of programs designed to deal with the economically disadvantaged and trainees from different socio-economic backgrounds. In addition, by 1966, the original act had been amended (in conjunction with the renewed interest in the poverty characteristics of the War on Poverty programs) to focus these training programs more specifically on the economically disadvantaged. This institutional training (mainly classroom oriented programs) continued until the early 1970s when CETA took over these programs (Kiefer, 1978: 111).

It is important to remember that these programs were designed to reduce the human capital gap between white and black workers (as well as other minorities) who possessed limited marketable skills. By preparing workers for better paying jobs by generally upgrading their skills, these programs attempted to make blacks and other workers more attractive to potential employers. Theoretically, then, employers would not tend to discriminate against such workers, assuming their skill levels corresponded to similarly qualified white men.

Numerous studies have been carried out that analyzed the MDTA programs operating in the 1960s and into the mid-1970s.[12] This research evaluated these employment and training programs by conventional criteria: income, occupational status, number of weeks employed, etc. For example, Corcoran and Duncan (1979) found that skill-acquisition programs alone could not reduce the earnings gap between white males and blacks, minorities and women. That is, equally productive workers were not necessarily paid equally. Other research has found that the impact of MDTA on male trainees was quite limited (if not non-existent) in two areas: employment and earnings. In effect, the trainees would have been better off, relatively speaking, if they had not participated in these programs and had instead continued to work in their former occupations. Furthermore, the study indicated that "It is therefore unlikely that training had any positive effect on the earnings of blacks. Indeed, trainees who stayed in the mean length of time seem to have experienced a relative decline in their weekly earnings." (Kiefer, 1978: 123).

Another program that was designed to upgrade skills, provide job placement, education and subsidize employment (to reduce the number of people on welfare) was WIN (Work Incentive Program). Unlike many other manpower training programs, this program enrolled mostly women and was geared only to AFDC recipients (of which a disproportionate number were blacks). A study carried out to assess this program found some blacks gaining from WIN programs. However, the average gain for blacks was far less than the average gain for whites. In fact, the income status of some blacks fell as a result of participation in the program. Some of the reasons why blacks experienced a relative drop in income as a result of these programs were that they

> ...probably experienced some discrimination by personnel who run programs... rational program administrators will exercise greater caution in placing Blacks in subsidized employment by matching them more closely to job requirement. The result is less upgrading for Blacks... and a smaller net income.... Whatever the actual explanation for observed racial differences... outright exclusion or more restricted access... the consequence of WIN program activities to date... [are] falling relative incomes.

Despite these findings for blacks, the study concluded "... that specific employment services, particularly on-the-job training and public service employment, can deliver impressive microeconomic benefits." (Schiller, 1978: 212, 216, 217)

Contrary to neoclassical interpretations of black labor markets, segmentation theorists argue that labor market discrimination and gaps in human capital oriented variables may persist in some forms but that historical and institutional factors are more decisive in determining why blacks are located in particular labor markets (Kerr, 1954; Piore, 1970, 1974, 1975, 1979; Doeringer and Piore, 1971; Reich, Gordon and Edwards, 1973).

Central to this research is the extent to which labor market conditions have changed historically for blacks and other minorities. Segmentation theorists argue that human-capital oriented explanations that stress that insufficient human capital investments account for the lag in income and occupational gains miss the important change in the structure of labor markets. Instead of looking at gaps in human capital variables, they argue that more emphasis should be placed on the principal division in labor markets between workers who participate in primary markets and those who work in secondary markets.

Different criteria are used by these theorists to define primary and secondary labor markets: median income, job characteristics, arbitrary judgement, industrial characteristics, economic sectors, etc. The above criteria indicate that segmented markets can be classified in many ways and that such classifications are needed to understand why certain workers are located in particular labor markets and occupations. Furthermore, other segmentation theorists have argued that it is difficult for workers in secondary labor markets to experience a change in their status to primary labor market workers because "... educational training, and geographic relocations are in themselves insufficient to enable workers to make the transition.." from secondary to primary labor market status. (Harrison and Sum, 1979: 693)[13]

Research in segmented labor markets has focused on refuting theoretical and empirical findings that deny or downplay the significance of structural differences in labor markets. The evidence presented earlier, on the increased importance of the service sector, adds another dimension to the structural problem blacks face in the labor market.

It is beyond the scope of this paper to explore all of the implications that emphasizing service occupations and industries has on segmentation theory. However, we suggest below some of the theoretical and empirical issues that need to be examined in further research.

It was noted earlier that service employment has grown quite rapidly in low-paying service-oriented occupations (including clerical workers) compared to high-paying ones. The growth of low-paying service-oriented jobs has increased the institutional rigidity of American capitalism that was already present in the past, further limiting black employment possibilities. Segmentation theorists, however, have not typically focused on the importance of the service sector but have placed increased importance on grouping jobs in either primary (or subdivisions within this segment) or secondary employment labor markets. While such analytical distinctions have yielded fruitful results, future research will have to account for why a large segment of blacks both continue to be paid poorly <u>and</u> are located in service industries and occupations. We elaborate on this point below.

Segmentation theorists have argued that job mobility from secondary to primary status is unlikely to occur because labor markets are individually defined. In certain industries this appears to be the situation. Low wage sales workers, for example, in the fast food restaurant industry, may be mired in secondary jobs with little possibility of experiencing job mobility. Yet every industry has different characteristics and different requirements for workers to experience occupational mobility. That is, whether occupational mobility is likely or unlikely within each industry (and in some cases by firm) needs to be examined separately within the industry's particular definitions of occupations. Thus one area of research that needs to be examined is to what extent service workers in particular low wage service industries have as much or less occupational mobility as do other low wage service workers (including clerical workers) in manufacturing. One recent study by Rumberger and Carnoy (1980) did find that there were some positive economic rewards associated with vocational training and with being married. Workers with these characteristics were found to have stronger attachments to secondary labor markets as well as higher earnings compared with other secondary workers. In addition, black workers in primary markets were found to face labor market conditions similar to the conditions faced by all secondary workers. Over time, the study indicates that "blacks also experienced downward mobility in primary independent jobs" (very skilled workers). (Rumberger and Carnoy, 1980: 122)

The research mentioned above suggests that segmentation theorists need to be more careful and clearer in defining the differences within and between primary and secondary labor markets. In addition they should look more closely at how different industries have developed different job structure systems with various job ladders that make it difficult to distinguish between primary and secondary workers. Regardless, segmentation theorists have contributed important insights on how labor markets function in contemporary capitalism. Future research should incorporate their insights with the role that service occupations and industries play in limiting the likelihood of job mobility.

CONCLUSION

The previous discussion indicates that in the last twenty years, except for the manufacturing sector, blacks did not gain access to very many high-paying jobs. Despite relatively more blacks being employed than ever before, the jobs and industries they tended to work in were not ones that promoted occupational advancement. For employed black workers there existed a continually large and growing number of jobs in service-related occupations that were relatively poorly paid compared with other occupations.

A quick perusal of a variety of journals and magazine articles indicates that a considerable amount of money and effort has been expended on evaluating why blacks are in poorly paid occupations. Academically authored articles and ad hoc news reports attest to the degree of confusion concerning the plight of the employed black workforce (including the black middle class and unemployed blacks). What can be said of these research efforts? First, one major reason why so many neoclassical studies have failed to even acknowledge that service employment and/or segmented labor markets are key factors in understanding the pattern of black employment, is probably accounted for by well defined ideological and political differences among neoclassical and radical economists in interpreting the evidence. These differences do not appear to be minor; they revolve around fundamental differences in emphasis with respect to the job structure system and the structure of the economic system. Neoclassical economists generally believe that the job structure system is flexible and open and therefore job mobility and the potential to experience higher earnings are characteristics of the fluidity of U.S. labor markets. It follows from this analysis that the present economic system needs to be left alone and these economists accept any rigidities within the system as essentially impregnable. Attempts to improve the potential for job mobility for employed blacks would lead, according to this view, to confusion and a misallocation of resources. Current legislative and Reagan administrative proposals to reduce the number of government sponsored or supported policy alternatives for blacks (and others) are geared towards having these workers rely more upon market forces. They assume that labor market discrimination considerations are irrelevant. Alternatively, radical economists believe that the institutional rigidity of the job structure system as well as differential job ladders by industry and firm makes the economic system considerably less flexible than neoclassical economists think it is.

Second, if proponents of human-capital theories fully acknowledged and accepted the alternative framework (service sector employment within a context of segmented labor markets), this would imply a change in the kind of policy prescriptions presented. This would mean that the historical reliance upon training and educational support programs initiated by liberal-oriented neoclassical economists would have to be radically altered. This does not mean that training programs emphasizing specific skill training would necessarily have to be scrapped. However, blacks and others being trained in such programs would have to be presented with a different set of incentives to avoid being placed in jobs which tend to be characterized by lower wages and less mobility than other occupations. New programs and policy initiatives would be required that are cognizant of the market realities facing blacks who seek employment. Within the context of the present set of policy and legislative goals outlined by the Reagon Administration, the likelihood of such programs emerging is bleak.

The neoclassical framework used to formulate a large amount of the poverty research on labor market conditions for blacks has had the unfortunate result of not acknowledging that the probability of successful economic achievement in this society is constrained. One constraining factor on blacks experiencing occupational mobility is the limited number of high-paying jobs currently available.[14] Also, different job structures within and among industries (as well as service employment) limit the number of high-paying jobs potentially feasible under the present economic system. Other factors such as geographic differences, private vs. public employment, quality and quantity of education, etc., have been discussed elsewhere in more detail. In the end, what this research signifies is that neoclassical explanations on how to solve labor market problems for blacks tend to be historically abstract and theoretically inconsistent. Concrete solutions, just like more high-paying jobs, remain difficult to find within the limits imposed by American capitalism.

NOTES

1. Some recent segmentation studies have focused on occupational and industrial divisions within the labor force. These studies analyze occupation and industrial segments at the same time to determine the effects of labor market discrimination on potential earnings. (Edwards, 1979; Rumberger and Carnoy, 1980; Reich, 1981).
2. No reliable data is available on black employment by industry prior to 1972. Other studies have used the non-white category as an appropriate proxy for changes in the occupational structure of the black labor force. While this presents certain data questions about the reliability of the generalizations being made, this study also considers the non-white category as a reasonable (although imperfect) indicator of changes in the black occupational structure.
3. Another important indicator of occupational changes would be the occupational distribution for race-sex groups within the service sector. Because of space limitations this data is not reported in this article but is available from the author.
4. Emphasis on changes in aggregate demand have been stressed by some economists (e.g., Thurow, 1969), but they have failed to couple these changes with changes in industrial categories, the job structure system, and more importantly, the tremendous growth in clerical and service-oriented jobs.
5. One important issue that is not explored in this paper is that while low-paying service sector employment is overwhelmingly characteristic of employed blacks to some extent irrespective of sex, the same cannot be said about whites. White males are

more likely to be in high-paying jobs while white women are more likely to be in low-paying occupations (Bluestone and Stevenson, 1980).

6. The number of non-whites employed in education-related areas rose sharply between 1962 and 1970 and then much slower between 1972 and 1980 (later years for blacks). No data is available to break down this category before 1972 to see how many non-whites were teachers, teachers' aides, librarians, etc. This data would be useful because there is a sizable difference in earnings associated with each of these sub-categories. Regardless, it is probably safe to assume that the majority of the new labor entrants were teachers during the 1960s and that their earnings rose considerably over the years. If this is accurate, it lends more evidence to the notion that segments of the service sector also contributed to the growth of the black middle-class and hence these numbers are not surprising.

7. The growth of service sector employment, however, has had different effects on white males versus white females. Unfortunately, the previously presented data cannot be broken down by sex at this time. We recognize that sex distinctions are important in understanding why a specific sexual division of labor has emerged where white women are more likely to be employed in low-paying occupations similar to black women and quite different than white men.

8. It is not surprising that service workers -- security guards, janitors, etc. -- experienced a decline in employment between 1972 and 1980. These jobs within the service sector were growing at a decreasing rate in most industries compared with the rise in the number of jobs for employed blacks in clerical occupations.

9. Men and women have different occupational profiles by race that is obscured by this data. Black women have shifted into clerical work and their occupational and earnings profile is now more similar to white women. However, both groups have failed to make progress with respect to white men (Beck, Horan and Tolbert, 1980; Hedges and Mellor, 1979: 36).

10. Two other industrial groupings experienced important changes over the years: educational services and business and repair services (two separate categories in Tables 12.1 and 12.2). During the 1960s education was a major growth area for employed blacks (see note 6). Growth continued in the 1970s but the occupational groupings remained virtually unchanged in the seventies. The bulk of the workers in this industry were either employed as teachers (professional and technical workers, 43.6 in 1972 and 42.2 in 1980) or as clerical and/or service workers (summed, 47.5 in 1972 and 47.4 in 1980). Thus, whatever inroads were achieved within the occupational structure in the 1960s they have not continued in the seventies.

Another area of growth within the service sector in the seventies has been business and repair services. It is useful to see if the number of blacks in high-paying jobs within these occupational groupings has changed since 1972. In these industries there has been a moderate increase in professional and technical workers (5.4 in 1972 and 6.8 in 1980) and managers and administrators (3.4 to 4.3, respectively). At the same time there has been a sharp decline in craft and kindred (22.0 to 18.8) and a large increase in clerical workers (15.1 to 18.5). Both transport and nonfarm labor declined and service workers remained unchanged over the years. The figures indicate that no significant inroads into higher paying jobs have been made in this industry and that over 50% of the workforce were employed in two categories that are characteristic of a substantial fraction of the employed black workforce, namely, clerical and service workers.

11. Neoclassical theorists who emphasize human-capital variables have explored these issues from the following perspectives: (1) that discrimination may be present but its effects are limited (Welch, 1967; Smith and Welch, 1977); (2) that discrimination depends on whether people have a "taste for discrimination" or on employers' perceptions of reality (Becker, 1971; Arrow, 1972, 1974); and (3) that industry and government-wide programs (affirmative action and manpower oriented) have had either a lot or a little effect on the occupational/earnings structure of black Americans (Freeman, 1973; Butler and Heckman, 1977; Beller, 1978; King, 1978). It is beyond the scope of this paper to present all of the different perspectives and themes neoclassical economists emphasize when discussing the problems blacks face in labor markets. Clear and insightful reviews of these theories and similar ones have been carried out by like-minded economists such as Marshall (1974, 1979) and Cain (1976), and from a non-neoclassical perspective by Harrison (1972), Harrison and Sum (1979), Rumberger and Carnoy (1980), and Reich (1981).

12. Other studies in the 1960s focused on the extent to which discrimination limited job prospects for blacks in different industries. They concentrated on reviewing the status of black workers in unionized sectors compared with non-unionized ones and demonstrated how difficult it was for blacks to gain union status and union work (Marshall, 1965; Marshall and Briggs, 1967; Ross and Hill 1967; Northrup, 1968a, 1968b).

13. In 1972 some economists recommended in Senate hearings that public service employment programs (such as CETA) be implemented for the purpose of placing disadvantaged workers into positions where they could seek employment in primary labor markets (Harrison, 1974: 26). Though it is difficult to know what impact these hearings had on the eventual passage

of CETA legislation, it is likely that this poverty research influenced policy makers.

14. High paying jobs are not the only problem. One recent study argued that welfare programs have failed to reduce poverty and that previously utilized training programs are not appropriate to solve today's problems. One of the main problems, structural unemployment, would still persist if the economy were to be at a full employment level. The only inroads against the incidence of poverty have been the growth of increase in cash and in-kind transfer payments (Danziger, Garfinkel, and Haveman, 1979). In addition there are many other structural problems that limit the potential for a capitalist country to solve these problems. These have been explored in Castels (1980) and Reich (1981). For another view, see Thurow (1975).

REFERENCES

Arrow, K.J. (1972) "Models of Job Discrimination" and "Some Models of Race in the Labor Market," Chapters II and VI in Pascal, A.H., ed., Racial Discrimination in Economic Life (Lexington, MA: D.C. Heath).
_____ (1974) "The Theory of Discrimination" in Ashenfelter, O., and Rees, A., eds., Discrimination in Labor Markets (Princeton: Princeton University Press).
Beck, E.M., Horan, P.M., and Tolbert, C.M. (1980) "Industrial Segmentation and Labor Market Discrimination," Social Problems, 28 (No. 2): 113-130.
Becker, G.S. (1971) The Economics of Discrimination, 2nd Ed. (Chicago: University of Chicago Press).
Beller, A.H. (1978) "The Economics of Enforcement of an Antidiscrimination Law: Title VII of the Civil Rights Act of 1964," The Journal of Law and Economics, 21: 359-80.
Bluestone, B. and Stevenson, M. (1980) "Industrial Transformation and the Evolution of Dual Labor Markets: the Case of Retail Trade in the United States," unpublished.
Butler, R. and Heckman, J. (1977) "The Government's Impact on the Labor Market Status of Black Americans: a Critical Review," in Hausmann, L.J., et al. (eds.), Equal Rights and Industrial Relations (Madison, Wisconsin: Industrial Relations Research Association).
Cain, G.C. (1976) "The Challenge of Segmented Labor Market Theories to Orthodox Theory: a Survey," Journal of Economic Literature, XIV (No. 4): 1215-1257.
Castels, M. (1980) The Economic Crisis and American Society (Princeton: Princeton University Press).
Corcoran, M. and Duncan, G.J. (1979) "Work History, Labor Force Attachment, and Earning Differences Between the Races and Sexes," Journal of Human Resources, 14 (No. 1): 3-20.

Danziger, S., Garfinkel, I., and Haveman, R. (1979) "Poverty, Welfare, and Earnings: a New Approach," Challenge, September/October.
Doeringer, P. and Piore, M.J. (1971) Internal Labor Markets and Manpower Analysis (Lexington, MA: D.C. Heath).
Edwards, R. (1979) Contested Terrain (New York: Harper and Row).
Freeman, R.B. (1973) "Changes in the Labor Market for Black Americans, 1948-72," Brookings Paper on Economic Activity, No. 1: 67-120.
Harrison, B. (1972) Education, Training, and the Urban Ghetto (Baltimore: The Johns Hopkins University Press).
_____ (1974) "Ghetto Economic Development, a Survey," Journal of Economic Literature, 12 (No. 1): 1-37.
_____ and Sum, A. (1979) "The Theory of 'Dual' or Segmented Labor Markets," Journal of Economic Issues, 13 (No. 3): 687-706.
Hedges, J.N. and Mellor, E.F. (1979) "Weekly and Hourly Earnings of U.S. Workers, 1967-1978," Monthly Labor Review, August, pp. 31-41.
Kerr, C. (1954) "The Balkanization of Labor Markets," in Bakke, E.W., et al., Labor Mobility and Economic Opportunity (Cambridge: MIT Press).
Kiefer, N.M. (1978) "Federally Subsidized Occupational Training and the Employment and Earnings of Male Trainees," Journal of Econometrics, 8 (No. 1): 111-125.
King, A. (1978) "Labor Market Discrimination Against Black Women," Review of Black Political Economy, 8 (No. 4): 325-335.
Mandle, J. (1978) The Roots of Black Poverty: The Southern Plantation Economies After the Civil War (Durham: Duke University Press).
Marshall, R. (1965) The Negro and Organized Labor (New York: John Wiley and Sons).
_____ and Briggs, V. (1967) The Negro and Apprenticeship (Baltimore: The Johns Hopkins University Press).
_____ (1974) "The Economics of Racial Discrimination: a Survey," Journal of Economic Literature, 12 (No. 3): 849-871.
_____ (1979) "Implications of Labor Market Theory for Employment Policy," in Swanson, G.I. and Michaelson, J. (eds.), Manpower Research and Labor Economics (Beverly Hills: Sage).
Northrup, H.R. (1968a) The Negro in the Automobile Industry (Philadelphia: University of Pennsylvania Press).
_____ (1968b) The Negro in the Aerospace Industry (Philadelphia: University of Pennsylvania Press).
Oaxaca, R.L. (1977) "Theory and Measurement in the Economics of Discrimination" in Hausman, L.J., et al. (eds.), Equal Rights and Industrial Relations (Madison, Wisconsin: Industrial Relations Research Association).
O'Connor, J. (1973) The Fiscal Crisis of the State (New York: St. Martins Press).

Piore, M.J. (1970) "Jobs and Training," in Beer, S. and Barringer, R. (eds.), The State and the Poor (Cambridge, MA: Winthrop Publishers).

_____ (1974) "Primary and Secondary Labor Markets: A Critique of the Dual Approach: Comment," Brookings Paper on Economic Activity, No. 3: 684-688.

_____ (1975) "Notes for a Theory of Labor Market Stratification," in Edwards, et al. (eds.), Labor Market Segmentation (Lexington, MA: D.C. Heath).

_____ (1979) "Conceptualization of Labor Market Reality," in Swanson, G.I. and Michaelson, J., (eds.) Manpower Research and Labor Economics (Beverly Hills: Sage).

Reich, M., Gordon, D.M., Edwards, R.C. (1973) "A Theory of Labor Market Segmentation," American Economic Review, 63, (No. 2): 358-365.

Reich, M. (1981) Racial Inequality (Princeton: Princeton University Press).

Ross, A.H. and Hill, H. (eds.) (1967) Employment, Race and Poverty (New York: Harcourt, Brace and World).

Rothschild, E. (1981) "Reagan and the Real America," New York Review of Books, February.

Rumberger, R.W. and Carnoy, M. (1980) "Segmentation in the U.S. Labour Market: Its Effects on the Mobility and Earnings of Whites and Blacks," Cambridge Journal of Economics, No. 4: 117-132.

Schiller, B.R. (1978) "The Pay-off to Training for Blacks: the WIN Experience," Review of Black Political Economy, 8 (No.2): 211-217.

Smith, J.P. and Welch, F.R. (1977) "Black-White Male Ratios: 1960-1970," American Economic Review, 67 (No. 3): 323-338.

Thurow, Lester (1969) Poverty and Discrimination (Washington: Brookings Institution).

_____ (1975) Generating Inequality (New York: Basic Books).

Welch, F. (1967) "Labor Market Discrimination: an Interpretation of Income Differences in the Rural South," Journal of Political Economy, 75 (No. 3): 225-240.

USES OF MICROSIMULATION IN APPLIED POVERTY RESEARCH

David Betson
David Greenberg

The tools for conducting empirical analyses of tax and transfer policies have become increasingly sophisticated in recent years. These tools include conceptual models of behavioral responses to tax and transfer programs, statistical techniques for measuring these behavioral responses, large micro-data files containing detailed information on representative samples of the nation's households, experiments and demonstrations to pilot-test proposed changes in policy, and microsimulation models. The development of microsimulation is particularly interesting because at its best this technique incorporates elements of all the other tools just mentioned in a way that makes it possible to predict the national costs and effects of proposed changes in tax and transfer policy. Microsimulation has been particularly useful for assessing the implications of proposals for changing the nation's welfare system.

Although several different microsimulation models have been used to predict the costs and effects of proposed alternatives to the existing welfare system, the most recently developed such model is known as the KGB model and was constructed within the Office of Income Security Policy of the Assistant Secretary for Planning and Evaluation within the U.S. Department of Health and Human Services. This model (which was named after its developers: Richard Kasten, David Greenberg and David Betson) uses micro-data on a representative sample of the nation's households to simulate the effects and costs of substantial changes in existing tax and transfer programs, including the guaranteeing of jobs. The model treats various interactions among transfer programs, public jobs programs, and the positive tax system, allowing for adjustments in work effort that result from different combinations of these programs. Over the last several years, the KGB model has been used extensively within the government to evaluate various welfare reform proposals, including the Carter Administration's 1977 Welfare Reform Proposal -- the Program for Better Jobs and Income. The KGB microsimulation model has also been used by both academic and government economists to conduct a substantial number of research projects.

This paper examines the use of microsimulation as a tool in applied poverty research, illustrating its use by focusing on the KGB model. The paper is divided into three major sections. The first provides a brief history of the development of microsimulation for purposes of analyzing anti-poverty strategies. A nontechnical description of how the KGB model operates appears in the second section. The third section describes some of the research and policy issues that have been examined with the KGB model. In illustrating various uses of the KGB model, particular attention is paid to those instances in which microsimulation has actually affected policy formulation in the anti-poverty area.

THE DEVELOPMENT OF MICROSIMULATION MODELS FOR ANALYSIS OF WELFARE ISSUES

Major Components of Microsimulation Models

For purposes of simulating welfare reform proposals, a fully-developed model should contain four component parts. The first of these, and indeed the starting point for virtually all microsimulations of proposed changes in the welfare system, is the ability to characterize the existing circumstances of representative individuals or households. This ability is mainly derived by using a high-speed computer to apply the rules and regulations of current tax and transfer programs to the characteristics of individual households, as reported in a nationally representative sample survey, and then computing these household's tax and transfer payments in a manner similar to the way they are actually calculated by the agencies administering these programs. In the second microsimulation component, a new regime (such as a new transfer program) is imposed and, given the new rules, the circumstances of the representative sample of households are recomputed. Comparisons of these altered circumstances with the pre-reform circumstances describe the initial, "first-round" effects of the new regime.

Until very recently, most microsimulations of welfare reform proposals stopped upon completion of the two steps just outlined. However, imposition of a new welfare regime will alter the framework underlying the economic decisions of those directly affected by the changes in programs; for example, because welfare programs affect the income level and tax rates of recipients, the work incentives of such persons may be influenced. Consequently, affected individuals may adjust facets of their behavior, such as the hours they work, in response to the new regime. This, in turn, will affect the costs and effectiveness of the new programs. Furthermore, other actors who are not directly affected by imposition of the new regime, such as employers, may nevertheless respond to behavioral adjustments, such as changes in labor supply, made by those who are directly impacted. Thus, the third and fourth components of a microsimulation model should take account of behavioral adjustments to the new regime by those who are directly affected and by those who are indirectly affected. To do this, microsimulation models must incorporate empirical estimates of response parameters that are imbedded within realistic theoretical constructs concerning household and individual behavior. Such behavioral response parameters can be obtained from previous empirical research in the social sciences, including that based on the various social experiments conducted in recent years; appropriate theoretical constructs are found in the corpus of social science theory.

Predecessors of the KGB Model

Efforts to construct simulation models that could be used for analysis of welfare programs began in the mid-1960s,[1] with the first government-sponsored effort leading to development of the RIM model at the President's Commission on Income Maintenance Programs.[2] This model was used during the late 1960s and early 1970s to estimate the cost of the Nixon Administration's Family Assistance Program and other proposed welfare reforms. RIM, however, consisted of only the first two of the microsimulation elements described above. That is, RIM essentially was a complex accounting mechanism that did not allow for possible behavioral responses to changes in existing programs.[3] In addition, RIM was used to attempt to accommodate an ever wider variety of purposes over the years and eventually became so large it was computationally unwieldly.

As a consequence of RIM's computational limitations, a redesigned, more modular version of RIM, known as TRIM, was developed in the early 1970s at the Urban Institute. TRIM has been used extensively by numerous government agencies (including the Congressional Budget Office, the Food and Nutrition Service, the Federal Energy Administration, the Treasury Department, and the Department of Health and Human Services) to examine a wide variety of tax and transfer policy issues. TRIM consists of a series of computer modules that apply the rules and regulations associated with various tax and transfer programs to the characteristics of households from a sample survey and calculate program outcomes. Proposed programs can be examined by simply allowing for changes in the rules and regulations by programming these changes into the various computer modules.[4] Like its predecessor RIM, however, TRIM does not take account of potential behavioral adjustments to these changes.

Variants of the TRIM Model are also found at Mathematica Policy Research, where the model is known as MATH, and at SRI International, where it is known as TATSIM. Since the different versions of TRIM are used by different groups of researchers and programmers, they have increasingly developed along divergent paths. For example, the Urban Institute, Mathematica, and SRI have all conducted independent reprogramming efforts on TRIM in recent years to make their versions more computationally efficient. Moreover, modules have very recently been added to the Mathematica and SRI variants of TRIM to allow for labor supply responses of transfer recipients to changes in income maintenance policy. As yet, however, none of the TRIM variants take account of possible "second-round" responses by political institutions, employers, and others -- the fourth of the microsimulation components discussed above.

The KGB Model

The KGB model was very much a child of necessity. It was developed in direct response to early Carter Administration welfare reform initiatives. Work on the model began soon after the Carter Administration took office, when it became clear that a welfare reform plan that combined a cash transfer program with a substantial public employment program was under serious consideration. Although the existing TRIM model and its variants could simulate reforms of the nation's cash transfer programs, a model did not exist at that time that could simulate a welfare reform package that combined cash programs with job programs.

Because information about the costs and effects of various combinations of cash and jobs was urgently needed so that major decisions about the Administration's welfare reform plan could be made, an intensive effort was initiated to develop the model as quickly as possible. The first usable output from the model was produced within about a month from the time its development began. As might be imagined, the earliest versions of the model were quite cumbersome, requiring over 8,000 individual steps and costing around $1,000 for a typical run that used the full data base. Since then, the model has been considerably streamlined and is now less than one-fifth as expensive to operate. The model has been improved in numerous other respects as well. Nevertheless, considerable important work remains to be done.

The speed with which the model was developed was only possible because many of the ingredients essential to it already existed. For example, high speed computer technology and survey data on representative households, which are prerequisites to any microsimulation effort, had been available for some time.[5] Moreover, certain existing modules from TRIM could be readily adopted for use in the KGB model. For example, as mentioned earlier, the Mathematica and SRI variants of the TRIM model allow for the fact that since transfer programs affect the tax rates and income levels of recipients, they would be expected to influence the work effort of these persons. The behavioral response parameter estimates that are used for this purpose were computed from data from the Seattle and

Denver Income Maintenance Experiments, a pilot test of alternative income transfer plans within a controlled experimental setting (Keeley, et al., 1978). The TRIM-type module developed to incorporate these parameters (which will be described in the next section) was subsequently modified and adopted for use in the KGB model.

Although in some instances appropriate TRIM modules were available for use in the KGB module, in other cases they were not, and it was necessary for the developers of KGB to construct their own. For example, as already suggested, TRIM and its variants did not have the capacity to simulate jobs programs; but a method of doing this was necessary for evaluating the Carter Administration's welfare reform initiatives. Fortunately, work on such a methodology had proceeded independently of TRIM and was completed in 1977 (Greenberg, 1978). After suitable modification, this methodology was incorporated into the KGB model. In simulating jobs programs, the Seattle-Denver behavioral response parameters are once again used to allow for adjustments in work effort, since, similar to transfer programs, jobs programs affect the wage rates and income levels of participants and, consequently, would be expected to influence their work incentives.

Somewhat uniquely, the KGB model also provides for some considerations of the demand side of the labor market. For example, the model attempts to allow for the fact that employers will retain some low-wage workers who would otherwise enter a public jobs program by raising the wages of these persons sufficiently to compete with the jobs program. In addition, the model has been used to examine the extent to which adverse effects on work effort that are initially induced by implementation of new income transfer plans might be partially ameliorated through "second-round" responses by employers and the unemployed (Greenberg, 1980).

The KGB model has also been used in conjunction with another microsimulation model -- the RESIND Model -- to simulate some of the distribution implications of the Carter Administration's Program for Better Jobs and Income (Haveman, et al., 1980). This simulation may be viewed as consisting of two stages. In the first stage, the KGB model was used to simulate the *net* change in the disposable incomes of households that would be attributable to the program, given predictions about family decisions on whether or not to participate in the public employment component of the program and on adjustments in hours of work by different household members. The second stage of the simulation, which was conducted by means of the RESIND Model, predicted how net changes in income would alter the level and composition of consumption spending. The model then traced the effects of these changes in consumption spending on the demands for goods and services produced by various industries and regions and ultimately on the derived demand for various categories of workers. Thus, by combining the KGB and the RESIND Model, it was possible to conduct a simulation that rather thoroughly incorporated all four of the microsmulation components discussed above.

In the next section of this paper, we provide a description of how the KGB model actually operates. First, however, it may be useful to briefly reconsider the progress that has been made in simulating welfare reform initiatives. Until the late 1960s, consideration of the costs and effects of such initiatives was mainly limited to fairly crude, "back of the envelope" calculations. Although the emergence of RIM and its successor, TRIM, permitted much more sophisticated analysis, these early microsimulation models did not allow for behavioral adjustments to changes in the welfare system and, consequently, were little more than large, complex accounting mechanisms. In the last several years, however, microsimulation models have exploited results from the Seattle and Denver Income Maintenance Experiments in a manner that permits analysts to account for the potential effects of simulated transfer programs on work incentives. This was an important step because it meant that findings from Seattle and Denver could be extrapolated to the nation as a whole and to transfer programs other than those directly tested in the experiment. By permitting this, microsimulation became a bridge between basic research, such as that represented by the Seattle-Denver Experiment, and policy analysis.

Development of the KGB model entailed at least two additional innovations. First the model takes at least some account of responses to changes in welfare policy by nonrecipients of welfare transfers and, hence, was the first of the models used to analyze welfare reform initiatives that contained elements of all four of the basic microsimulation components listed at the beginning of this section. Second, the model was the first to simulate jobs programs as well as transfer programs. To do this, moreover, estimates of work responses from the Seattle-Denver Experiment were used. Thus, empirical results derived from examining one policy (transfer programs) were utilized to analyze another policy (jobs programs).

THE KGB SIMULATION MODEL[6]

The KGB microsimulation model -- which, as previously noted, was expressly designed to examine alternative reforms of the tax-transfer system, including the provision of public employment programs -- proceeds in four major steps:

1. Characterization of U.S. population in absence of reform,
2. Characterization of the reform of policy interest,
3. Prediction of how individuals would alter their hours of work in response to the reform, and
4. Prediction of which eligible individuals would enter Public Sector Employment (PSE).

Characterization of the Pre-Reform Population

In the first KGB step, the Survey of Income and Education (SIE) is used to characterize the pre-reform economic status of a representative sample of the nation's families in 1975. The SIE is a large micro data base containing various detailed demographic and economic information (such as family size, composition, earnings, and hours worked) on over 175,000 households. Although many of the variables needed for use in the model appear in the SIE, others such as the receipt of benefits from government programs must be imputed to the data base from other sources of information. Currently, the list of existing government programs explicitly considered by the model include AFDC, SSI, Food Stamps, General Assistance, Unemployment Compensation, Federal and State Income taxes, and payroll taxes. Upon completion of this first step, the model will have characterized each SIE household's first pre-reform economic status in terms of its disposable income and the net return from work (the net wage rate) received by its members.

The Impact of the Reform in the Absence of Any Behavioral Adjustment

In the second step, the values of net wage rates and disposable income are adjusted to what they would be were the simulated reform measure implemented, but work effort and earnings remained unchanged. For workers who are eligible for a public service employment job, it is necessary to compute what these values would be if: (1) the worker leaves the regular labor market to take a public employment job (which is characterized as the "pure strategy"); (2) he remains attached to the regular job sector and takes a public employment job only when he is unemployed (the "mixed strategy"); or (3) he does not participate in public employment at all (the "private strategy").

Prediction of Labor Supply Adjustments to Implementation of the Reform

The model's third step consists of adjusting the values of the post-reform variables to account for labor supply responses to changes in wage rates and disposable income under each public employment strategy. The values obtained from the first two steps are used to calculate the changes in net wage rates[7] and disposable incomes that would result from the welfare reform, prior to any labor supply responses. Predictions of the effects on work hours of the reform are then derived by multiplying these calculated changes by appropriate labor supply parameters that were estimated from the Seattle and Denver Income Maintenance Experiments.[8] Once these labor supply adjustments are computed, they are used to determine the number of hours individuals would work during the post-reform period. Given these estimates of the hours family members would work, household earnings, transfer payment receipts, and tax payments can then be recomputed.

Individual Decisions on Participation in Public Employment

The first three steps of the simulation procedure provide estimates of post-reform income and hours of work for a sample of households. When a household member is eligible for a public service employment job, it is necessary to compute alternative sets of post-reform income and labor market measures for each of the three PSE strategies listed under Step 2. The final step in the simulation involves using these measures to determine whether an individual who is eligible for public employment will take such a job whenever he is in the labor force, only when he is unemployed, or not at all. Since this is probably the most novel feature of the simulation methodology, it is discussed in some detail.

It seems reasonable to view individuals who are eligible for public employment as engaging in a comparison between the jobs program and their best opportunity within the regular job sector and as choosing the alternative that makes their family best off.[9] In general, one would expect that the chosen alternative would offer the highest income level at a fixed number of hours worked.[10]

As indicated earlier, however, an individual is not confined to an all or nothing choice between public and regular employment. He may also participate in public employment only during his weeks of unemployment, returning to the regular job sector when an opportunity becomes available. This "mixed strategy" seems, in fact, to be the possibility stressed by most advocates of large-scale public employment programs. Under certain circumstances, however, the mixed strategy may not be a viable alternative. Some unemployed persons may be unwilling to participate in public employment if the program wage is below their usual market wage and some may be unwilling to relinquish unemployment compensation to accept a public employment job. Moreover, public employment programs may require a "waiting period" before an unemployed person becomes eligible for participation and this waiting period may exceed the length of his spell of unemployment. These considerations are explicitly treated by the simulation procedures used in the KGB model.

To determine whether various persons would participate in given PSE programs and whether they would select the pure or the mixed approach if they do participate, it has been necessary to develop a participation test. The test we use is based on the assumption that individuals will choose the strategy that maximizes the expected value of their family's stream of future disposable income after all labor supply adjustments have taken place.[11]

USE OF THE KGB MODEL IN POLICY FORMATION AND APPLIED RESEARCH

As stated earlier, the initial impetus for the development of the KGB model was the need of the Carter Administration to predict the cost and effects of its proposed welfare reform. The question of ultimate costs was of utmost importance because the Carter Administration initially hoped to develop a reform package that would enhance the adequacy of the welfare system and maintain incentives to work, but not increase government spending. Since the KGB model was used to predict the cost of budget outlays, it was not surprising that it came to play an important role in the policy process that determined the actual design of the reform package. One example of this was in the design of the jobs component of the welfare reform package.

The initial Department of Labor (DOL) proposal for this jobs component would have had the federal government guarantee any member of a household with children a job at the prevailing wage. Since the United States had no recent experience with a public jobs program of this type, the first questions that needed to be addressed were: how many individuals would take the government up on their offer of a prevailing wage job and how much would this cost the government? The intial cost estimates produced by the KGB model suggested that this proposal would at least double federal transfer and jobs expenditures on the low income population. Additional simulations further suggested that a large proportion of the newly created jobs would go to the nonpoverty population. After examining these initial KGB estimates, analysts at DOL and the Department of Health, Education, and Welfare (DHEW), refined the eligibility criterion for public employment jobs in the jobs component by restricting the jobs to primary earners and reducing the wage rate paid to the federal minimum. The simulation model indicated that these modifications of the initial proposal not only greatly reduced costs, but also resulted in substantially improved targeting of the jobs on the poor.

Although, more often than not, potential costs of the reform package were the cutting edge on decisions, it was also very important to the Carter Administration that the reform not increase disincentives to work. While provision of the guarantee of a job was seen as essential to achieving this goal, analysts at DHEW and DOL were also concerned with the accumulation of tax rates, especially where various tax and transfer programs overlapped.

One area of particular concern was the overlap of the cash assistance component of the welfare reform package with the existing Federal Income Tax. In this region of overlap, the marginal tax rate on the earnings of two-adult households would have been at least within the 70 to 80% range, and thus seemed likely to be associated with substantial work disincentives. To reduce these high tax rates, the Carter Administration's original reform proposal contained a provision that would have provided "tax credits" equal to 20% of earnings that were above the income level at which the Federal income tax liability began, but below the natural phaseout point of the reform package's cash assistance component. (The 20% figure was chosen because it roughly offset the income tax liability facing those on the lowest rung of the Federal Income Tax ladder.) The tax credit was to be reduced by 20 cents for each dollar of income above the cash assistance component's phaseout point. Thus, marginal tax rates facing those who qualified for cash assistance payments would have been reduced by the tax credit plan, while tax rates facing those with incomes slightly too high to qualify would have been raised. Both groups, however, would have received some tax relief.

The tax credit provison of the Administration's reform plan was proposed before any simulations of its potential effects were made. It was simply assumed that it was important to minimize work disincentives facing those cash assistance recipients who were also liable for federal income taxes. When simulation of the tax credit provision were finally conducted, however, they indicated that the provision would add $72 million of cost to the Administration's reform plan, but that increased work incentives would only result in an additional $60 million in earnings. Thus, the simulations suggested that the tax credit's effects on work incentives were likely to be quite small relative to its costs and the additional administrative burden that it would entail. As a consequence, the provision was quietly dropped during deliberations by the special House Subcommittee on Welfare Reform.

Although the KGB model was developed in direct response to a particular policy initiative and has been used extensively to simulate alternative welfare policies, the model has also been utilized for exploring more basic research questions. One example of its use for this purpose can be found in a recent simulation study by Betson, Greenberg, and Kasten (1982). The central question explored in this study can be stated as follows: Is it preferable from the viewpoint of economic efficiency to "tax" the poor at the same rate as the rest of society, or at a higher rate or a lower rate? While the theoretical literature on optimal taxation has produced many fruitful theorems on the structure of the optimal tax-transfer system, it has not yet yielded the answer to this particular question. Theoretical work has shown, however, that the optimal structure of tax rates will depend largely on the labor supply behavior of the individuals in the economy. Hence, a natural line of research is to ask what reasonable assumptions can be made about the labor supply behavior of individuals and what is the optimal structure of tax rates implied by these assumptions. Further, it is important to ask how sensitive the results are to the particular assumptions chosen.

The 1982 Betson, Greenberg, and Kasten study concluded that various tax-transfer structures did not differ very much in terms of their effects on economic efficiency and, consequently, other criteria would have to be used to choose among alternative tax structures. Moreover, this conclusion appeared to be relatively insensitive to the set of labor supply assumptions chosen. The study also found that by consolidating and simplifying the existing patchwork of tax and transfer programs into a single integrated system, it was possible to increase output in the economy, while at the same time redistributing greater amounts of income to the poor. More specifically, it was found that although low income families who received increased transfer benefits would decrease their hours of work, higher income households -- who were subjected to the tax increases required to pay for the additional transfer benefits received by the low income population -- would actually increase their work hours. Moreover, the additional earnings resulting from these increases in the hours of higher income households would be sufficient to offset most or all of any earnings reductions by transfer recipients. Once again, this result was maintained even when several different alternative sets of estimated labor supply parameters were used in conducting the simulations.

CONCLUSIONS

In this paper, we have reviewed the historical development of microsimulation modeling in the areas of applied poverty research and the formation of welfare policy alternatives, particularly highlighting the KGB model. Two important functions of microsimulation models were pointed out. First, the models have served as a mechanism by which knowledge gained from other modes of basic research -- for example, results from income maintenance experiments -- can be generalized so that their implications for national programs can be drawn. Second, microsimulation models have given researchers a form of analysis that allows them to quantify both the aggregate and the distributional consequences of proposed governmental policies.

The benefits to policymakers of these microsimulation activities are obvious. They can go far to decrease the range of uncertainty that would exist in the absence of a formal microsimulation efforts. For example, more reliable cost estimates of proposed policy intiatives and improved information about who is likely to benefit and who is likely to be hurt under the initiatives can be obtained.

Even while acknowledging the usefulness of microsimulation in analyzing anti-poverty policy, however, it is important to recognize its limitations -- many of which stem from the heavy reliance of microsimulation models on household survey data and on theoretical and empirical studies of behavioral responses to anti-poverty programs. Survey data files, for example, do not contain all the information that would be useful for simulation purposes and even the information that is available is invariably measured with some error. Theoretical and empirical research on human behavior is also subject to major limitations.[12] Moreover, the very attempt to model behavior realistically within a microsimulation context results in large, complex computer programs that are difficult to manage and potentially subject to hard to discover programming errors.

The problems just listed imply that the reliability of microsimulation results should be of major concern to users of the models. However, methods that can be used for validation purposes are not obvious. In this respect, microsimulation models might usefully be contrasted with macrosimulation forecasting models, which are frequently used to predict trends in the performance of the national economy. The reliability of these forecasting models can be tested by simply comparing their predictions for a particular time period with actual events during the period. Predictions by a microsimulation model, in contrast, are mainly counterfactual -- asking what would have happened had some given policy modification been adopted. However, unless the simulated policy is actually initiated -- an event that only rarely occurs -- validation of the model's predictions is not really feasible. Thus, the confidence that is placed in the model must usually depend upon subjective judgements as to whether the model's conceptual analytical structure appears reasonable and its predictions seem plausible and internally consistent.

The issue raised by the fact that microsimulation models cannot be adequately validated is a serious one. However, because policymakers are increasingly requesting quantitative predictions of the potential costs and effects of various policy proposals, a choice must be made between using microsimulation techniques to meet the needs of policymakers or simply relying on "back of the envelope calculations." In our view, the superiority of the former is obvious. Microsimulation is based on more explicit and less arbitrary assumptions. Thus, results based on microsimulations can be recomputed by others and underlying assumptions can be debated. As a consequence, the potential for manipulating analysis to produce desired results is considerably more limited than less formal methods of predicting the costs and effects of policy proposals. Furthermore, as suggested earlier, microsimulation techniques make much more comprehensive use of available data sources and evidence from previous research studies.

NOTES

1. Although much of the initial motivation behind the development of microsimulation models was the hope of facilitating evaluation of proposed welfare reform alternatives, a considerable number of microsimulation models have emerged since the mid-1960s that mainly serve other purposes. (Many of these models are described in Microeconomic Simulation Models for Public Policy Analysis, edited by Robert H. Haveman and Kevin Hollenbeck, Academic Press, 1980.) Because of space limitations, we focus here on only those models that were mainly developed to simulate changes in welfare policy and that are therefore direct predecessors of the KGB model.
2. See Gail R. Wilensky (1970), and Nelson McClung (1970). For an interesting discussion of pertinent events and technique innovations that preceded the development of RIM, see Robert Harris (1978).
3. However, in the late 1960s, initial attempts were made elsewhere to acount for work responses in a simulation context. See David H. Greenberg and Marvin Kosters (1973). Greenberg and Kosters' treatment of existing tax and transfer programs, however, was considerably cruder than that found in the RIM model.
4. For a more detailed description, see Margaret Sulvetta (1976).
5. However, at the time the KGB model was being developed, a new survey -- the 1975 Survey of Income and Education (SIE) -- became available that provided a data base superior to previous surveys. These data, which were collected by the Census Bureau, include good measures of many of the key variables needed by the model. Moreover the SIE provides a statistically reliable sample for individual states, permitting the effects of welfare reform measures on individual states to be examined.
6. Because of space limitations and the complexity of the model, it is only sketched here. Greater detail, as well as an examination -- and in some cases sensitivity tests -- of major assumptions that underlie the KGB simulation methodology, may be found in Betson, Greenberg, and Kasten (1980).
7. An individual's "net" wage rate is simply his nominal wage times one minus the cumulative tax rate he faces.
8. These parameters are estimated by two variables that represent the net changes caused by the various payment plans in the experiment. The first variable measures the change in family income resulting from the experimental treatment in the absence of any adjustment in hours worked. The second is the change in an individual's net wage rate due to the program's benefit reduction rate. The estimates produced by this procedure indicate how individuals will adjust their work effort in response to given changes in the amount of transfer payments

they receive or in the size of the benefit reduction rates they face. The regression model that was used to obtain these estimates was developed by Keeley, Robins, Spiegelman, and West (1978).

9. The simulation methodology assumes that this choice is made on the basis of perfect information about the alternatives, an assumption that probably results in an overstatement of the public employment supply population. Unless persons are aware of public employment and know something about it, the program is not a viable employment alternative for them. Knowledge of the program is likely to be positively related to the publicity given the program, the length of time the program has been in operation, and the size of the program.

10. For purposes of the simulation, it is assumed that an individual will participate in public employment whenever the program is viewed by him as marginally superior to his best conventional sector alternative. In actual practice, however, a substantial differential between public and conventional employment may be necessary, if only to overcome inertia. Nevertheless, many of the frictions that exist in labor markets would be reduced over the long-run. For example, many persons may not actively consider voluntarily leaving their present job to participate in public employment; but once they have been terminated or laid off they may seriously examine PSE as a possible alternative to available regular employment opportunities. Thus, the methodology is best viewed as being based on a static model of economic behavior; the adjustments to the introduction of a PSE program would not take place instantaneously, but only over time. The larger the comparative advantage of public employment, the more rapidly the adjustments would be expected to occur.

11. This procedure does not allow for the fact that individuals may not always be able to choose freely the total number of hours they work, at either a regular or a public employment job. In such cases, income might be higher if an individual picks one strategy over the other, but only because he would work longer hours. If so, the individual must trade-off a higher family income against lower hours, and his choice will only be clear with knowledge of his utility map. Betson (1980), however, has developed a technique that utilizes income and substitution effect estimates, such as those from the Seattle and Denver Income Maintenance Experiments, to derive the information needed about households' underlying utility surfaces. Preliminary tests of this utility technique suggests that it produces simulation results that are very similar to those obtained from the simpler procedure discussed in the text.

12. For some specific examples of the effects of such limitations on the KGB model, see Betson, Greenberg, and Kasten (1980).

REFERENCES

Betson, David (1980) "Labor Supply Functions an Expenditure Functions: Theoretical Derivatior. _ to Microsimulation Analysis," unpublished thesis, Univ_. Wisconsin-Madison.

Betson, David, David Greenberg, and Richard Kasten (1982) "A Simulation Analysis of the Economic Efficiency and Distribution Effects of Alternate Program Structures: The Negative Income Tax Versus the Credit Income Tax," in Income-Tested Programs: The Case for and Against, edited by Irwin Garfinkel, Academic Press, New York.

_____, (1980) "A Microsimulation Model for Analyzing Alternative Welfare Reform Proposals: An Application to the Program for Better Jobs and Income," in Microeconomic Simulation Models for Public Policy Analysis, Vol. 1, edited by Robert Haveman and Kevin Hollenbeck, Academic Press, New York.

Greenberg, David H., (1978) "Participation in Public Employment Programs," in Creating Jobs: Public Employment Programs and Wage Subsidies, John Palmer (ed.), The Brookings Institute, Washington, D.C.

_____ (1980) "Employers, the Unemployed, and the Effects of Transfer Programs on Hours of Work," Technical Analysis Paper, U.S. Department of Health, Education, and Welfare, Office of Income Security Policy.

Greenberg, David, and Marvin Kosters (1973) "Income Guarantees and the Working Poor," in Income Maintenance and Labor Supply, Cain and Watts (eds.), Markham Press, Chicago.

Harris, Robert (1978) Microanalytic Simulation Models for Analysis of Public Welfare Policies, The Urban Institute, Washington, D.C.

Haveman, Robert, Kevin Hollenbeck, David Betson, and Martin Holmer (1980) "The Poverty Institute Regional and Distributional Model -- Its Application to the Program for Better Jobs and Income," in Microeconomic Simulation Models for Public Policy Analysis, Vol. 2, Robert Haveman and Kevin Hollenback (eds.), Academic Press, New York.

Keeley, Michael C., Philip K. Robins, Robert G. Spiegelman, and Richard W. West (1978) "The Estimation of Labor Supply Models Using Experimental Data," The American Economic Review, 68:873-877.

McClung, Nelson (1970) "Estimates of Income Transfer Program Direct Effects," in the President's Commission on Income Maintenance Programs: Technical Studies, U.S. Government Printing Office, Washington, D.C.

Sulvetta, Margaret (1976) "An Analyst's Guide to TRIM: The Transfer Income Model," Urban Institute Paper, Washington, D.C.

Wilensky, Gail (1970) "An Income Transfer Computational Model," in the President's Commission on Income Maintenance Programs: Technical Studies, U.S. Government Printing Office, Washington, D.C.

EVALUATING POVERTY PROGRAMS: THE USEFULNESS OF DYNAMIC CONTINUOUS SIMULATION MODELLING

John Dixon
Barry Nagorcka
James Cutt

All poverty programs have a set of beneficiaries and a set of net contributors, and how each group responds to the provision of cash transfers and the payment of income tax and compulsory contributions will determine the cost-effectiveness of such programs over time. A generous poverty program that may discourage work effort or savings on the part of its beneficiaries, while at the same time alienating its net contributors, who may decide to reduce their work effort or to obtain compensating adjustments to their real incomes so as not to bear the real program cost, may be well-intentioned but not a cost-effective means of reducing poverty. Thus an evaluation methodology if it is to be useful, must provide insight into the possible economic and distributional consequences of the range of empirically-based hypotheses relating to the possible behavior modifications that may be induced by poverty programs. The methodology used to evaluate poverty programs must allow these hypotheses to be fed-back into an information system that generates a set of program cost and performance indicators.

We have undertaken a major evaluation of poverty program options in Australia (Cutt, Dixon, and Nagorcka, 1977). We have constructed a simulation model of the Australian income redistribution process that explicitly incorporates time in a continuous manner, so as to explore the _dynamic_ impact of a selection of poverty programs on a comprehensive range of cost and performance indicators.

The purpose of this paper is to demonstrate the usefulness of the dynamic, continuous macro-simulation modelling technique when evaluating poverty programs.

EVALUATING POVERTY PROGRAMS

The objective of any poverty program evaluation methodology is the provision of improved information to political decision-makers on the cost and performance implication of the alternatives. Such an analysis requires the modelling, in one form or another, of the system in which cash transfer payments are made and financed, and, by definition, to which new programs will be directed. The first step is the determination of a set of appropriate program objectives and the specification of a set of performance indicators that are relevant to those objectives (for a discussion of the practical program design problems and trade-offs present in any income maintenance system seeking to achieve multiple objectives see Lerman and Townsend (1976)). Table 14.1 contains a set of poverty program objectives and related performance indicators. We believe that it is essential for the comprehensive evaluation of poverty programs that the objective function contain a selection of macroeconomic variables (including inflation, unemployment and Gross Domestic Product) for their inclusion not only widens the context within which poverty programs can be assessed but also stresses the consequences of such programs on absolute as distinct from relative income. Moreover, we contend that a poverty program's cost effectiveness over time is clearly determined by its impact not only on poverty and inequality but also on inflation, unemployment and economic growth. Of crucial concern then is, first, the likely impact of receiving cash transfers on the recipients' work effort, savings behavior and willingness to take up the transfer; and second, the likely impact of paying income tax or compulsory contributions on the net contributors' work effort or willingness to pay the real cost of the poverty program.

THE BEHAVIOR OF BENEFICIARIES

For those eligible for cash transfers the behavior modifications of concern to decision-makers relate to work effort, the desire to save and the willingness to seek cash transfers.

The Labor-Supply Response of Cash-Transfer Recipients

Whether or to what extent transfer recipients who are capable of contributing to the total labor supply reduce their work effort upon the receipt of cash transfers is an issue of policy relevance. In fact, there seems to be a general preoccupation with the work incentive aspects of poverty programs, probably for the following reasons. First, the cost of a particular poverty program over time depends to some extent on the degree of work curtailment it encourages. Second, the political acceptability of a particular program likewise depends, as least in part, on this work-disincentive effect. Finally, the impact of a particular program on inflation, unemployment and economic growth depends in part on its effect on the supply of labor over time. This preoccupation with work incentives is a recognition of, first, a political attitude that society is not eager to enact any poverty program that gives the poor

TABLE 14.1

A Set of Poverty Program Objectives
and Related Performance Indicators

Objectives	Performance Indicators
To reduce absolute poverty	The poverty gap
To reduce income inequality	The Gini Co-efficient[1]
	The Affluence Margin[2]
To achieve the lowest possible degree of work disincentive	Total number of hours worked per year
To achieve the smallest possible:	
1) inhibition of economic growth; and	Gross Domestic Product[3]
2) growth in inflation and unemployment.	Inflation and unemployment

Notes

1. The "Gini Coefficient" is a mathematical measure of relative income inequality. As the co-efficient approaches zero, the degree of income inequality diminishes.

2. The "Affluence Margin" is measured by the sum of the incomes of families above a set of income levels that demarcate the "affluent" families in various population categories. These income levels may be defined as a multiple of the poverty line appropriate to the population category.

3. Defined as the total market value of goods and services produced in Australia after deducting the cost of intermediate usage of goods and services but before deducting allowances for the consumption of fixed capital.

assistance and yet allows them to work less; and second, a concern for economic reality -- that the level of absolute incomes over time is the primary determinant of wellbeing.

A great deal of rhetoric and mythology surrounds the issue of the work-disincentive effect of cash transfers. Opinions abound on the extent to which the receipt of cash transfers reduces work effort; facts are rare. Assertions as to the consequences of any such reduction of work effort are commonplace; documented arguments are not. Undoubtedly the work-leisure decision calculus is complex. Many factors determine whether an individual works or not, including the nature of income support available, the state of the labor market, work motivation, health status and family responsibility (Goodwin, 1972). There is, however, no comprehensive social theory which allows us to integrate all the factors that impinge on people's work-leisure decision. Thus the extent to which individuals adjust their work effort after receiving cash transfers remains an empirical question. (The body of literature on this subject is immense (Cameron, 1972:141-150); we recommend U.S. Congress (1974) and Lampman (1978).)

We postulate that the labor-supply response of cash transfer recipients depends on the magnitude of the basic allowance or basic income guarantee; the level of earned income up to which no reduction is made to the basic allowance (defined as threshold income); the rate at which the basic allowance is reduced as earned income rises above the threshold income; and the circumstances of transfer recipient families, with allowances being made for the number of dependent children and the sex of the family head. Moreover, any resultant reduction in work effort manifests itself in any of three ways: a total withdrawal from the work-force; a partial withdrawal from the work-force (in the form of either continuous part-time or discontinuous full-time employment) or a fractional reduction in hours worked, by means of reduced overtime or reduced multiple job-holding.

The point we emphasize is that a labor-supply response of any magnitude will cause a disturbance to the economic system, the possible consequences of which must be explored as part of a comprehensive poverty program evaluation strategy. Figure 14.2 contains three feedback loops that indicate the possible economic consequences of the work disincentive effect of the cash transfers. Loop 'a' is an example of a positive feedback loop, which indicates that any reduction in work effort (measured in terms of hours worked) will reduce production and thus profits, investment and productivity. This will further reduce production. Loop 'b' is also a positive feedback loop. It suggests that any reduction in work effort will reduce production and thus increase prices, wages and unemployment, which will further reduce production. Loop 'c' is a negative feedback loop where we have assumed that any reduction in work effort reduces production and causes prices and thus wages to rise.

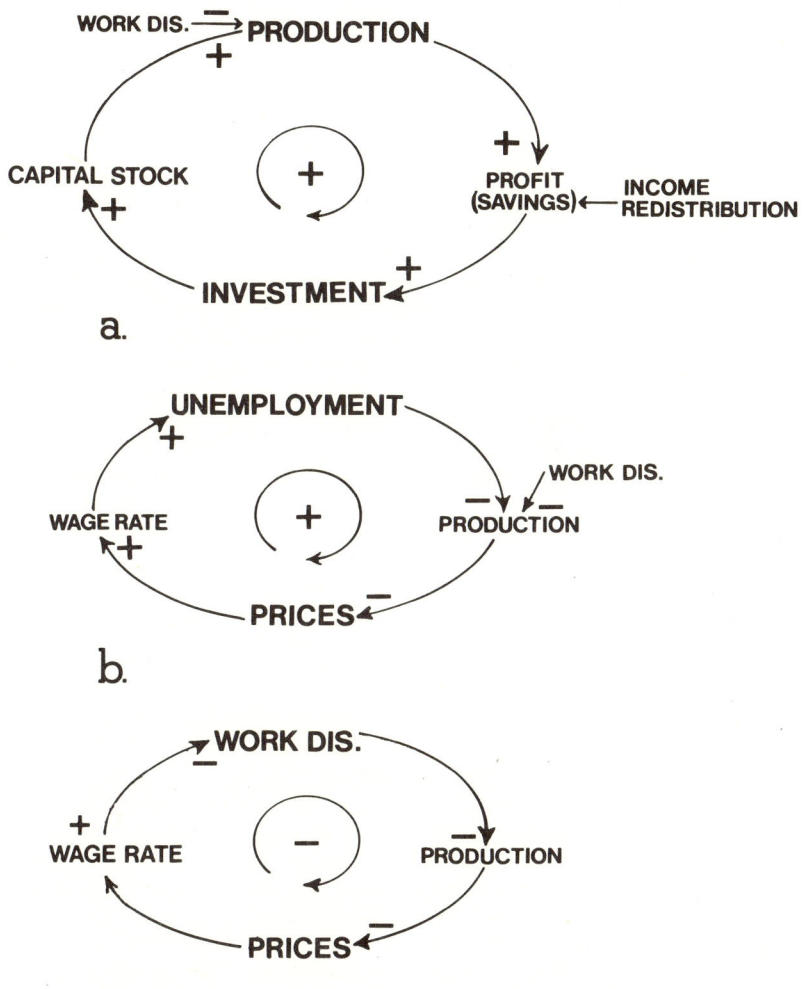

Figure 14.2 Work Disincentive Feedback Loops

Assuming that this reduces the real value of the cash transfer, then work effort increases as a result of a reduced work disincentive effect. All these loops, therefore, should be considered in any assessment of alternative poverty programs.

The Savings Response of Cash-Transfer Recipients

If individuals are guaranteed income-security then the conventional view is that the precautionary savings motive may well be weakened. But, as Pechman, et al. (1968:183) argue, poverty programs "... may well provide an incentive for individuals to save more: with major hazards already covered, other savings goals may appear to be within reach." Moreover, poverty programs may stimulate savings, as Munnell (1974; also, see Feldstein, 1974) suggests, first, by encouraging individuals to retire early and thus forcing them to save over a shorter working life for a longer retirement period; and second, by providing individuals with a base on which they could build towards an adequate retirement income. The extent to which individuals adjust their savings behavior remains an empirical issue. Our point again is that the possible consequences of any changed savings behavior must be explored as part of a comprehensive poverty program evaluation strategy.

We incorporate this response into our model by assuming that the average propensity to save decreases after the introduction of a poverty program.

The Take-Up Response of Eligible Cash-Transfer Recipients

The take-up rate may be defined as the proportion of eligible population receiving cash transfers (MacDonald 1975; Bickell and MacDonald, 1975; Lidman, 1975). It is determined by the following factors: the degree of stigmatization attached to a particular poverty program, which, in turn, depends on the degree of selectivity defined in its eligibility criteria, the degree of inquisition involved in the granting of its benefits, and the social values associated with the receipt of those benefits; the degree of generosity of the program's payments; the availability and cost of information about the program; the range of supplementary benefits attached to the program; and the economic circumstances of the potential transfer recipients' family. The take-up response is an important determinant of both the cost and the effectiveness (in terms of reduced poverty) of poverty programs and its implications must be explored in a comprehensive evaluation strategy.

We exogenously specify the take-up rates in our model.

THE BEHAVIOR OF NET CONTRIBUTORS

For net contributors the behavior modifications of concern to decision-makers relate to work effort and the desire to maintain real income shares.

The Labor-Supply Response of Net Contributors

Static economic theory postulates that an increase in income tax rates reduces after-tax income, which not only increases the need to earn more income if after-tax income is to be restored, but also decreases the price of leisure in terms of earned income. The net effect on work effort, and thus earned income, depends on which of these countervailing forces predominates. A priori reasoning cannot establish unambiguously whether or not an increase in income-tax rates reduces work effort. Unfortunately, empirical evidence is sparse; a few attempts have been made to obtain information on this relationship, but they are scarcely definitive. (OECD, 1975; Cutt, Standish and Walsh, 1975; Kesselman, 1974). We contend, however, that a defensible hypothesis relating to this response must be incorporated into a comprehensive poverty program evaluation strategy.

We include this response in the model by postulating a relationship between the marginal tax rate and the number of hours worked by net contributors.

The Maintenance-of-Real-Income-Shares Response of Net Contributors

The alleviation of absolute poverty is an objective which might be acceptable across the political spectrum. Certainly any program designed specifically to alleviate poverty will have gainers and losers (net contributors), but the costs involved are generally spread widely enough to ensure that the losers will not become hostile, or behave in such a way as to offset the effects of the poverty alleviation measures. Redistribution is quite another matter. By definition, a program designed to redistribute income significantly involves a specific group of losers, who are expected to accept a relative, or perhaps even an absolute, loss of real income in favor of a specific group of gainers. A poverty program couched explicitly in this way is more likely to create political opposition, which may hinder its effective implementation. But, more importantly, attempts to redistribute income may prove to be self-defeating. The question of trade-offs over time between redistribution and economic growth, and the whole dilemma of absolute income levels and relative income shares become central. It may well be that income shares are resilient to equalization attempts, largely because of the capacity of powerful groups in the economy -- including trade unions -- to shift tax burdens and to fix the price of their services. Thus the initial relative income structure over a significant range of incomes may eventually be restored but, in the process, absolute incomes may be lower than they might have been in the absence of the redistributive policy. The income-redistributive process is only poorly understood, and it is a complex social issue on which reasonable people may disagree. We argue that a comprehensive poverty program evaluation strategy should attempt to explore the consequences of the net contributors being unwilling to pay the real cost of a poverty program.

We accommodate this response by maintaining the real income shares of net contributors by automatically adjusting wages in accordance with price and productivity changes generated after introducing a range of poverty programs.

MODELLING AN INCOME-DISTRIBUTION SYSTEM

The methodology used to evaluate poverty programs requires not only the definition of the income distribution system within which such programs operate but also the modelling of that system over time. A model is a simplified abstraction of the real system and, in this sense, is always an analogue of reality. While there are many ways in which an income distribution system may be modelled, including the popular qualitative and intuitive approach, we have chosen to represent the structure of the system and the relationship between its variables mathematically by means of a simulation modelling technique that explicitly incorporates time in a continuous manner (Goodman, 1974). We stress that the primary function of a system model is explanatory. It must, therefore, account for the operation of a particular system over time, and thus its basic structure must first, describe the behavior, or the transformation relationships of the variables representing the system (the state variables); and second, present information to the decision-maker in the most useful manner.

The operation of the model is defined by the transformation relationships (a set of rate-of-change-over-time equations) incorporating delays in the adjustments of some variables to changes in others, and sequences of responses in the state variables, following a perturbation of the system. The transformation relationships in a dynamic model, therefore, incorporate the fundamental concept of feedback. Three feedback examples relating to the effect of work disincentives on inflation, unemployment and production were given in Figure 14.2. A full flow diagram of our model is given in Figure 14.3.

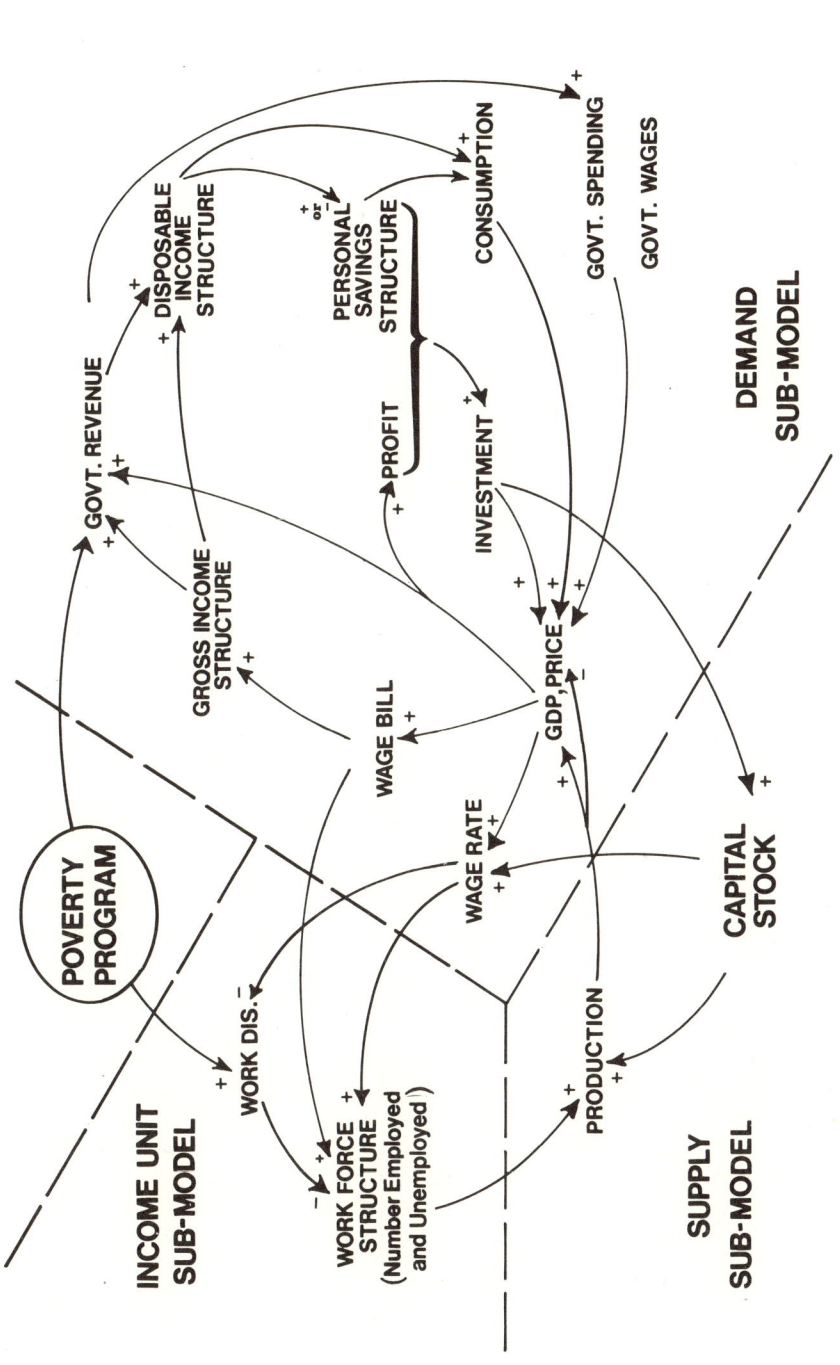

Figure 14.3 Causal Loop Diagram of the Whole Model

A DYNAMIC CONTINUOUS SIMULATION MODEL OF AN INCOME DISTRIBUTION SYSTEM

We will now briefly describe our model. It is convenient to consider it as having three sub-models: an income-unit, a demand and a supply sub-model.

The Income-Unit Sub-Model

This is the largest and most complex of the three sub-models and its tasks are to maintain information on the income status of 'income units', and to provide information on the level of employment and the number of hours worked by individuals, which is used in the supply sub-model.[1] It contains income units which are initially classified into categories by age, sex, marital status and number of children, and then further classified and reclassified, continuously according to workforce participation and gross wages. This process involves three steps (see Figure 14.4). In the first step the initial categories of income units are further classified by gross wage ranges. A set of hours worked is then associated with each wage range, allowing us to estimate the total number of hours worked by the population. The second classification step involves altering the set of wage distributions, the average number of hours worked, or both, in response to the behavioral adjustments made by adults who receive cash transfers or pay income tax. To determine the work disincentive effect of cash transfers we postulate that the percentage reduction in hours worked is directly related to the magnitude of the basic income guarantee and inversely related to the difference between the after-tax income obtained by the income unit when the individual is working and when he is not working. We recognize that there may be a significant delay between receiving a cash transfer and any labor supply response, and such a delay has been incorporated in the model. Because of the lack of data to determine the work disincentive effect of income tax payments we arbitrarily postulate that taxpayers will reduce their hours worked by up to 20 percent as the marginal tax rate increases beyond 50 percent.

The final classification step involves the adjustments resulting from the mismatching of the demand and supply of labor. We determine the supply of labor by adding together all adults in all non-zero wage groups for all non-aged income-unit types. We compare the demand and supply of labor in each of the wage ranges and the levels of employment (by wage range) and involuntary unemployment are obtained on the basis of the mis-matching of the demand and supply of labor. The model has the capacity to allow unemployed income earners to adjust their wages to find work or to allow some employed income earners to move to vacancies in higher wage ranges.

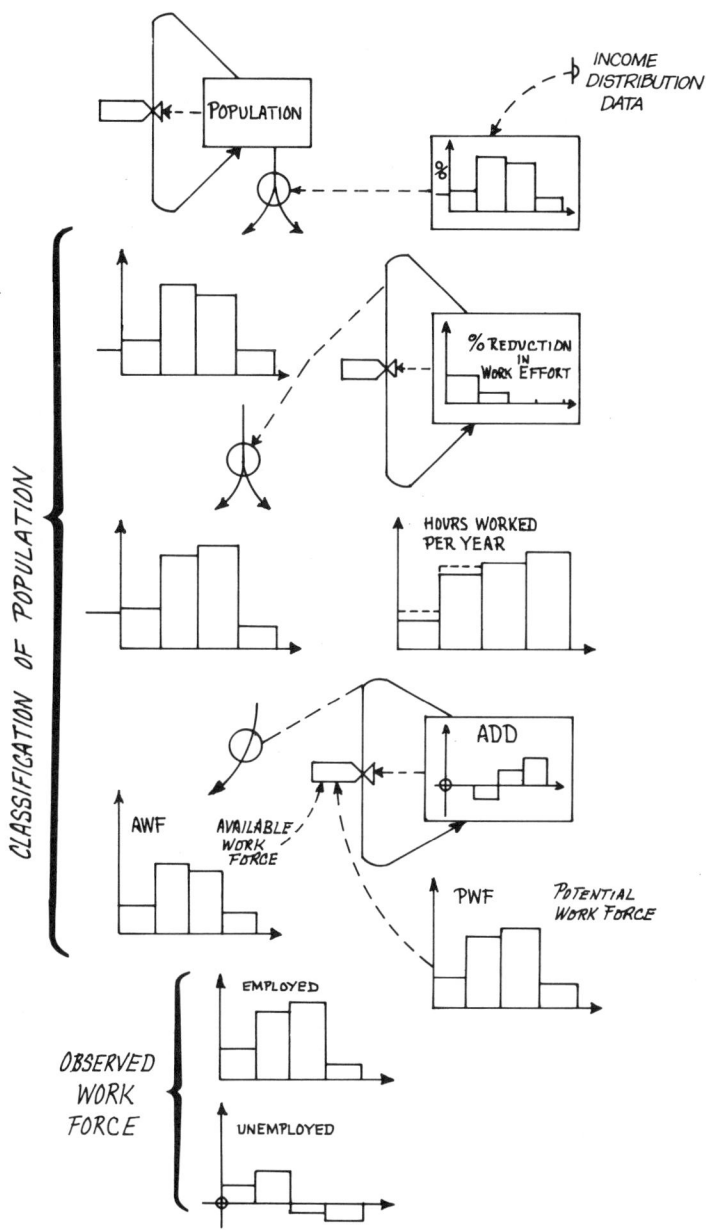

Figure 14.4 Income-Unit Sub-Model

The Demand Sub-Model

This is the core of the dynamic model for it provides a macroeconomic context which allows us to gather information on the effects of various poverty programs and their attendant methods of financing on aggregate demand, economic growth, personal income levels and the cost of poverty programs. The <u>demand sub-model</u> contains a pool of money which is acquired and dispersed by income units, enterprises and the government (see Figure 14.5). For convenience the <u>demand sub-model</u> may be sub-divided into four sectors. The <u>household sector</u> centers on the derivation of income from various sources by income units and the dispersal of that income to various ends. The income status of income units gathered in the <u>income-unit sub-model</u> provides the basis of this sector. It is in this sector that we introduce modification to the savings behavior of cash transfer recipients. The <u>business sector</u>, which involves the determining and financing of private investment. The <u>government sector</u>, which does not incorporate the characteristics of a federal political system, includes the collection and spending of government revenue. It is in this sector that we introduce modifications to the willingness of the eligible population to seek cash transfers. The <u>production sector</u> focuses on the sources and uses of Gross Domestic Product. It is in this sector that we introduce the proposition that net contributors may seek to maintain their real income shares by means of compensating real income adjustments. At this point we must explain two fundamental modelling assumptions. First, we determine exogenously the money supply, and increases in that supply, which are related to the growth in GDP, enter the model through the <u>government sector</u>. Second, we ignore external economic disturbances by assuming that exports are offset by imports. These constraints can be removed if desired.

The Supply Sub-Model

This is concerned with, first, the supply of goods and services; and second, the reconciliation of demand and supply to determine the price level (see Figure 14.6). We postulate that aggregate supply is functionally related to productivity, which we make dependent on investment, through the capital-labor ratio, and on the total number of hours worked. The investment rate is determined in the <u>demand sub-model</u> and hours worked in the <u>income-unit sub-model</u>.

DATA REQUIREMENTS

The model can be operated in either the historical or the forecasting mode. We chose the historical mode because of data

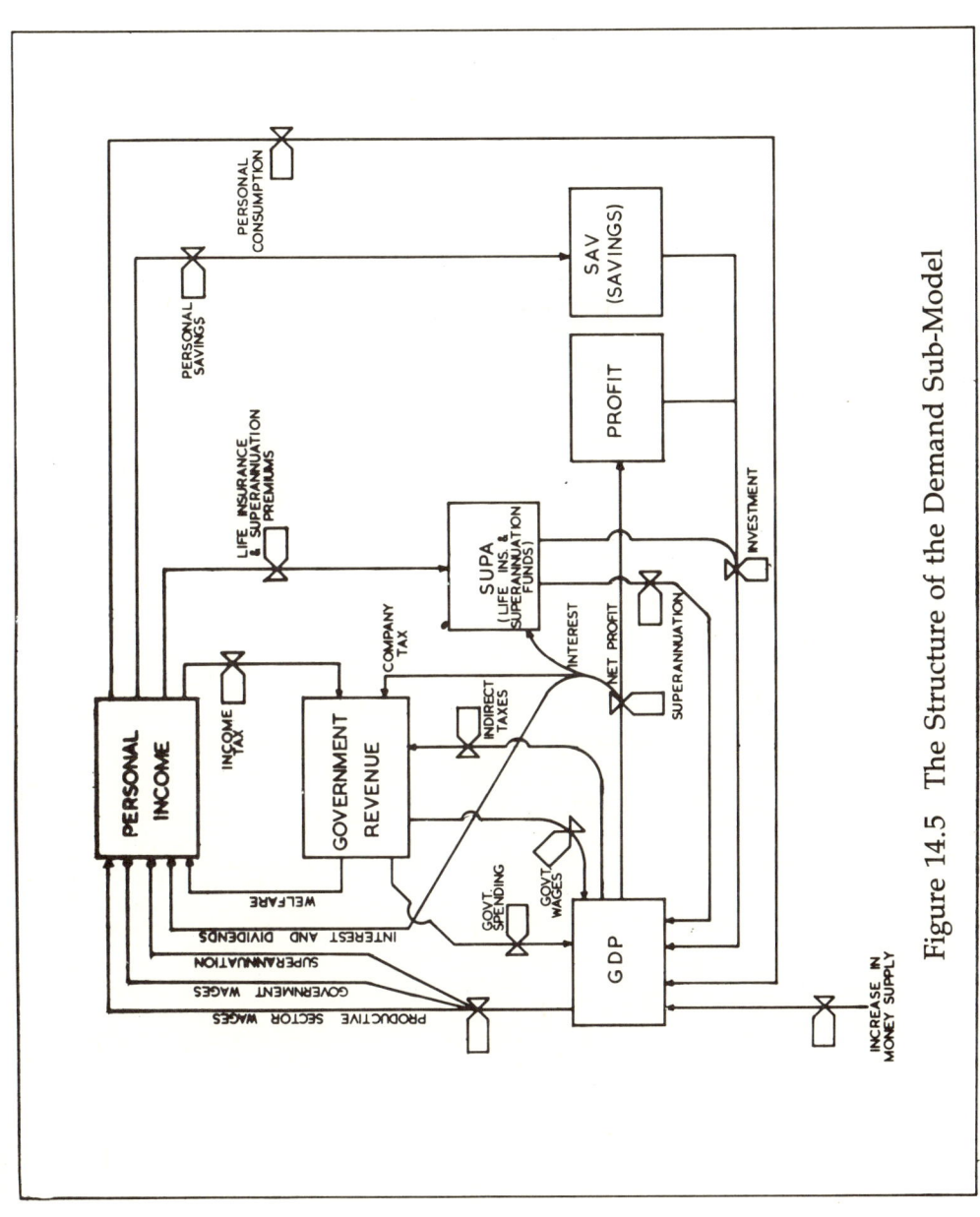

Figure 14.5 The Structure of the Demand Sub-Model

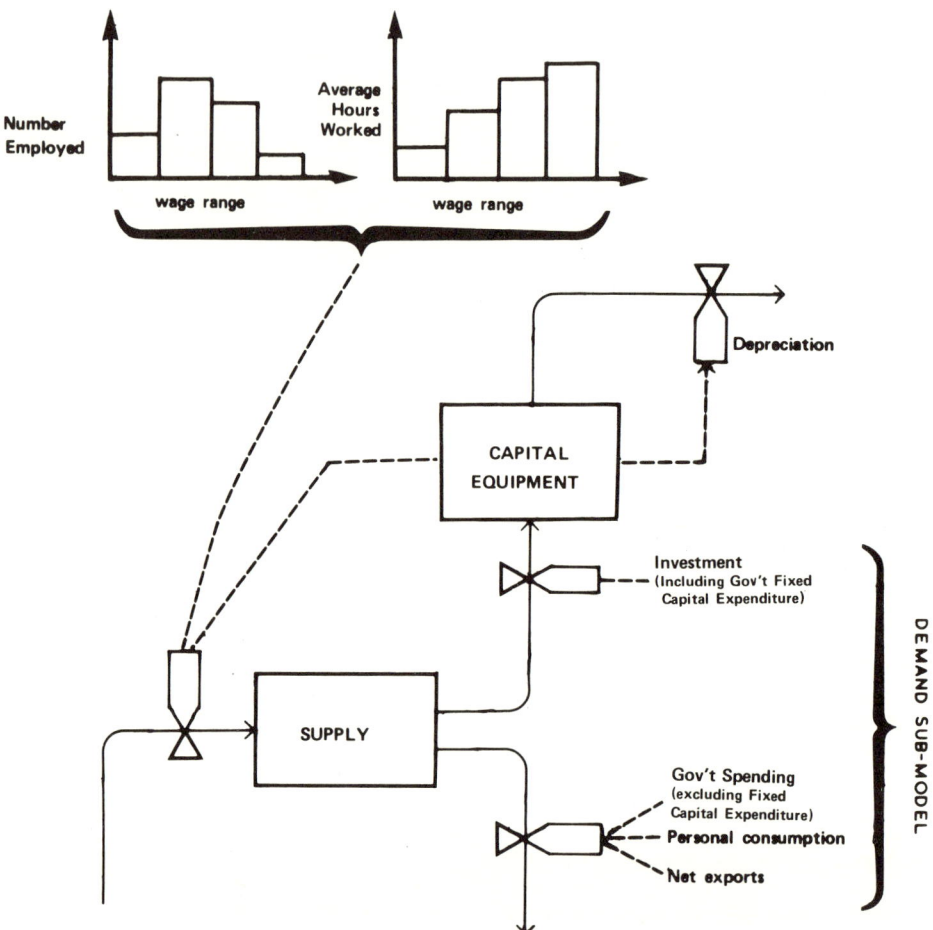

Figure 14.6 The Structure of the Supply Sub-Model

constraints. We decided to address the question: What would have been the macroeconomic and redistributive consequences for Australia of introducing various poverty programs over the period 1963 to 1973.

Thus we were able to compare the model's performance with actual data collected during this period, and to assess the usefulness of the dynamic simulation technique in this context. Used in the historical mode the model's data requirements are quite modest.

The state variables in the income-unit sub-model are based on income distribution data disaggregated by income-unit type (that is, by age, workforce participation, sex and marital status). To a very large extent the richness of the income distribution data base determines the degree of disaggregation that is possible and thus the extent to which a poverty program's likely impact on a particular population category can be ascertained.

The state variables in the demand and supply sub-models are based on the national economic accounts framework and capital stock data.

The data requirements are more demanding when determining the model's various transformation relationships -- the set of differential equations that define the rate of change of state variables -- and delays, which cushion the response of the system to changed input conditions. Data on the various behavioral adjustments outlined above is sparse. Our approach is to postulate hypothetical relationships based on the best available empirical evidence. It goes without saying, however, that the determining of realistic transformation relationships is perhaps the most important, and certainly one of the most time-consuming, aspects of dynamic modelling.

Once we move to the forecasting mode the modeller must estimate the transformation relationships and delays that in the historical mode were available in the historical data base. This is a more complex exercise without the benefits of hindsight that the historical mode allows.

MODEL PERFORMANCE

The model is coded using the FORTRAN-based continuous simulation language ACSL (Advanced Continuous Simulation Language). We used the model to simulate the income status of income units and the major economic variables in Australia for the period 1963 to 1973. Despite the many assumptions and approximations made in constructing the model, most of which were necessary because of the lack of appropriate data, the model's simulation of the Australian economy for the period 1963 to 1973 closely approximated national accounting data in its long term (or trend) behavior.

MODEL RESULTS

We used our model to explore the socio-economic consequences over a ten-year period that might have followed if Australia had adopted any of a set of alternative poverty programs in 1963 (including negative income tax and universal demogrant proposals), given a defensible set of behavioral adjustment assumptions. We found that although the panacea proposals would have been more successful in alleviating poverty and reducing income inequality, in the short-run at least, than Australia's existing non-contributory, selective-categorical, flat-rate programs, each had a significant economic growth cost. Although the <u>relative</u> incomes of those in the various target groups improved, their <u>absolute</u> incomes were, on average, lower than they would have been in the absence of such programs. When we introduced the proposition that net contributors seek to protect their real income shares by tying their income to the growth in productivity and inflation, the macroeconomic implications for both the negative income tax and, more particularly, the universal demogrant proposals became very serious indeed, for both inflation and unemployment accelerated. This result somewhat surprised us, for it was not anticipated. In essence, the introduction of a more generous poverty program under these conditions has the following consequences in the model. The modest reduction in hours worked (5-6 percent) causes the growth in production to slow down, which accelerates inflation and pushes wages up. This makes labor relatively more expensive and thus involuntary unemployment rises, which further reduces the net supply of labor (measured in terms of hours worked). This further slows down the growth in production and another round of price-wage spiralling is initiated, followed by a further rise in unemployment. Production is further curtailed and ultimately the system collapses. Under these economic circumstances the intended target groups found their real incomes diminished and their employment opportunities seriously curtailed. The growing unemployment, in fact, causes the poverty gap to widen dramatically. Moreover, the continuing inflation-unemployment spiral markedly increases the growth in income-support expenditure, while income tax revenue grows at a somewhat slower rate, because of the reduction in the number of taxpayers caused by the growth in unemployment. <u>The important implication of this, of course, is that if net contributors refuse to pay the real cost of a poverty program, it cannot be sustained.</u> It also brings into question the cost-effectiveness of poverty programs that might elicit such a response from its net contributors. Our purpose in outlining this possible scenario is to emphasize the importance of considering the dynamic implications for the macroeconomy of the introduction of any poverty program. We recognize that the initiation of an inflation-unemployment spiral will almost certainly lead to numerous behavioral adjustments by the various actors in the economic system. We have not attempted to predict or incorporate into our model such behavioral changes. Nevertheless, we believe that we have established a _prima facie_ case in support of a policy analysis delving more deeply into the dynamic macroeconomic implications of various poverty programs.

CONCLUSION

We have, we believe, established the need for analysts to evaluate poverty programs in a dynamic context, giving special consideration to the magnitude and the consequences of the possible behavioral adjustments associated with the receipt of cash transfers and the payment of income tax or compulsory contribution. The information generated by means of a dynamic continuous macro-simulation model, one that considers both the expenditure and financing aspects of poverty programs and that enables the feedback consequences of induced behavior modifications to be explored, is crucial if the decision-maker is to consider the full consequences over time for the intended target groups.

NOTE

1. An 'income unit' is a grouping of individuals into units comprising an adult head, a spouse (if head married) and any dependent children.

REFERENCES

Bicknell, Garry and Maurice MacDonald (1975) "Participation Rates in the Food Stamp Program: Estimated Levels, by State." Discussion Paper 253-75, Institute for Research on Poverty, University of Wisconsin.

Cameron, Colin (1972) _Income Support Schemes: Bibliography and Annotations to Academic Literature including References to Newspaper Citations._ Madison: Institute for Research on Poverty.

Cutt, James, John Dixon, and Barry Nagorcka (1977) _Income Support Policy in Australia: A Dynamic Approach._ Research Monograph No. 2, Administrative Studies Program, Australian National University.

Cutt, James, P.E.M. Standish, and C. Walsh (1975) "The Relationship Between the Progressive Income Tax and Labor Supply." _Administrative Studies Discussion Paper_, Administrative Studies Program, Australian National University.

Feldstein, Martin (1974) "Social Security, Induced Retirement and Aggregate Capital Accumulation." _Journal of Political Economy_ 82:905-926.

Goodman, Michael R. (1974) *Study Notes in System Dynamics*. Cambridge, Mass.: Wright Allen Press.

Goodwin, Leonard (1972) *Do the Poor Want to Work? A Social-Psychological Study of Work Orientations*. Washington, D.C.: Brookings Institution.

Kesselman, Jonathan R. (1974) "Tax Effects on Job Search and Work Effort." Discussion Paper 74-12, Economics Department, University of British Columbia.

Lampman, Robert J. (1978) "Labor Supply and Social Welfare Benefits in the United States." Special Report 22, Institute for Research on Poverty, University of Wisconsin.

Lerman, Robert I. and Alair A. Townsend (1976) "Conflicting Objectives in Income Maintenance Programs." *American Economic Review* 64:205-211.

Lidman, Russell M. (1975) "Why is the Rate of Participation in the Unemployed Fathers Segment of Aid to Families with Dependent Children (AFDC-UF) So Low?" Discussion Paper 288-75, Institute for Research on Poverty, University of Wisconsin.

MacDonald, Maurice (1975) "Why Don't More Eligibles Use Food Stamps?" Discussion Paper 292-75, Institute for Research on Poverty, University of Wisconsin.

Munnell, Alicia H. (1974) "The Impact of Social Security on Personal Savings." *National Tax Journal* 27:553-567.

OECD (1975) *Theoretical and Empirical Aspects of the Effects of Taxation on the Supply of Labor*. Paris: OECD.

Pechman, Joseph A., Henry Aaron and Michael K. Taussig (1968) *Social Security Perspectives for Reform*. Washington, D.C.: Brookings Institution.

U.S. Congress, Joint Economic Committee (1974) *How Income Supplements Can Affect Work Behavior*. Studies in Public Welfare, Paper No. 13.

PART IV

ALTERNATIVE POLICY PERSPECTIVES: THE SUBJECTS OF POVERTY RESEARCH

INTRODUCTION

Richard Goldstein
Stephen M. Sachs

> In the manner of professors, I resorted to reason: Was it not the case, I asked, that a very considerable number of poverty programs had been begun in Roxbury in recent years? (The Boston Globe was shortly to publish a special supplement describing 262 such programs spread about the city as a whole.) "Exactly, " came the retort, "but do you notice they only fund programs that don't succeed?"
>
> Moynihan, 1969:3

Policy perspectives as used here refers to both the policies that are or are not studied and to the policy perspective inherent in the method of study. This second part of the meaning is closely related to what was called "alternative research perspectives" in the preceding section in the sense that a research study that studies only individuals, say, is constrained in the types of policies that it can "see" as solutions to the problems studied. Of the five articles in this section, two contain arguments concerning the policies studied, while the other three contain arguments relevant to the policy perspectives that are inherent in certain forms of research.

The phrase, "the policies that are or are not studied", is very broad. For our purposes, two particular dimensions are of prime importance in assessing poverty research. The first, and much narrower, dimension is the dimension usually meant by policy researchers when they use a phrase of this kind. For these people, this phrase

> means such things as (1) do we provide for compulsory or optional caseworkers, (2) do we provide for a uniform national floor with regard to welfare payments, (3) do we include abortions as a welfare benefit, (4) should lawyers be appointed to represent welfare recipients filing complaints concerning terminations, eligibility, or benefit levels . . . (Nagel, 1981)

This dimension is not represented in this book. In fact, the second dimension, which asks, for example, if welfare as we know it in the United States is a desirable policy at all, is different from the first dimension in kind, not in degree. That is, this second dimension of alternative policy perspectives rejects the types of issues that the first dimension is concerned with. Rather than saying, is this the right road for getting us in our car to point A, the second perspective would say, is a car the right way to get to point A?

However, even narrowing the meaning of alternative policy perspectives to this second dimension does not make its meaning clear enough. One possible specification would be to see problems such as poverty as conflicts of interest rather than just as problems of deciding on the best means to get to an agreed upon end. That is, maybe poverty programs don't work because there are many who don't want them to work since this would hurt the interests of some people. (See Rule, 1978; Ryan, 1971.)

Joseph Nalven's paper is an example of this idea of problems as conflicts of interest. Nalven looks at the debates, both among researchers and among policy-makers (legislators, members of the executive branch, and courts), concerning the health of undocumented immigrants. He considers what, if anything, these various parties believe should be done about these issues, and shows how the material interests of various parties affect their points of view.

Another possibility might be to compare the rhetoric of social reformers and social reform agencies with the programs actually put in place by these people and these groups. Some authors have done this and found that while in most cases the rhetoric and programs were consistently individualistic, in other cases the rhetoric and the program were not consistent. In these cases the rhetoric was structural and the programs were individualistic. For example, Helfgot (1981:54) found that the organizers and administrators of Mobilization for Youth in New York City believed that teachers were unprepared because of their own training, because of school department personnel policies, because of the inadequate supplies made available to them, and because of the poor curriculum and poor conditions. But, the organization only tried to change the behavior of the teachers. Furthermore, the organization tried to change this behavior without changing the system of rewards and punishments for the teachers, and without providing any other institutional changes that could facilitate or justify such changes in behavior on the part of the teachers. Other examples occurred in Office of Economic Opportunity programs (Patterson, 1981:151). Blau and Meyer (1971:115-116) draw a parallel between the occurrence of this form of inconsistency in the war on poverty and Michels' "Iron Law of Oligarchy."

Another possible meaning of alternative policy perspective is to examine the structural effects on communities of the structure of programs. That is, rather than examining the effects on individual enrollees (and a "control" group) one might see what the effect of a program was in community terms. Although we know of no one who has done this, Helfgot (1981) has made a start. He examined the effect on a community of the structure of applying for funding of programs. He found that since the procedure turned community groups into competitors, this application structure had the consequence of splitting up the community. This kind of effect is very unlikely to lead to the amelioration or eradication of poverty in such a community, especially when community residents learn that they also have to compete with (or join with) professionals for these funds. When poor residents realize that as far as the funding agency is concerned there must be professionals involved, they often sense that the game is up. Residents are supposed to be helped and served by professionals, but the history of professionals in anti-poverty shows that often they are no help. It has even been charged that at best professionals have their own axe to grind; at worst, they do not want to be so successful that they do themselves out of a job. (Helfgot, 1981:146-9, 187, 201)

There is another possible sense of "structural" as used above, namely, an attempt to extend the actual structure of (part of) society to the rest of the society. (See the Introduction to Part I for a general discussion of "structure".) That is, one can argue that part of the problem of poverty is that the successful economic structure of the rest of society is not replicated in poor areas. This supposition is behind much of the community economic development and community action program parts of the War on Poverty. (Title VII of the Economic Opportunity Act, as amended, contains the economic development portion, and was the funding authority for the Community Development Corporations. Title II was the authority for the CAPs.) This supposition is also behind a British program which appears to have been modeled after the U.S. community action program (Loney, 1980). However, to the extent that these programs only change who is employed or when people work, and do not increase the size of the economy and the number of people working, they only move poverty around and do nothing to reduce it. Unfortunately, this was the case with the design of many of the War on Poverty programs.

Where programs engage in authentic economic development,[1] real reductions in poverty can result, as has been achieved spectacularly by the Mondragon co-operatives in the Basque area of Spain (Oakeshott, 1978), and has been proposed for the United States by Sachs (1975) and attempted in a few cases (for example, see Maher, 1980, and Sachs, et al, 1982; Harrell Rodgers' paper in this section discusses some of these issues in his consideration of labor market strategies).

Given the important role played by professionals in poverty programs, another policy perspective would be to ask, "why have we been blind to the way in which our professional institutional roles and broader social values profoundly influence our approach to social problems?" (Guttentag, 1970:15) Professionals have been integrally involved in all poverty programs in the U.S. to date. Why? Can one group be truly necessary in every case? Further, what role have professionals played in the success, or lack of success, of these programs? Though a start has been made on these questions, and these questions are, at least implicitly, dealt with in many of the articles in this book, we still are not close to satisfactory answers. (For example, see Lee Fremont-Smith's article.)

A final possible policy perspective is to ask why researchers have not looked into policies that have not been tried in the United States. Partly, of course, the answer is in our bias for studying what *is*, but this cannot be the entire reason, especially given the presence of many varieties of programs in Europe that have never been tried in the U.S. These European programs are not brand-new innovations. As Walter Korpi (1980:287) has recently said,

> in examining the present social policy agenda in the United States, the European observer finds lively debates on issues that he or she has previously met only in the more or less dusty pages of historical accounts of the development of social policy at home. (See also Patterson, 1981:30, 33, 72-87, 166.)

Many of the different programs that exist widely throughout Europe are briefly described in Harrell Rodgers' article. One article is too short a space for detailed presentation of these programs and the issues raised by them. But Rodgers does clearly lay out the skeleton of many of the most important differences between European and U.S. policy. He also presents some data on the different positions of the poor in these countries. While we cannot say to what extent these differences are due to the differences in programs, this is, at the least, an interesting hypothesis for future investigation.

There has of course been some start at investigating and debating the desirability of using some of the same principles in the U.S. that are used in Europe. Some of this work is cited by Rodgers. In addition, several years ago, the Institute for Research on Poverty held a conference on Income-Tested versus Universal Transfer Programs ("The Issues at the Conference", 1979). However, none of this literature examines in detail the reasons why more has not been done, at least by researchers, in the United States.

The other three articles in this section examine the policy perspective inherent in some part of a method of studying certain issues. Leon Ginsberg provides several examples of research that "worked", largely because of who performed the research and why. Ginsberg argues that had the Welfare Department that he is Commissioner of farmed out this research to others (either commercial firms or academics), the desirable results would not have occurred. The most interesting aspect of Ginsberg's article is the set of issues it raises concerning how research is used. In this case research is used as a means of informing the public about poverty policy issues. The extent to which government agencies make information available to the public honestly, openly, and in an unbiased manner determines the extent to which official information contributes to the democratic process or constitutes manipulation. Lee Fremont-Smith makes many of the same points from a different perspective.

The final paper in this section presents a different political problem. Kenneth Neubeck, discussing the income maintenance experiments, argues that if the aim of poverty research is to benefit the poor, it is counter-productive to engage in research confined to the viability of specific pilot programs where it is politically impossible for those programs to be established. This returns us to points made in the Introduction to Part I, to Goldstein's paper, and to the Introduction to Part III and the papers by Rist and Ferleger.

NOTES

1. There is a distinction between economic growth (increase in output or in income per capita) and economic development (a change in the underlying economic structure such that the standard of living increases for the poorest members of society). This meaning of economic development is what we mean by "authentic economic development". For discussions of this difference see Conroy (1975:1), Hagen (1968:29), or Tussing (1975:74).

REFERENCES

Blau, Peter M. and Meyer, Marshall W. (1971) <u>Bureaucracy in Modern Society</u>. New York: Random House, Inc., Second Edition.
Conroy, Michael E. (1975) <u>The Challenge of Urban Economic Development</u>. Lexington: Lexington Books.
Guttentag, Marcia (1970) "The Insolence of Office..." <u>Journal of Social Issues</u> 26:11-17.
Hagen, Everett E. (1968) <u>The Economics of Development</u>. Homewood: Richard D. Irwin Inc.
Helfgot, Joseph H. (1981) <u>Professional Reforming</u>. Lexington: Lexington Books.
Korpi, Walter (1980) "Approaches to the Study of Poverty in the United States: Critical Notes from a European Perspective." In <u>Poverty and Public Policy: An Evaluation of Social Science Research</u>, edited by Vincent T. Covello. Cambridge: Schenkman Publishing Co.
Loney, Martin (1980) "Community Action and Anti-Poverty Strategies: Some Transatlantic Comparisons." <u>Community Development Journal</u> 15:91-103.
Maher, Timothy (1980) "The Indianapolis-Mondragon Experiment Revisited." <u>Self Management</u> 8, No. 1:21-22.

Moynihan, Daniel P. (1969) "The Professors and the Poor." In <u>On Understanding Poverty</u>, edited by Daniel P. Moynihan. New York: Basic Books, Inc.

Nagel, Stuart (1981) Personal Communication.

Oakeshott, Michael (1978) <u>The Case for Workers Co-ops</u>. London: Routledge and Kegan Paul.

Patterson, James T. (1981) <u>America's Struggle Against Poverty, 1900-1980</u>. Cambridge: Harvard University Press.

Rule, James B. (1978) <u>Insight & Social Betterment: A Preface to Applied Social Science</u>. New York: Oxford University Press.

Ryan, William (1971) <u>Blaming the Victim</u>. New York: Vintage Books.

Sachs, Stephen M. (1975) "Self-Management: The Core of an Effective Program to Eliminate Poverty." In <u>Analysing Poverty Policy</u>, edited by Dorothy James. Lexington: Lexington Books.

Sachs, Stephen M. and Axelson, Cathy (1982) "Building Workplace Democracy in the U.S." <u>Communities</u> 55.

"The Issues at the Conference" (1979) <u>Focus</u> 3:10-14.

Tussing, A. Dale (1975) <u>Poverty in a Dual Economy</u>. New York: St. Martin's Press.

WHO BENEFITS FROM KNOWLEDGE ABOUT THE HEALTH OF UNDOCUMENTED MEXICANS?

Joseph Nalven

INTRODUCTION

When the question of the health of undocumented Mexicans in the United States is raised, there are two prominent and generally unrelated responses. The first response springs from the maturing research on the health of Mexican Americans (California Raza Health Alliance, 1979; Hayes-Bautista, 1980; Keefe, Padilla, and Carlos, 1979; Shearer and Donahue, n.d., U.S. Department of Health, Education and Welfare, 1979); the second response comes out of the national debate on undocumented immigration to the United States in which a significant number of immigrants is represented by individuals of Mexican origin.[1] When these two separate lines of inquiry are brought together, the dilemma for health researchers is obvious: the asking of immigration status in a health survey to determine how such status might influence the health care and health condition of a large number of undocumented individuals who reside in the United States might prejudice the person being interviewed and undermine the successful implementation of the survey.[2] Furthermore, there is a positive, ethical bias among health researchers. The object of health research is intended to include the target population in the existing system of health care (Andersen et al., 1980:4-5; California Raza Health Alliance, 1979:7, 162). However, the information gathered about an undocumented population might be "abused" (as viewed from the perspective of individuals who hold an inclusionary bias) by government officials who emphasize fiscal restraint and by a general public that is antagonistic to undocumented immigration. This latter view can be described as an exclusionary perspective.

Until the contest between those individuals who wish to include and those who wish to exclude undocumented immigrants from the government-reimbursed system of health care is resolved, there are important health issues that will only be partially addressed in the years to come: does the legal barrier to health care create public health risks in the wider community as well as among the undocumented population? Does the limitation of access to prenatal care increase the incidence of morbidity among the children of undocumented women? (Note that these children, by virtue of birth in the

United States, are citizens of the United States.) Does the exclusion of undocumented workers from health services create a less than charitable, if not immoral, situation in which the workers who are more likely to be exposed to occupational health dangers are also those who are deterred from obtaining treatment from a fear of deportation and are probably left ignorant of the risk to which they are exposed?

Data-gathering and research on undocumented immigrants cannot be viewed in the same, social action paradigm of "normal" applied poverty research. Gone is the assumption that an improved understanding of a poverty-related situation, process, or problem provides an improved grounding for re-designing existing programs or advocacy for new ones. In place of this assumption is the opposition of two, divergent, social-action contexts: the inclusive and exclusive contexts for applying knowledge about the life style and community impacts of a specific population segment, namely, undocumented immigrants. It is important for the applied poverty research community to grasp these divergent contexts, not simply to understand how applied poverty research is foreshortened when the study population is undocumented, but also to consider how an expansion of an exclusionary policy context, proposed by "conservative" legislators and administrators, might affect research on other poverty, population groups.

The question for researchers who study poverty-related themes is whether legislative or administrative decisions to alter the definition of poverty actually aggravate the poverty condition. For example, a halving of the poverty-line may save millions in fiscal dollars that had been targeted for social services to the poor. Does this definitional change of what is to be considered poverty actually change the indices used to describe poverty? If not, does the short-term fiscal saving get shifted to other sources (such as a new settlement-house movement), or displaced to possible, future impacts? Advocates who hold that individuals are (or at least should be) responsible for their living condition will likely hold forth for a massive wave of Horatio Alger-success stories, or, in the event that these do not transpire in sufficient numbers, point out that the victims are the cause of their own problems. Advocates who hold that the environment can be controlled or influenced through intervention -- and here we have a range of government, intervention programs being targeted for reduction or elimination -- will argue that withdrawal of assistance to the poor will not magically transform these individuals into independent and successful members of the working masses. The researcher may, once more, have a new opportunity to investigate individual-environment controversies -- an opportunity set in motion by executive and legislative action being generated from an exclusionary context.

THE INCLUSIONARY CONTEXT

The inclusionary perspective towards the undocumented immigrant generally begins with a statement about the economic role the undocumented worker plays in the United States. The undocumented worker takes jobs which American workers generally discard as being too hard and without adequate compensation. These individuals pay social security and other deducted payroll taxes just as other citizens do (Cardenas and Flores, 1980:30; Community Research Associates, 1980:82-9, 316-23). In effect, they are "undocumented taxpayers." Thus, the exclusion of these individuals and their dependents from government reimbursed services can be viewed as hypocritical insofar as government is only too willing to accept their tax contributions. Additionally, the exclusion of these individuals from services is detrimental both to themselves and to the wider community (Cornelius, 1980; Van den Noort, 1980). Excluding them from health services creates a potential health hazard and may lead to higher rates of handicapped children and mortality because of poor prenatal, maternal care. These indirect health consequences may end up costing the government more in the long run than what is saved in immediate expenses.

Beyond weighing costs and benefits, there are two legal considerations which buttress the inclusionary context. First, based on the equal protection clause of the Fourteenth Amendment, the undocumented immigrant may be viewed as having a right to services until such time as he or she is deported by immigration authorities. Second, even if there is no right based on equal protection considerations, the undocumented immigrant may be extended services based on the semantics of residency and socio-economic characteristics, not on legal immigration status; because legal status is not included in the definition of eligibility, undocumented immigrants cannot be excluded from services available to residents.[3]

Legal-Administrative Considerations

It could be argued that a trend is developing, particularly in the judiciary, for including undocumented immigrants in the system of rights and responsibilities of American citizens. First, there was the question of whether these persons should be counted in the 1980 census. After all, it was argued, millions of dollars in federal spending was at stake, not to mention several Congressional seats: if these decisions were to be based on the number of people in the United States, let them be citizens. The Supreme Court, in letting stand a lower-court decision, ruled against this view: the Constitution speaks of "whole persons," and no mention is made of legal (or lawful) immigration status (Mann, 1980:8).

Second, a Texas judge ruled that a 1975 law that excluded children of undocumented parents from schools was unconstitutional.

The Fifth U.S. Circuit Court of Appeals reversed this decision, but their ruling was in turn reversed by Supreme Court Justice Powell. The U.S. Supreme Court ruled that the State of Texas could not exclude undocumented children from the Texas school system (Plyler v. Doe, 1982). Powell's interim decision viewed the "balance of harms" weighing more heavily on the children than on the school districts. Powell argued that "not only are the children consigned to ignorance and illiteracy, they are also denied the benefits of association in the classroom with students and teachers of diverse backgrounds." Continuing in an area that touches on the health of these children, Powell observed, "the children remain idle or are subject prematurely to physical toil, conditions that may lead to emotional and behavioral problems" (San Diego Union, 1980: A-1). It could also be observed that to the extent that these children are involved in farm work, they will receive a longer exposure to the heavy pesticide burden that is suspected among farm laborers (see research cited below).

Finally, the landmark Graham Vs. Richardson decision (which parallels Powell's argument above) explicitly removes equal protection considerations from fiscal ones. The decision states that "since an alien [note that "alien" is not "undocumented" alien in this case] as well as a citizen is a 'person' for equal protection purposes, a concern for fiscal integrity is not a compelling justification for the questioned classification."[4] How far this rationale can be extended from "citizen" to "whole person," thereby including "undocumented" persons as well, remains to be tested.

Administrators can also play an important role in interpreting the equal protection rationale, particularly by emphasizing "residency" over "immigration status" for determining eligibility.[5] For example, the Director of California's Department of Health Services argued, in a memorandum to the State's Attorney General, "that Counties should be encouraged to provide health care to all who need it and to seek reimbursement for that care consistent with the promotion of accessible, acceptable, quality health care services."[6] This opinion adheres to the State's Welfare and Institution Code which requires counties to provide health care to indigents. However, the State Attorney General rejected this view and asserted that "County employees may be personally liable for knowingly authorizing the expenditure of public funds for, or providing health care services to, illegal or undocumented immigrants."[7] This issue has not yet been resolved in court.

Research Considerations

There is scant research on the health of lawfully-admitted immigrants to the United States.[8] "Research"--in the strict sense of the term -- on the health of undocumented immigrants is nonexistent. What does exist are inferences drawn from samples which include many undocumented immigrants (but which do not use immigration status as an independent variable), from health-care-provider utilization reports, and from reports describing the poverty-related health problems that exist in the undocumented worker's home country. Let us examine the health profile of undocumented persons developed from these data sources.

Van den Noort, in an attempt to portray the health status of undocumented immigrants in Orange County, California, readily admits to the weakness of hospital admission and referral reports as a valid data base for his enterprise:

> What are the medical needs of the population? People who come here are generally young and this means a high incidence of injuries, a high birthrate, and lots of children. The frequency of serious infectious diseases such as tuberculosis and parasitic infestation is relatively high. In other aspects they resemble the indigenous indigent population with the usual range of diseases, most of which are detected in a late stage as a medical emergency. They are not welcome in most hospitals and in most physicians' offices. For the most part, they come to [the University of California, Irvine, Medical College] or CCOC which is also operated by UCI... We cannot [quantify] this suffering or measure its cost. We do have case by case information of individuals who have refused care rather than apply for Medi-Cal. We do have information that Medi-Cal application has caused [the Immigration and Naturalization Service] to contact certain patients. We do know that 20-30% of CCOC patients, UCIMC pediatrics patients, and obstetrical patients are uncertified aliens. (Van den Noort, 1980:20-1)

The bill collection process "kicks out," as it were, indigents who cannot be certified as eligible, almost exclusively because they are undocumented immigrants. However, hospital records do not identify undocumented immigrants who do pay (out of fear of deportation, many do pay). Thus, the "data base" is skewed towards medical emergency cases of those undocumented immigrants who are unable to come up with a payment plan. Moreover, hospital records are untenable as a data base for reflecting the health status of all the undocumented immigrants in the community in which the hospital is located.

Since most undocumented immigrants in California are from Mexico, it is understandable that health professionals in California might want to augment their understanding of the health problems of undocumented Mexicans in the United States by adding the complex of poverty-related health problems that undocumented immigrants bring with them from Mexico. These health problems would be compounded by the life style and oftentimes difficult working conditions of an undocumented work force. An example of how "Raza" health professionals in California have attempted to extrapolate the health care needs of undocumented workers can be found in "The California Raza Health Plan: An Action Guide for the Promotion of Raza Health in California."

> ... little is known about the health status and health service utilization of the Raza undocumented population. Because of the population's illegal character, they are difficult to identify and assess. In many ways, their socio-economic and cultural characteristics are similar to the Chicano population before World War II: predominantly monolingual Spanish, largely rural, traditional Catholic, median education under 8 years, majority below the poverty level and little formal contact with a Westernized medical system. Though much of this population is young (i.e., 20-30 years), the health disorders that have been identified are dramatic. Due to a generally deprived history of public health [intervention] in Mexico, much of the undocumented suffer from a variety of disorders (e.g., hypertension, tuberculosis, syphilis, salmonella); the poor and stressful working conditions are an additional catalyst to many disabling and disease conditions. An accurate assessment of these conditions must be carried out by mandated public agencies ... (California Raza Health Alliance, 1979:161).

The portrait of the undocumented individual given above continues to be fairly accurate. However, there are important details that should be added to this portrait. With the dramatic urbanization of less developed countries over the last half-century, including Mexico, the "rural" proletariat is giving way to an "urban" proletariat. Mexico continues to send short-term migrants to work in U.S. agriculture. However, it may now be that the larger proportion will soon be permanent residents working in urban settings.

Best-guess estimates of all undocumented persons in the United States have been in the range of 3 to 6 million individuals with Mexicans representing about half this number. However, recently released survey results by Mexico's Department of Labor Statistics, CENIET, have placed the number of undocumented Mexicans in the United States between .5 and 1.25 million at any one time. To bring this survey result into accord with U.S. estimates of all undocumented persons, either the percentage of undocumented Mexicans as part of all undocumented persons would have to be lowered or the total number of undocumented persons would. At present, these estimates have been left to stand independently, especially since no one truly knows what the precise size or composition of this population is.[9]

What is interesting about the Mexican survey results, however, is that only 13.1% of undocumented Mexicans were found to be residing outside the U.S. Southwest. 50.8% of all undocumented Mexicans were believed to be in California and 24.7% in Texas. Thus, a national policy could be developed along bilateral lines with Mexico that emphasized a regional strategy for jobs and social services.

Returning to the portrait of the undocumented person, we must recognize that since World War II, there has been a revolution in communications and transportation which has broken down the insulation of rural and urban processes. In both settings in the U.S., however, the undocumented worker continues to occupy secondary-sector jobs, those which are at the bottom of the ladder of success, often "stoop" labor, low paid, and, if hazardous, less likely to be given the more rigorous protections given to citizens. The undocumented worker often works in a context of exploitation, characterized by low pay and poor working conditions.[10] In this context, the employer gives occupational health and safety regulations low priority. Since the undocumented worker rarely calls official attention to this work context out of fear of deportation, the regulatory agencies are not pressed to review these work situations as often or as thoroughly as they might if the workers were citizens or lawfully-admitted residents.

One notable exception to the undocumented worker's reluctance to press for equal protection under existing State and Federal labor codes calls attention to the way in which low wages are linked to hazardous work conditions. A dozen workers on a Southern California avocado grove filed a complaint with the U.S. Department of Labor that they were not being paid the minimum wage. (Labor officials do not use legal immigration status to decide whether they will investigate a complaint.) Two of the workers described their working conditions:

> Roberto Lopez Sanchez, 16, told how workers suffer infections and other ailments caused by the chemical sprays used in the avocado groves. Sanchez . . . said, "They don't give us masks or gloves when we spray and the chemicals can get on you and cause a rash or sores."
> Ambrize added, "I have headaches sometimes from the spraying. My nose dries up and I start coughing and my lungs feel hot." But the working conditions didn't concern these men so much as their belief that their previous employers had underpaid them. . . . The men contended in interviews that at the last place they worked they had not been paid the minimum wage for working in the avocado groves, had received no overtime for long days and were suspicious of deductions from their pay. (Montemayor, 1980:26)

While this information about the health status of undocumented workers is anecdotal, it directly identifies the probable link between illegal immigration status and a higher health risk than that run by individuals who are citizens or individuals who are lawfully-admitted to the U.S. What research does exist fails to control for immigration status as a variable. For example, a study on the health effects of exposure to pesticides among farm workers in a county adjacent to the one cited in the preceding example came up with a complementary finding. The study found that farm worker children suffered birth defects at a rate thirteen times the national average. A suggested cause was genetic, pesticide poisoning.[11] In this case, the study population probably included permanent residents (many of whom live in the nearby Mexican city of Mexicali and are referred to as "commuter" workers) as well as native Mexican Americans. In this study, the issue may properly be more one of ethnicity (Mexican or Mexican origin) than one of immigration status. It is well to recognize the historical pattern where owners of small farms of non-Mexican heritage have been supplanted by large-scale agribusiness and, in this process, there has been an associated shift to farm workers of Mexican origin (Moles, 1979:20-7). Many of the short-term agricultural workers on these farms are likely to be undocumented Mexicans. However, in the border region, the picture becomes complicated by the choice of many permanent residents of Mexican origin who choose to live in Mexico (the "commuter" worker). To the average Anglo-American these distinctions are lost, and all are subsumed under "Mexicans." However, to health researchers, these differences may be significant; the configuration of health effects and immigration status, clearly, would be different in rural and urban work settings as well as in border and non-border settings. In a critique of another health study, and one that would be applicable in the study cited here, the author noted:

> Nor did the sample systematically stratify first generation Mexican-born and second and third generation American-born members, although such distinctions may drastically affect the variables of language, education, <u>immigration status</u>, familiarity with services, and level of acculturation; <u>all of these in turn affect health and use of services</u> (Salcido, 1979:375). (emphasis added)

Although it would appear from the preceding discussion that immigration status should be considered as a factor in explaining health status and lower utilization rates, there is little treatment of this theme in the literature on Latino health in general and Mexican American health in particular. Furthermore, in the brief treatment that is given, it is unclear whether the researchers see the variable of immigration status as co-varying with education, income, and ethnicity, thereby undercutting its priority as an independent variable, or whether the methodological difficulty in interviewing individuals when immigration status is asked for precludes researchers from adequately treating the immigration variable.

In a review of the literature, Weaver pointed out the salience of the mass deportations of Mexicans in the United States, the most recent being "Operation Wetback" in the 1950s. The trauma associated with these experiences may partially explain the "Mexican American's habit of associating health workers with 'authorities' and their resultant reluctance to contact them" (Weaver, 1973:96). Yet, despite this acknowledgment of lack of legal immigration status as a barrier to health service -- whether as the act of reporting suspected undocumented individuals to the Immigration and Naturalization Service or as an internalized fear among the undocumented population -- the research aims Weaver suggests make no mention of immigration status as a potentially useful explanatory variable. He asks,

> Is utilization of public and private providers a function of cost, location or information; or is symptomatology, socio-economic status or age the principal determinant(s)? We have seen claims that Mexican Americans avoid "Anglo Medicine," preferring to rely on curanderos, family or friends. Other research suggests that the fee system, or availability and ease of access, or the patient's education and acculturation is the controlling factor (Weaver, 1973:101).

Seven years after Weaver's review, at a time when the focus on undocumented immigration had been dramatically heightened with the work of the Select Commission on Immigration and Refugee Policy, a paper titled, "Access to Medical Care Among the Hispanic Population of the Southwestern United States" made no mention of undocumented immigration status. The paper was presented at the American Public Health Association in a session sponsored by the Latino Caucus of the APHA and the National Center for Health Services Research (Andersen et al., 1980). Once again, the issue was avoided: was this because these researchers saw undocumented immigration status as 1) having low theoretical significance for health research or 2) having low priority on the research agenda because using immigration status raises a difficult methodological problem?

The question becomes yet more complicated when the relation of the soon-to-be-created Latino health data base and health care service programming is raised. If undocumented immigration is associated with additional health problems, either in type or magnitude, and recognizing that the Latino health survey will not control for the immigration variable,[12] then it follows that the data base that will be used by administrators and health planners will influence their programming decisions in unknown ways. The nub of the problem arises when it is remembered that services which are reimbursed by government programs such as Medicaid or Medi-Cal will not be covered if the client is determined to be undocumented. Thus, the data base -- because it is inclusive -- will lead to "ghost" programming inasmuch as some of the statistically covered persons are excluded from receiving reimbursement for the targeted health service. To be sure, there are areas in the health care delivery system in which there is tremendous slippage: the personnel in these areas have a good, working knowledge of the problems of undocumented persons and are giving health services to these individuals. However, these services are not being "officially" targeted to such persons and may result in a financial drain on the service provider (Young, Hall, and Collins, 1979); here we enter into an area of ethics and advocacy of health care personnel who recognize a responsibility to provide health care that is based on need, not on legal immigration status. By not screening out undocumented individuals from receiving health care services, the potential for "ghost" programming may be unwittingly minimized; and to the extent that it exists, it can be viewed perversely as the costs due a bureaucracy that imposes an immigration model on a system for health care.

There is another line of inquiry that focuses on health and the undocumented immigrant: this line of inquiry, however, is not concerned with the specific health profile of undocumented immigrants, but rather with the allegedly minimal cost impacts they presently have on the health care system. This type of research serves as a counter-argument to the "proof" of a fiscal burden that local jurisdictions claim.[13] The under-utilization of health services by undocumented immigrants, however, is a status quo argument. If services are made available to them, it would appear that utilization would increase, at least to the level of under-utilization of native-born Latinos in the United States.[14]

THE EXCLUSIONARY CONTEXT

Recent opinion polls reaffirm the majority's antagonistic view towards undocumented immigration to the United States (Loveman and Hofstetter, forthcoming; Gallup, 1980: A-21). This antagonism is based on one or more of the following considerations: first, the set of laws and agencies that operate on the assumption of national boundaries which have integrity and are enforced tends to be undermined by the "silent invasion" at the U.S.'s southern border (Carter, 1977; San Diego Union, 1978); second, the growing national consciousness and desire for a "quality of life" social and physical environment -- a goal that is undermined by undocumented population growth, especially by individuals who do not adhere to zero population growth fertility patterns (Conner, 1979; Select Commission on Immigration and Refugee Policy Newsletter, 1980:4-5); third, the reservoir of nativist and racist sentiment for a "White America."[15] Furthermore, even if undocumented workers displace only a minimum of U.S. workers, the recessionary climate and substantial unemployment reinforce the paranoia of many labor organizations towards the loss of jobs to a work force that generally accepts its exploitative work situation. When the focus shifts from jobs to social services, there is a popular perception -- that undocumented immigrants are a fiscal burden (Bustamante, 1980). Given the dramatic rise in costs in the health care industry for U.S. citizens, the thought of undocumented immigrants getting government-reimbursed services becomes intolerable.

Legal-Administrative Considerations

It is important to recognize the inconsistent way in which immigration law is conceived and implemented. A good example of the selective nature of immigration law is the penalty against harboring undocumented persons. It is a felony to give room and board to an undocumented person, unless such aid is given as compensation for work. Employers are exempt from legal sanctions for hiring undocumented workers -- with the few exceptions in State law going unenforced (U.S. Commission on Civil Rights, 1980:60; General Accounting Office, 1980:47). However, if new legislation were passed, making employers liable for hiring undocumented workers, employers would be placed in a role of immigration officers in their seeking to determine the immigration eligibility of the worker. Because such eligibility tests would be an onerous burden, employers would likely simplify the hiring procedure: discriminate against individuals who have the same physical and/or cultural characteristics of the popular stereotype of undocumented workers. In the U.S.-Mexico border region, this procedure would result in widespread discrimination against individuals of Mexican origin. To compensate for this possibility, policy-makers are considering taking the immigration eligibility step out of the hands of employers: all U.S. workers would have to carry a national, worker identification card and having such a card would certify the worker's eligibility to work in the U.S. However, this compensating measure has, in turn, aroused the ire of civil libertarians who fear the potential administrative abuse of a centralized information bank. (Louv, 1980a:95).

While the national debate on immigration policy continues, employers remain beyond the pale of legal sanctions for "harboring" undocumented workers (insofar as their "harboring" is a marketplace transaction, not an altruistic one). For employees and officials of government agencies which provide social services, the immunity from sanctions is less clear. Government employees could claim, like private-sector employers, that they do not knowingly aid undocumented individuals. However, if the immigration eligibility step is inserted into their procedures (for admitting children into public school, for granting Medicaid or Medi-Cal reimbursement for health services, and so forth), then government workers require screening units or procedures to eliminate undocumented immigrants from receiving services. Such a doubling up of immigration eligibility steps with the existing set of eligibility requirements leads to discrimination against citizens and permanent residents who have the same physical and/or cultural characteristics as the prototypical undocumented immigrant -- Latinos. One doctor at a hospital in San Diego refused admission of a Mexican-American youth who had accidentally shot himself saying that the hospital did not want "Mexican aliens laying around the ward, eating up our funds."[16] The doctor was acting contrary to his oath of office: he was acting as an administrator, concerned with the cost of treatment, not with the care of a human being.

The exclusionary perspective which motivated this doctor's admission refusal is reinforced by the legal opinion of California's Attorney General. This opinion states:

- Counties are not authorized to provide non-emergency (elective) services to undocumented immigrants under Welfare and Institution Section 17000.
- Counties may provide non-emergency services to undocumented immigrants if the client applies for Medi-Cal and in the course of applying claims that residency status is legal.
- County employees may be personally liable for knowingly authorizing the expenditure of public funds for, or providing health care services to, illegal or undocumented immigrants.[17]

The County of San Diego, for example, had a screening unit set up in the County-University Hospital.[18] Although the Immigration and Naturalization Service said that they did not ask the hospital to provide them data on possible undocumented persons, the County screening unit requested checks on suspected individuals if they did not pay for the health services received. The County was intent on proving their financial liability in a law suit against the Federal government. The burden of this health cost, in the County's view, is part of the overall failure of Federal immigration law and its lack of enforcement. The County's action coincides with the Attorney General in litigation of local-level costs and federal-level responsibilities and benefits (from the tax contributions of undocumented workers).

The Attorney General's Office has not only taken California agencies and their employees to task for providing services to undocumented immigrants; it has also sought to exclude undocumented immigrants directly from receiving benefits under California laws. In a court case heard in Los Angeles, the Attorney General argued that two undocumented persons were ineligible to receive benefits under the victims of crime legislation. Although the court held that they <u>were</u> eligible for benefits, the lone dissenting opinion argued, consistent with the Attorney General's view, that "legality of residence does not add a requirement but rather, in further defining eligible persons, simply recognizes and reiterates the self evident fact that, to be a qualified resident, one must ordinarily be legally within the state."[19] The key issue is whether the undocumented person is in the United States: in terms of physical presence, the answer is "yes;" in terms of legal presence, the answer is "yes" and "no." The legal presence is ambiguous because of the clash of views on residency and equal protection. The majority opinion held that the "addition of the word 'lawful' as a modifier of the term 'resident of California' is clearly unwarranted" (Cabral and Vasquez Vs. State of California Board of Control, 1980:7). This court decision is not decisive in the contest of inclusionary and exclusionary perspectives toward undocumented immigrants. The attempts to fashion new Federal legislation may seek to override such judicial decisions, especially where the climate of public opinion weighs heavily against undocumented immigration.[20]

Research Considerations

It is important to grasp that impact studies of undocumented immigrants are rarely requested by government agencies and elected officials with the idea of providing better services to undocumented immigrants; rather, these studies are generally motivated by a desire to determine the fiscal costs, job displacement and other community-wide burdens that may be attributable to undocumented individuals.[21] Local-level governments, for example, may not necessarily wish to remove these individuals but to establish a basis for Federal-level reimbursement. The National Association of Counties Task Force on Aliens, Refugees and Migrants adopted a set of resolutions that had originated with the County of San Diego regarding undocumented immigrants. These resolutions were directed to the Select Commission on Immigration and Refugee Policy in an attempt to make the local-level viewpoint felt by the Commission and with the hope that the Commission would incorporate this viewpoint in its final report to the President. Recommendation #4 dealt with health and social services:

> That the federal government reimburse State and local governments for the costs of health and social service benefits provided by them to indigent undocumented aliens. Since immigration laws and policies are a federal responsibility, the Board of Supervisors believes that the federal government should bear the costs of necessary medical services for these people. In San Diego County the cost of medical care for all indigent undocumented aliens during 1979 was approximately $4 million (County of San Diego News Release, 1980:5-6).

This projected cost impact for all San Diego hospitals (with the County-University Hospital absorbing about 20% of this amount) was about 1% to 2% of all patient costs for 1979 (Community Research Associates, 1980:xiv). The costs of undocumented immigrants may have been proportionately higher if other elements of the health care system, such as clinics, had been factored in the County of San Diego-generated study. Still, the bottom line for the elected officials is: are these costs tolerable? Who should pay for them? While the costs reported for the County of San Diego were tolerable to the extent that the Board of Supervisors did not call for deportation (in fact, arguing for recognition of their overall positive impact on this border county), the Supervisors sought reimbursement from the Federal government.

A Los Angeles County study put the health care costs for undocumented immigrants for the County at 8.3% to 12.4% -- or between 40 and 60 million dollars (Flores, Moore, and Schey, 1979:24). While the manner of estimation may be called into question, the stakes are clearly higher. Los Angeles County instituted more rigorous screening procedures to save on these costs. However, the question of what effect this "saving" has on the overall public health is not raised by officials asking about fiscal costs. The association of fiscal saving and public health costs was raised in a study conducted in Orange County, California:

> Only a year and a half after the county began requiring everyone who could not pay for medical care to apply for Medi-Cal -- and reporting to the INS those who refused to apply and those who were without proof of residency -- medical problems multiplied:
>
> -Extrapulmonary tuberculosis increased 57%
> -Salmonellosis increased 47%
> -Infectitious hepatitis increased 14%
> -Rubella increased 53%
> -Syphilis increased 153% (Flores, Moore, and Schey, 1979:47).

Is the missing factor the exclusion of undocumented immigrants? Possibly. Such correlations are highly suggestive of the health impacts that can be attributed to the exclusion of undocumented immigrants from health care service. However, such impacts have not motivated government-sponsored research into this area of inquiry.[22] The general absence of this line of research can be explained by 1) the lack of interest in the negative consequences of exclusionary practices by those officials who are concerned with fiscal impacts, and 2) the possible fear of those officials (who would like to provide services to undocumented immigrants) that research which showed these negative consesquences -- especially where these were community-wide, public health consequences -- would be counter-productive. The demonstration of public health problems due to exclusionary health-care-provider practices would, given the public's sentiment against undocumented immigration, not persuade officials to open up services to these individuals, but rather persuade officials to deport the "problem."

The American public should fully consider the types of impacts that could result from excluding undocumented individuals from the health system, not only as they affect undocumented persons, but also citizens and permanent residents. The first type is a public health impact. The widespread use of undocumented labor in restaurant kitchen crews (as cooks, food "preps," and dishwashers), especially in the Southwest, raises the potential problem of the spread of infectious disease. The County of San Diego, for instance, recently instituted a food-handler course as a result of a rash of infectious hepatitis cases among kitchen staff, including at one of San Diego's fine tourist restaurants. While no link was established with undocumented workers and the hepatitis outbreak, the potential is there. The exclusionary practice would not, to be sure, "cause" the disease transmission (nor would an inclusionary practice necessarily prevent it); it would simply undermine the maintenance of a sound public health program.

The second type of health impact is individual-centered. It must be remembered that the children of undocumented women, if born in the United States, are not undocumented: they are United States citizens. Thus, the exclusion of the mothers of future United States citizens can be surmised to raise the incidence of pre- and post-natal problems, which, in turn, would lead to long-term fiscal impacts. Such fiscal impacts could be avoided by including these women in health programs normally provided to pregnant women in the United States in line with standard eligibility requirements --that is, eligibility based on income level and residency, not immigration status.

More than likely, the American public will take far greater interest in the first type of impact (the public health impact) than the second type of impact (the health of U.S.-born children of undocumented parents). Nevertheless, both impacts fall on U.S. citizens and permanent residents.

CONCLUSION

The rationally-seductive solution to undocumented immigration would be to grant widespread "amnesty" (normalization of the "illegal" immigration status) to undocumented immigrants who reside in the United States, favor Mexico with a higher immigration quota and/or a limited, foreign-worker program, and modernize and strengthen the Immigration and Naturalization Service. The thrust of this solution would be to avoid the draconian measures needed to deport undocumented immigrants already in the United States, to accept some poverty-generated migration from Mexico, and to permit the agency which is designated as the manager of our border's integrity to accomplish its task. Mexico would be given priority in dealing with the much vaster potential for undocumented immigration because of the historical relationship the U.S. Southwest has with Mexico and because a strict law enforcement solution to undocumented migration would force the U.S. to militarize a 2,000-mile border. If such a solution were implemented, the exclusionary context would be pushed back to the borders of the United States: if the government is to exclude assistance to individuals who are living in poverty or who fall within the definitions used to provide social service assistance, then would it not be better to give the action inter- rather than intra-national force? Just as the United States has felt the limitations of its ability to be the policeman of the world's morality, the United States is limited in its ability to provide the world -- or to the Third World countries truly in need of assistance -- a standard of subsistence that would parallel its own. Even humanism must be pragmatic.

However rational or pragmatic the suggested solution is, it is doubtful that legislators will be able to pass the appropriate legislation.[23] Public sentiment is strongly antagonistic to giving "amnesty" to undocumented immigrants. Public sentiment was also strongly against giving "amnesty" to the youth who avoided the Vietnam War. Symbolically, "amnesty" is difficult to achieve as a broad-based measure. Thus, the exclusionary context is likely to continue to influence the way in which illegal immigration status is handled in research directed at the Mexican-origin population in the United States, namely, avoidance of immigration status as an explanatory factor in the health status, the access to health services and the types of strategies employed by Latinos for health treatment, especially in the U.S. Southwest border region. Health researchers may find this outcome acceptable, especially since the only research conducted by individuals and agencies with an exclusionary bias has thus far been limited to program evaluation and fiscal-oriented studies. "Research," in such an exclusionary framework, may be considered definitionally to be not "real" research.[24] The limitations of time and budget and the frequent attempt to flag the public's attention by policy-makers with the study's results severely test the empirical value of this type of data-gathering enterprise. Even so, such "research" may be in greater demand in a fiscally conservative administration and legislature -- at least, insofar as the scope of services for poverty-related programs narrows.

The applied poverty research community might do well to ask whether their research would be affected with the expected narrowing of the definition of program eligibility. Perhaps, the equal protection guarantees for U.S. citizens will forestall the type of schizophrenic response to research on undocumented immigrants: that is, applied poverty researchers will continue to do research as usual since there will be no equivalent to the fear of deportation in the targeted, study populations; the only change will be in the number of individuals who will qualify for services and in the number of programs that will continue to be funded. Another and more disheartening possiblity is that what one U.S. Senator refers to as America's "compassion fatigue," when talking about the plight of the undocumented immigrant, will encompass the wider domain of poverty problems: the audience for applied poverty research will turn a deaf ear to the concerns raised by investigators as they confront the outcomes of a fiscal narrowing of what government programmers consider poverty to be.[25,26]

NOTES

1. The work of the Select Commission on Immigration and Refugee Policy has summarized this national debate and made recommendations for modifying U.S. immigration laws and quotas in a report to the President. Many of these issues are also discussed by another federal commission, U.S. Commission on Civil Rights, holding hearings at about the same time as the Select Commission on Immigration and Refugee Policy. See also Teitlebaum, 1980:21-59.
2. The methodological problem of asking for immigration status in a large-scale survey is discussed in the plans for the first major survey of Hispanics ("Latinos" is preferred by this author). National Center for Health Statistics, 1980:23.
3. An excellent overview of the legal issues related to Medicaid can be found in a report prepared for the Department of Health, Education and Welfare by Grace Flores, Joan Moore, and Peter Schey. See also Salazar, 1979:4-12.
4. Graham Vs. Richardson, 403 U.S. 376 (1971). Cited in Flores, Moore, and Schey, 1979:7.
5. Letter from State of California Superintendent of Schools, May 10, 1978, referring to Education Code 48200 to County Superintendents of Schools indicates that the Education Code makes a distinction about state residency, not lawful immigration status, on whether a child should attend school or not in California.
6. Memorandum from B. Myers.
7. California Attorney General Legal Opinion, CV 78, February 9, 1979.
8. "Primary Health Care Needs of Immigrants," Senate Report 96936, 1980:2. The California Policy Seminar of the State Legislature of California and the University of California has funded a two-year, preliminary study on health problems among Mexican immigrants. See Jones and Cornelius, 1980.
9. There is no definitive census-type survey to accurately evaluate the patterns of migration and settlement. The U.S. Bureau of the Census reviewed available studies for the Select Commis-

sion on Immigration and Refugee Policy and observed that "Researchers and policy-makers will have to live with the fact that the number of illegal residents in the United States cannot be closely quantified." Siegel et al, 1980:20. Recent studies in the urban areas have shown that undocumented immigrants also settle there, generally on a longer-term basis than those individuals who participate in agriculture. See studies conducted by Cardenas and Flores (Houston), Community Research Associates (San Diego), and Maram (Los Angeles). For a view that favors the greater impact of short-term, agriculture-related migrancy patterns, see Cornelius, 1979:111-121. His review was written before the three, urban-based studies were completed. Mexico's survey on Mexican nationals who were undocumented individuals in the United States is summarized in CENIET, 1977, and subsequent occasional reports. A new study by the Census Bureau estimates that the 1980 Census enumerated approximately 2 million undocumented persons, 45.5% of whom were from Mexico (Warren and Passel, 1983).

10. During the last two years, the State of California, Department of Industrial Relations, Division of Labor Standards Enforcement and the U.S. Department of Labor, Employment Standards Division, have conducted surveys among the type of firms most likely to hire undocumented workers. The object of the enforcement surveys was "to remove the economic incentive from employers who hire undocumented workers." U.S. Department of Labor Highlights, January 8, 1980:2. In an evaluation of existing, though limited data, the California Raza Health Alliance infers that the Raza (Latino) citizen and undocumented worker "would be subject to a high number of work disabilities when compared to the Anglo workforce." This higher disability rate can be attributed to the work environments in which many Latinos work and "which are unsafe and offer little opportunity for improvement through union health and safety provisions from bargaining agreements." California Raza Health Alliance, 1979:76,77.

11. Louv, 1980b:A-3, and Schwartz and Heifetz, n.d.

12. "Hispanic Health and Nutrition Examination Survey (HHANES) Supporting Statement for Preliminary Plans." The Deputy Assistant for Health Research, Statistics and Technology has stated that "undocumented persons will be included in HHANES but will not be identified as such. ... The data base will not address the issue of whether programs should be created for the use of undocumented persons." Hanft, 1980:1.

13. Cornelius, 1980:221-222. But see "Commentary on the Cornelius Report Appearing in Congressional Record, December 13, 1979, S 18455," David S. North, for a critique of how data is misused to assess the undocumented immigrants' service utilization rate.

14. An analysis of Silva-Bell cases--a group of undocumented individuals who were able to apply for legal residency status in the United States -- suggests that the rate of utilization for this group will approximate that of the overall population when the legal barrier to services is removed. Community Research Associates, 1980:178-188.
15. Loveman and Hofstetter, forthcoming, and Condon, 1980.
16. San Diego Evening Tribune, April 24, 1979:B-1.
17. California Attorney General Legal Opinion CV78, February 9, 1979.
18. The County of San Diego has since sold the County Hospital to the University of California. The screening unit will be maintained under the new management.
19. <u>Cabral and Vasquez Vs. State of California Board of Control</u>, 1980:9.
20. The interplay of judicial decisions and State and Federal legislation in the area of immigration law has created some ambiguity as to what is legally correct. Although Federal legislation excluded normal employment practices from harboring penalties, several states have enacted laws which make it illegal for employers to "knowingly" hire an undocumented worker. The California law was ruled to be constitutional by the Supreme Court, but goes unenforced because a Los Angeles County Superior Court issued an injunction pending new, comprehensive Federal legislation. Thus, though it is constitutional for states to have employer sanction legislation, and several states do have such legislation, none have contemplated enforcing these laws (except for two pending cases in Massachusetts). For a fuller discussion of employer sanction legislation, see General Accounting Office, 1980:39-49.
21. The California Department of Health Services' Director has voiced the Department's concern with the reluctance to grant <u>all</u> residents health care. There has not been a corresponding research effort to show the consequences of having an exclusionary practice in administering health care services.
22. An example of the type of inferential analysis that could be undertaken, in the absence of direct data on immigration status, can be found in Medina, 1980:21,2:1-7. Medina notes that there is an increase in health care service utilization in a clinic that is culturally sensitive to the lifestyle of Hispanics (with an avoidance of immigration inquiries) and, moreover, there is a corresponding decrease in fetal, neonatal and perinatal death rates for Hispanics in the county in which the clinic was located. Although the data was inadequate to show that the clinic was directly responsible for lowering these death rates, the author argues that this inclusion is justifiable because one can assume "(1) that many if not most Hispanic mothers in Alameda County used [the clinic], and (2) that its work is in large part responsible for the improvement shown." By

contrast, in another northern California county selected for purposes of comparison, there was no change in the Hispanic fetal and infant death rates and there was no similar clinic outreach efforts to Hispanics.
23. For an overview of the undocumented immigration dilemma as it confronted the Select Commission on Immigration and Refugee Policy in its closing months of existence, see "Flood of Immigrants Into U.S. Stirs Clamor to Shut the Door," New York Times News Service (1980).
24. For a discussion of program evaluation in the contrast of basic and applied research, see Dynes, no date.
25. Senator Alan K. Simpson, a member of the Select Commission on Immigration and Refugee Policy, used the phrase "compassion fatigue" to explain the overwhelming public sentiment against undocumented immigration. New York Times News Service, 1980:A-1.
26. An analysis of the competing altruistic and economic motives guiding the delivery of social services to undocumented immigrants can be found in "Gifts to Strangers: Public Policy and Delivery of Health Services to Illegal Aliens." Cohen, 1973:183-195.

REFERENCES

Andersen, Ronald; Zelman Lewis, Sandra; Giachello, Aida L.; Aday, Lu An, and Chiu, Grace (1980) "Access to Medical Care Among the Hispanic Population of the Southwestern United States," Center for Health Administration Studies, University of Chicago, revised paper originally presented at the American Public Health Association Meetings, Los Angeles, October 1978.

Bustamante F., Jorge A. (1980) "La Migracion Mexicana de la Dinamica Politica de las Percepciones," El Colegio de Mexico, presented at Trabajadores Indocumentados (conference), Tijuana, B.C.

<u>Cabral, Francisco, and Vasquez, Gabriel Vs. State of California Board of Control,</u> Court of Appeal, State of California, Second Appellate District, December 8, 1980, Los Angeles Superior Court.

California Attorney General Legal Opinion (1979) CV 78, February 9, 1979. Cited in Community Research Associates 1980:130.

California Raza Health Alliance (1979) "The California Raza Health Plan: An Action Guide for the Promotion of Raza Health in California," issued as a Memorandum, California Department of Health Service, Office of External Affairs, October 1979.

California State Superintendent of Schools (1978) Letter referring to Education Code 48200 to County Superintendents of Schools, May 10, 1978.

Cardenas, Gilbert, and Flores, Estevan T. (1980) "Social, Economic and Demographic Characteristics of Undocumented Mexicans in the Houston Labor Market: A Preliminary Report," prepared for the Gulf Coast Legal Foundation.

Carter, President Jimmy (1977) "Undocumented Aliens Message to the Congress," Cited in Mexican Workers in the United States. Edited by George C. Kiser and Martha Woody Kiser. Albuquerque: University of New Mexico Press, 1979, pp. 207-214.

CENIET (1977) Analisis de Algunos Resultados de la Primera Encuestra a Trabajadores Mexicanos No Documentados Devueltos de Los Estados Unidos.

Cohen, Lucy (1973) "Gifts to Strangers: Public Policy and the Delivery of Health Services to Illegal Aliens," Anthropology Quarterly, July, 1973:183-195.

Community Research Associates (1980) Undocumented Immigrants: Their Impact on the County of San Diego. County of San Diego, May 1980.

Condon, George, Jr. (1980) "Metzger Attacks Aliens, Jews in Picnic Address," San Diego Union, September 15, 1980:B-1. (Tom Metzger is the Ku Klux Klan leader in San Diego, California.)

Conner, Roger (1979) "Abolishing Illegal Immigration," Address to the Select Commission on Immigration and Refugee Policy, San Antonio, Texas, December 17, 1979.

Cornelius, Wayne (1980) "Undocumented Immigration and Access to Health Care: Short-Term 'Savings' vs. Long-Term Costs," Address delivered at a conference on "Mexican Migration: Health Care Needs and Resources," San Diego Health Council, National Association of Social Workers.

_____ (1979) "Mexican Migration to the United States (with comparative reference to Caribbean-Basin migration): The State of Current Knowledge and Recommendations for Future Research," Program for United States-Mexican Studies, University of California, San Diego.

County of San Diego (1980) News Release [on Immigration impacts], Fact Sheet, November 21, 1980.

Cross, Harry E., and Sandos, James A. (1979) "The Impact of Undocumented Mexican Workers on the United States," Battelle PDP Working Paper No. 15, Washington, D.C.

Dynes, Patrick S. (no date) "Improving Methods of Program Evaluation for Congressional Use: Prospects and Problems," Institute for Program Evaluation, General Accounting Office.

Flores, Grace; Moore, Joan, and Schey, Peter (1979) "Unpaid Medical Costs and Undocumented Aliens," prepared for the Department of Health Education and Welfare, Contract No. HEW-100-76-0216.

Gallup, George (1980) "Most U.S. Citizens Favor a Hard Line Toward Illegal Aliens," San Diego Union, November 30, 1980:A-21.

General Accounting Office (1980) <u>Illegal Aliens: Estimating Their Impact on the United States</u>, PAD-80-22.

Graham Vs. Richardson (1971) 403 U.S. 376. Cited in Flores, Moore, and Schey, 1979:7.

Hanft, Ruth (1980) Letter to Congressman Bob Wilson, December 9, 1980:1 from the Deputy Assistant for Health Research, Statistics and Technology.

Hayes-Bautista, David (1980) "Identifying 'Hispanic' Populations: The Influence of Research Methodology Upon Public Policy," <u>American Journal of Public Health</u>, 70,4:353-6.

Jones, Oliver W. and Cornelius, Wayne A. (1980) "Health Problems and Health Service Utilization Among Mexican Immigrants in San Diego County," estimated date of completion, July, 1982.

Keefe, Susan E.; Padilla, Amado, and Carlos, Manuel (1979) "Mexican-American Extended Family as an Emotional Support System," <u>Human Organization</u>, 38,2:144-152.

Louv, Richard (1980a) "The Temporary Visa: Part of the Answer?" in <u>Southwind</u>, San Diego Union.

_____ (1980b) "Valley Study Links High Rate of Birth Deformities to Pesticides," <u>San Diego Union</u>, October 27, 1980:A-3.

Loveman, Brian, and Hofstetter, C. Richard (Forthcoming) "American Perceptions of Undocumented Immigrants: Political Implications," <u>New Scholar</u>, Special Border Issue.

Mann, Jim (1980) "Court Voids State Ban on Federal S&Ls," <u>Los Angeles Times</u>, March 18, 1980:8.

Maram, Sheldon (1980) "Hispanic Workers in the Garment and Restaurant Industries in Los Angeles Counties," California State University at Fullerton, State of California Contract #1-9101.

Medina, Antonio S. (1980) "Hispanic Maternity Care: A Study of Deficiencies and Recommended Policies," <u>Public Affairs Report</u>, 21,2:1-7.

Moles, Jerry A. (1979) "Who Tills the Soil? Mexican-American Workers Replace the Small Farmer in California," <u>Human Organization</u>, 38,1:20-27.

Montemayor, Robert (1980) "Legal Pleas Seek to Assist Workers in Avocado Groves," <u>Los Angeles Times</u>, December 15, 1980:26.

Myers, B. (1978) Memorandum to E. Younger, Attorney General, State of California. September 12, 1978. (From Director of Health Services, State of California)

National Center for Health Statistics (1980) "Hispanic Health and Nutrition Examination Survey (HHANES) Supporting Statement for Preliminary Plans."

New York Times News Service (1980) "Flood of Immigrants Into U.S. Stirs Clamor to Shut the Door," <u>San Diego Union</u>, December 28, 1980:A-1.

North, David S. (1980) "Commentary on the Cornelius Report Appearing in <u>Congressional Record</u>, December 13, 1979, S 18455," TransCentury Foundation, Washington, D.C.

Orange County Task Force on Medical Care for Illegal Aliens (1978) The Economic Impact of Undocumented Immigrants on Public Health Services in Orange County (Calif.): A Study of Medical Costs, Tax Contributions, and Health Needs of Undocumented Immigrants.

Plyler v. Doe and Texas v. Certain Named and Unnamed Undocumented Children (1982), Nos. 80-1538 and 80-1934, United States Supreme Court, June 15.

Salazar, Sandra A (1979) "The Politics of Health Care Services for Undocumented Persons," prepared for the First Annual California Raza Health Planning Conference, Pomona, California.

Salcido, Ramon (1979) "Needed: Hypertension Research for Mexican-Americans," Public Health Reports, 94,4.

San Diego Evening Tribune (1979) "Probe of Emergency Care Welcomed," April 24, 1979:B-1.

San Diego Union (1980) "Court Orders Texas Schools to Enroll Aliens," September 5, 1980:A-1,6.

_____ (1978) "Colby Cites Mexican Peril," June 7, 1978.

Schwartz, David and Heiftez, Ruth (no date) Unpublished study cited in Louv 1980b.

Select Commission on Immigration and Refugee Policy (1981) U.S. Immigration Policy and the National Interest, Staff Report, April 30, 1981.

_____ (1980) "Consultations Update, Immigration and Resources," Newsletter, No. 10, August.

Shearer, Elizabeth and Donahue, Charles (no date) "Health Problems and Barriers to Care for Spanish Speaking and Spanish Surname Populations in the United States: An Annotated Bibliography," Boston University Center for Health Planning (probably 1980).

Siegel, Jacob et al. (1980) "Preliminary Review of Existing Studies of the Number of Illegal Residents in the United States," for the U.S. Census Bureau.

Teitelbaum, Michael S. (1980) "Right versus Right: Immigration and Refugee Policy in the United States," Foreign Affairs, 59,1:21-59.

U.S. Commission on Civil Rights (1980) The Tarnished Golden Door, Civil Rights Issues in Immigration. Washington, D.C.

U.S. Department of Health, Education and Welfare (1980) "Primary Health Care Needs of Immigrants," Senate Report 96936, pursuant to Section 116a Public Law 95626:2.

_____ (1979) "California Conference on High Blood Pressure in the Spanish-Speaking Community, Summary Report," NIH Publication No., 79-1959.

U.S. Department of Labor (1980) Highlights, January 8, 1980.

Van den Noort, Stanley (1980) "The Politics of Providing Health Care to the Undocumented," address delivered to the conference on "Mexican Migration: Health Care Needs and Resources," originally presented in 1977 in Orange County, California.

Warren, Robert and Passel, Jeffrey S. (1983) "Estimates of Illegal Aliens from Mexico Counted in the 1980 United States Census," U.S. Bureau of the Census, Population Division, Presented at the Population Association of America, Pittsburgh, April 14-16.

Weaver, Jerry L (1973) "Mexican American Health Care Behavior: A Critical Review of the Literature," <u>Social Science Quarterly</u>, 54:1.

Young, Christine L; Hall, William T., and Collins, Jane (1979) "Providing Health and Social Services to Illegal Alien Families: A Dilemma for Community Agencies," <u>Social Work in Health Care</u>, Spring 1979, 4,3:309-318.

CHANGING PUBLIC ATTITUDES ABOUT PUBLIC WELFARE CLIENTS AND SERVICES THROUGH RESEARCH

Leon H. Ginsberg

Public welfare is the major institution serving the low income population of the United States. This network of state and local organizations spends over $85 billion in state, local, and federal funds, provides cash assistance, food stamps, and, in most states, pays medical care for low income individuals and families.

PUBLIC HOSTILITY TO PUBLIC WELFARE

Since the 1960's, when public welfare clients grew in number because of economic and government policy changes, the term "welfare" has become inflammatory. Merely mentioning it ignites the passions of some citizens. For a variety of reasons too complicated for this paper, many believe millions of people receive public welfare assistance because they are unwilling to work, choose to become public charges, and therefore live on the tax payments of the rest of the population. Those who are directly involved in public welfare believe that is largely incorrect for many reasons. For example, many people confuse public welfare services with other federal, state, and private programs, such as workmen's compensation; Social Security payments to the retired, widowed, handicapped, and dependent children; Supplemental Security Income; Veterans Administration benefits; and private pensions. These programs, which are designed to reach many of the same ends as public welfare, enjoy better reputations than the public welfare cash and social assistance programs.

Nevertheless, the myth of the welfare cheat or loafer is strongly held. Even aspiring recipients of public assistance often prefix their requests with, "Now, everyone knows there are many people receiving welfare who don't deserve it. But believe me, I am not one of them. I need and am worthy of public aid." Belief in the existence of cheats is so strong that even those who need help assume they are exceptions rather than typical financially needy families. They do not understand the public welfare system as one that largely helps people surmount short-term difficulties.

These attitudes toward welfare services have negative consequences for the poor in the United States. The myth of the welfare cheater makes welfare budgets prime candidates for budget reductions. Alleged welfare abuses are subjects for discussion in the media and wherever non-recipients gather. As a result, those who operate public welfare programs have a responsibility to affect public attitudes toward public welfare, both to ensure continued support for welfare services and to minimize the demoralization of those who need public welfare's help.

This writer, as commissioner of the state public welfare agency in West Virginia, decided to publicize some specific research findings as one means of changing public attitudes toward public welfare.

RESEARCH AS A MEANS OF INFLUENCING PUBLIC ATTITUDES

The conduct of research and the dissemination of research findings are among the means used by public welfare agencies to influence public attitudes towards public welfare. That research includes contract research by private organizations, projects conducted by institutions of higher education, student research projects undertaken to fulfill course or thesis requirements, and studies conducted by the agency with its own staff and resources. The results of many projects are released to the media, to legislatures, and to others who may want to use them in understanding and evaluating welfare programs.

In addition to research, public welfare agencies also use public relations campaigns to achieve specific goals. Press releases, television spots and radio announcements, are used to recruit foster parents and volunteers, to explain new services or modifications in old services, and to achieve better understanding of welfare services.

This paper describes three studies which were initiated because of controversial stories in the media and in response to questions from reporters. Because the stories were current, the reporters wanted prompt, factual information which was not immediately available from the agency. If the information was to be provided while the stories were still current, there would not be sufficient time for contracts to be negotiated with outside research organizations. Such contracts require several weeks to be executed and it was likely the stories would have been stale before the research began. Because the reporters sought facts, the exhortations of a public relations campaign would not have met their needs. Therefore, to meet the deadlines of the reporters whose questions initiated the studies, the agency decided to conduct the research itself, with its own resources. Although other more complex questions might have required other research strategies, this in-house research was satisfactory to the reporters, who were informed of the methodology used and who were invited to speak personally to those who conducted it.

THREE STUDIES

The first of these studies dealt with the consequences of changing the method of distributing school clothing allowances for children in public assistance and foster families from an annual voucher to a check. The change had aroused public concern and some were quoted in the press saying the money might be used for purposes other than purchasing clothing for the children. Reporters wanted facts on the real consequences of the change.

In the second project, the department studied the length of time families actually received assistance. A widely held belief about public welfare is that once on the assistance rolls, a family remains for generations. Data on the turnover of the case load could be used to assess the reality of that stereotype.

A third project was an analysis of the numbers of public employees receiving services from the public welfare agency. At the time, in early 1977, the federal government, through its Department of Health, Education, and Welfare, was matching lists of federal employees with lists of public assistance recipients in the District of Columbia. There was concern that many public employees were receiving assistance although they were already fully employed at relatively high wages. On the state level, public employee listings were matched with state public assistance listings when a reporter asked if the state had conducted or could conduct a similar study.

The reporters who had raised the questions followed the progress of the research, both to plan stories about it and to ensure that they would have first access to the information -- a key consideration for reporters. Each was promised and received first access to the information their questions generated.

The School Clothing Allowance

Although there had been relatively little disagreement with the state's helping low income families purchase school clothing each fall, a change in providing that assistance aroused protest in 1977, the first year of a new governor's administration. Under the previous governor, allowances were vouchers which could be spent in retail outlets. The state waived sales tax on these purchases and many merchants gave special discounts to voucher bearers. In 1976, however, federal authorities insisted that the use of vouchers violated federal regulations which forbid states from making "restricted payments" to all welfare clients. The state may suggest a use of funds but, except for a small percentage of client families, who are demonstrably irresponsible with their grants, assistance must be non-restricted. The state could, of course, choose to use only its own funds to provide school clothing vouchers but if it wanted federal money it would have to provide the allowance in the form of checks. Because federal matching funds of some 70% were available if federal rules were followed, the state decided to provide school clothing assistance checks rather than vouchers.

All the assistance families with school age children received checks accompanied by letters specifying school clothing as the intent of the special aid. When the change to checks was announced there was public complaint because many believed the funds would be used for items other than school clothing. Merchants, some legislators, and some newspapers said they were concerned that the funds could be misused.

Some critics of the clothing checks had proposed that client families be required to bring receipts for school clothing to welfare offices to prove the funds had been properly spent, which would have been administratively cumbersome and in violation of federal policies.

Instead, the department research staff conducted a mail and telephone survey of 1,286 clients, school personnel, clothing merchants, and randomly selected members of the general public. Each group was asked different questions to determine, as accurately as possible with such methodology, how the money was used and how some non-clients perceived the program.

Among the 305 school administrators and teachers who were surveyed, three-fourths were aware of the program and a similar number said they knew students who were eligible for the clothing assistance. Of those who knew children who were eligible, 58.8% said that the children's personal appearances indicated they had benefited from the program, although 14.1% said the children's personal appearances did not indicate any benefit from the program. The rest did not know. Seventy-five percent of the administrators and teachers said that the state should use a restricted voucher, even if it meant using only state funds for the program. The following year, when budget constraints threatened the survival of the school clothing allowance, pressure from school personnel was a major factor in convincing the governor and the legislature to continue the program.

Of the three hundred clothing merchants interviewed, 88% were familiar with the program and had processed the vouchers in the past. When the merchants were asked if the change from vouchers to checks had affected their sales of school clothing, 59.1% said it had. However, the balance of the respondents said that the change either had no effect (25.7%) or that they could not determine whether or not it had had an effect (15.2%). When the merchants were asked about the "frugality" of families in purchasing school clothing, 52.3% said the families were less frugal when using checks than they had been with vouchers. Although 34.4% said they did not know, 13.3% believed the families spent their checks as wisely as they had their vouchers. When asked if there was ample evidence that the allowances were being spent for school clothing, 47.4% thought there was not ample evidence but the rest said they either did not know or that there was good evidence of such expenditures. Those who thought there was such evidence -- 17.8% -- were a clear minority. And 75% of the merchants said that the allowance ought to be given in the form of a restricted voucher, even if it cost the state three times as much.

Of the 300 members of the general public who were polled by telephone, a minority, 44.3%, knew that there had been a clothing allowance. 80.7% of the respondents favored the state helping with such a program. But, when the difference between a voucher and a check was explained to them, 66.3% of the respondents believed that a restrictive voucher was more desirable than an unrestricted check, even if federal funds were lost.

But those recipients who received the help had a different point of view. A total of 642 clients received questionnaires and 417 of those were returned to the researchers within a few weeks after the checks were mailed. By that time, 97.8% of the clients, which included low income and foster parents, had spent their total allowances and nearly half had used their money in more than one store. This flexibility represented an advantage of the checks over the vouchers, which had usually required the recipient's spending the entire check in one store, whether or not the store had what they needed. The clients reported purchasing ordinary clothing -- undergarments, shirts, blouses, jeans, coats, boots, shoes, and sweaters. When asked if they had found it necessary to spend some or all of their allowance for items other than school clothing, 9.6% said that they had but, in almost every case, the expenditures reported were for other school items such as notebooks and pencils or for clothing needed by pre-school children who were not eligible for the allowance. A handful of respondents used part of the money for other basics such as food, rent, utilities, and medical expenses.

When asked if they preferred a check or a voucher, 62.6% of the clients preferred checks and 6.7% vouchers, but 30.7% had no preference or did not respond to the question.

The study, which received widespread coverage in the media and which was used extensively with legislators in 1977 and in subsequent years when the same issue arose, confirmed the marked difference of opinion between clothing vendors and clients. It demonstrated that whether a check or a voucher was used made little difference in the client expenditures for school clothing or at least in the way those clients reported their expenditures. And it also demonstrated that the public attributes little importance to whether the state or the federal government is the source of funds, although that is a major consideration for government officials.

The opinions of clients differed significantly from the other

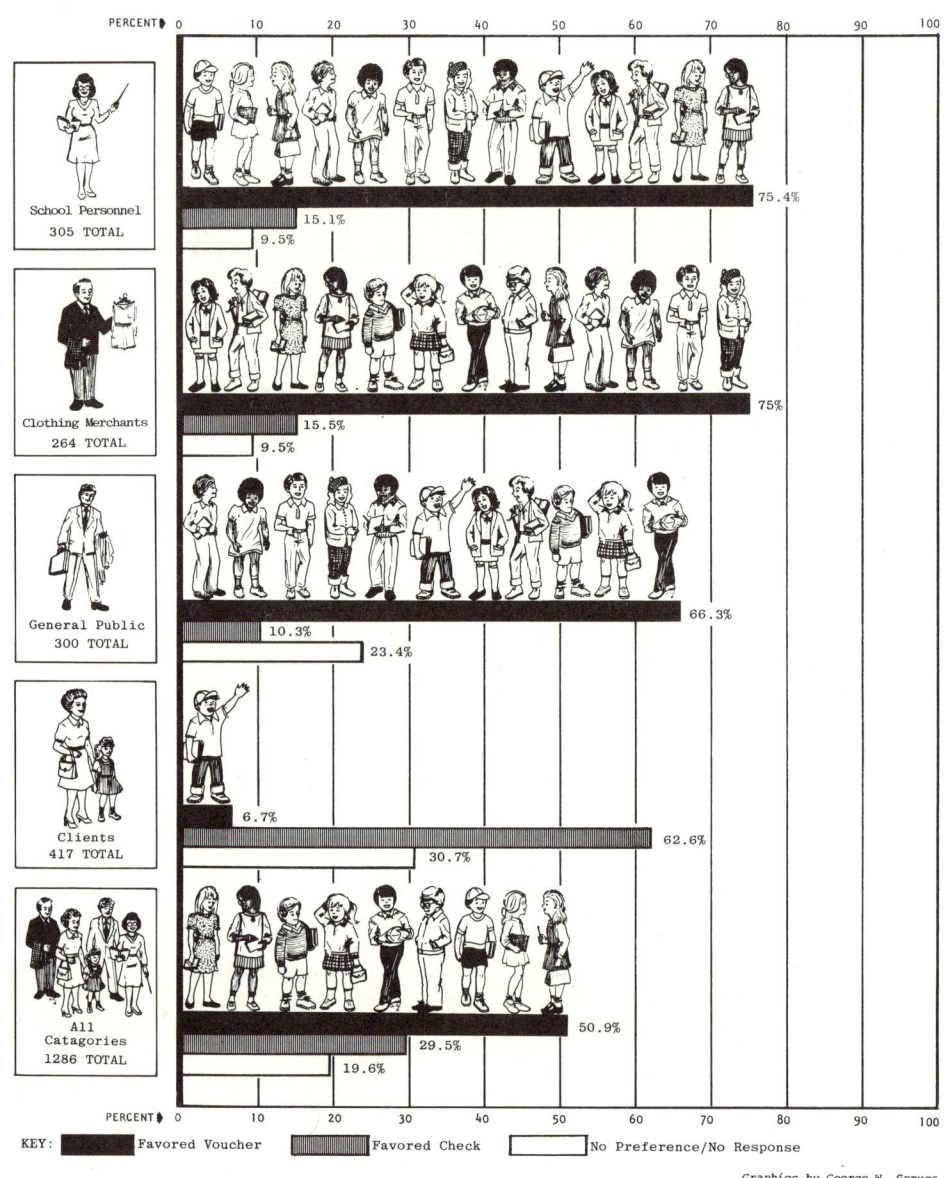

Figure 17.1 School Clothing Allowances; Distribution Method Preferences

three groups. But the clients seemed more concerned with receiving the help than with the form in which it was provided.

The research may have changed some public attitudes about clients and their uses of school clothing assistance. It also communicated to those who were concerned that the public welfare agency cared enough to follow up on the use of the checks. Although it is unlikely that many attitudes were changed about the relative virtues of checks and vouchers, the positive elements of the program received media coverage and helped balance the public image of the allowances.

The Turnover of Cases Receiving Public Assistance

A second study examined one of the tenaciously held stereotypes of public assistance recipients -- that families receive aid for several generations over several decades. That notion is even occasionally reinforced by social scientists attempting to document the existence of a "culture of poverty." As the story goes, a welfare-assisted woman raises a daughter who, as soon as she is able to do so, produces a child of her own and promptly becomes a welfare recipient. And that child eventually becomes a recipient of help, the stereotype continues.

There are such families in the case loads of every public welfare department. Some non-recipient families either know such families or think they do. But research on welfare-assisted families demonstrates that most families use welfare as a temporary expedient and that few families receive assistance for even a year, much less a generation. Federal studies of welfare clients consistently show that to be true.

The short-term nature of public assistance in West Virginia was documented in 1978 when another study was initiated to analyze the turnover rate of the families being served. Welfare department researchers established that 28% of the families receiving assistance received it for no more than two months. Those figures applied to families whose cases had ended between March 6, 1977, and March 6, 1979. Of the cases active on March 6, 1979, a time of poor economic conditions, the mean length of time for receiving assistance was 28.2 months and the median was twelve months. Of the active case load, some 20% received assistance for two months or less but only 10% for more than six years.

These data were used to demonstrate the impact of some means used by the agency to reduce the case load such as work training and job placement for clients. Other factors, such as a child reaching his or her majority, which would disqualify the family from receiving assistance, were also described. Marriage, remarriage, and other changes in the family situation were also discussed to explain the many ways in which families leave the welfare rolls.

Public welfare staff members recognize that there are two basic groups of people who use the public assistance program. One is the family which needs help because of a crisis. The desertion of a breadwinner, death, or long-term unemployment, are among the typical crises that cause many families to need public help. There are also marginally employed people who, when the economy falters, find that they need public assistance. When the economy improves, they become employed once again.

Although the myth of the generational welfare family persists, research findings do not support its existence. The cyclical need for public assistance is based upon economic changes and probably not by family tendencies to use public help. When the economy is strong, even many of the most unemployable people find work and leave the public assistance rolls. This study helped document and clarify the short-term nature of most public assistance.

Public Employees Receiving Public Assistance

A third study followed some analyses by federal officials. Early in the Jimmy Carter administration, Secretary of Health, Education, and Welfare Joseph Califano, and his Inspector General suggested that public assistance was being obtained by federal employees in the District of Columbia. Computer matches were run between Washington's public assistance rolls and federal employment listings. The Department discovered that there was a significant crossover --that many federal employees were recipients of some sort of public assistance. The implication was that these recipients were defrauding the public welfare system by drawing adequate salaries and public aid as well.

A reporter from one of West Virginia's largest daily newspapers asked what the state's situation was -- were a number of public employees also receiving public welfare?

Although the department had current listings of its employees who received assistance from the department's programs, it did not know about other state employees. So a study was initiated to answer the reporter's questions.

The study identified 1,253 state employees receiving public welfare assistance. In every case, the recipient was fully eligible for the aid.

The analysis showed that of the 1,253 state employees whose names also appeared on welfare rolls, 648 were employed under the Comprehensive Employment and Training Act program, a federally funded, state operated employment program for disadvantaged people. These were low income people, many of whom had received welfare assistance before being employed and who continued receiving some aid after becoming state employees under the CETA

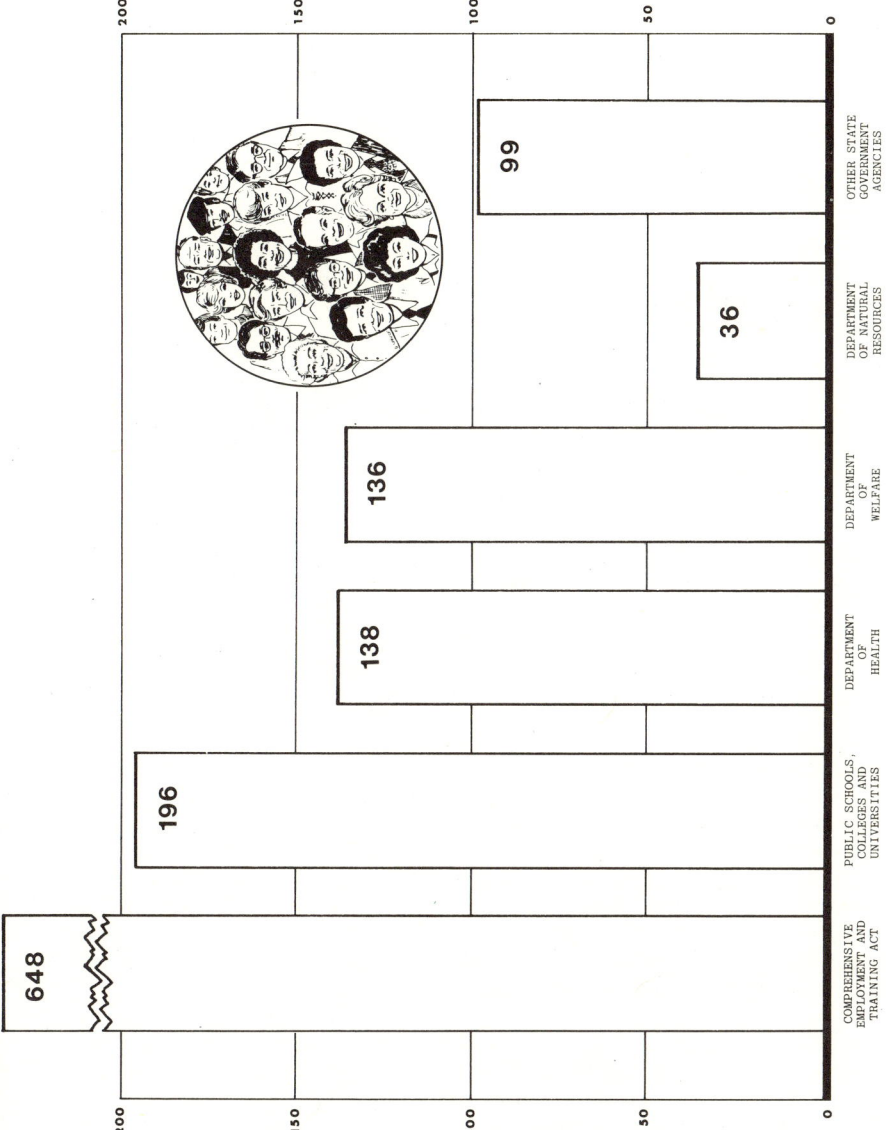

Figure 17.2 Public Employees Receiving Welfare Services by Agency

program, which placed them throughout state government but carried them as employees of the CETA program.

The most commonly provided service was day care, which made it possible for many of the CETA employees to work. Six hundred and eleven of the 1,253 recipient families used only day care services. Most of the state-employed recipients were receiving help so they could work and not require other forms of public aid.

Four hundred and twenty-five employees received only food stamps or a combination of food stamps and day care. Two hundred and nine families received public cash assistance. However, 133 of those were CETA employees and many of the rest were grandparents who received checks for the support of dependent grandchildren but no aid for themselves.

Each of the cases was individually checked and the department verified that every individual receiving every service was unquestionably eligible for the services received.

The results led to several widely publicized conclusions. One was that the welfare department was careful about providing assistance and that the people receiving assistance were eligible for it.

West Virginia's state employee-welfare client match uncovered no cases of welfare fraud or abuse. It demonstrated that one could be employed full time by the state and remain eligible for some welfare help. The research focused attention on low public employee salaries including CETA salaries and on the agency's efficiency in providing help to only those who are entitled to it.

Several newspaper editorials and columns were devoted to the low public employee compensation. A state association of public employees organized and publicized West Virginia's low ranking in public employee wages.

BENEFITS AND COSTS TO THE POOR

Research of the kind described here and its dissemination benefit the poor in a number of ways. Because it reflects positively on welfare recipients, such research tends to forestall reductions in appropriations for welfare services and helps maintain increased funding, which are major concerns when budgets are tight. The more generous the appropriations for welfare services, the more poor people can be served and the more generous are the benefits they receive.

Of some importance, too, are the improvements in the images of welfare recipients. Research which demonstrates public assistance recipients spend their children's clothing allowances wisely, receive help for only short periods of time, and are eligible only after careful screening to establish need, helps the recipient feel somewhat better about needing and using public aid. The demoralization of those poor enough to receive public help, including the demoralization of impoverished children, is a significant problem. Research that helps counter their poor public image can, in turn, help welfare recipients have better self images and better treatment by those with whom they come in contact.

The costs of conducting the kind of research described here are minimal. The information, with the exception of the surveys (of school personnel, clothing merchants, and the general public), for the school clothing allowance study, was already collected and simply had to be reorganized. Regular state and federal reporting requirements necessitate the maintenance of the rest of the data at all times. There was no cost for preparing the material in the form of press releases. The information was given to the reporters and they wrote the stories. Even mailing costs were avoided because the Associated Press and United Press International circulated the stories throughout the state at their own cost.

Each of these studies led to some changes in the way the press covered all three issues. For example, the coverage on the school clothing allowance consisted, before the research, of negative comments on the use of checks instead of vouchers by several clothing merchants and some key members of the state legislature. After the research was published, the criticism ceased until the following year when the same comments were made by some of the same people. Reiterating and updating the research findings helped mitigate against the charges of waste and misuse of school clothing money.

The study of caseload turnover was also covered throughout the state. Reporters tend to keep records and when those who remembered the study covered speakers who asserted that people received assistance for many generations, the reporter either ignored their comments or referred back to the research in their stories. These research results are also handy for responding to anti-welfare editorials and for testifying on budget requests before legislative committees.

When the federal studies of federal employees on welfare rolls were first publicized, the immediate public conclusion seemed to be that some fraud was occurring -- that federal insiders were taking care of themselves through public aid programs. The West Virginia study of state employees receiving welfare help demonstrated that it was possible to be a state employee and also qualify quite legitimately for aid; that the welfare department carefully checked for eligibility before providing help; and that there was less fraud than many people imagined. A strong movement for improved public employee salaries grew out of the research and although West Virginia's state employees still have low salaries compared to their counterparts in some other states, there is greater public support for improving their wages. This research improved the credibility of the welfare program and helped humanize welfare recipients. Instead of some distant "they," the public could now visualize recipients as ordinary, fully employed people who were poor. Several editorials, columns, and newspaper stories covered this research in a way that had positive consequences for the poor and for the agency with which they are most intimately involved.

CONCLUSION

Public welfare is the major program for serving the poor in the United States. As such, public knowledge and acceptance of public welfare programs is crucial to its success. A hostile public may result in reduced appropriations for public welfare and, therefore, to less aid for the poor.

Although the research described here is neither exhaustive nor definitive on the issues studied, it served its purpose of providing rapid feedback to reporters who sought responses to well-publicized charges about welfare programs. In doing so, the research helped the economically disadvantaged by portraying their behavior with a high degree of accuracy and from a different perspective than their critics had. By doing so, it could assist in helping improve the public understanding of the poor as well as the self-images of the poor themselves.

INCOME MAINTENANCE EXPERIMENTATION: CUI BONO

Kenneth J. Neubeck

Who benefits from research on the poor? Does social science research adequately address the obstacles to the mitigation of poverty? What new directions might poverty researchers consider pursuing? Such questions arise in conjunction with a major research effort whose preliminary findings have kindled some controversy: income maintenance experiments. The purpose of this paper is to comment on these experiments and questions.

The limits to existing approaches to the mitigation of poverty became apparent in the 1960s. Progressive critics of traditional welfare programs -- from political liberals to the militant National Welfare Rights Organization -- expressed a variety of concerns. Many poor persons who were financially eligible were not receiving aid. Eligibility rules were often overly complex and restrictive. Payment levels were inadequate, doing little to move recipients out of harsh poverty circumstances. Recipients were stigmatized by negative stereotypes and often condemned for their lack of financial independence.

Nor did the War on Poverty programs of the 1960s go unscathed by criticism. Instead of putting more cash directly into the hands of the poor, the War on Poverty entailed a "service approach". Operating under the assumption that the "culture" of the poor needed changing -- i.e., their attitudes, motivation, and achievements -- programs such as Head Start and the Job Corps were launched. Community action programs were begun to encourage the poor to "pull themselves up by their own bootstraps." Such programs were underfunded and reached only part of the poverty population. Progressive critics were, moreover, uncomfortable with the assumption that poverty was a matter of deficits among the poor rather then a problem of how income and wealth were distributed (Valentine, 1968).

An alternative to traditional welfare programs and the War on Poverty -- the negative income tax or NIT -- began to receive serious discussion by the mid-1960s (Theobald, 1966). Under an NIT a minimum guaranteed income would be provided for all members of the poverty population. Persons with no other source of income would be granted a basic benefit. For those with outside earnings this benefit would be less and would decrease to zero as earnings rose to an established eligibility cutoff point.

Economists favoring an NIT saw it as a replacement for most existing welfare programs. They pointed to its apparent administrative simplicity and the likelihood an NIT would eliminate a good deal of endemic poverty. Even as the War on Poverty began there was some interest in the NIT concept within federal policy circles, in particular at the Office of Economic Opportunity (OEO), the principal anti-poverty agency.

Staff at OEO initiated a series of multi-million dollar, large-scale experiments involving an NIT (Levine, 1975). Economists were enthusiastic because such experimentation provided an opportunity to test the so-called work/leisure hypothesis. The latter posited that a guaranteed income, under certain conditions, could have a negative effect on work effort. The NIT experiments were to provide a test of this hypothesis under a variety of benefit and wage-earner "tax" rates (Ferber and Hirsch, 1978).

Of more practical concern to policy-makers in OEO was the question of the costs of an NIT. Any reductions in work effort could add to its overall costs. This possibility would also be of concern to those involved in the formulation and appraisal of NIT legislation. In its later stages the experimentation would also come to focus on the impact of an NIT on marital stability. Increased stabilization or destabilization of family life among the poor could have additional cost implications.

Research commenced in 1967 with the New Jersey Income Maintenance Experiment (Kershaw and Fair, 1976; Watts and Rees, 1977). This was followed by further experimentation in Gary, Indiana (Kehrer, 1977), and rural North Carolina and Iowa (U.S. Department of Health, Education and Welfare, 1976). In 1971 experimentation was begun in Seattle and Denver (Journal of Human Resources, 1980). The Seattle/Denver Income Maintenance Experiment (SIME/DIME) will be our primary concern here, given the significance that has come to be attached to its findings.

SIME/DIME involved assessing the effects of a variety of NIT formulas on a group of low income families (in contrast to a control group of families not receiving "treatment" with an NIT). By the late 1970s preliminary findings began to be generated and were disseminated widely. A great deal of publicity was given to two areas of inquiry among many actually encompassed by the research: work effort and marital stability.

Briefly, preliminary findings from SIME/DIME were as follows. While varying in amount depending upon the type of NIT formula applied to them, experimental families reduced work effort. Similarly, the amount once again depending on the type of NIT scheme involved, marital dissolution was increased. Many technical questions bearing on the precision of the findings (and extrapolations from them) were acknowledged by the researchers. However, the overall message of the preliminary findings quickly became reified:

an NIT, if implemented nationally, promised to reduce the incentive to work and to break up marriages among the poor.

These preliminary findings have helped to generate political indifference or hostility to any NIT-type guaranteed income plan (Neubeck and Roach, 1981a). For example, during the Carter Administration a modified NIT plan (the Program for Better Jobs and Income), coupled with a work requirement for many recipients, was presented to the Congress (U.S. Department of Health, Education and Welfare, 1978). The work requirement was attached, in part, to take early SIME/DIME findings on work effort into account. The Carter Administration's proposal died in the Congress, a victim of the credibility and importance being attached to preliminary SIME/DIME findings within political circles.

The findings could also not help but strengthen the hand of the Reagan Administration when it came to dealing with the poor. The Republicans came into office with a party platform that included the following statement: "We categorically reject the notion of a guaranteed annual income, no matter how it may be disguised, which would destroy the fiber of our economy and doom the poor to perpetual dependence" (Republican National Committee, 1980).

In early 1981 the Reagan Administration made clear its intentions with regard to poverty policy. Aid through traditional welfare programs was to be reduced, efforts to root out fraud and waste were to be stepped up, and states were to be encouraged to experiment with "workfare" programs. In the latter, the relatively small percentage of adult able-bodied welfare recipients would be required to work in return for the benefits they received. Minimum welfare payments would be maintained as a "safety net" for the "truly needy" and aid would provide less relief for the working poor. As one Reagan Administration budget official put it, "The policy decision is that welfare is a safety net and not an income supplement program" (Rosenbaum, 1981).

The preliminary findings of SIME/DIME and the political uses to which they have been put have helped to undermine any consideration of a guaranteed income program. However, the actual political importance of SIME/DIME has been far less than it appears to be. Even if the SIME/DIME research showed no effects or even mildly positive effects on work effort and marital stability, the implementation of such a program was and is unlikely. This can be seen in two ways: in the context of America's economic problems over the last decade or so and, more fundamentally, in the context of underlying systemic obstacles to a guaranteed income. These obstacles are rooted in the political economy of American capitalism.

Present-day economic problems began their development in the late 1960s. These problems have been reviewed by Paul Blumberg (1980) as they bear on class inequality and poverty. The main features of the situation have been high levels of inflation, economic stagnation, and high levels of unemployment. The costs of living have risen while real wages have declined for the average worker.

Consequently, members of the working and middle classes have been experiencing serious economic stress.

Public sentiment has slowly shifted in favor of restricted government spending so as to stabilize (if not reduce) tax burdens. Even liberal political elites have had to acquiesce to this sentiment. The outcome has been a widespread willingness to allow "public goods and services to be sacrificed upon the altar of private consumption" (Blumberg, 1980: 224).

In such a climate, concern for the poor has been overridden by concern for economic self-interest among the non-poor. As part of a more general thrust toward restricted government spending, social welfare programs -- lacking any appreciable political backing by the late 1970s -- have become increasingly vulnerable to attack. The preliminary findings of SIME/DIME helped to buttress opposition to a guaranteed income program. However, the troubled state of the economy (and reactions to this by the public and political elites) would have precluded the spending necessary to such a program in any event.

There are also underlying systemic obstacles to a guaranteed income that are rooted in the political economy of American capitalism. These obstacles likewise would help to bar such a program even if the ultimate SIME/DIME findings provide ammunition to its advocates (Neubeck and Roach, 1981a). These larger contextual factors too often go ignored by poverty researchers. This is evident in recent overviews of research conducted to date (see, e.g., Covello, 1980). Here space allows only a short enumeration of some of the obstacles a guaranteed income program must face.

1. A meaningful guaranteed income would move the poor up to or beyond the official poverty line. This could force employers who were dependent on low-wage labor to raise wages to retain or attract workers. Such employers could be expected to resist this change in poverty policy. So would other employers whose workers were further up on the wage hierarchy, knowing they might expect heightened wage demands. A guaranteed income program would help to mitigate poverty, but it could also destabilize the wage hierarchy from which employers of wage labor draw substantial benefits (Edwards and Gordon, 1978).

2. If implemented, a guaranteed income program could prove attractive to persons with wages just above the guarantee level. Since it would be clear that one could survive without work, persons in this wage situation could seek to opt out of the labor force or pose problems of control and discipline on the job. Employers could be expected to resist policies that threatened to promote such outcomes.

3. A largely overlooked obstacle to a guaranteed income program, and to progressive welfare reform in general, is racism. There is research indicating that hostility to welfare and welfare recipients is somewhat racially based. Further, this hostility is

reflected in restrictive policies of aid for the poor. Some have linked this restrictiveness to the desire by employers of low-wage labor for a plentiful supply of minority group members in need of work (Neubeck and Roach, 1981b).

4. The poor, it is widely held, are to blame for their plight. Prevailing ideology suggests that the solution to poverty lies in their own individual efforts to escape it. The implementation of a guaranteed income program would be at odds with this ideology. It could help to legitimize the dissonant belief that political and economic institutions should accomodate to the needs of people much more than they do now. Those who benefit from the status quo are unlikely to endorse a program that could undermine the notion that poverty is a matter of personal responsibility.

5. Finally, strain would be placed on the state by a guaranteed income program that would mitigate poverty. The anticipated costs of such a program could not easily be absorbed by the state. The latter faces constant demands -- particularly in times of economic stagnation -- to devote substantial resources toward assisting the corporate sector in capital accumulation. This, as seen in Reagan Administration economic policies, often requires limits if not cutbacks in social programs. The state must have a healthy economy if it is to have sufficient revenues, even if the pursuit of capital accumulation means that the immediate needs of the poor must go unmet (O'Connor, 1973).

Income maintenance experimentation was initiated with the idea of developing data to guide policy formulation in the quest for a solution to poverty. But developments thus far make it apparent that the poor have not and are unlikely to benefit from this research. Nor will researchers' current efforts to refine their analyses necessarily increase the prospects for progressive welfare reform somewhere down the line. That is, not if the kinds of obstacles previously enumerated are as important as stated.

The immediate beneficiaries of this research are those who are or have been involved in conducting it. The experiments have provided researchers with employment, professional visibility, publications, and enhanced relations with funding institutions. The availability of voluminous amounts of data for future analysis, along with models and statistics developed in conjunction with the research, will insure that many academics will have hypotheses to explore for years to come.

Important social scientific and even administrative knowledge (e.g., how to set up an NIT) may well be coming out of the research activity. However, the benefits accruing to white-collar professionals from this research are far more apparent than benefits to the poor. And, to reiterate, this would most likely be true even if the final research findings were to provide a more positive case for progressive welfare reform.

In the larger picture benefits flow to the non-poor in general and the affluent in particular. Progressive welfare reform means tampering with the class structure of American society. In the absence of a major shift in spending priorities by the state, e.g., away from war preparation and defense, such reform could well require significant changes in the taxation structure. Such changes would be necessary to redistribute income to the one out of seven Americans who are "poor". Research findings that suggest new economic and social costs associated with a more generous income maintenance policy undermine arguments for income redistribution. Such redistribution is unlikely in any event, given the upper class economic affiliations of political elites and their financial backers.

The next needed step in poverty research seems clear, although it is not so clear who would fund it, not to mention how it would become "applied." Nor is it a foregone conclusion that its results will alleviate the conditions of the poverty-stricken, given that such matters are so eminently political.

At present, policy research concentrates too much on the poor rather than economic inequality as a systemic phenomenon. This constricts informed debate over the degree to which it is possible to mitigate poverty without broader institutional changes. Rather than continuing to focus on the poor -- their behavior, their psychological states -- research must focus on the ways in which the American political economy informs and constricts poverty policy. Included here would be a focus on ideology pertaining to poverty and the structures responsible for ideology generation; the material interests of the non-poor (from individual taxpayers to employers) as these pose obstacles to or place limits on poverty policy; and the functional needs of our capitalist economy and state, particularly in periods of fiscal crisis, that shape the parameters within which change and reform are possible.

It is time we ceased studies of the conditions for misery and rejoicing among the most victimized members of American society. Poverty research must now seek to understand and lay bare the powerful groups and institutions that control the destiny of the poor. Alternatively, researchers might gear up their instruments and models to study a new wave of underclass unrest.

REFERENCES

Blumberg, P. (1980) *Inequality in an Age of Decline*. New York: Oxford University Press.
Covello, V.T., ed. (1980) *Poverty and Public Policy*. Cambridge, MA: Schenckman Publishing Co.
Edwards, R.C. and D.M. Gordon (1978) "Divisions in the Labor Force." Pp. 200-205 in R.C. Edwards, M. Reich, and T.E. Weisskopf (eds.), *The Capitalist System*. Englewood Cliffs, NJ: Prentice-Hall.

Ferber, R. and W.Z. Hirsch (1978) "Social Experimentation and Economic Policy." Journal of Economic Literature 16: 1379-1414.

Journal of Human Resources (1980) 15.

Kehrer, K.C. (1977) The Gary Income Maintenance Experiment: Summary of Initial Findings. Gary, Indiana: University of Indiana.

Kershaw, D. and J. Fair (1976) The New Jersey Income Maintenance Experiment, Vol. I. New York: Academic Press.

Levine, R.A. (1975) "How and Why the Experiment Came About." Pp. 15-24 in J.A. Pechman and P.M. Timpane (eds.), Work Incentives and Income Guarantees. Washington: Brookings Institution.

Neubeck, K.J. and J.L. Roach (1981a) "Income Maintenance Experiments, Politics, and the Perpetuation of Poverty." Social Problems 28: 308-320.

_____ (1981b) "Racism and Poverty Policies." Pp. 153-164 in B.P. Bowser and R.G. Hunt (eds.), Impacts of Racism on White Americans. Beverly Hills, CA: Sage Publications.

O'Connor, J. (1973) The Fiscal Crisis of the State. New York: St. Martin's.

Republican National Committee (1980) 1980 Republican Party Platform. Washington, D.C.: Republican National Committee.

Rosenbaum, D.E. (1981) "Study Shows Planned Welfare Cuts Would Hurt Poor Workers the Most." New York Times, March 20: A1.

Theobald, R., ed. (1966) The Guaranteed Income. Garden City, NJ: Doubleday Anchor.

U.S. Department of Health, Education and Welfare (1976) Rural Income Maintenance Experiment: Summary Report. Washington, D.C.: DHEW.

_____ (1978) Seattle-Denver Income Maintenance Experiment: Mid-experimental Labor Supply Results and a Generalization to the National Population. Washington, D.C.: DHEW.

Valentine, C.A. (1968) Culture and Poverty. Chicago: University of Chicago Press.

Watts, H.W. and A. Rees, eds. (1977) The New Jersey Income Maintenance Experiment, Volumes II and III. New York: Academic Press.

EMPLOYMENT DEMONSTRATIONS: A STRATEGY FOR POLICY FORMULATION

Lee Bowes Fremont-Smith

> The world is disenchanted. One need no longer have recourse to magical means in order to master or implore spirits ... Technical means and calculation perform the service.
>
> Weber, 1946 (1918): 139

During the 1970s, there emerged a great variety of employment programs which provided job training for the unemployed and disadvantaged. In addition to such multibillion dollar federal programs as the Comprehensive Employment and Training Act (CETA), training for those on welfare (WIN), and the Vocational Rehabilitation Acts, there were a number of demonstration programs. The latter were designed to test new employment approaches for groups of disadvantaged individuals. On the basis of carefully evaluated results, a program would be considered for expansion. Demonstrations, generally with an evaluation design that emphasized cost-benefit analysis, included the Minnesota Work Equity Project, Workfare, Employment Opportunity Programs (EOPP), and the Youth Entitlement Project; but the largest and most comprehensive was the Supported Work Demonstration. With 6,600 individuals in a controlled experiment, it started in 1974 and continued through 1981.

This paper explores the Supported Work Demonstration. It looks first at its research design and its program operation, then uses the demonstration to examine broader issues in social policy formulation.

During 1980-1981, shapers of the national demonstration at the Ford Foundation failed to gain acceptance for their recommendations. The program ended nationally in 1981, then the sites began closing down locally. By 1983, only remnants of the original demonstration remained. The question for this paper is, why weren't the recommendations adopted?

AN OVERVIEW OF THE RESEARCH

The National Supported Work Demonstration grew out of a program operated by the VERA Institute of Justice. In New York VERA had designed a program for ex-addicts and alcoholics that offered them high support in supervised public work. The Ford Foundation, which funded the project, was encouraged by VERA's early research results and moved to establish a national demonstration and research program. One of its purposes was to provide transitional work experiences for seriously disadvantaged individuals. However, the summary of the national demonstration's research findings makes the following statement:

> Its objective was not to create a new, all-purpose antipoverty program, not to serve as a pilot effort for general welfare reform or as a guaranteed jobs program. Instead, the purpose was to test the feasibility and impact of a tightly designed employment program. Previous social experiments tested alternative support systems, such as restructured welfare payments or housing subsidies; the supported work demonstration was the first major effort to test an employment program by means of a set of complex yet sharply defined experimental methods built around the random assignment of applicants to experimental (participant) and control (comparison) groups. In many respects it was, therefore, also a demonstration of the feasibility of running a large and complex operating program under the controlled conditions of a social experiment. (Manpower Development and Research Corporation, 1980: 1-2)

The program was carefully evaluated between 1975 and 1978 through research conducted at fifteen locations across the country. Some of these were new non-profit agencies established to operate the program, others had been incorporated into existing community-based agencies with broader social purposes. In either case, the purpose was to improve the employability of people least likely to succeed in the job market. Target groups in the demonstration included women who had been on AFDC for long periods of time, drug addicts, individuals who had criminal records, and young people under eighteen who had dropped out of school.

The demonstration was designed to place people in transitional work experiences that would include close supervision and intense support services. It made use of elements such as work crews, with resulting peer group support, and carefully graduated expectations; it offered bonuses and pay raises as incentives. Though supported workers were on the payroll of the local program operator they were placed at work sites in the community. Funding came from revenue received for services, from national sources through the Ford

Foundation and the Department of Labor, from such local sources as CETA, and through diversion of welfare grants. The cost of the demonstration and research was $82.4 million: $49.5 million from the national sources, and $32.9 raised locally.

The work sites, often revenue-generating, were almost all in the public sector or in public businesses. Training was given in maintenance, repair, assembly, clerical, construction and related jobs. The length of time in the program averaged 6.9 months, although a stay of up to 18 months was possible. At the end of the demonstration phase in 1978, the rate of those placed in jobs or in other training was 31.7 percent. Since the public cost averaged out to $6,627 for every person in the program during the four year period and less than a third of those participants were placed, the cost of each placement was $20,905.

These performance statistics represented all groups but there was considerable variation among the groups themselves; in the bridge year 1979, the placement rate of AFDC recipients had climbed to 41 percent, while that of ex-addicts remained at 20 percent.

Highlights of the findings included the following: (1) the program was effective in placing women welfare recipients in jobs; for the AFDC group it was cost-effective; (2) the ex-addict population did better at getting jobs than the control group; also, those in the experiment were less likely to engage in criminal activity; (3) the program had a marginal impact on ex-offenders, and for the youth group it yielded no long-term positive results.

At the conclusion of the demonstration in 1980, policy recommendations were made to expand the programs for AFDC recipients and ex-addicts through national initiatives at the Departments of Labor and Health and Human Services. Use of intermediaries such as the Manpower Demonstration and Research Corporation (MDRC) and research and demonstration programs on new groups were also to be continued.

THE ROLE OF ECONOMICS

In the seventies, the use of economic analysis in formulating social policy increased. This was a change from the sixties when it was believed that technical solutions could be found for social problems perceived as minor imperfections on a basically fair structure. Through social science, solutions could be found and reforms achieved (Helfgot, 1981). Yet by the end of the decade the soundness of many sixties programs was in doubt; the public had begun to view them as failures. But failures in comparison to what? What criteria were used to measure these failures? It was partly to find answers to these questions that those responsible for programs in the seventies turned heavily to research. It was used not only to formulate social policy but to evaluate programs and demonstrations.

The seventies, too, saw widespread dependence on employment as a way of solving social problems. The major forms of intervention during the sixties had been counseling, transfer payments, education, group work, and recreational activities. Although there were some jobs programs in 1968 (e.g., MDTA, Neighborhood Youth Corps, and New Careers) training and employment accounted for only five percent of all human services expenditures. During the early seventies, CETA, the Vocational Rehabilitation Act, and WIN were established and employment programs were on the rise. But by 1978 they still represented only ten percent of human services expenditures (including welfare, counseling, housing, etc.). And by then a gap between traditional social services and the new employment programs was evident.

Many social reformers felt that employment programs were actually punitive measures directed against the poor, the handicapped, and others of the disadvantaged. They saw the programs as calls for retreat in the War on Poverty and as a means of forcing poor people into low-paying jobs. For this reason some schools of social work refused to recognize manpower programs as legitimate social services. In a similar reaction, Community Action Programs (CAPs) often charged that the new CETA system took away their authority over local programs and handed them over to politicians. CETA was a smokescreen, they said, behind which the programs would be used as sources of political patronage. Both splits were part of a broader philosophical disagreement as to how the problem of poverty should be addressed, one that left the new employment programs without advocates and consequently without a professional base in the traditional social services. It was then that labor economists became the spokespeople for the new programs of the seventies. After all, employment and training were areas that they had written about and analyzed.

When the board of MDRC was formed under Eli Ginsberg, seven of the ten members were labor economists. As a majority, they dictated the style which emphasized research on the project. Because of them, cost-benefit and impact analysis was used to the exclusion of almost any other research technique in evaluating the MDRC demonstrations.

Labor economists have frequently relied on the results of the MDRC experiments in comparative analysis for job creation or wage subsidy programs in the United States or European countries. But, as of 1983, CETA directors, Labor Department officials, local employment directors, and other employment professionals had made little use of it.

CRITIQUE OF THE RESEARCH

The quality of the cost-benefit and impact research could not be questioned. There was, however, an important missing link: the process analysis and the documentation analysis were never adequately conducted. The few documents produced were not comprehensive reports of what was going on in the program as a whole. For example, supported work, treated as a single variable in the research, contains in itself many independent variables: the paycheck, working environment, supervision, peer group relationships, and local management, among others. Process and documentation analysis could have looked at those variables and, in a substantial way, tested important elements of the program (Cook and Campbell, 1979).

The overall effect of the nationally emerging CETA system and the wide use of employment programs in general, cannot be overlooked. First, work experience, special projects and youth programs had many elements similar in design to the supported work program. This was less true in the late sixties when the program was conceived by VERA than in the seventies when billions of federal dollars went into employment programs, many of which served the same target groups. Program designs often shared many, if not all, of the characteristics of the supported work design. Lack of careful process documentation of the components made it easy to confuse the effects of supported work with a variety of other available programs.

The emergence of the CETA system also affected the program in other ways. Many of the control groups were being served in programs similar to the supported work model. Ultimately, the success of the program was seriously impeded by the fact that the researchers could no longer "control" the environment. Research on youth in the supported work program was especially difficult because many participants, originally in the control group, had become involved in CETA programs. These programs were similar to the Supported Work Program. This negated the difference between them and the experimentals. With other groups (i.e., ex-offenders, ex-addicts and welfare recipients), however, it was not a question of supported work versus no training or jobs programs. It was supported work versus everything else that was available. While the program's true value might have been revealed through a more qualitative process evaluation, researchers leaned toward a rigorous econometric study. As a result, only limited information was gained and many programs appeared less valuable than they may indeed have been.

PROGRAMMATIC ISSUES

Funding, design, performance, and other programmatic issues constricted the operation of the National Supported Work Demonstration.

Since the national demonstration raised only 60 percent of the total funds, local operators were required to make up the difference. Much of management time during the first year was spent on this effort rather than in delivering quality programs. Although the demonstration was touted nationally as a long-term experiment to be unaffected by year to year funding constraints, the truth was somewhat different. Each year the money was in jeopardy so a great deal of time had to be spent on short-term funding issues. Process and documentation analysis was not undertaken, in large part because the intermediary's interest and time had been consumed by the fundraising activity.

The design was said to have a number of waivers which allowed it to operate differently than other Department of Labor funded projects; for example, use of public service money in revenue generating jobs, the exclusion of Davis-Bacon restrictions, and the tracking of private-sector revenues. As time went on, however, it became clear these waivers were not in effect; MDRC had been unable to obtain them. This caused tremendous design problems as, after-the-fact, local operators attempted to fit their program design into the national research on the one hand and local and national restraints of CETA funds on the other.

Ultimately, the program's placement rate of less than 32 percent overall at a cost of almost $21,000 each did not compare favorably with those of other employment programs. It has been argued that other programs do not deal with as significantly disadvantaged individuals; however, the short-term results of classroom training, WIN, STIP, and other activities appear to yield a greater number of placements at lower cost. A recent study of classroom training programs under CETA showed a 52 percent placement at a $3,100 cost per placement (Taggart, 1982).

As a program operator in the national demonstration, it is clear to me that the demonstration suffered from its emphasis on a controlled design. The lack of flexibility in the design made the overall results limited in terms of placements and costs. After the demonstration phase ended, many programs were able to lower their costs substantially by altering the design of the program. One program, Transitional Employment Enterprises of Massachusetts, was successful in lowering its costs per placement to $4,000 (from $12,000) after the demonstration ended, and in increasing the percent of people going into unsubsidized employment to 68 percent. As a program operator at TEE, even before the demonstration ended, I became concerned that the research was controlling the direction of the national demonstration. The main concern of MDRC was to objectively report findings to the Department of Labor, not to advocate for the program, but to advocate for the value of research. The over-emphasis on a controlled research experiment not only led to an inflexible program design but also caused the demonstration agency (MDRC) to be objective about the program itself rather than being advocates for the program. Although MDRC contracted both the research and the program operations to outside agencies (Mathematica and the Institute for Research on Poverty did the research while local non-profit agencies operated the program), they identified with the research role, and they were fearful that a lack of objectivity would mean their research was not valid. So, for example, even though the program proved effective for women on welfare, MDRC did not want to make any policy recommendations until the demonstration was over. This made it impossible to gain support for the program.

TEE in Massachusetts took the position that policies were formed through advocacy supplemented with hard data, not research alone. Beginning in 1979, TEE conducted limited research on its programs. This research looked at the cost of the program, pay-back to the government and qualitative information on how the program affected the lives of women on welfare. The research results and brief descriptive information were presented to state legislators in briefings. One person decided to go out and see the program itself.[1] After talking to women in the program, he introduced legislation creating funding to run the program statewide.

Today, the program is operated in twelve agencies statewide and serves 1,500 people yearly at a cost per placement estimated at $2,800. The Massachusetts model is being examined by other states as a prototype and is being considered for further expansion in Massachusetts. The number of people served in the first year of operation in Massachusetts alone exceeded those served in the start-up of the national demonstration.

Although the purpose of this paper is to discuss the National Supported Work Demonstration, the results of the Massachusetts experience provides an alternative which has a useful lesson for the role research should play. TEE first fought the rigid demonstration design by altering its program. This lowered the costs. It conducted its own research which was short-term and results-oriented. TEE then helped initiate two new policies by educating the state Legislature about long-term cost savings of helping people obtain jobs. By contrast, MDRC's approach was to conduct rigorous detailed research and withhold information until the results of the demonstration were completed.

RESEARCH, POLITICS AND SOCIAL POLICY

> Politics is a strong and slow boring of hard boards. It takes both passion and perspective. Certainly, all historical experience confirms the truth that man would not have attained the possible unless time and again he had reached out for the impossible (Weber, 1946 (1918): 128)

Perhaps the greatest shortcoming of the Supported Work Demonstration was its failure to create strong support for a new policy initiative, one that would provide jobs for people on welfare. This "bread upon water" approach failed (Rein and Miller, 1967).

MDRC assumed that the research could and would speak for itself and therefore MDRC did not act politically. The demonstration was not adopted because it lacked political persuasiveness. Legislators were made aware of the program only at the last moment, in 1981, as it was about to be defunded. The history of social policy formulation, particularly of those policies that affect services for the poor, confirms the obvious fact that new programs must be based on political forces, coalitions and power.

A second factor, clear to Weber sixty years ago, was that the methods of research and those of politics are quite different. Research assumes a rational world in which technical solutions can be discovered and applied. Politics seeks to lead or drive people to conclusions that have been predetermined. As a result there were seeds of conflict in MDRC's role during the demonstration. After having contracted for objective research, MDRC still tried to control and manage that research rather than attend to the politics of the organization's long-term goals. With its board of economists and its large research staff, the organization saw itself as an objective manager of the research and hence duplicated the role of its own subcontractors.

The shapers of the National Supported Work Demonstration are defensive about their program's outcome. They maintain that if the federal government had not pulled back services, or if the political climate had been more receptive, or, indeed, if more people had really wanted an employment program for disadvantaged adults, the demonstration would have worked. They cite the extensive volumes of data from the program, unequalled by others such as CETA and are satisfied a documented history will justify its existence. Already they look at the developing local supported work programs and say, "See! It has all been worthwhile." Moreover, the research design was itself a technique; it allowed the service to be delivered. Further, of the ten thousand people in the demonstration many would not have been reached by any other program. It was, in fact, the research that gave the program credibility and enabled the funding to continue for seven years.

If the lesson learned from the sixties was not just to throw money at social problems, the lesson of the seventies may have been not to form social policy on research alone. Research is useful in shaping social policy but only as a tool in the hands of advocates with the expertise to carve out meaningful, productive programs; not through "recourse to magical means" but by "technical means and calculation." If the myths and illusions that have surrounded the poor, the unemployed, and the disadvantaged were dissipated so that viable means of helping them became clear, then the Supported Work Demonstration did not fail. Because of it, to some extent, "The world is disenchanted."

NOTES

1. This was Senator Chester Atkins who was concerned about the state's need to respond to the harsh effects of the national policy cut-backs on the poor in general. He also is Chairman of the Senate's Ways and Means Committee which controls spending.

REFERENCES

Cook, Thomas D. and Donald T. Campbell (1979) Quasi-Experimentation: Design and Analysis Issues for Field Settings. Chicago: Rand McNally College Publishing Company.

Helfgot, Joseph H. (1981) Professional Reforming: Mobilization for Youth and the Failure of Social Science. Lexington, MA: Lexington Books.

Manpower Demonstration Research Corporation (1980) Summary and Findings of the National Supported Work Demonstration. New York.

Rein, Martin and S.M. Miller (1967) "The demonstration project as a strategy of change." In Martin Rein, Organizing for Community Welfare. New York: Random House.

Taggart, Robert (1982) A Fisherman's Guide: An Assessment of Training and Remediation Strategies. Kalamazoo, MI: The W.E. Upjohn Institute for Employment Research.

Weber, Max (1946 (1918)) "Science as a Vocation," and "Politics as a Vocation." In H.H. Gerth and C. Wright Mills (eds.) From Max Weber: Essays in Sociology. New York: Oxford University Press.

SOCIAL WELFARE PROGRAMS: LESSONS FROM EUROPE,
THE NEED FOR COMPARATIVE ANALYSIS

Harrell R. Rodgers, Jr.

Studying social welfare programs in the western industrialized nations provides an important comparative perspective to the analysis of U.S. anti-poverty efforts. This is not because these nations have succeeded in eradicating poverty. A few nations, such as Sweden, West Germany, Austria, Switzerland and Norway, do have very little poverty but other nations, such as France and Britain, have a rate of poverty quite similar to America's. What is important is that the variety of anti-poverty strategies employed by these nations provide a basis for weighing alternatives to U.S. approaches. This is an extremely important undertaking because almost all poverty research undertaken in the United States has been narrowly framed, most often evaluating programs only in their own terms, with little if any in-depth consideration given to the advantages and disadvantages of alternative strategies.

Below we discuss five anti-poverty strategies and programs found in Western Europe that suggest valuable options for reforming and improving America's social welfare programs. These include the preventative and universal design of many European social welfare programs and Sweden's labor market strategy. Also discussed are the implications of the decision of many nations to finance pension programs in whole or part from general tax revenues rather than strictly from taxes on recipients and employers. Last, we examine the consequences of Sweden's decision to design its social welfare programs with the intent of achieving specific philosophical goals.

PREVENTION

European social welfare programs are much more often designed to prevent social problems than are American programs. Because they seek to prevent a problem, rather than administer to the crisis that lack of prevention causes, they are more likely to be effective.

The European programs tend to be based on the understanding that to be truly preventative, social welfare programs must be comprehensive. Programs must be designed, in other words, so that citizens cannot fall through the cracks. There are at least three major policy areas which demonstrate the commitment of various European nations to the prevention of social ills. These are family, health care, and housing policies.

Family Policy

All the European nations have been more astute than has America in understanding the need for supportive services for families. In the European nations there seems to be a clearer understanding that a healthy environment is essential to stable family-life and good child development. As Kahn and Kamerman (1977: 172) note:

> What the Europeans apparently know but what many Americans do not yet perceive is that social services may support, strengthen, and enhance the normal family -- and that failures in social provision may undermine our most precious institutions and relationships. The issue is not whether or not government will intervene. It will. The question is will it intervene for enhancement and prevention or to respond to breakdown, problems, and deviance alone.

There also seems to be a better understanding in Europe that family policy can promote specific societal goals such as child bearing, low infant mortality rates, and women's liberation.

The point of departure for family policy in Europe starts with paid maternity leaves for working women, pre-natal and post-natal mother and child care, family allowances, and child care. As we detail below, in most of the nations there are also specific programs designed to assure families of adequate housing.

Most of the European nations provide working women with generous maternity benefits under a national insurance scheme. In all the Scandinavian nations, in Britain, West Germany, France, and Belgium, among others, working women receive maternity benefits under the national insurance scheme. Sweden's program is one of the best. Mothers normally receive a 36 week leave, but it can be extended under some circumstances. After the birth of the child, either the mother or father can take the leave. The parent on leave is assured 90 percent of his/her normal pay. In West Germany the leaves are extended only to women who belong to an approved sickness fund (which includes most workers), and the leave is 14 weeks. The mother receives 100 percent of her normal income. In England the leave is for 18 weeks, in France 14 weeks. In France the mother only receives 50 percent of her normal income (Social Security Administration, 1977: 78). In Israel and Japan the leave is 12 weeks (Takahashi, 1975: 406). In Japan the leave is often paid by the employer. With increases in women workers and the debates about women's liberation, many of the European nations have been improving benefits in recent years.

As part of their medical systems, all the major Western European nations have special programs to look after the health care needs of pregnant mothers and young children. The benefits under these programs include pre-natal and post-natal mother and child care. In the Scandinavian nations there are maternity centers where expectant mothers receive free pre-natal and delivery care. Once the child is born the centers provide regular checkups and care for any problems found. For mothers who cannot travel to the centers there are health visitors (trained nurses) who make home visits. Almost all mothers in these nations use the maternity centers. One clear result is that the Scandinavian nations have the world's lowest rate of infant mortality, while the U.S. ranks 19th.

The French also have a system of maternity centers. Parents cannot receive their family allowances unless they take their children to the centers for periodic checkups (Jordan, 1977: 20). In England, West Germany, and Belgium pre-natal and post-natal services are provided as a regular part of the nation's health care system. Israel also provides pre-natal and post-natal care in special maternity centers. Children in Israel receive close follow up until they enter elementary school.

Another common feature of European family policy is family allowances. Family allowances are designed to encourage population growth and/or good family environments by paying part of the cost of child support. In the Scandinavian nations, Canada, and Belgium, among others, the allowances are universal and tax free. All families, in other words, receive the allowance, regardless of the family's income. In Britain and France only families with two or more children receive an allowance. West Germany has the least coverage because an allowance is provided only to families with two or more children, and the program is means-tested. Only families below a certain income level are eligible. The universal programs are by far the best because they do not carry a welfare stigma, which can discourage participation. One of the most positive aspects of the maternity leaves and pre-natal and post-natal care programs discussed above is that they are not means-tested. This encourages participation, and furthers the program's goals.

One last feature of family policy discussed here is the existence in many nations of a network of state administered and subsidized child care centers. The best child care centers are found in Sweden, Norway, and Denmark (see Wagner and Wagner, 1976). In each of these nations child care centers have been developing rapidly since the 1960s. The child care centers tend to be neighborhood based and supervised by a board composed of parents and professional child-care workers.

The centers are designed primarily to meet the needs of working parents, but they also often serve other groups as well. In all the centers the children receive educational, nutritional, and medical care. The educational program varies according to the age of the children, becoming rather sophisticated by the fourth and fifth year. Good nutrition is stressed through instruction and through meals. Medical and dental checkups are scheduled throughout the year. The centers care for pre-school children, and also provide after-hour care for school children. Some centers are open 24 hours a day to accommodate families that work night shifts. Parents may also leave children with a center for only a few hours while they run errands. Senior citizens also frequently use the center's facilities.

Child care is rarely proprietary in Scandinavia. The state subsidizes the centers, establishes the regulations and guildelines for them, and specifies the training and certification for child-care personnel. It is up to the local community, however, to actually establish the centers and set up boards to supervise them. The families who use the center elect one or more representatives from among themselves to serve on the board. The families also pay some of the costs of the operation of the center. The fees charged the parents vary by the number of children the family has in the center and the parents' income. The fees are kept modest so that center use will not be discouraged.

France and Israel also have a good system of child care, but in these two nations the centers are primarily designed for children three to five years old. The centers serve as pre-schools, or kindergartens. Most of the Israeli Kibbutzim provide day care for working mothers, including children under age three (Jordan, 1977: 18-19). In recent years France, England, and West Germany have been expanding child care facilities, but in the latter two countries parents still rely primarily on private care for their children.

The advantages of a good child care system should be obvious. The centers free the parents for work or education and they provide a wide range of beneficial services to the children. Good child care also makes it easier for women to combine motherhood with a career. Child care also allows single parents to work, instead of staying at home on welfare. Moreover, healthy, well-nourished children are likely to have fewer problems later in life and well-educated children are more likely to adapt to society and the job market. Hence, good child care has the potential to both increase the quality of life and reduce later public and private costs.

Housing Policy

Most of the European nations have concluded that it is in society's best interest to see that all citizens have good quality housing. There are two broad types of policies that can be used to advance this goal. First, a nation may help expand the housing base by financing, subsidizing, and/or regulating home construction. These policies can be quite comprehensive or they can be designed primarily to subsidize and stimulate the private housing market (Heidenheimer, Heclo, and Adams, 1975: 69-96). All of the western industrialized nations have developed policies to increase the availability of good quality housing, and many of them are quite comprehensive.

In Britain, for example, the government has expanded the housing base by building a great deal of good quality public housing. Public housing in Britain is not just for the poor. All income groups, except perhaps the richest, can be found living in publically built and locally managed flats. By the mid-1970s one household out of every five in England was living in public housing.

Sweden has also played a large role in improving its housing inventory. There are three housing sectors in Sweden. The first is the public sector which has built about 45 percent of all housing since WW II. The second is consumer cooperatives which have built about 20 percent of all housing. Last, is that private sector which has built about 35 percent of all housing (Headley, 18978: 45). Regardless of the sector, the Swedish government provides most of the financing. Since WW II some 90 percent of all housing construction in Sweden has been financed by the government.

The government's financial contribution has given it great leverage over home builders. The government plans housing construction in a very comprehensive manner. The government designs satellite cities, and establishes building standards and location requirements. One of the government's standards is that builders must cater to the needs of all income groups. The result of Sweden's comprehensive housing policy is that, along with Switzerland, it leads the western world in dwelling units per capita, and in the amenities of units (Headley, 1978: 47). There are no slums in Sweden, and low and moderate income citizens are probably housed better in Sweden than in any other country (Furniss and Tilton, 1979: 138-142). Housing in Sweden is also quite equalitarian. Neighborhoods do not reflect a particular income class, because housing projects accomodate a mix of income levels.

France, West Germany, and The Netherlands also have comprehensive housing policies. These nations do not directly own a large proportion of the housing sector, but like Sweden they subsidize quasi-public housing authorities and private home builders. Of these three nations the French government plays the largest role in the housing market. The French government also licenses and regulates all housing construction. Tax programs are also used to stimulate investment in the housing market. In France, as in Sweden and England, the housing built by quasi-public authorities is available to all income groups, and is, therefore, economically heterogeneous (Heidenheimer, Heclo and Adams, 1975: 92).

The second method of improving the quality of housing is through housing allowances. Sweden, West Germany, Britain, and France, among others, have a housing allowance program. The allowance in all the countries is designed to help low and moderate income citizens afford decent housing. In Sweden some 40 percent of the population is eligible for a housing allowance. Sweden and West Germany provide special benefits to one-parent families. France stresses aid to the poorest citizen, and England's plan is designed to aid citizens whose rent is high in relationship to their income.

While the housing policies of these nations are far from perfect, there is no doubt that the programs have greatly improved living environments. None of the countries with housing programs have the type of big city ghetto areas found in America where housing problems are acute. England and France do have housing that is grim, but it is still superior to the worst American neighborhoods. In Sweden, West Germany, Switzerland, Norway, Austria, and Denmark, among others, rural housing is on average far superior to that found in America; and, there is little or no real slum property in the cities of these nations.

Health Care

All the western European nations have adopted health care programs that extend comprehensive medical services to all citizens, regardless of their income level. These health programs include benefits such as maternity and sickness allowances, and pre-natal and post-natal care. These programs are designed, in part, to prevent poverty by promoting good health. They also prevent poverty because a family cannot be bankrupted by medical expenses, and they help the poor who do fall ill get back on their feet through medical and other supportive services. Some of the nations, such as Germany, have distinctly oriented their health care systems toward preventative health care, rather than the acute health care system found in America (Leichter, 1979:110-156). The preventative orientation seeks to prevent lost productivity and even poverty through a healthy and medically informed public. All the nations, therefore, have a health care system that does a much better job than the American system of serving the needs of low-income citizens, and of preventing poverty.

All the major western European nations, with the exception of England, have adopted national health insurance. These programs are generally made available to the public through the job market, and are financed by a tax on workers and employers. They are also usually subsidized by general tax revenues. Medical services are comprehensive, but there is generally some cost-sharing. The patient, in other words, often must pay a modest fee for certain types of services, particularly dental, medical appliances, and sometimes drugs. These systems are normally administered and regulated by the state. England is somewhat unique in having a socialized medical system, rather than national health insurance.

UNIVERSALITY

Social welfare programs are generally less categorical in Europe than they are in America. Rather then being designed just for the poor, they are often designed for all citizens, regardless of wealth. This is true, of course, of European housing and health care programs, and, as noted above, generally true of policies designed to assist families. Additionally, the European nations' are also much more inclined to believe that all the poor should receive assistance, regardless of their personal characteristics.

For example, European income maintenance programs for the needy differ significantly from America's Aid to Families with Dependent Children (AFDC) program. Under AFDC, and often under state assistance programs, single males, male-headed families, and families with a head in the workforce are often excluded from assistance. Public assistance programs in Europe tend to be means-tested, and the benefits do vary from family size. But in virtually all the European nations, families are not excluded from assistance simply because they are intact, in the workforce, or because the family head is male. Single males can also receive assistance in most of the European nations. These differences result from the fact that in most European nations there is a greater willingness to believe that most economic hardship is caused by events beyond the control of the individual, and that society has an obligation to succor those facing temporary or permanent hardship. There is also a belief that it is in society's interest to see that none of its citizens is desperately poor.

There are at least two major advantages of a universal as opposed to poverty-specific programs. First, a universal program is much more likely to be acceptable to the public. A program designed just for the poor carries a stigma, and generally receives less political and public support. A poverty-client program can also discourage even the needy poor from utlizing it because of the shame associated with participation. The stigma associated with poverty programs in America explains in part why only about half the families who could qualify for food stamps apply for them.

Second, since universal programs are for all or most of the public, they tend to be much better designed. In part, this is because the programs have better public support and because the programs do not have the punitive orientation of poverty-client programs. Being more broadly oriented, the goals of a universal program can be more positive, and policies can be designed to achieve those goals. This is in part why housing and medical programs in Europe have a much more positive impact on poor citizens than do poverty programs in American such as Medicaid and public housing.

LABOR MARKET STRATEGY

A labor market strategy is simply a series of techniques designed to promote public well-being and equality through the economy. A good market strategy creates a healthy economy that meets the needs of most citizens and thereby decreases the need for social welfare programs, allowing the nation to deal more effectively and generously with those citizens who cannot meet their needs through the market. A good strategy also contributes to public growth and dignity by allowing the public to shape the economy to meet their needs, rather than allowing the economy to force the public to adapt to its priorities.

Sweden has one of the best articulated and most successful strategies of any major nation. Sweden's strategy is based on three major philosophical decisions.[1]

Full Employment

The Swedish practice what they call maximalist full employment. This policy involves two major elements. First is a policy decision to try to provide every citizen who wants a job with one. Second, the job should pay a decent wage and be satisfying. The Swedish feel that every citizen should have the right to quit a job and train for a new one if he/she is seriously dissatisfied with his/her job. The Swedish, in fact, are concerned that a constant effort be made to continue to upgrade the work environment of all employees. A 1976 law requires all firms to earmark 20 percent of net profits for improvements in the workplace environment (Furniss and Tilton, 1979:127).

The Swedish have been quite successful in insuring full employment. The unemployment rate averaged 1.8 percent between 1960-73, and 1.9 percent between 1974-80 (New York Stock Exchange, 1981:43). Employment policy is in part a critical form of preventative social policy. By assuring citizens of a good job, the nation avoids much of the costs associated with unemployment compensation, and many of the social problems spawned by economic deprivation.

Economic Efficiency

The Swedish believe that their economy must be economically efficient. This means that industry must constantly innovate to promote productivity, and that weak, inefficient businesses must be weeded out. Union featherbedding is not allowed because it reduces productivity. Workers and unions do not have to struggle to protect obsolete jobs because if workers' jobs are abolished, they are assured of other equally good jobs. The Swedish goal is a modern, highly-productive economic system that enables businesses to successfully compete in international markets.

The Swedish do not emphasize economic efficiency to encourage materialism. They encourage efficiency to produce the surpluses needed to provide a wide range of supportive human services. Thus, efficiency is employed to enhance human welfare.

Public Control of the Economy

The Swedish philosophy is that the public should run the economy, rather than be run by it. To control the economy, the Swedish decided to control major investment decisions, rather than by nationalization of industry. While most industry remains in private hands, the state makes many of the most important decisions about when, where, and what industry produces. Business still probably makes 80 percent of all investment decisions, but the government exercises control over the most important decisions involving energy and other markets critical to the nation's well-being.

The United States, of course, does not employ a market strategy of this type, and the consequences are obvious. The nation's high unemployment and subemployment rates cause millions of Americans to be economically deprived, while undermining and increasing the costs of the nation's welfare programs. All the major proposals to reform the American welfare system in the last 15 years have proposed, in one form or another, the adoption of a negative income tax and/or a guaranteed income (Rodgers, 1979). But it should be obvious that this type of reform would be extremely expensive unless a market strategy was used to alleviate the poverty of most of the nation's able-bodied poor and their dependents. The realization that the nation's high rate of unemployment would make reform proposals extremely expensive played a significant role in convincing Congress not to support them.

PUBLIC FINANCING

By the 1950s most of the European nations had gotten past a psychological barrier that still hampers American social-insurance programs. By the 1950s the major European nations had concluded that social-insurance benefits need not be tied to past earnings and contributions. Most of the major nations concluded that certain groups -- the aged, disabled, involuntarily unemployed -- should as a matter of simple justice be maintained at a decent income level, despite past earnings. Other groups, such as single parents, have often been added to the list.

As in America, all the western nations have agonized over whether the state should give cash grants to needy citizens, and, if so who should receive the grants, how generous they should be, and how they should be financed. The transition from poor relief to social insurance resolved for a time part of this problem. Workers who contributed to a plan could count on receiving a retirement pension or other benefits as a matter of right. Politicians could defend the system because it was financed by worker and employer contributions.

Social insurance, however, raised new issues. Where the aged were concerned, three questions were prominent. What should be done about aged citizens who were not covered by an insurance scheme during their working years, leaving them in poverty during retirement? Similarly, what should be done about those aged citizens who contributed to the social insurance scheme but because of low wages and low contributions were eligible for only inadequate benefits? Last, what should be done if outlays for the program started to outstrip contributions?

By the 1950s most of the major western nations had resolved at least the first two questions. All the major nations had decided that where the aged were concerned the state had an obligation to provide assistance, regardless of the contribution record of the retiree. In fact, by the late 1960s many of the western nations had decided that all aged citizens should receive a guaranteed minimum income, an income that would assure them of a reasonably decent lifestyle. Sweden, England, Norway, Belgium, the Netherlands, Australia, New Zealand, and Canada all made the decision that the aged should have a guaranteed minimum income. This decision required the nations to sever the link between contributions and benefits, and accept the obligation of seeing that the aged were cared for despite their past earnings record.

Some of the nations were also faced with the issue of program financing. If benefits were larger than contributions, should contributions be raised, or benefits reduced, or should other sources of income be found? Canada, Australia, and New Zealand solved the problem simply by financing pensions entirely from general tax revenues. In these nations a pension is a guaranteed right, regardless of the retiree's work record. Most of the western industrial nations dealt with the problem by subsidizing the social insurance fund from general tax revenues.

These European programs differ from the American approach in two ways. First, Social Security benefits are still tied to individual contributions to the program. A retiree may receive more benefits than he/she paid for during his/her work years, but benefits still reflect contributions. Those who paid more in receive more, regardless of need. In 1981 Congress voted to repeal the Social Security Program's guaranteed minimum to the aged of $122 a month. Some of the aged who lost this benefit will be covered by Supplemental Security Income, but, SSI benefits are very modest. Thus, unlike many other countries, America has still not made the commitment to provide decently for all the aged. In many of the European nations an aged person could remain in poverty only by failing to apply for benefits. Failure to apply, in fact, is the major cause of poverty among the aged in some European nations.

Second, the Social Security program is strictly financed by employee-employer contributions. As the Social Security program has incurred increasing financial problems, debate about how to solve the problem has centered primarily on which Social Security benefits to cut. The option of financing social security in whole or part from general tax revenues is anathema. With few exceptions, the American attitude is that benefits for the aged must be self-financed. The lifestyle of the retired, therefore, is more likely to reflect past earning records in America then in many other nations.

A PHILOSOPHICAL FOUNDATION

A few of the European nations have begun to develop a distinct social philosophy about the obligations of citizens to one another and the desirable goals of national policy. This philosophy serves to guide policy-makers in the design of social welfare programs. A review of the philosophical foundation of one nation's welfare structure provides insights into the positive impact of a theoretical consensus, creating a more comprehensive, logically designed, and effective set of policies.

In Sweden the political parties, academics, and unions have developed and promoted a rather specific idea of the type of society they would like to create, and have formulated many of the social policies that would be necessary to achieve that society. No one would argue that the ideals of the society have been achieved, that a perfect consensus on these ideals has been reached, or that specific programs are as well designed as they could be. Still, the comprehensiveness of the Swedish social policy is quite impressive. An examination of the Swedish approach suggests the value of a philosophical orientation for social welfare policies.

While it does violence to the richness of the philosophical base the Swedish have developed over the last several decades, the major elements of the Swedish approach can be easily, but incompletely, summarized under three major headings (see Furniss and Tilton, 1979:Chapter 6).

A Free, Equal, and Secure Society

The Swedish philosophy is that every citizen has a right to live in a democratic society which guarantees its citizens freedom, equality and personal security. Free people have a right, within reason, to choose their own lifestyle, participate in the rule of society, and have their fundamental rights guaranteed. Participatory democracy is also required so that all groups can have their interests considered.

Equality goes beyond equal opportunity and assumes that a society will be as free as possible of class barriers. This means that differences in income should not be so great as to create social classes. The Swedish unions have sought to implement this goal through solidaristic wage policies. A solidaristic wage policy means that wage negotiations are designed to reduce as much as possible the range between the lowest and highest paid workers. This promotes equality and a sense of fraternity among workers. Of course, Sweden has also used the income tax to reduce the discrepancy between incomes.

Last, the nation assumes the responsibility of seeing that all citizens have at least a decent lifestyle. In part, this means that society should protect citizens against the hardships of illness, old age, and other misfortunes. Society is also obligated to provide its citizens with decent opportunities in the job market so that they can, as much as possible, take care of themselves.

Preventative Social Policy

The Swedish belief that the state should guarantee every citizen a secure lifestyle orients social policy toward prevention of social problems rather than crisis relief. The Swedish believe that it makes more sense to spend the money necessary to prevent problems that it does to pay for the inevitably costly consequences of deprived and strife-ridden families. This philosophy reflects understanding on the part of Swedish policymakers that public deprivation is never cost free. A nation can pay the cost of providing all individuals with a decent environment, or it can suffer the costs of welfare, loss of productivity, crime, etc.

The Swedish also understand that to be really preventative, social policy must be comprehensive. It does not make sense to educate children while neglecting their nutrition, basic health, or housing needs. Thus, Swedish family policy includes children's allowances, paid maternity leaves, well-baby clinics, basic health care for all, free hot school lunches for all children, housing subsidies for many, and child-care centers. This network of policies is designed to deal with the whole range of family and child needs, and not allow needs to compete with one another.

Labor Market Strategy

An important component of Sweden's public philosophy is the market strategy discussed above. The goals of this strategy, of course, are to solve most of the nation's problems through the market, while enhancing public growth.

America would greatly benefit from a debate on the goals of America's large and very expensive social welfare programs. This is true because America's welfare system has grown not by design but instead in response to crisis. The result is an expensive, diverse, and uncoordinated set of programs that often conflict and even negate one another. A debate would be difficult because America is still the most reluctant of the welfare states. At the same time that America spends over half its budget on social welfare expenditures, while subsidizing and protecting business, most public officials still want to think of America as a free enterprise, capitalist nation. These public officials also want to think of social welfare programs as aberrations or at least temporary measures grafted on to the free enterprise system.

This is hardly realistic, but it presents a real barrier to a more rational aporoach. What public officials could at least do is face certain realities, the most obvious of which is that huge social welfare expenditures are here to stay. In fact, over the next two decades social welfare programs will surely grow, becoming more comprehensive in design and coverage. This is true in part because of the increasing power of special interest groups in America, and because of the aging of the American population. It is also true because public officials from both parties have come to accept the necessity of social welfare programs. The parties now restrict their differences to questions of level of funding, not to the existence of programs. Witness the debate that occurred in the first session of the 97th Congress with Reagan in the While House and a Republican majority in the Senate. The Republican party fought to lower the cost of social welfare programs, but did not argue that they should be abolished. Indeed, the Republicans found themselves under intense pressure over program cuts. Reactions to arguments that programs such as food stamps or Social Security should be abolished would certainly be severe enough to turn the Republican party out of office.

Public officials could, at least, then, accept the fact that social welfare programs are here to stay and that they should be designed to maximize their cost efficiency. A program is cost efficient when it accomplishes agreed-upon goals. We need to accept the fact that a program is not necessarily efficient just because benefits under it are modest.

CONCLUSIONS

There is much that American policymakers can learn from European social welfare and economic policies. This is true despite the fact that the European nations have certainly not solved their social and economic problems. On specific points, however, European social welfare programs have a number of advantages over the American approach. First, they have a broader orientation. Unlike American programs they are less categorical, and often designed for all individuals and families, not just the poor. This not only removes the social stigma from programs, it often makes them much more effective.

Second, European social welfare programs are often more sensibly financed. A social insurance program financed by a tax on workers and employers provides benefits to workers as a right, while being self-financing. Financing old-age pensions in whole or part through general tax revenues also allows benefits to the aged to be more generous, while leveling less burdensome taxes on middle and lower-income workers. Third, European social welfare programs are much more often designed to be preventative. Because they seek to prevent a problem rather than administer to the crisis that lack of prevention causes, they are more likely to be comprehensive and effective.

The design of some nation's welfare programs is also more logical, in part because they are based on a more well-thought out philosophy. The distinct philosophical base that underlies the Swedish welfare state, for example, gives its welfare and economic strategies a coherent design. Knowing the goals it wishes to promote, it is much more likely to achieve them. America has certainly not agreed on or even debated such issues as the kind of society it wishes to achieve, or even what society's obligations are to the poor and needy. Thus, welfare policies are more likely to be ad hoc, conflicting, and even self-defeating.

Some of the specific programs employed by the European nations are far superior to those found in America. Family policy and health care is superior in most of the nations, and the minimum income and housing programs found in some of the nations are much better designed and more effective than the American counterpart.

Last, the concept of a market strategy, epitomized so well by the Swedish approach, is critical to any nation that really wants to eliminate poverty. A viable market strategy not only takes care of most of the public's needs, it creates the surpluses needed to succor those citizens who cannot participate in the market.

NOTE

1. This summary is drawn from Furniss and Tilton's excellent study (1979); see especially Chapter 6.

REFERENCES

Furniss, N. and Tilton, T. (1979) <u>The Case for the Welfare State: From Social Security to Social Equality.</u> Indiana University Press, Bloomington, Indiana.

Headley, B. (1978) <u>Housing Policy in the Developed Economy: The United Kingdom, Sweden and the United States.</u> Croom Helm, London.

Heidenheimer, A. J., Heclo, H. and Adams, C.T. (1975) <u>Comparative Public Policy: The Politics of Social Choice in Europe and America</u>. St. Martin's Press, New York.
Jordan, R. (1977) "Child Care: The Need for Commitment." <u>American Federationist</u>. Section: 20.
Kahn, A.J. and Kamerman, S.B. (1977) <u>Not for the Poor Alone: European Social Services</u>. Harper Colophon Books, New York.
Leichter, H.M. (1979) <u>A Comparative Approach to Policy Analysis</u>. Cambridge University Press, London.
New York Stock Exchange (1981) <u>U.S. Economic Performance In a Global Perspective</u>. Office of Economic Research, New York.
Rodgers, H.R. (1979) <u>Poverty Amid Plenty: A Political and Economic Analysis</u>. Addison-Wesley Publishing, Co., Reading, Mass.
Social Security Administration (1977) <u>Social Security Programs Throughout the World 1977</u>. Government Printing Office, No-78-11805, Washington, D.C.
Takahashi N. (1975) "Child Care Programs in Japan." Pamela Roby (ed) <u>Foreign and Domestic Infant and Early Childhood Development Policies</u>. Basic Books, Inc., New York.
Wagner, M. and Wagner, M. (1976) <u>The Danish National Child-Care System</u>. Westwood Press, Boulder, Colorado.

PART V

CONCLUSION

POLITICS, ETHICS, AND POVERTY RESEARCH

Stephen M. Sachs
Richard Goldstein

Reviewing the contributions to this volume one is immediately struck by the exceedingly political nature of poverty research, and by inference, of public policy related research in general. What is to be researched, by whom, using what assumptions, and which methodologies, how the research is to be utilized and publicized are all decisions which have broad political implications and which may well be made on the basis of political considerations. To say such decisions are political is not to make a value judgement but rather to recognize their far reaching importance and sensitivity.

The problem of defining poverty and determining eligibility standards for poverty programs (discussed in the second section of this volume) exemplifies the political nature of poverty policy. Technical issues aside, there is no natural and immediate basis for establishing such standards. Whether to use absolute or relative measures, and having decided that to choose a particular level as appropriate requires deliberation of fundamental value questions. While some of the researchers have seriously examined those basic policy questions, one is struck by the arbitrariness of the official actions in defining poverty and program eligibility. At the beginning, as Rodgers shows, a standard was simply grabbed up because it was available and was used without any real consideration of its appropriateness. Then, when that standard, which already appeared low according to the logic upon which it was supposed to be based, seemed too high to obtain full funding, it was simply adjusted by the amount deemed necessary to make the final figure politically viable and the decision appear scientifically arrived at. This kind of expediency is hardly decision-making based upon careful policy analysis and it raises serious ethical questions.

Budget considerations certainly have to be taken into account in setting program eligibility, but it is one thing to say we can't spend as much as our analysis indicates would be desirable and another to adjust the analysis to make it appear that what an agency is doing is what it should be doing. Similarly, practical decisions on progam levels often must involve compromises between positions with different principles. But in this case the policy determination process, which is a kind of applied research, simply appears unprincipled.

Some of the complexity of the politics of poverty research is indicated in Fremont-Smith's analysis of the Supported Work Demonstration. The experiment was initiated because of change in public opinion about poverty and a change in national administration from the mid 60's to the 70's. The experiment was opposed by much of the poverty establishment, not because of any belief in the intrinsic characteristics of employment programs, but because of how they believed (quite possibly correctly) such programs would be used. The program was ended, in large part because the researchers failed to build a political base for it, though local staffs in a few states were able to build a sufficient base to continue the project locally. Since several of these local operations have been modified to be cost effective, they appear to be providing working examples that are being used to build broader support for the basic concept.

The political nature of poverty research is perhaps most clear where an agency uses research to provide information to the public. In the case of the West Virginia Department of Public Welfare, as described by Ginsberg, the process appeared to be open and honest and thus contributed to the democratic process of policy discussion. The fact that the research results either answered current public questions or tended to correct public misconceptions appears quite positive. Moreover, the way in which the agency carried out its research in conjunction with the press tended to open up its operations to media scrutiny and hence increased the agency's public accountability.

On the other hand, where research results are adjusted by the agency and selectively released for its own purposes without any public oversight, the use of "research" as information constitutes a dangerous manipulation. An extreme example is the case in the late 1960's of the U.S. Military Command in South Vietnam changing the estimates of the number of Vietcong and North Vietnamese in that country to make it appear, not only to the public, but also to the Congress, the White House and the Pentagon, that they were winning the war of attrition. (C.B.S. Reports, 1982).

Political and ethical issues also arise in answering the question of what to study and how to carry out the research. As Ray Rist and others point out, a great deal of poverty research is very narrowly conceived to examine only existing programs, often using methodologies so uncritically designed that the research is not adequate for its immediate purpose and does not provide a basis for comparison with other studies, particularly with later research that could reveal something about change and long term impacts. The fact that in a very large number of instances research is restricted to evaluating either pilot cases of proposed policies or ongoing programs seriously limits the contribution of research to the policy making process. Certainly there needs to be a considerable amount of these types of research, but if this is not balanced by a sufficient quantity of serious studies of alternative types of policies used elsewhere, as suggestd by Rodgers' review of European practices, or by simulating completely new types of programs, as discussed by Betson and Greenberg, the overall effect of poverty research in the nation as a whole is to tend to limit public debate of poverty policy to issues relating to established policy and to deny the public the opportunity of considering the most fundamental issues. The reason that this occurs has a great deal to do with the shortrun interests and perceptions of those who fund research. In some instances this occurs because of a narrowness in the professional outlook of the research designers. In the Supported Work Demonstration, for example, the principal investigators, almost entirely economists, restricted their inquiry to cost benefit analysis. Unfortunately, as Fremont-Smith points out, the research seems to have made the program exceedingly costly, so that without other kinds of qualitative analysis supported work appeared less viable than it probably was, and this in turn contributed heavily to its demise.

Regardless of whether the restricted character of research is politically calculated or follows from the limited outlook of the investigators, the result is that, instead of leading the political debate by contributing deep insights and new perspectives, research has too often followed politics and simply reinforced established interests by its narrowness of scope and methodological limitation. Moreover, as Ferleger shows in his examination of Black employment, the limitation of research perspectives may lead to programs being established upon false assumptions, thus leading to small advances at great expense (in at least one instance, it turned out the participants would have been better off not to have joined in the program). This in turn may produce sufficient frustration concerning government anti-poverty efforts among both the poor and the general public as to create the belief that poverty programs are not worth pursuing.

Another discouraging aspect of poverty research in the United States is its cyclical history (discussed in the introduction to the book). Every few years there is an awakening of public interest in poverty and a new round of poverty research rediscovering the problem all over again, repeating much of what has been said before. For a while new agencies and programs are established only to be cut back when public support declines until the next rediscovery of poverty some years later when research starts up again with little reference to past work. Even research in the same period by the myriad of separate concerned agencies is often undertaken with little reference to other research so that studies are often noncomparable and do not present or lead to generalized conclusions. This isolated "pluralism" of poverty research reflects the political weakness and fragmentation of those concerned about eliminating poverty. By contrast research in the area of commerce is far more consistent and comparable.

An additional dimension of poverty research (and of social research in general) is raised by Nalven's study of research relating to health care. The Heisenberg effect is as much an element of social as it is of physical science research. Research itself may have consequences for the population studied, and those consequences may be negative. This raises ethical and political problems that researchers should consider carefully before undertaking a study. Failure to do so may have adverse effects for those studied which may also cause them to respond in ways that invalidate the research.

A more general problem is that the subjects of most poverty research have no say about how the research is conducted though they have considerable interest in the outcome: an interest that may be vastly different from that of the researchers and those that fund the researchers. Since the design of research will directly affect its results, and the results may have serious consequences for future policy, lack of an effective voice by the low income people being studied can lead to results that are prejudicial to the interests of the subjects. In this regard the case of the evaluation of the Title VII Community Development Corp. by Abt Associates Inc. is illuminating ("The Abt Evaluation, What Happened": 1977:32). This evaluation contained two interim reports, one year apart, and then a final report. A committee of CDC's and related parties was set up to review Abt's work. A report from this committee appeared in each of the interim reports, though nothing from them appeared in the final report. Their comment in the second interim report (Phase II) is most important for this issue. Practically the first thing said by this committee in the second (the Phase II Report) was:

> We find ourselves somewhat dismayed to note that the issues raised below, almost without exception, were discussed in the committee's previous written comments. In the intervening year, apparently, we have had little impact on Abt's view of the SIP [Special Impact Program -- the official name for Title VII's program] and the appropriateness of its approach and methods.

The same comment could have been repeated in the final report if it had been allowed.

The legitimate interests of those being studied can be protected by giving them a meaningful voice in the research process. As the Vedlitz and Alston article indicates, participation of low income people in evaluating programs or conditions related to them not only represents their concerns, but provides a source of essential data.

There are many related ethical issues involved in all forms of social research, too many for us to adequately deal with here. We do want to point out, however, that the way that most social scientists tend to deal with these issues is not satisfactory in a way similar to our dissatisfaction with applied poverty research: that is, social scientists deal with many of these issues only from the perspective of the researcher while ignoring the perspective of the subject. This applies to issues such as "harm" and "freedom of research" as well as to an issue that many ignore, the dignity and privacy that each person, including the subjects of our research, should be allotted.[1]

Returning to our opening question then, who benefits from poverty research? This short study has only begun to consider the question. Obviously, the answer varies with the particular case and even the overall impact can only be tentatively assessed on the basis of this volume. We have strong indications that a great deal of poverty research could have been much better conceived and carried out than it has been. Clearly many researchers and the poverty research community have benefited in terms of income and professional prestige from participating in what has been undertaken. But they might have benefited even more if their research had been better conceived, if for no other reason than better research might have increased program successes leading to more programs and more research. Have the program agencies benefited? That depends on the case and the perspective. Some research has been good and helped improve program performance. Other research may have benefited an agency's short term budget interests by satisfying the requirement for review without pointing up difficulties with the program. But that, and other cases of overly narrow or deficient research, may have detracted from the long term interests of at least some agencies and their personnel by failing to show how the programs could be improved. Of course where programs would have had to have been totally replaced to be adequately improved, producing that information might not have been in the interest of the agency or its personnel. Has poverty research helped the poor? Perhaps sometimes, clearly not in others, and in some circumstances it appears to have had harmful effects. But even if one ultimately concludes that all that has been done has been more beneficial than if nothing had been done, it is also clear that the poor would be much better off today if that research had been carried out more correctly, particularly along the lines suggested above. Finally, has the public and the public interest benefited from poverty research? In some cases yes, and in others no (at considerable cost both in terms of paying for the research itself and suffering the consequences of misguided policy). Perhaps overall there has been more benefit than if no research were undertaken, even with all the costs. But more important, it is clear that the public and the public interest would have benefited considerably in terms of better programs resulting in less poverty and a far higher quality democratic policy making process had a far higher proportion of the research undertaken been more broadly conceived and more carefully designed. We can proceed a lot better than we have in the past, and it's time we did so.

NOTE

1. Two excellent articles from a legal scholar dealing with many of these issues are, Robertson, 1977 and 1979. From a social

science perspective, many of these issues are confronted in the following "debates": Pool, 1979, Boulay, Goldstein and Zisk, 1980, and Pool, 1980; Baumrind, 1979, Baron, 1981, and Goldstein, 1981. It should be noted that in some instances harm resulted (or could have resulted) when legal authorities obtained research data. A review article, for which the authors identified 18 subpoena incidents is, Knerr and Carroll, 1978. Papers dealing with specific instances include Kershaw and Small (1972) and Walsh (1969). Kershaw and Small discuss the New Jersey Negative Income Tax Experiment. Walsh discusses an OEO research situation in which the subpoena came from Congress. Although the researchers here were told that Congress would maintain the confidentiality of the data, confidentiality was breached by Congressional personnel.

REFERENCES

"The Abt Evaluation: What Happened" (1977) In A Review of the Abt Associates, Inc., Evaluation of the Special Impact Program. Cambridge: Center for Community Economic Development.

Baron, Robert A. (1981) "The 'Costs of Deception' Revisited: An Openly Optimistic Rejoinder." IRB: A Review of Human Subjects Research 3, No. 1:8-10.

Baumrind, Diana (1979) "IRBs and Social Science Research: The Costs of Research." IRB: A Review of Human Subjects Research 1, No. 6:1-4.

Boulay, Harvey, Goldstein, Richard, and Zisk, Betty (1980) "Protecting Human Subjects of Research: Proposed Amendments to HEW Policy: Comment on Pool's Analysis." PS 13:202-203.

C.B.S. Reports (1982) "The Uncounted Enemy: A Vietnam Deception."

Goldstein, Richard (1981) "On Deceptive Rejoinders About Deceptive Research: A Reply to Baron." IRB: A Review of Human Subjects Research 3, No. 8:5-6.

Kershaw, David N. and Small, Joseph C. (1972) "Data Confidentiality and Privacy: Lessons from the New Jersey Negative Income Tax Experiment." Public Policy 20:257-280.

Knerr, Charles R. and Carroll, James D. (1978) "Confidentiality and Criminological Research: The Evolving Body of Law." The Journal of Criminal Law & Criminology 69:311-321.

Pool, Ithiel de Sola (1979) "Protecting Human Subjects of Research: An Analysis of Proposed Amendments to HEW Policy." PS 12:452-455.

Pool, Ithiel de Sola (1980) "Response." PS 13:203-204.

Robertson, John A. (1977) "The Scientist's Right to Research: A Constitutional Analysis." Southern California Law Review 51:1203-1279.

Robertson, John A. (1979) "The Law of Institutional Review Boards." <u>UCLA Law Review</u> 26:484-549.

Walsh, John (19 September 1969) "Antipoverty R&D: Chicago Debacle Suggests Pitfalls Facing OEO." <u>Science</u> 165:1243-1245.

INDEX

Abt, Clark, 11, 33, 34, 37.
affirmative action, 153, 164, 171.
affluence margin, 193.
affluent, 49.
Aid to Families with Dependent Children (AFDC), 56, 67, 83, 88, 90, 96, 138-146, 165, 181, 262, 263, 276.
anarchist, collective, 17ff.
Anderson, Martin, 77, 82, 94, 99.
anthropology, 18, 128.
Australia, 191, 205, 206.

Basque, 214.
Bell, Daniel, 15, 23.
beneficiary, 7, 30, 82, 96-98, 139-146, 191, 192.
benefits, 37, 82, 83, 86, 96-98.
blacks, 30, 66, 95, 97, 131, 136, 139, 145, 146, 148-172.
block grants, 90, 92, 103, 112.
Booth, Charles, 5.
Budgets for Retired Couples, 65, 66.
Bureau of Labor Statistics (BLS), 54, 55, 65, 66, 96.

Califano, Joseph, 94, 99, 136, 249.
capitalism, 16, 18, 22, 166, 167, 169, 172, 256, 257.
Carter, 77, 78, 90, 92, 93, 94, 123, 136, 175, 178, 179, 183, 238, 249, 256.
Census, Bureau of, 47, 55, 65, 66, 67, 76, 81, 82, 87, 93, 95, 98, 100, 114, 117, 234.
Chicano, 223.
classical liberals, 14ff.

client, 138, 140, 141, 142, 144, 226, 244, 245, 248.
Community Action Program (CAP), 214, 254, 264.
Community Development Corporation (CDC), 214, 291.
community economic development, 214.
Comprehensive Employment and Training Administration (CETA), 98, 164, 171, 249, 251, 261-268.
Congressional Budget Office (CBO), 58, 62, 67, 75, 83-87, 95-99, 177.
conservatives, 8, 15, 20, 21, 219.
Consumer Price Index (CPI), 43, 45, 51, 66, 67, 74, 81, 117.
cost-benefit analysis, 33, 61, 138, 264.
Council of Economic Advisors (CEA), 50, 74, 97.
Current Population Survey (CPS), 47, 65, 83, 95, 96.

data "aging", 83.
Department of Agriculture, 47, 50, 56, 65, 74, 94, 100, 102, 111.
Department of Health and Human Services (DHHS), 11, 55, 67, 76, 175, 177, 263.
Department of Health, Education and Welfare (DHEW), 44-48, 55, 60, 70, 76, 106, 136, 146, 183, 184, 234, 240, 244, 256, 260.
Department of Labor, 183, 184, 224, 235, 240, 262, 263, 264, 266.

discrimination, 153, 164, 165, 168, 169, 171, 228.
disincentives, 15, 69, 70, 98, 184, 194, 196, 199, 200.

earnings capacity, 46.
economic development, 214, 216.
economic growth, 8, 54, 66, 150, 192, 202, 206, 216.
education, 3, 15, 19, 36, 44, 67, 100, 102, 103, 104, 107-111, 124-130, 153, 155, 165, 223, 225, 243, 264, 273.
educational, 34, 168, 170, 273.
elderly, 43-50, 64-74, 84-87, 96.
employment, 92, 93, 126-130, 145, 150, 153, 157, 165, 200, 258;
    black, 119, 148-172, 290.
    youth, 119, 133, 135, 136.
equal protection, 220, 221, 224, 230, 233.
equality, 21, 113, 277, 280-281.
equity, 46, 146.
ethics, 9, 288, 291.
evaluation, 17, 20, 33-36, 96, 119, 126-129, 135, 139, 141, 146, 187, 191, 233, 235, 237, 261, 263.
exclusion criteria, 73.
exclusionary perspective, 218, 219, 227-232, 233, 236;
    legal-administrative, 228-230.
    research, 230-232.
Exemplary In-School Projects, 125, 134.

families, 43, 44, 55, 60, 68, 74, 97, 119, 121;
    poor, 78.
family, 50, 51, 54, 93, 94, 271.
Family Assistance Plan (FAP), 6, 90, 177.
food budgets:
    economy, 50, 51, 55, 65, 94.
    low-cost, 50, 56, 74.
    thrifty, 47, 55, 56, 65, 74, 94.

Food Stamps, 56, 67, 69, 70, 72, 73, 77, 78, 82-86, 92, 98, 181, 282.
foster parents, 243, 244, 245.
foundations, 17-19.
free market, 14, 15, 18, 22.

General Accounting Office (GAO), 17, 34, 123, 236, 237.
Gini coefficient, 193.
government services, 16, 47, 102, 103, 104, 106, 108, 112;
    poverty, 102, 103, 105, 106, 109, 111, 112.
grants, 17, 19, 34, 244, 278.
Great Society, 108, 164.

healthcare, 51, 70, 71, 218, 221, 222, 223, 227-231, 236, 271, 275-283, 290;
    pre-natal, 219, 220, 271, 272.
    post-natal, 271, 272.
Helfgot, Joseph, 6, 8, 9, 12, 23, 25, 30, 32, 38, 214, 216, 263, 269.
Hispanic, 95, 136, 139, 234, 236.
Hoagland, G. William, 77, 83, 84, 85, 86, 87, 95, 96, 97, 99.
households, 44, 58, 61, 67, 72, 84, 97, 98, 121, 153, 175, 176.
housing, 67, 74, 77, 78, 86, 90, 271;
    policies, 271, 273-275.
    public, 69, 78, 82, 83, 86, 276.
    subsidized, 70, 71, 72, 78.
human capital, 69, 73, 148, 149, 150, 164, 165, 166, 168, 171.

incentives, 10, 168, 176, 179, 183, 192, 235.
inclusionary perspective, 218, 220-227, 230, 232;
    legal-administrative, 220-221.
    research, 221-227.
income maintenance, 9, 16, 192, 254-259, 276;
    experiments, 21, 216, 258.

Index

New Jersey, 132, 255, 293.
President's Commission on, 49, 62, 177.
Seattle/Denver (SIME/DIME), 179, 180, 182, 188, 255.
inequality, 8, 18, 66, 192, 206, 256, 259.
inequities, 44, 70.
inequity, 71.
inflation, 90, 149, 192, 198, 206, 256.
in-kind benefits, 21, 44, 45, 47, 56, 58, 60, 62, 67, 78-98.
in-kind transfers, 69, 73, 78, 81, 82.
institutional, 35, 71, 214, 257.
institutionalized, 65, 213.
institutions, 47, 65, 118.

KGB model, 175-189.

labor markets, 93, 149, 171, 188, 194;
　segmented, 164-167.
labor market strategy, 214, 270, 277-278, 281-282.
Latino, 225, 226, 227, 233, 234, 235.
liberals, 16-22, 254, 257.
libertarians, 14, 16, 17, 21.
life-cycle hypothesis, 68.

macroeconomic, 83, 192, 202, 206, 207.
macrosimulation, 96, 121, 191-207.
Manpower Demonstration Research Corporation (MDRC), 262-269.
Manpower Development and Training Act (MDTA), 164, 165, 264.
Marxists, 19, 20, 22.
MATH, 177.
media, 243, 248.
Medicare, 67, 69, 71, 72, 78, 82, 84, 96, 98.
Medicaid, 7, 56, 58, 69, 70, 71, 73, 78, 82, 83, 84, 85, 95, 96, 97, 98, 226, 229, 234, 276.
Mexican-Americans, 218, 225, 226, 229.
microsimulation, 83, 85, 121, 175-189.
minorities, 92.
Mondragon, 214.
Moynihan, Daniel P., 15, 16, 21, 26, 121, 122, 131, 147, 212, 217.

National Health Insurance, 275.
Negative Income Tax (NIT), 206, 254, 257, 278.
neoconservatives, 15, 16, 21.
net contributors, 191, 192, 197-198, 202, 206.
net worth, 68, 95.
nonwhites, 87, 110, 111, 151, 153, 169, 170.

Office of Economic Opportunity (OEO), 213, 255, 293.
Operation Wetback, 226.
Organization for Economic Cooperation and Development (OECD), 54, 60, 62, 208.
Orshansky, Mollie, 47, 48, 50, 62, 65, 68, 74, 75, 76, 81, 94, 99;
　index, 43, 46, 50.

Paglin, Morton, 86, 87, 93, 97, 100.
pluralism, 17.
politics, 9, 20, 46, 135, 267, 268, 288.
poor:
　control of, 118.
　deserving, 5, 6, 7, 9, 15.
　underserving, 5, 6, 7, 9.
poverty:
　causes of, 6, 7, 9, 16, 18, 120.
　culture of, 5, 6, 8, 9, 15, 20, 121, 248, 254.
　European programs, 8, 215, 270-283.
　extent of, 77, 82, 83, 95.

gap, 6, 45, 96, 206.
individual approach, 6, 30, 33, 213.
line, 5, 6, 43, 45, 47, 50, 54, 56, 60, 64, 66, 68, 71, 73, 78, 81, 82, 83, 87, 92, 94, 96, 102-105, 109, 113, 257.
line, absolute, 43, 49, 50, 64, 81, 106, 109, 110, 192, 194, 278.
line, implicit, 65, 71, 72, 73.
line, permeability of, 45.
line, relative, 44, 47, 49, 50, 60, 62, 64, 81, 103, 192, 194, 278.
policy, 14, 18, 19, 22, 49, 78, 102, 215, 257, 278.
prevention of, 5, 6, 270-275, 281, 183.
programs, 3, 6-9, 14, 18, 30, 31, 102, 191-207, 214, 233, 268, 270, 276, 278.
rate, 65, 82, 83, 85, 87, 92, 96.
structural approach, 6-9, 33, 119, 148, 172, 213.
praxis, 23.
press, 17, 18, 19, 243, 252, 279.
production, 150, 199, 202.
productivity, 33, 149, 150, 151, 199, 202, 206, 277.
Program for Better Jobs and Income (PBJI), 78, 92, 94, 175, 179, 256.
public services, 14, 16.

qualitative, 119, 198, 265, 290.
qualitative research, 127, 128, 134;
 advantages of, 129-133.

Reagan, 7, 15, 27, 77, 78, 90, 92, 93, 98, 168, 169, 256, 258, 282.
regulations, 14, 18, 21, 176, 177, 244, 273.
research:
 contract, 243, 266.
 controls, 120.
responses:

behavioral, 121, 122, 139, 175, 177, 179, 187, 200.
labor supply, 178, 181, 182, 192-196, 197, 200.
maintenance of real income, 197-198.
savings, 196.
take-up, 196.
revealed preferences, 104, 113.
RIM, 177, 180.
Rothschild, E., 150, 155, 174.

safety net, 15, 112, 256.
sectors:
 manufacturing, 151, 153, 155, 167.
 service, 149, 153, 155, 157, 166, 168, 169, 170, 171.
sensivity, 288;
 analysis, 96, 122, 187.
simulations, 74, 84, 96, 121, 122, 177, 183, 191, 200, 205.
Social Security, 15, 54, 56, 58, 67, 69, 74, 90, 220, 242, 279, 282;
 Act, 7.
 Administration (SSA), 43, 50, 54, 55, 58, 62, 65, 66, 73, 284.
 services, 15.
socialists, 16, 17, 19, 20, 21, 22.
Supplemental Security Income (SSI), 56, 67, 69-74, 83, 93-96, 181, 242, 279.
Supported Work Demonstrations, 261-267, 290.
Survey of Income and Education (SIE), 181, 187.

target efficiency, 31.
TATSIM, 177.
Townsend's deprivation standard, 61.
transfers, 78, 82, 95, 97;
 cash, 67.
 income, 77, 85, 90, 92, 93, 96.
 in-kind, 69, 86, 172.
 medical, 82, 84, 85, 86, 96.

Transitional Employment Enterprises, (TEE), 266-267.
TRIM, 177-180.
truly needy, 77, 90, 93, 94.

underemployed, 7.
underemployment, 119.
undocumented:
　aliens, 221.
　immigrants, 213, 219-237.
　Mexicans, 10, 218, 223, 224, 225.
　persons, 221, 223, 224, 227.
unemployed, 7, 14, 123, 168, 278.
unemployment, 33, 56, 67, 92, 119, 123, 125, 126, 129, 135, 172, 192, 198, 200, 206, 249, 256, 277.
universal, 206, 270, 272, 276.

wages, 7, 153, 155, 168, 194, 200, 257.
War on Poverty, 3, 5, 7, 15, 77, 87, 102, 164, 213, 214, 254, 255, 264.
Welfare, 14-18, 21, 49, 61, 62, 70, 72, 77, 78, 85, 90, 92, 93, 138, 146, 172, 175-189, 215, 242-253, 254, 255, 262, 270, 278, 282;
　benefits, 195, 212.
　clients, 242-253.
Work Incentive Program (WIN), 165, 261, 264, 266.
workers, 32, 92, 164;
　clerical, 149, 167.
　service, 149, 167.
workforce, 92, 93.

Youth Employment Demonstration Projects Act (YEDPA), 124-126, 133.
Youth Employment and Training Program (YETP), 124, 126.
Youthwork National Policy Study (YNPS), 127, 128.

CONTRIBUTORS

JON P. ALSTON, Ph.D., Professor of Sociology at Texas A&M University, has published numerous scholarly articles. His research interests include the influence of religious beliefs on behavior and secular attitudes, the cultural foundations of the Japanese managerial system, and how organizations relate to their members and clients. He has recently published in <u>Business Horizons, Futures, American Journal of Sociology</u>, and <u>Sociological Quarterly</u>. He is currently completing a book on how Americans can adopt selected features of Japanese management.

DAVID BETSON is a member of the Economics Department at the University of Notre Dame. Prior to this appointment, he was a Research Associate at the Institute for Research on Poverty, University of Wisconsin-Madison. Between 1975 and 1979, he worked in the Office of Income Security Policy of the Assistant Secretary for Planning and Evaluation in the Department of Health, Education and Welfare where he was involved in the design and planning of the Carter Administration's reform of the welfare system. His published work has been mainly in the area of the efficiency and distributional effects of the tax-transfer system.

JAMES CUTT is Professor of Public Administration at the University of Victoria, British Columbia. He is the author of numerous books (including <u>A Planning Programming and Budgeting Manual</u>) and articles. His major research interests are policy analysis and human resource economics.

JOHN DIXON is a Lecturer in Economics at the Canberra College of Advanced Education, Canberra. His books include <u>The Chinese Welfare System 1949-1979</u> and <u>Australia's Policy Towards the Aged 1890-1972</u>, and he has published various articles on social welfare in Australia and in China. He is a member of the International Institute of Social Economics. He is the Academic Director of the Management and Policy Studies Centre at the Canberra College of Advanced Education in Australia.

LOUIS FERLEGER is an Assistant Professor of Economics at the University of Massachusetts in Boston. He worked in the post office for eight years. He received his Ph.D. from Temple University and has taught at LaSalle College and the University of New Hampshire. He is co-author of <u>Statistics for Social Change</u> (1980) and has authored several articles on the postbellum southern economy, the latest appeared in Louisiana History. He is currently engaged in research on politics, the use of statistics, and industrial relations in the U.S. auto industry.

LEE BOWES FREMONT-SMITH has been Executive Vice President of Transitional Employment Enterprises, Inc. in Boston for five years. Prior to that, she was the Executive Director of a CETA agency. She recently completed her Ph.D. in Applied Social Science at Boston University.

LEON H. GINSBERG is Commissioner of the West Virginia Department of Human Services and is on leave from the West Virginia University School of Social Work, where he served as Dean and Professor from 1969 until 1977. His Ph.D. is in Political Science and he also holds the Master of Social Work degree. He is the co-author of a text entitled Human Services for Older Adults and his latest book is The Practice of Social Work in Public Welfare. He has also written extensively on rural social work, civil rights of the mentally disabled, and various issues in social welfare policy, social work education, and social welfare administration.

LORI B. GIRSHICK is a doctoral student in the Social Economy and Social Policy Program in Sociology at Boston College. Her present research interest is ideology and social change with a focus on local level political education programs, particularly those offered at the workplace by labor unions.

RICHARD GOLDSTEIN is a free-lance consultant and a senior member and director of a new research firm (Qualitas, Inc.) in Boston which specializes in support of public interest litigation and quality control of research, especially data quality control. As a consultant, he specializes in (1) research design, and, (2) statistical analysis for litigation, particularly in the area of employment discrimination. His most recent publications appeared in Evaluation & the Health Professions, and IRB: A Review of Human Subjects Research.

DAVID GREENBERG is currently a Visiting Professor of Economics at the University of Maryland Baltimore County. After receiving his Ph.D. in Economics from MIT in 1966, Dr. Greenberg was employed as a labor economist by the Rand Corporation. In 1968-69, Dr. Greenberg served on the staff of the President's Commission on Income Maintenance Programs and, in 1974-75, he took a year's leave of absence at the University of Wisconsin as a Visiting Associated Professor of Economics and a Fellow of the Institute for Research on Poverty. In 1975, he became an economist at the U.S. Department of Health and Human Services' Office of Income Security Policy and in

1976-77 served as acting director of that office. From 1980 to 1982, Dr. Greenberg was employed by SRI International.

RONALD B. LARSON is a graduate research assistant in the Department of Agricultural and Applied Economics, University of Minnesota.

BARRY NAGORCKA is a Senior Research Scientist with the Commonwealth Scientific and Industrial Research Organization's Division of Computing Research, Canberra. His main interest is in the field of mathematical modelling of continuous dynamic systems. He has published many papers in this field. He is a Councillor of the Simulation Society of Australia.

JOSEPH NALVEN is senior researcher at Community Research Associates, Inc., San Diego, California. His curent research interests focus on the U.S.-Mexico border region. While he held a Rockefeller Postdoctoral Fellowship in Environmental Affairs, he studied the cross-cultural context for air-pollution control policy and planning in the San Diego-Tijuana air basin. Since then, he has been co-author and principal investigator for Undocumented Immigrants: Their Impact on the County of San Diego (1980) and Employers of Undocumented Workers: Implications for a Guest-Worker Program (1981), respectively.

KENNETH J. NEUBECK is an Associate Professor of Sociology at the University of Connecticut-Storrs. A Ph.D. from Washington University in St. Louis, he is the author of two books: (Corporate Response to Urban Crisis and Special Problems: A Critical Approach) as well as articles in such journals as Social Policy and Social Problems. Dr. Neubeck's current research interests are on class inequality and political-economic obstacles to the elimination of poverty.

RAY C. RIST is Deputy Director of the Institute for Program Evaluation, United States General Accounting Office. He has also served as Associate Director of the National Institute of Education and as a Senior Fulbright Fellow at the Max Planck Institute in Berlin. He received his Ph.D. from Washington University, St. Louis (1970). He is the author or editor of ten books, most recently EARNING AND LEARNING (1981); CONFRONTING YOUTH UNEMPLOYMENT (1980); and GUESTWORKERS IN GERMANY (1979). Academic affiliations have included Cornell University, George Washington University, and a number of Visiting Professorships.

HARRELL R. RODGERS, JR., Professor of Political Science at the University of Houston, received his Ph.D. from the University of Iowa. He is the author of Community Conflict Public Opinion and the Law; Crisis in Democracy; Poverty Amid Plenty; and Ending Poverty In America. He is co-author of Law and Social Change; Racial

Equality In America; Unfinished Democracy and Coercion to Compliance. He is editor of Black Political Attitudes, and Alternatives to Racism and Racial Inequality.

STEPHEN M. SACHS is an Associate Professor of Political Science at Indiana University-Purdue University, Indianapolis. He is the editor of Workplace Democracy, and has written articles on workplace democracy for a number of different journals. He is also interested in and has written about worker co-operatives as a method of economic development. He is active in the Caucus for a New Political Science, and was a founder of the Conference for a Relevant Social Science. He is presently editing a book on consciousness and social change.

TIMOTHY SMEEDING is an Associate Professor of Economics at the University of Utah, and has been an American Statistical Association Research Fellow at the U.S. Bureau of the Census. He compiled the first indepth study of the impact of in-kind transfers on poverty in 1975, and has recently authored the first U.S. Census Bureau report to Congress on valuation of in-kind transfers. He is a long-time research affiliate at the Institute for Research in Poverty at the University of Wisconsin and has written several journal articles on poverty and income distribution in the United States and abroad.

THOMAS F. STINSON is an economist with the Economic Research Service, U.S. Department of Agriculture, and Associate Professor, Department of Agricultural and Applied Economics, University of Minnesota. He has written extensively on the finances of local governments, concentrating particularly on problems of non-metropolitan communities.

ARNOLD VEDLITZ serves as Associate Dean for Research and Director of the Public Policy Resource Laboratory in the College of Liberal Arts in Texas A&M University. He is also an Associate Professor in the Department of Political Science. During 1980-81, Dr. Vedlitz was on leave from Texas A&M serving as a senior associate analyst with the Office of Services Delivery Assessment in the U.S. Department of Health and Human Services. In this capacity, he acted as a principal investigator on nationwide evaluations of DHHS programs. Dr. Vedlitz's scholarly articles have appeared in The American Journal of Political Science, The Journal of Politics, Social Science Quarterly, Political Methodology, Urban Affairs Quarterly, The Annals of the American Academy of Political and Social Science, The Journal of Black Studies, The Journal of Negro Education, The Western Journal of Black Studies, and The Negro Educational Review.

JOHN WILLIAMSON is Associate Professor of Sociology at Boston College. He is director of the Applied Social Research Sequence and a former chair of the Poverty, Class and Inequality Division of the Society for the Study of Social Problems. He has written extensively in the areas of poverty and social gerontology. His books include: <u>Strategies Against Poverty in America</u>, <u>The Politics of Aging</u>, <u>Growing Old: The Social Problems of Aging</u>, <u>Aging and Society</u>, <u>Social Problems: The Contemporary Debates</u>, and <u>The Research Craft</u>.